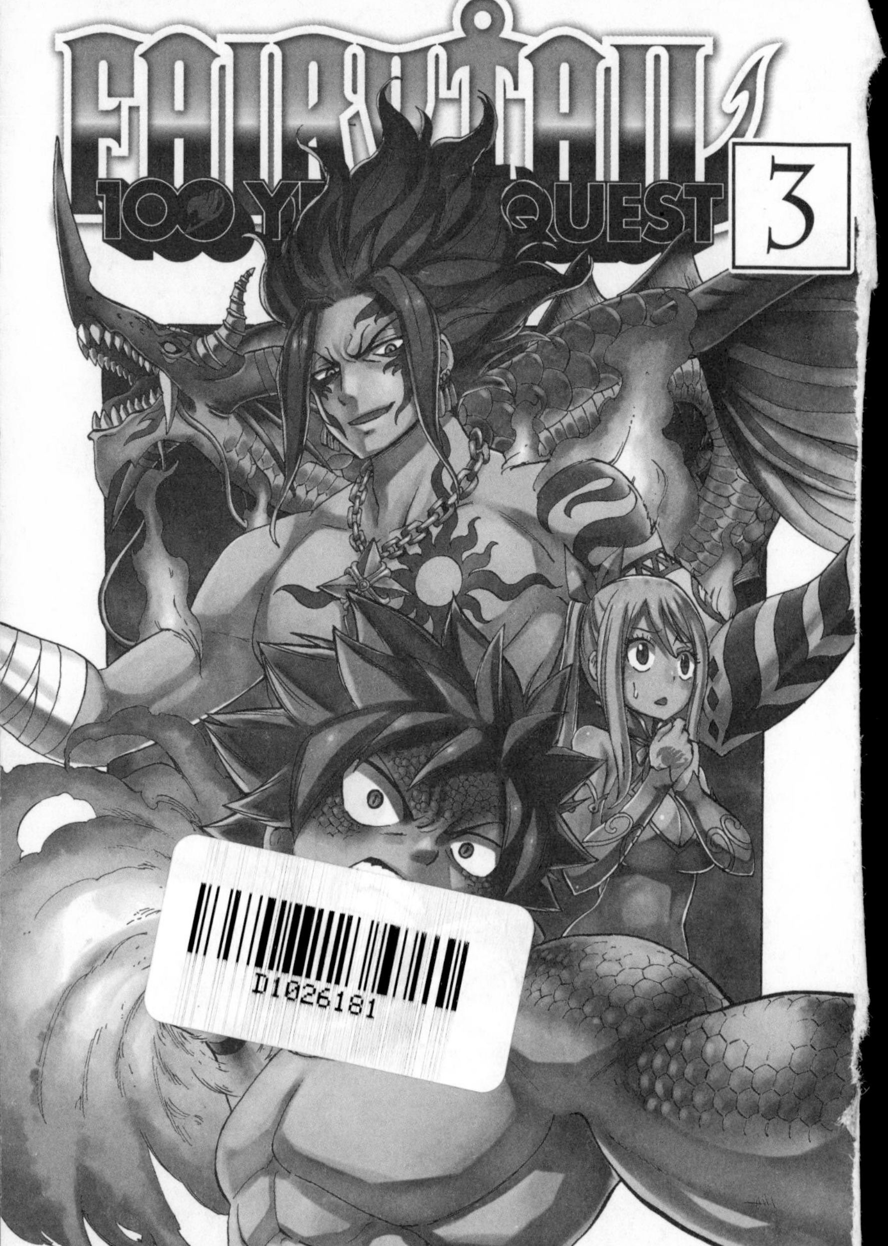
FAIRY TAIL
100
QUEST
3

HIRO MASHIMA ATSUO UEDA

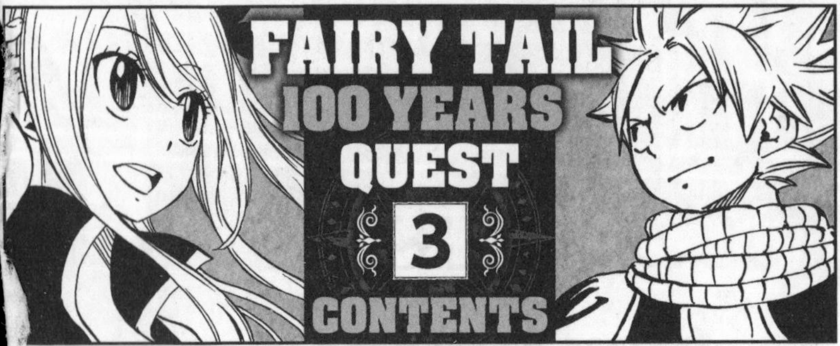
FAIRY TAIL
100 YEARS
QUEST
3
CONTENTS

FAIRY TAIL 100 YEARS QUEST

Chapter 19: From the Depths

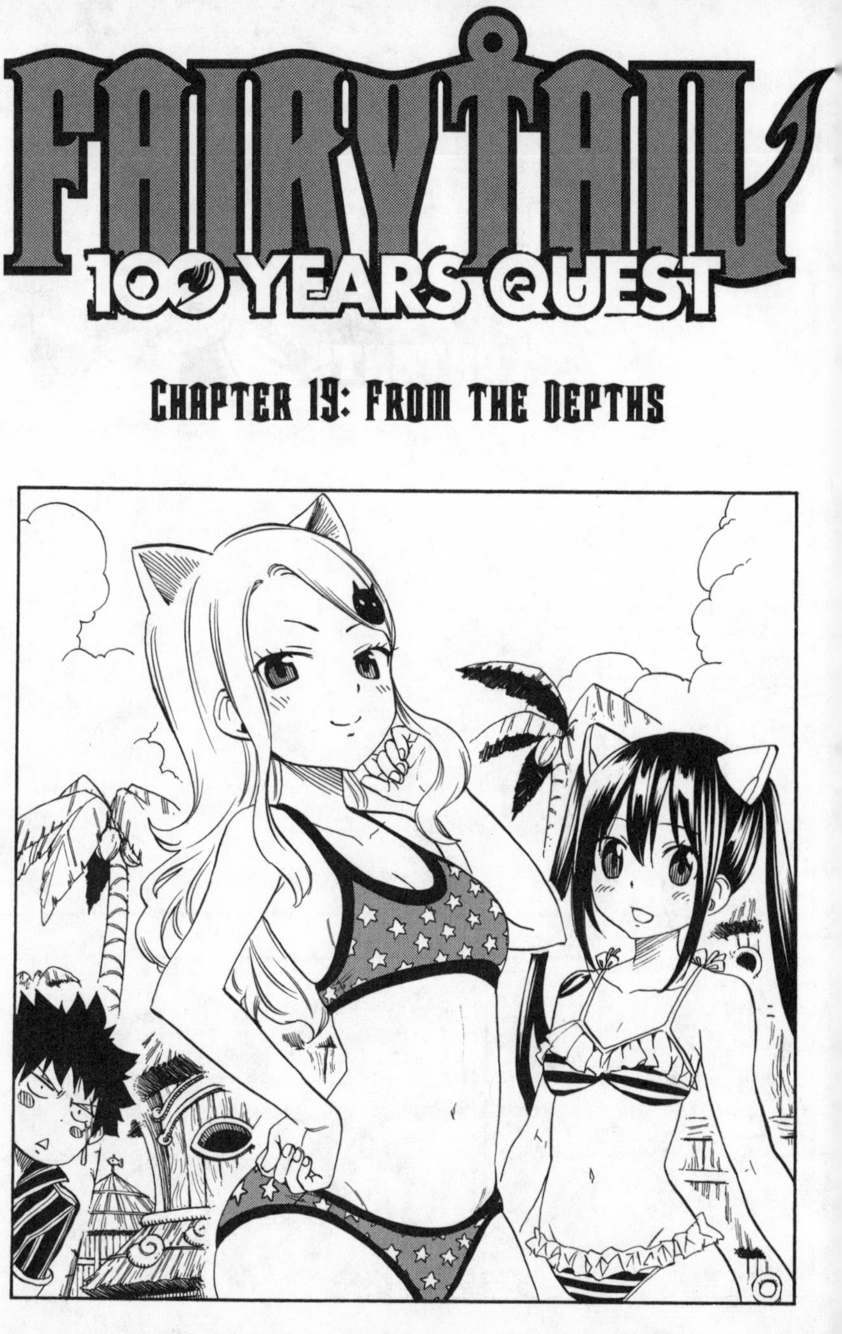

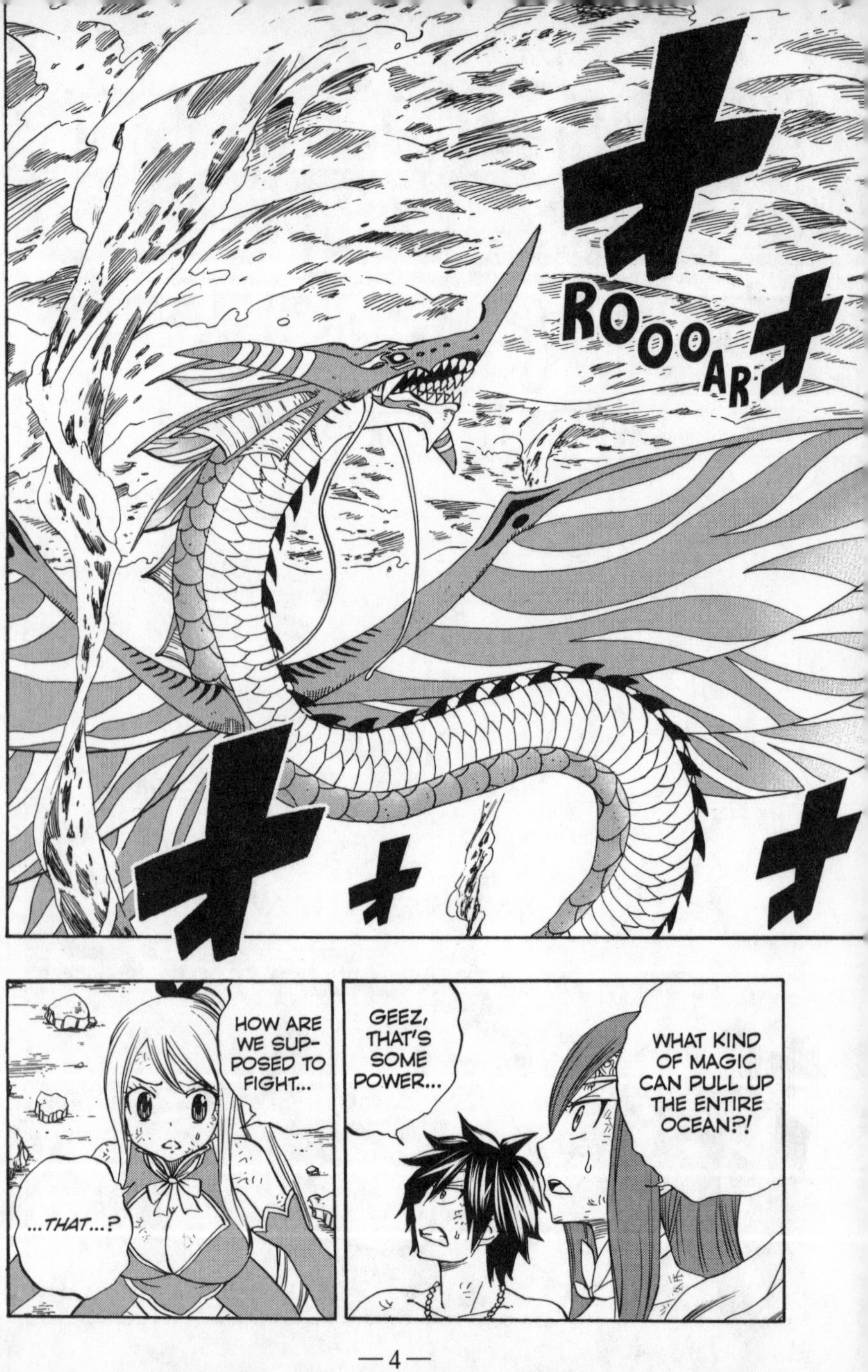
ROOOOAR
WHAT KIND OF MAGIC CAN PULL UP THE ENTIRE OCEAN?!
GEEZ, THAT'S SOME POWER...
HOW ARE WE SUP-POSED TO FIGHT...
...THAT...?

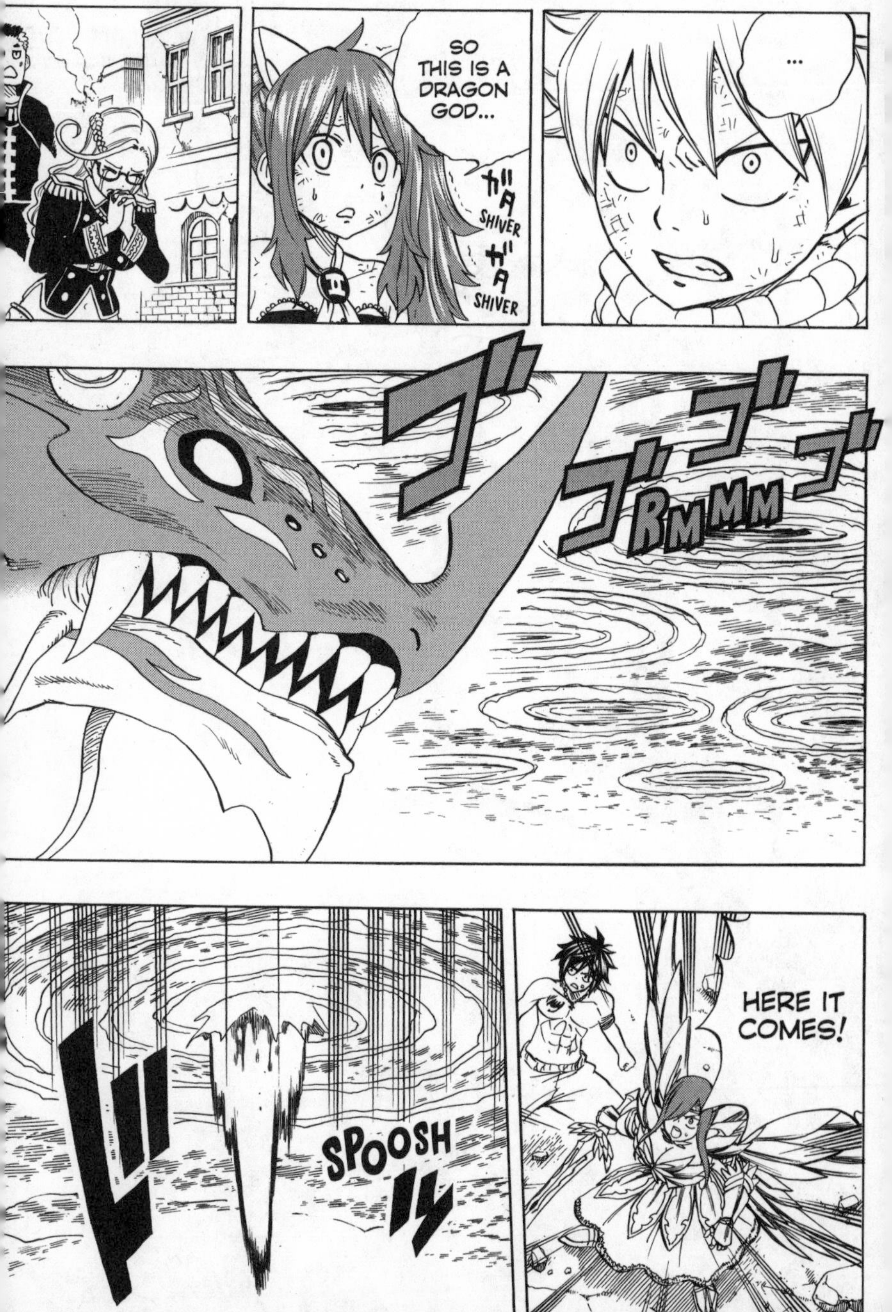
...
SO THIS IS A DRAGON GOD...
ガタ
SHIVER
ガタ
SHIVER
ゴ
ゴゴゴゴ
RMMMM
HERE IT COMES!
SPOOSH

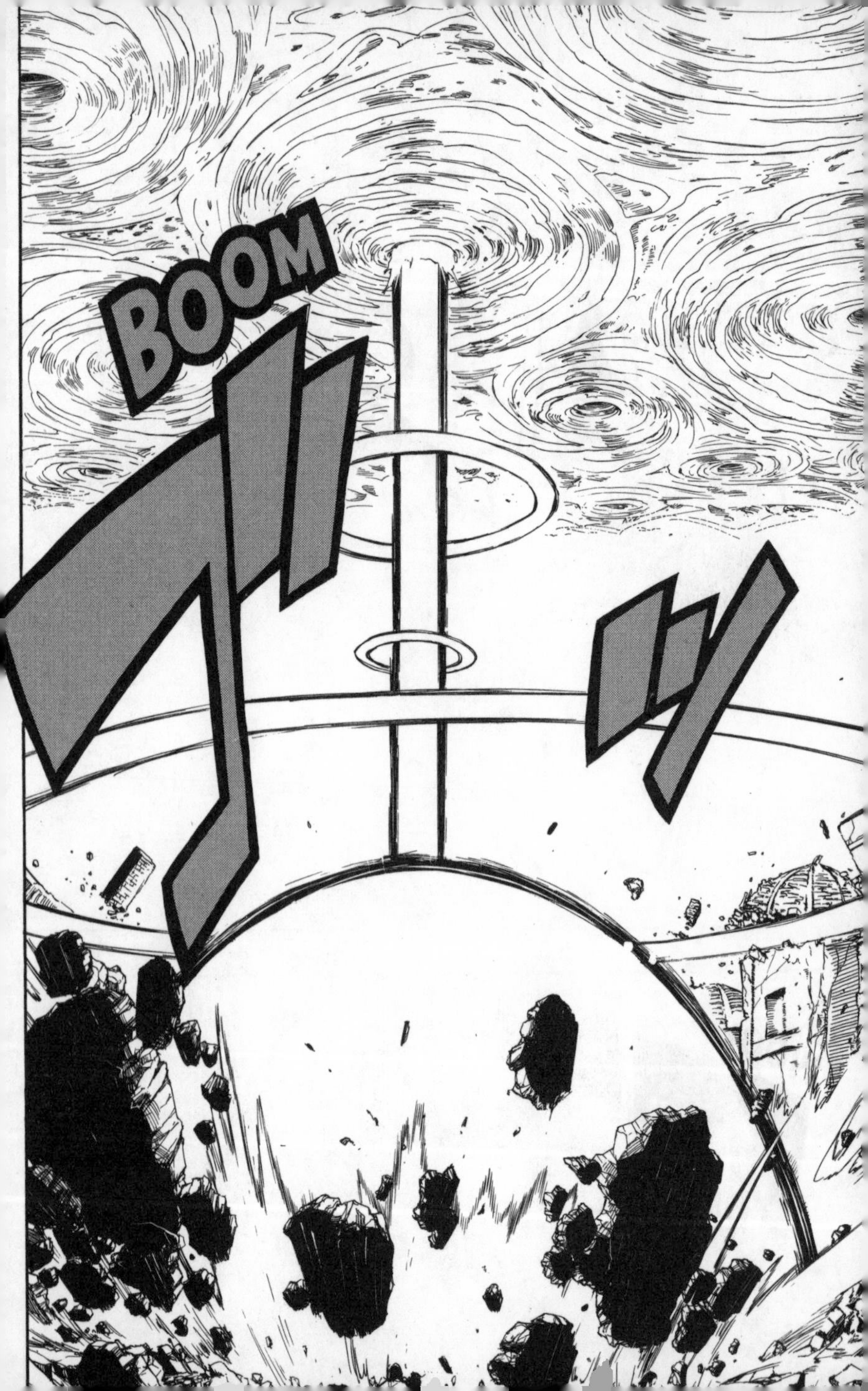
BOOM

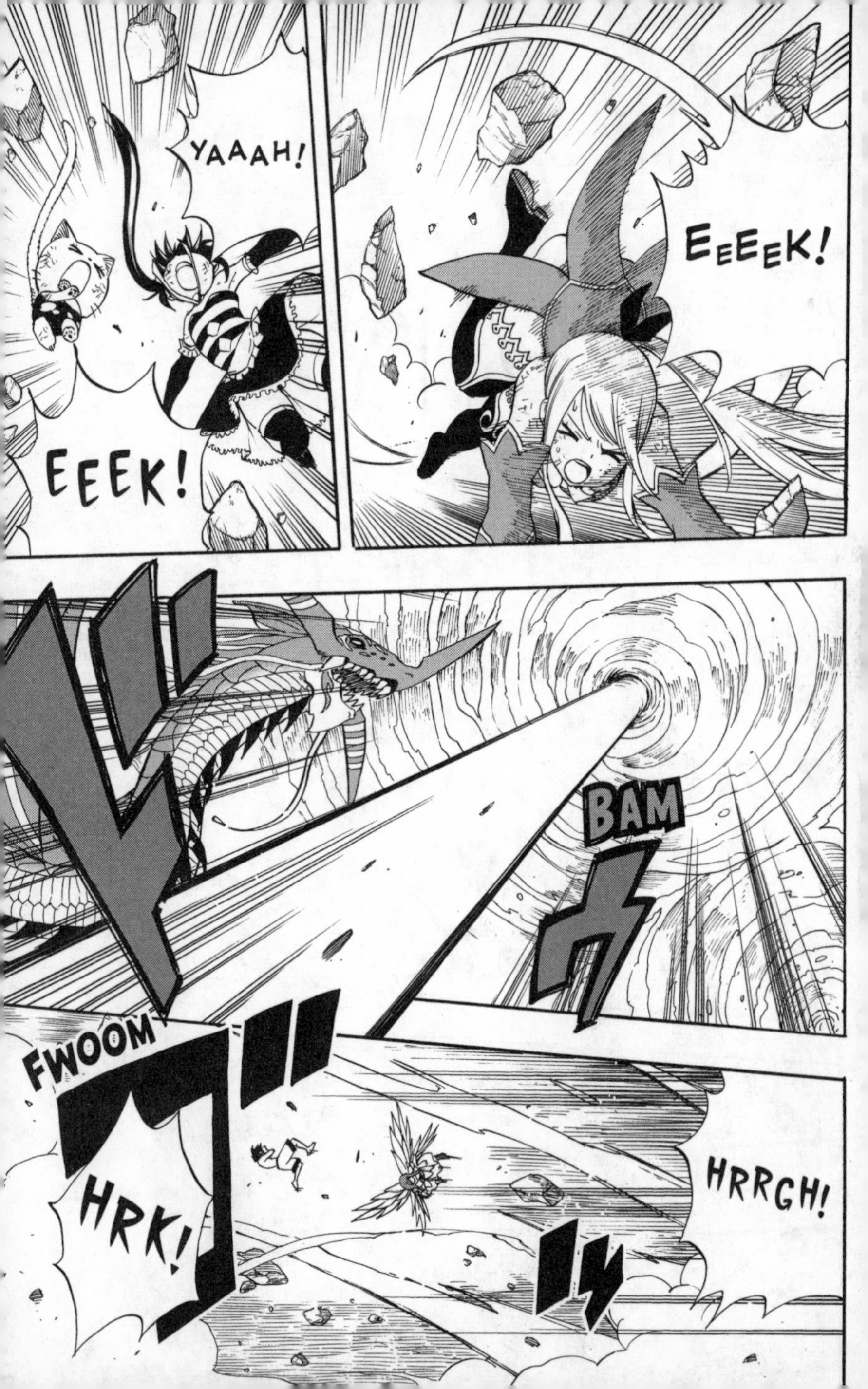
EEEEK!
YAAAH!
EEEK!
BAM
HRRGH!
FWOOM
HRK!

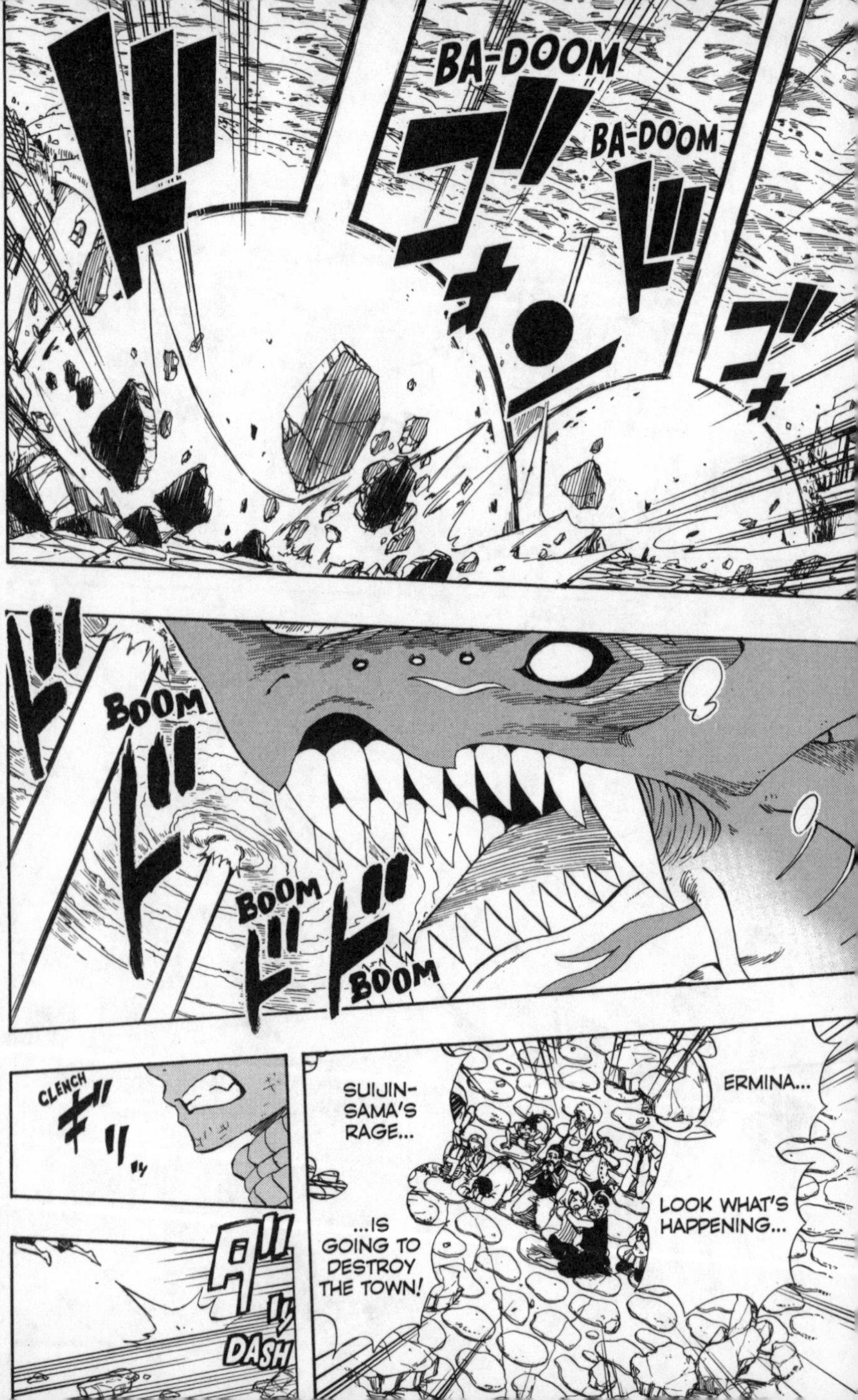
BA-DOOM
BA-DOOM
BOOM
BOOM
BOOM
ERMINA...
LOOK WHAT'S HAPPENING...
SUIJIN-SAMA'S RAGE...
...IS GOING TO DESTROY THE TOWN!
CLENCH
DASH

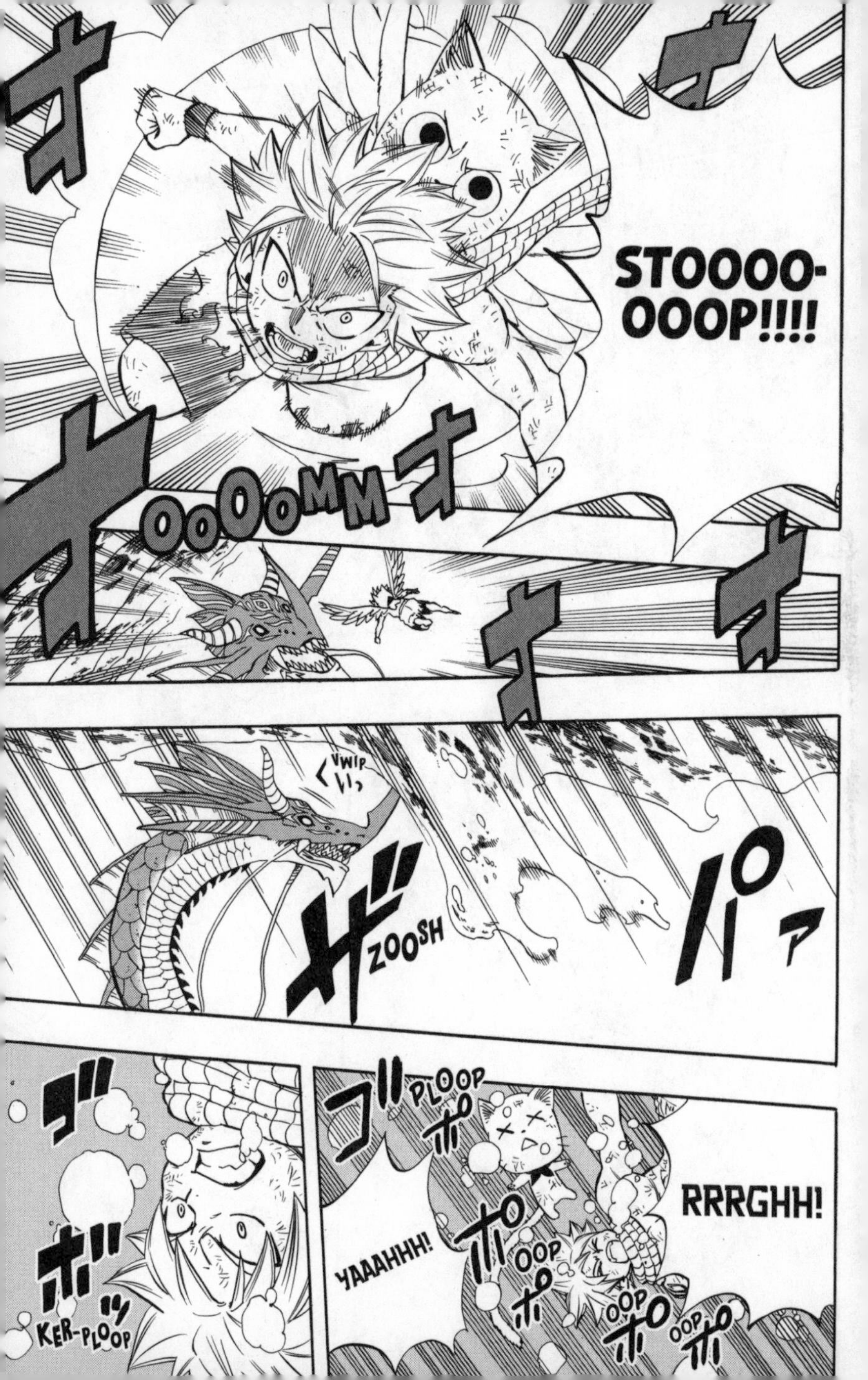
STOOOO-OOOP!!!!
OOOOOMM
VWIP
ZOOSH
PLOOP
RRRGHH!
YAAAHHH!
OOP
OOP
OOP
KER-PLOOP

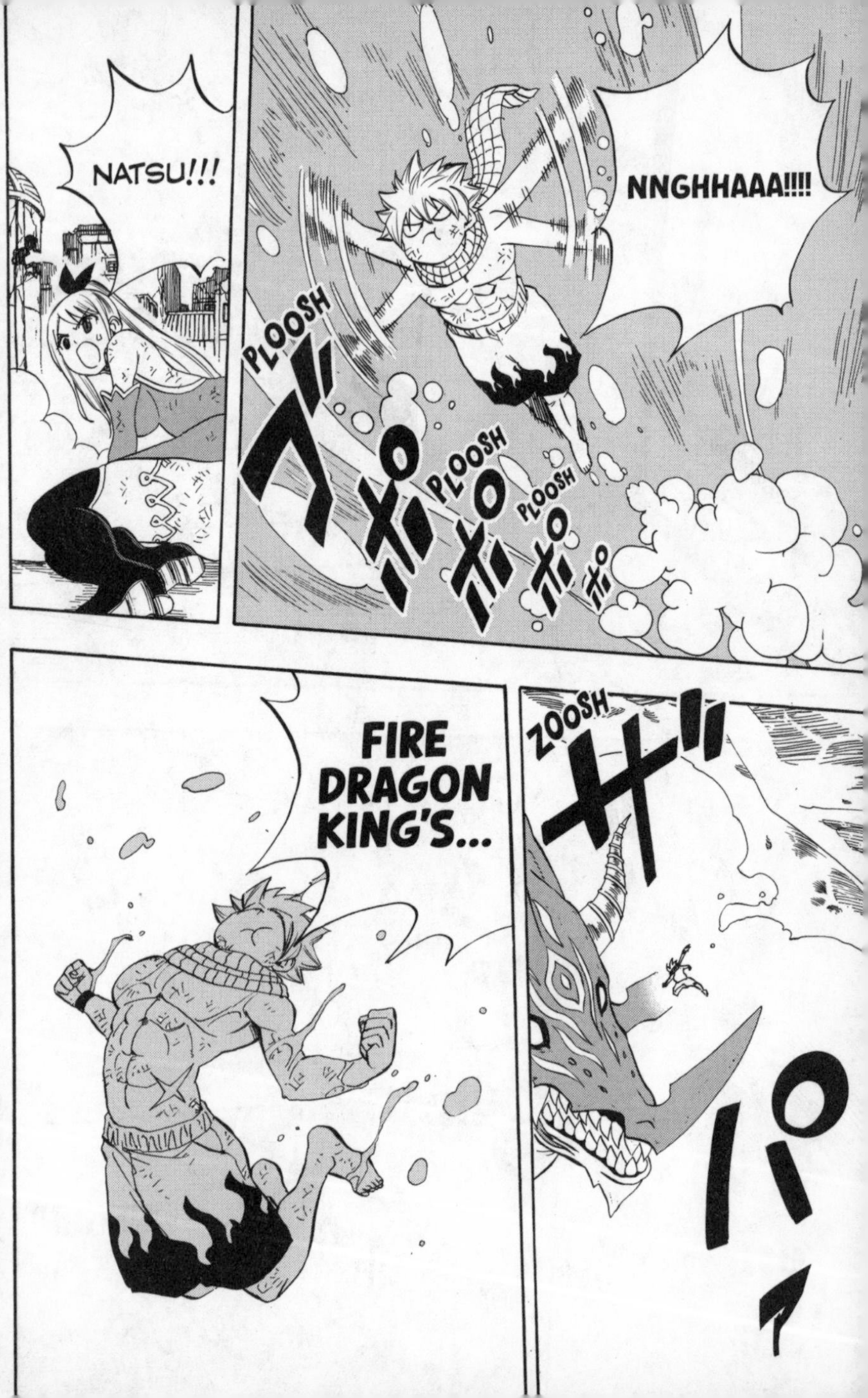
NNGHHAAA!!!!
PLOOSH
PLOOSH
PLOOSH
NATSU!!!
ZOOSH
FIRE DRAGON KING'S...

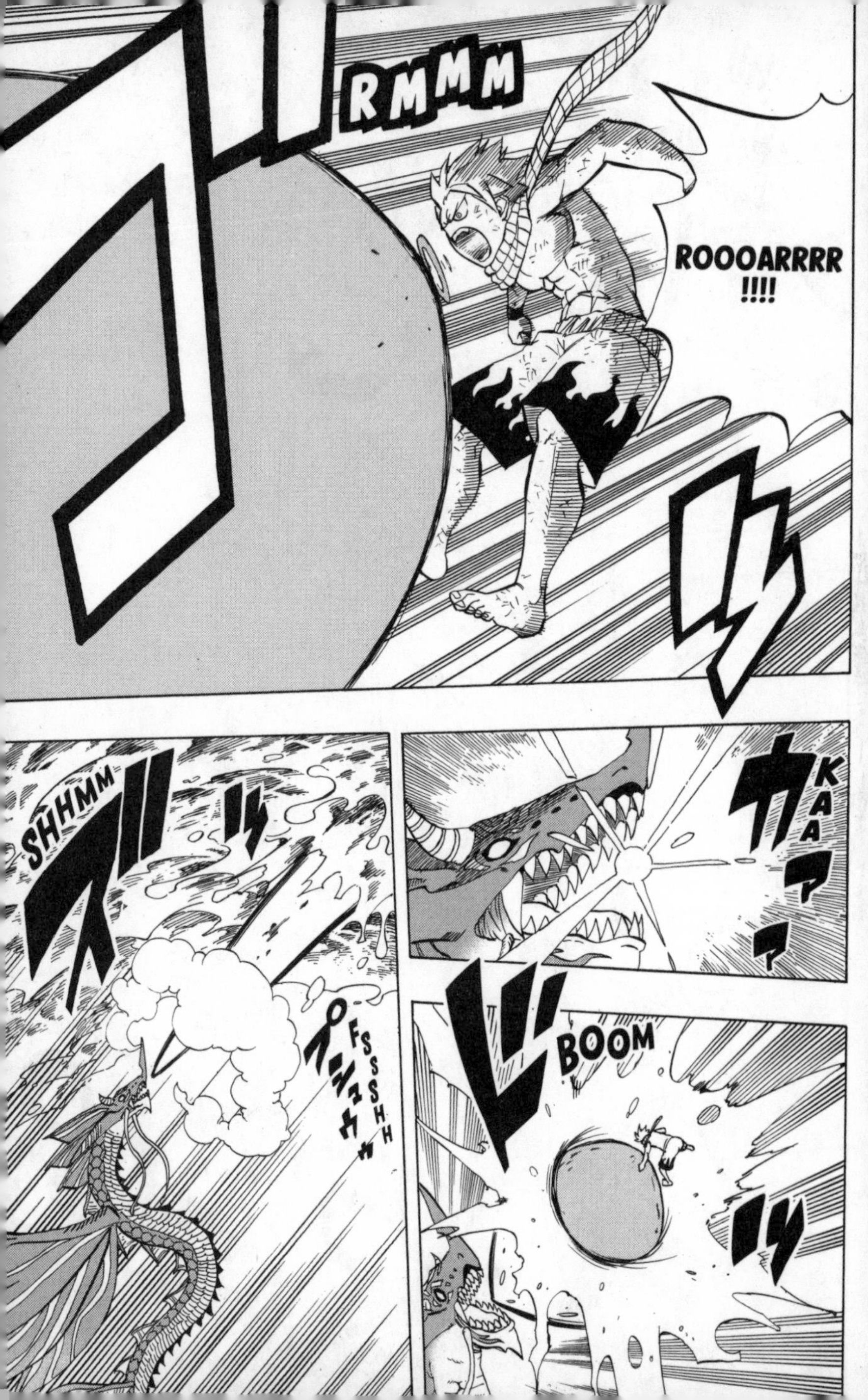
RMMM
ROOOARRRR !!!!
KAA
BOOM
SHHMM
FSSSHH

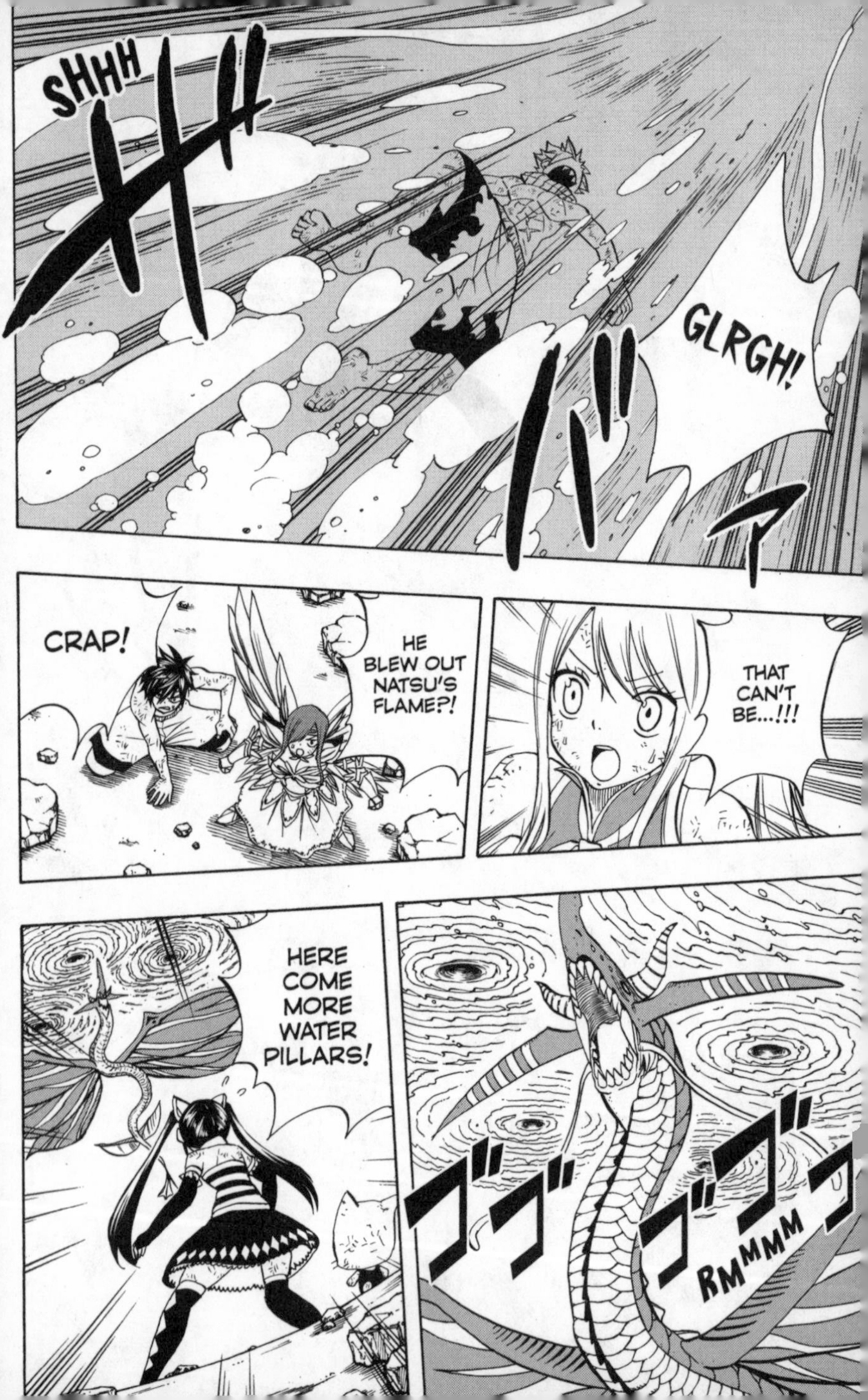

SHHH
GLRGH!
THAT CAN'T BE...!!!
CRAP!
HE BLEW OUT NATSU'S FLAME?!
RMMMM
HERE COME MORE WATER PILLARS!

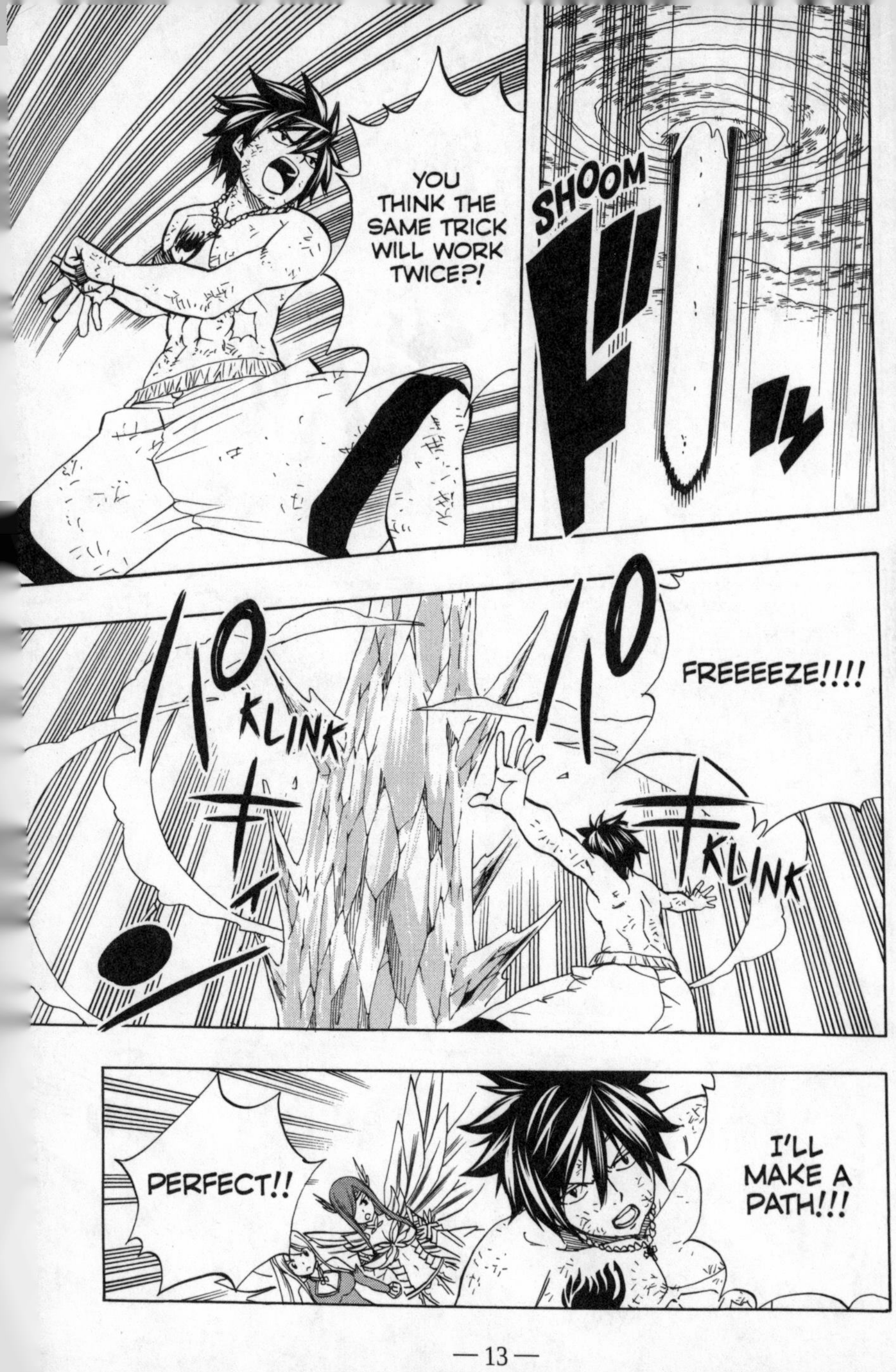
SHOOM
YOU THINK THE SAME TRICK WILL WORK TWICE?!
FREEEEZE!!!!
KLINK
KLINK
I'LL MAKE A PATH!!!
PERFECT!!

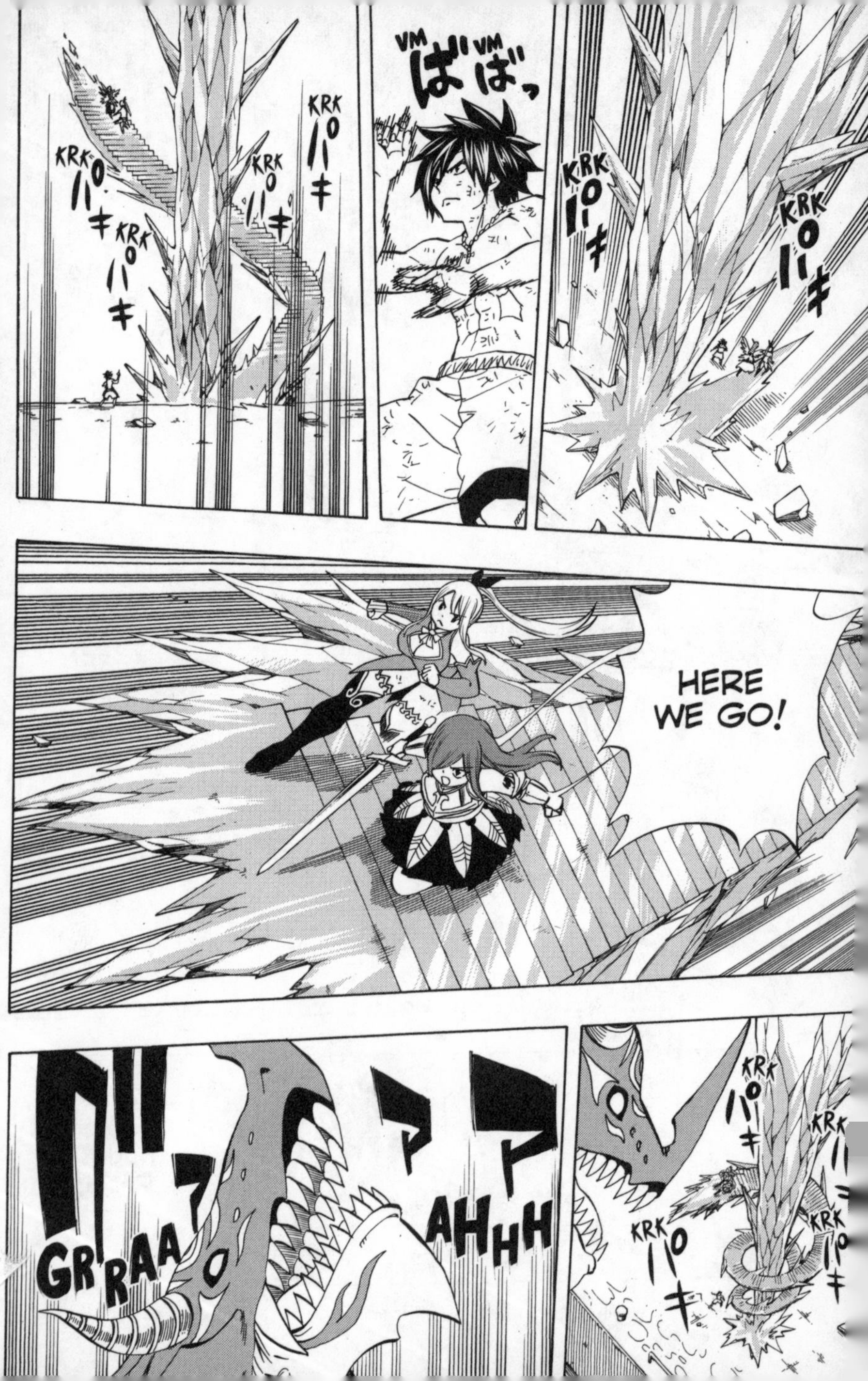

KRK パキ
KRK パキ
VM VM ばばっ
KRK パキ
KRK パキ
KRK パキ
KRK パキ
HERE WE GO!
KRK パキ
KRK パキ
KRK パキ
GRRAAAHHH

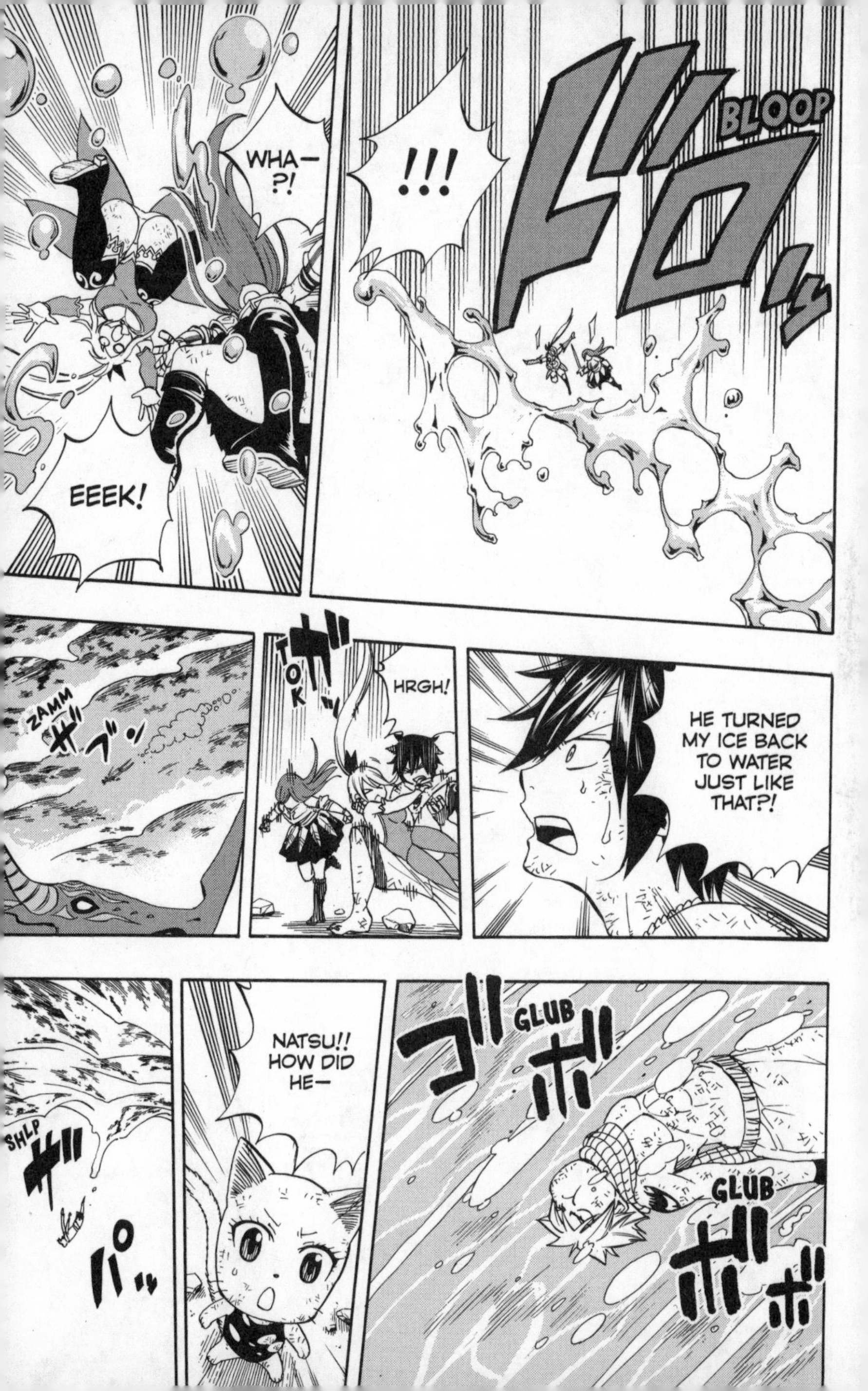
BLOOP
!!!
WHA— ?!
EEEK!
HE TURNED MY ICE BACK TO WATER JUST LIKE THAT?!
TOK
HRGH!
ZAMM
GLUB
GLUB
NATSU!! HOW DID HE—
SHLP

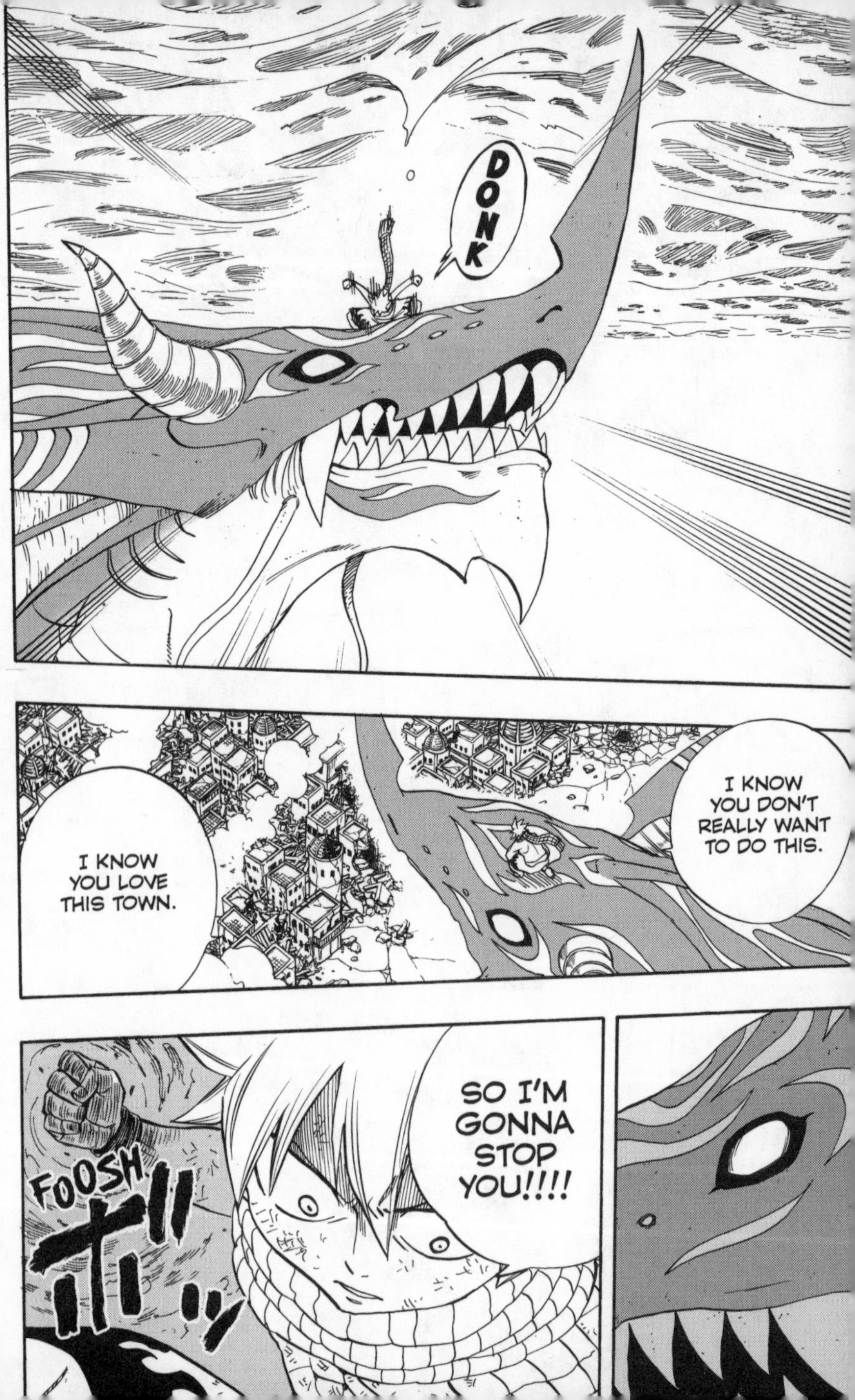
DONK
I KNOW YOU DON'T REALLY WANT TO DO THIS.
I KNOW YOU LOVE THIS TOWN.
SO I'M GONNA STOP YOU!!!!
FOOSH

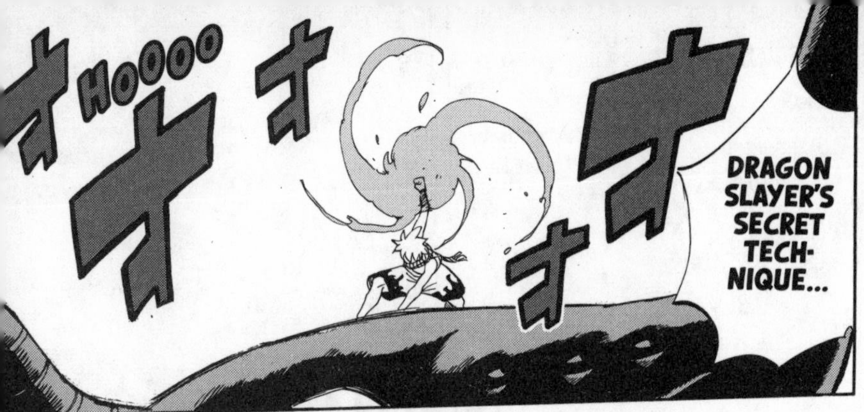
DRAGON SLAYER'S SECRET TECH-NIQUE...
HOOOO

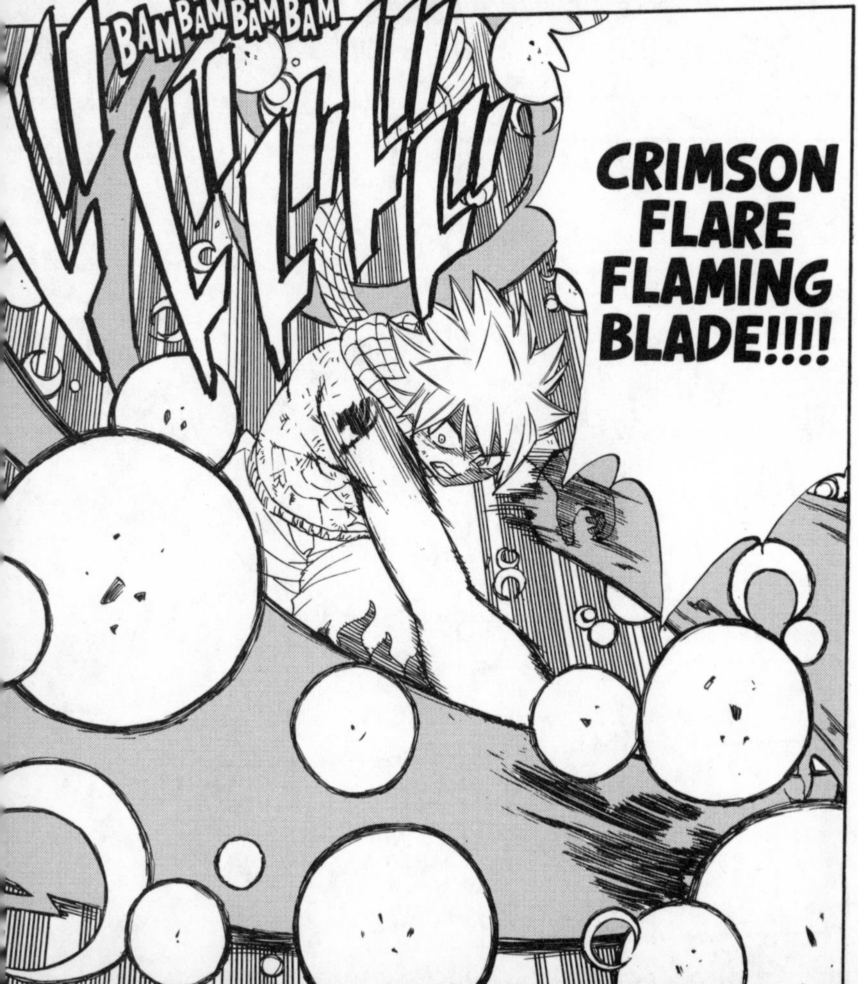
CRIMSON FLARE FLAMING BLADE!!!!
BAMBAMBAMBAM

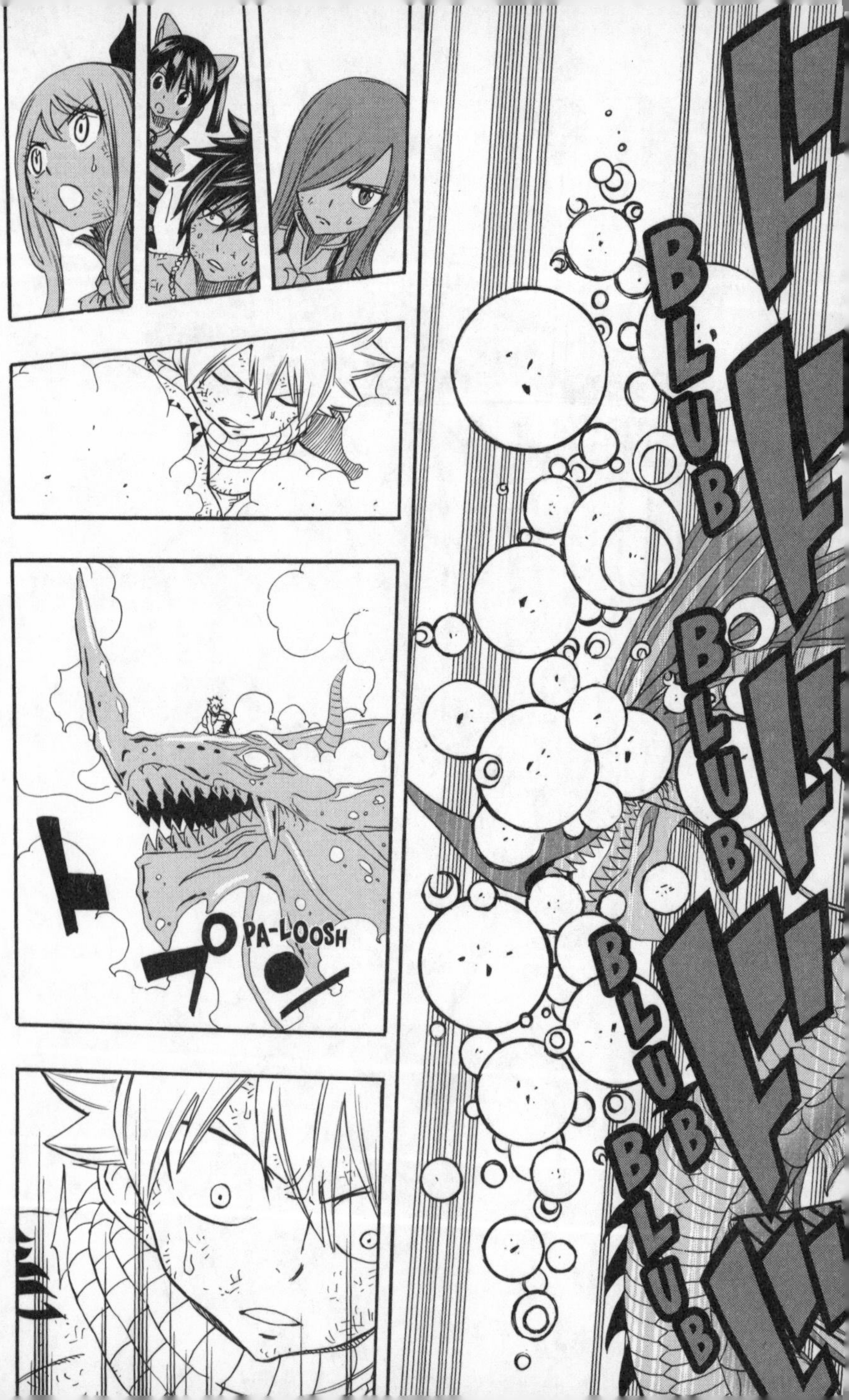
BLLUB
BLLUB
BLLUB
BLLUB
PA-LOOSH

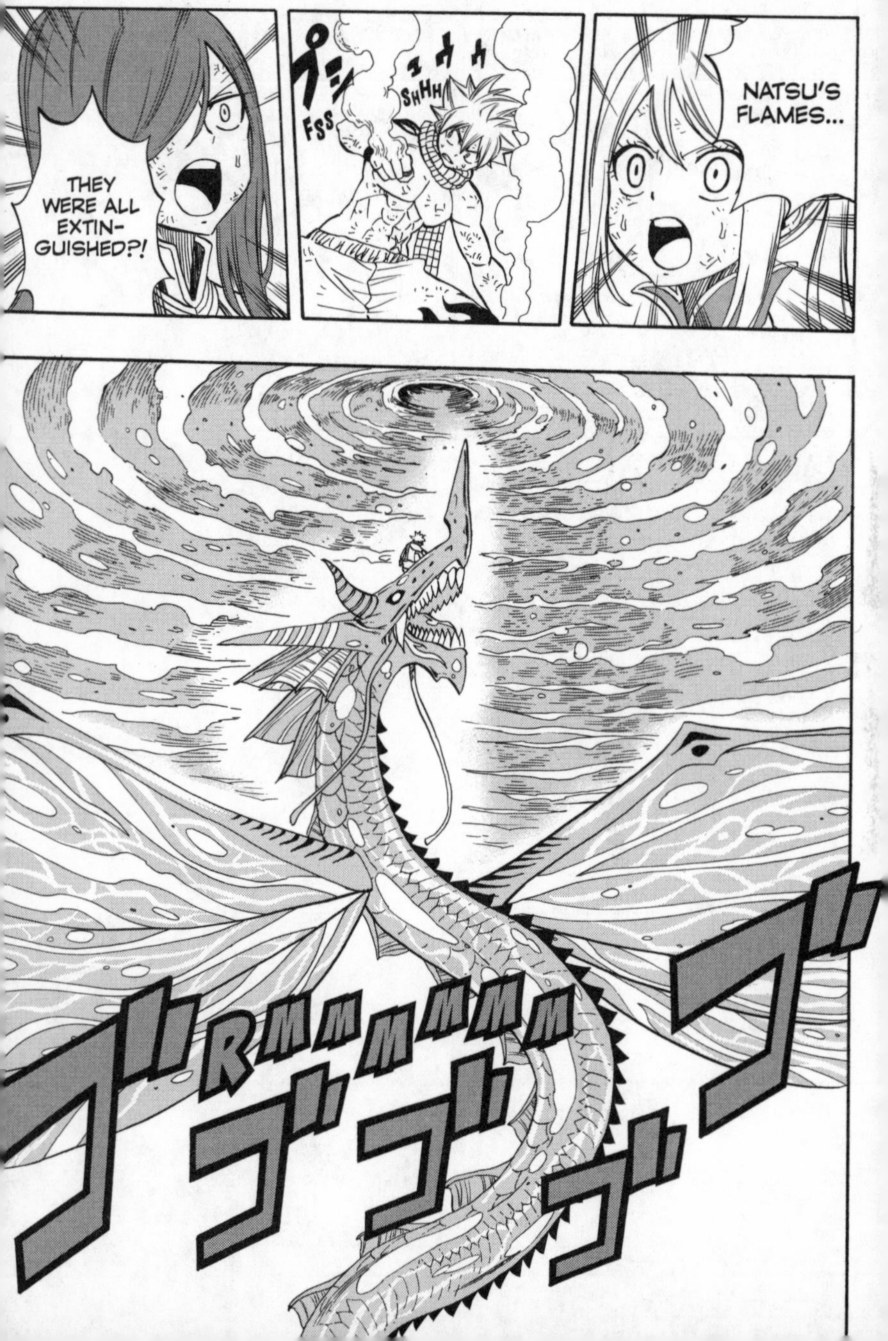
NATSU'S FLAMES...
FSS
SHHH
THEY WERE ALL EXTIN-GUISHED?!
RMMMMMMM

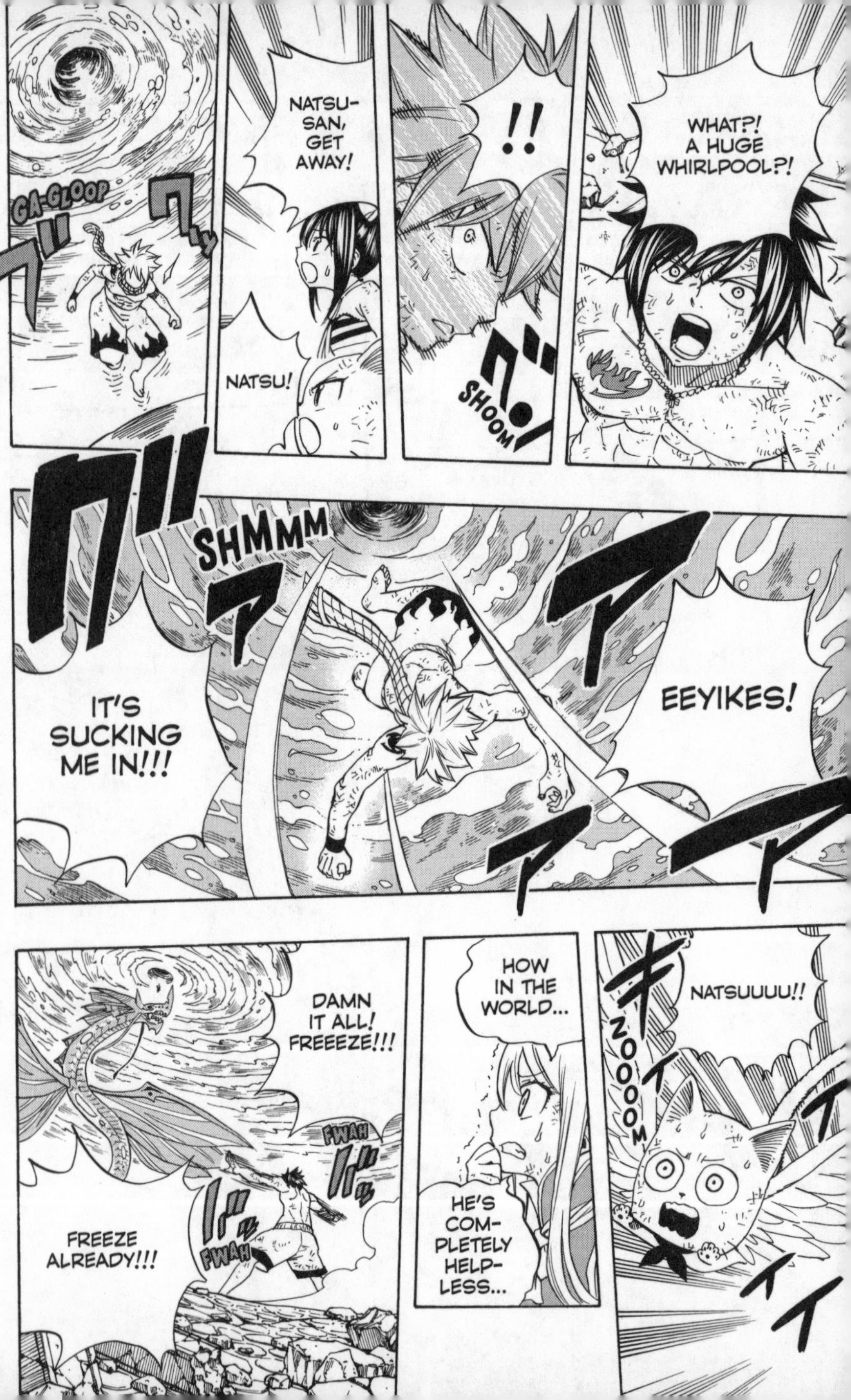
WHAT?! A HUGE WHIRLPOOL?!
!!
SHOOM
NATSU-SAN, GET AWAY!
NATSU!
GA-GLOOP
EEYIKES!
SHMMMM
IT'S SUCKING ME IN!!!
NATSUUUU!!
ZOOOOM
HOW IN THE WORLD...
HE'S COM-PLETELY HELP-LESS...
DAMN IT ALL! FREEEZE!!!
FWAH
FREEZE ALREADY!!!
FWAH

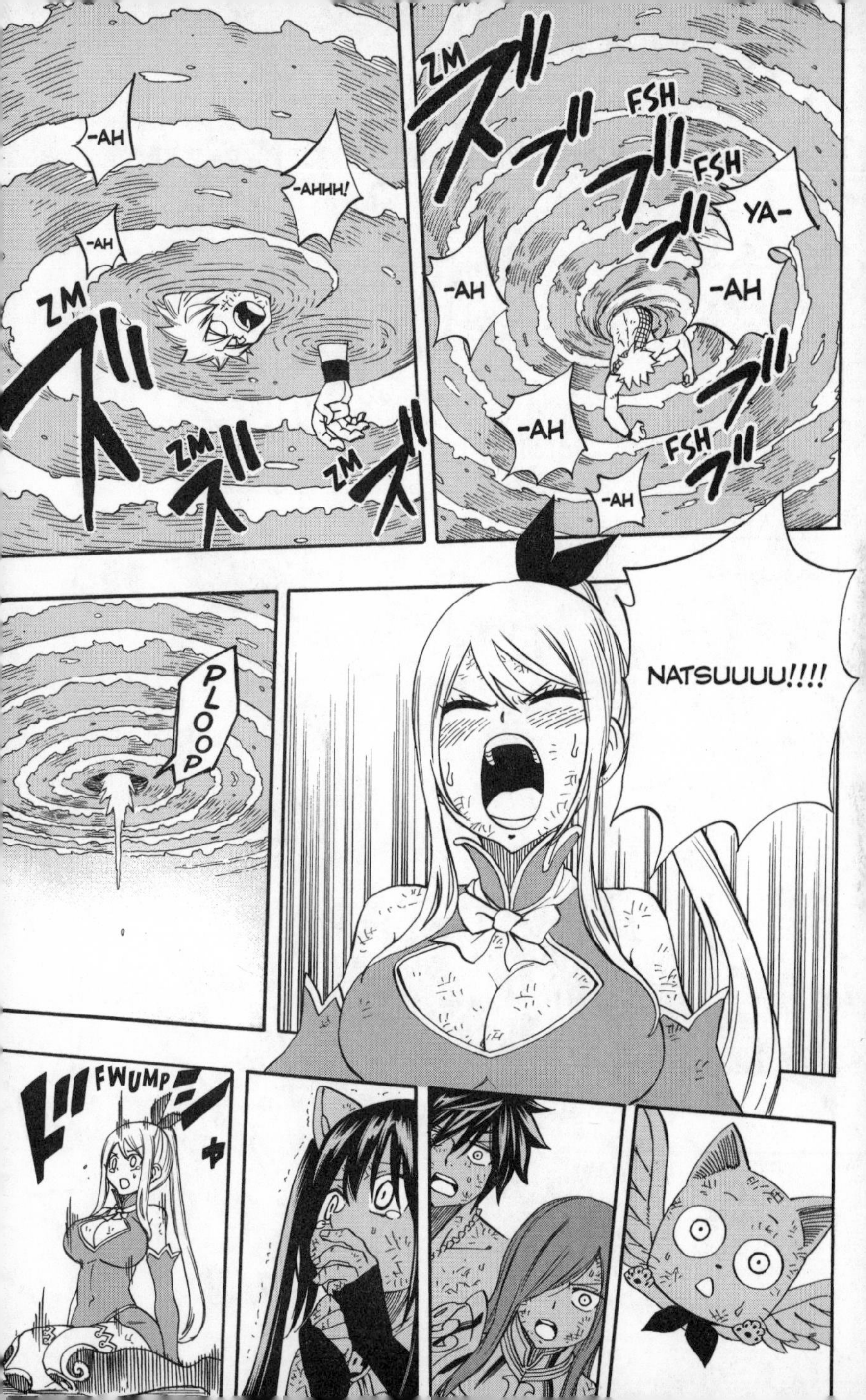
ZM
FSH
FSH
YA-
-AH
-AH
FSH
-AH
-AH
-AHHH!
-AH
-AH
ZM
ZM
ZM
NATSUUUU!!!!
PLOOP
FWUMP

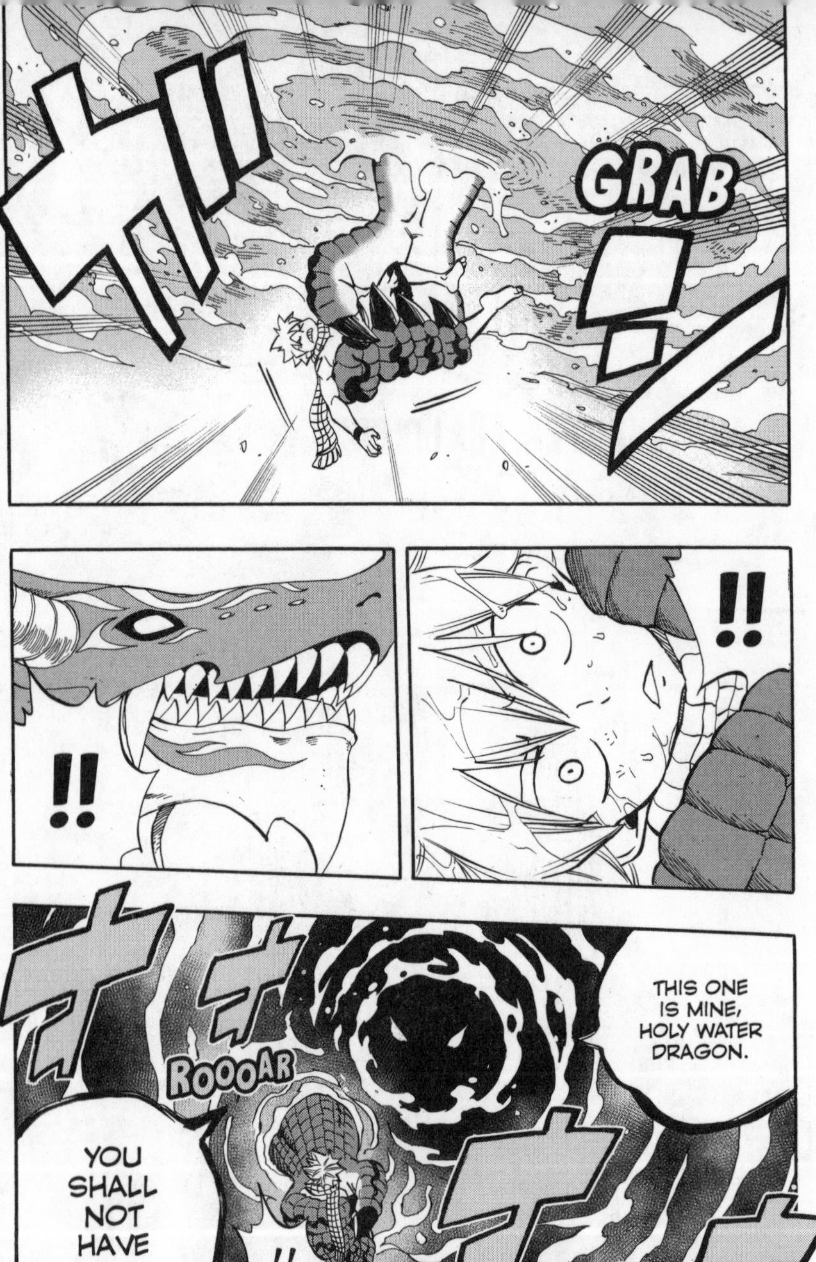
GRAB
!!
!!
THIS ONE IS MINE, HOLY WATER DRAGON.
ROOOAR
YOU SHALL NOT HAVE HIM.
!!

FAIRY TAIL 100 YEARS QUEST

Chapter 20: Lineage of Fire

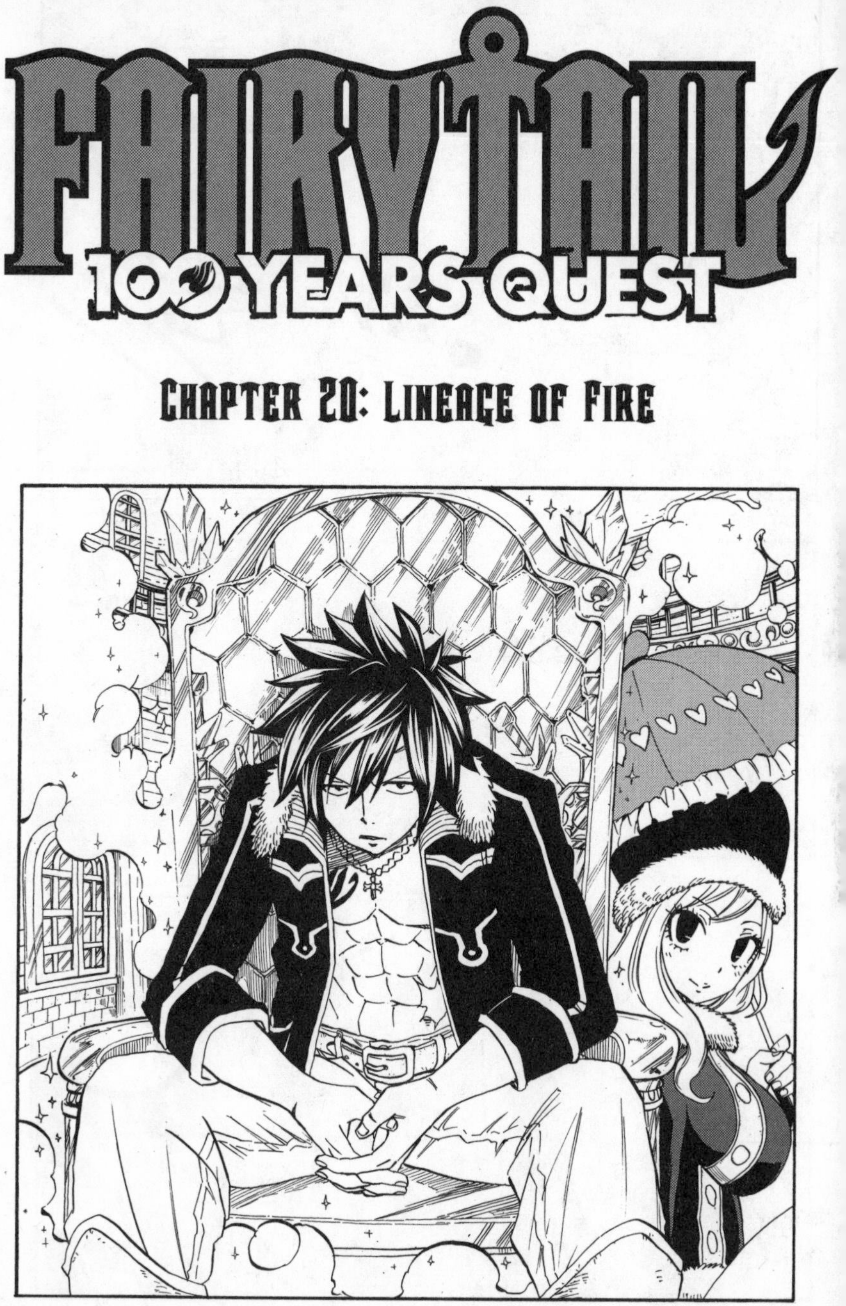

ゴゴ ゴゴ ゴゴ ゴゴ...

RMMMMMMM

WH—

WHAT'S WITH THE HAND?!

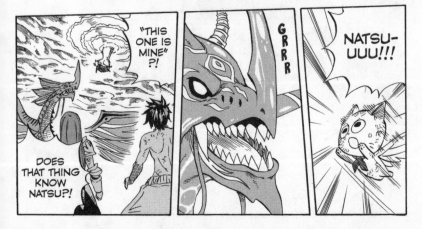

"THIS ONE IS MINE"?!

DOES THAT THING KNOW NATSU?!

GRRR

NATSU-UUU!!!

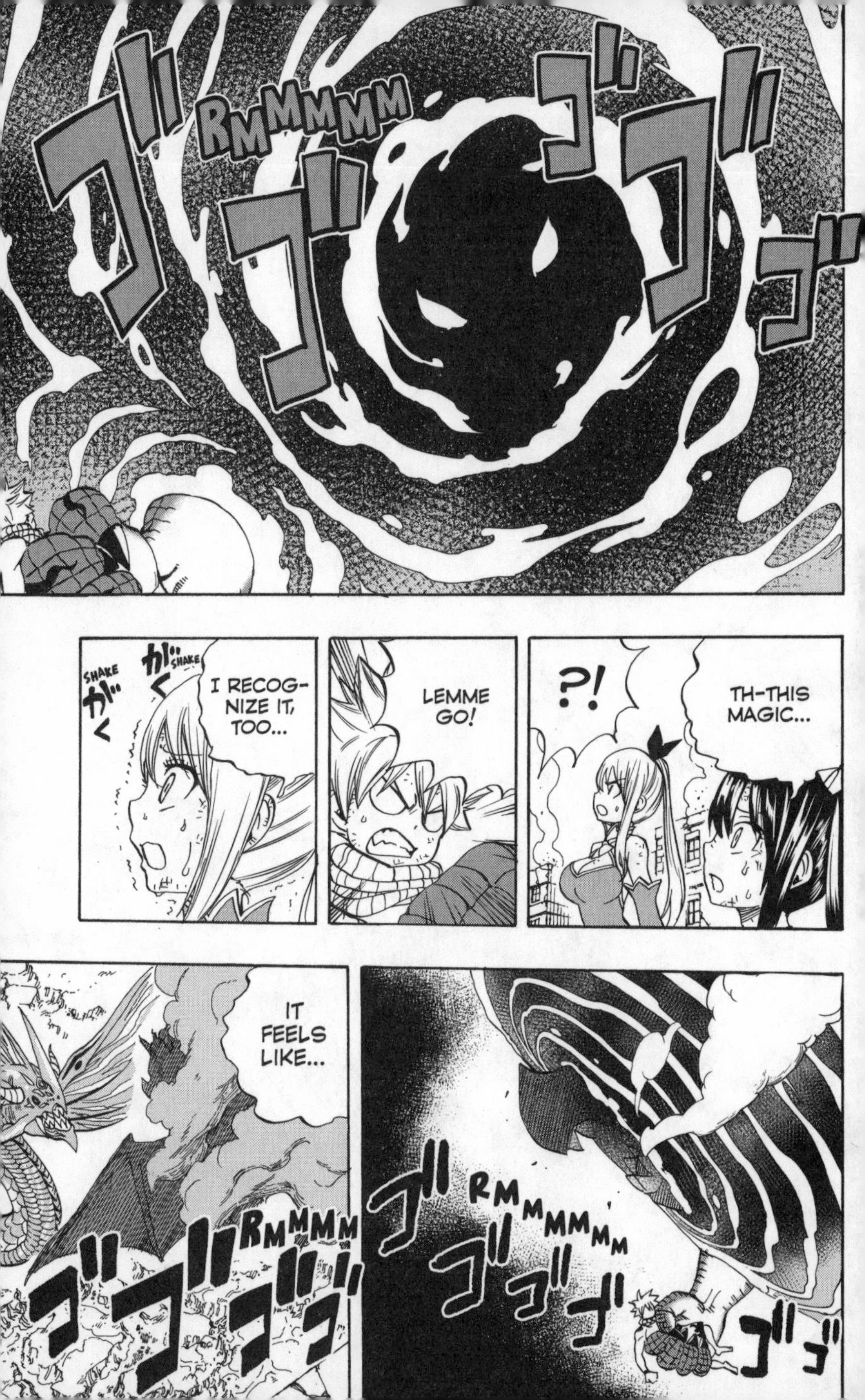
RMMMMMM
TH-THIS MAGIC...
?!
LEMME GO!
I RECOG-NIZE IT, TOO...
SHAKE
SHAKE
RMMMMMMM
IT FEELS LIKE...
RMMMM

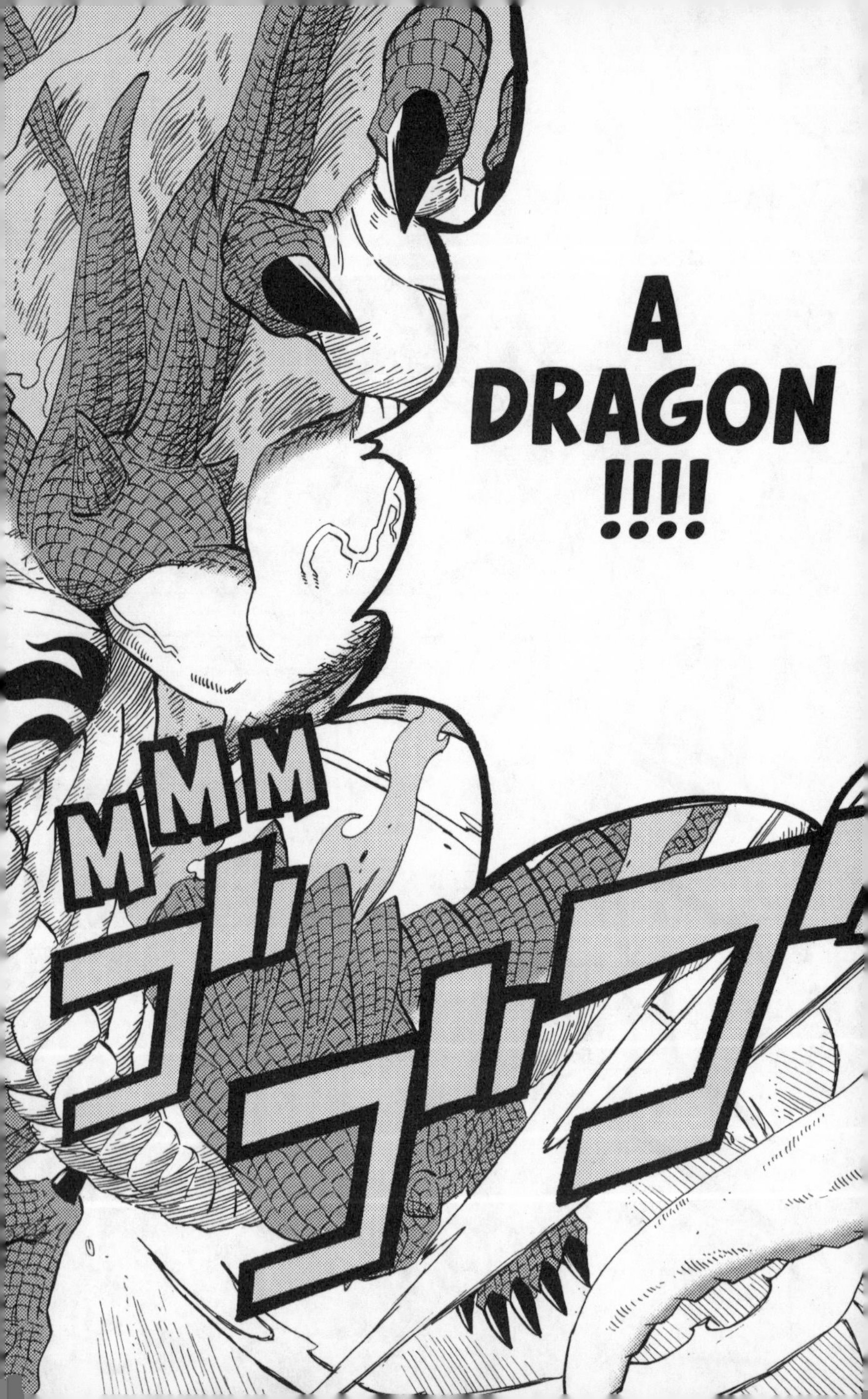
A DRAGON !!!!
MMM
ゴゴゴ

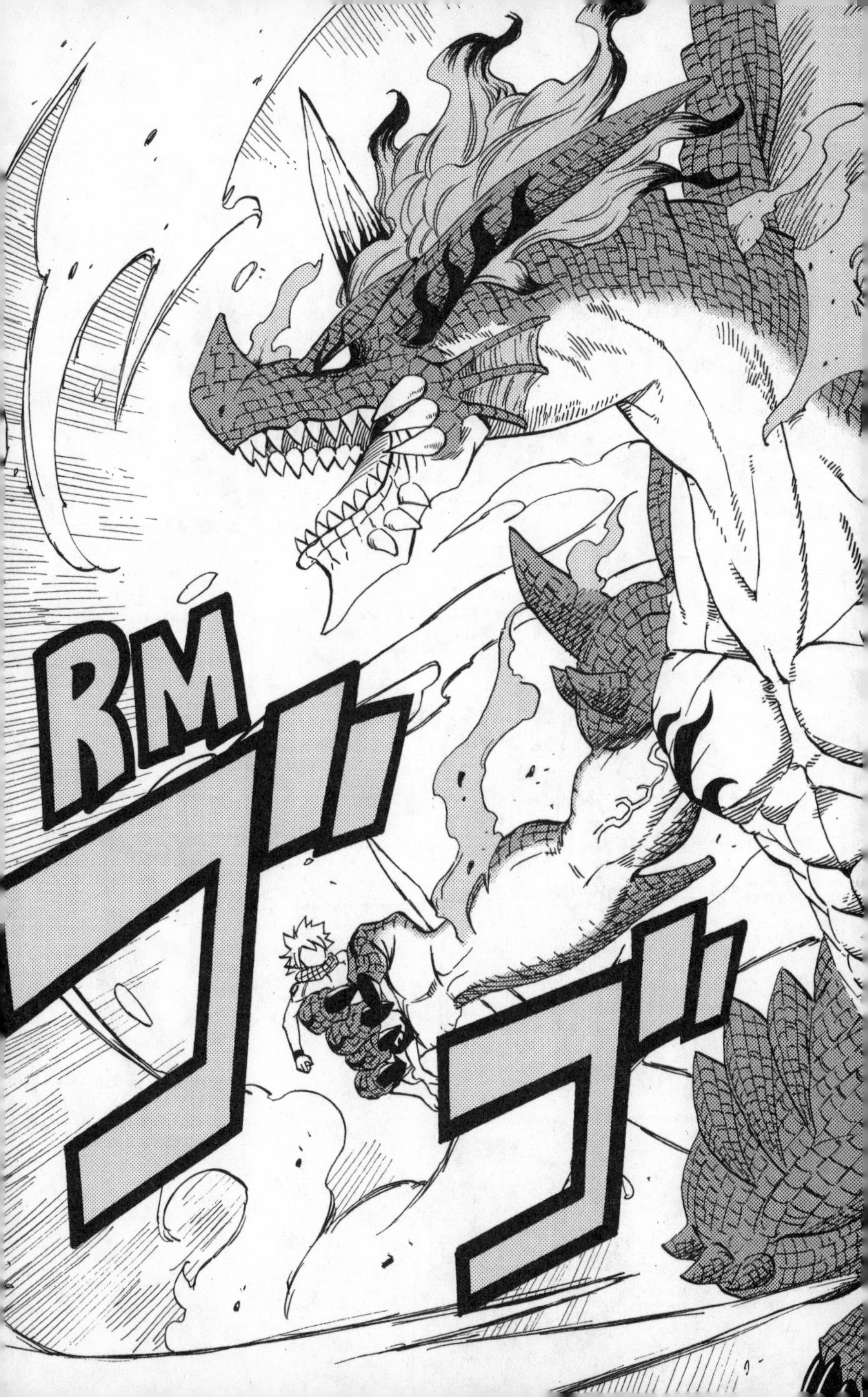
RM
ゴゴ

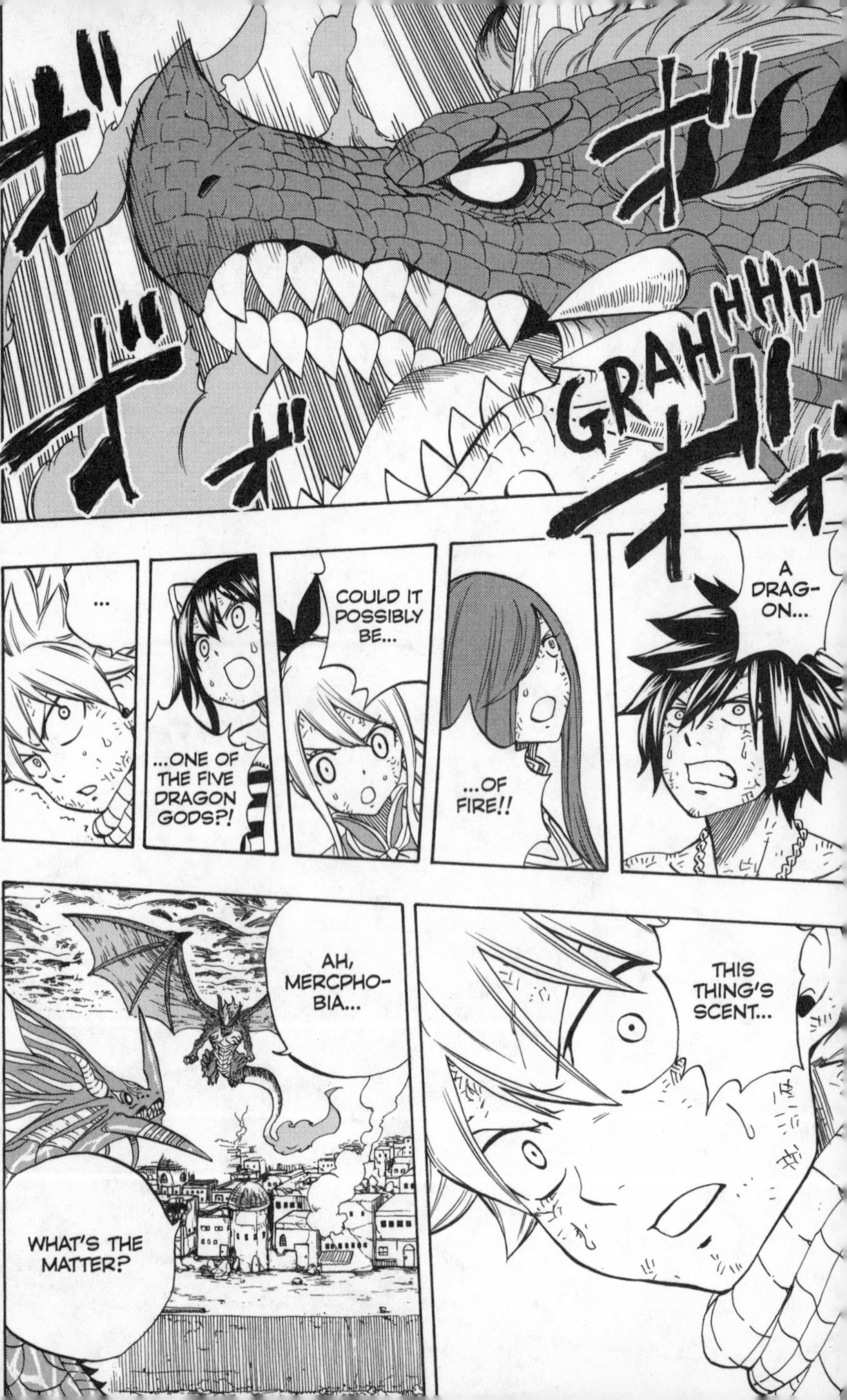
GRAHHHH
A DRAG-ON...
...OF FIRE!!
COULD IT POSSIBLY BE...
...ONE OF THE FIVE DRAGON GODS?!
...
THIS THING'S SCENT...
AH, MERCPHOBIA...
WHAT'S THE MATTER?

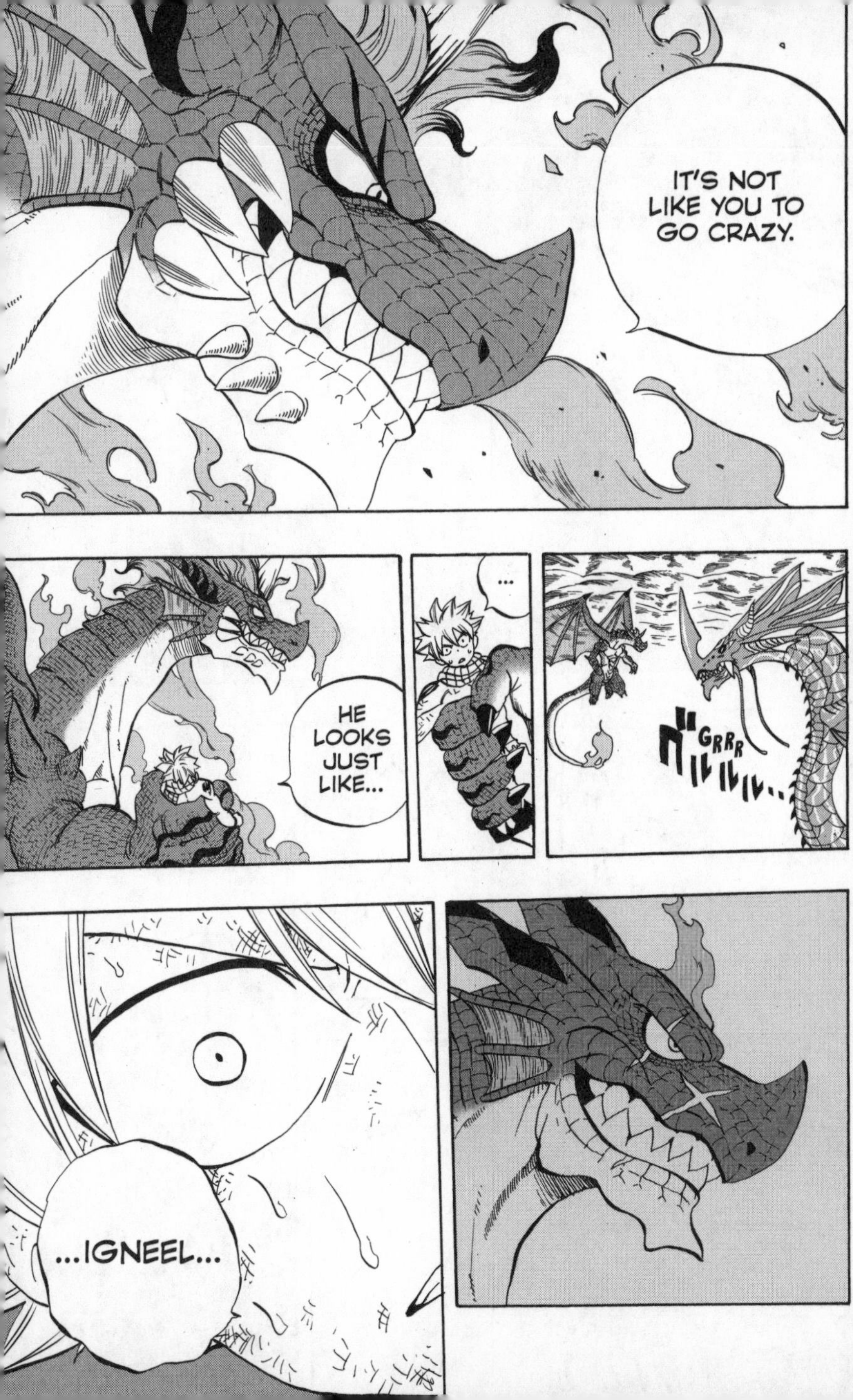
IT'S NOT LIKE YOU TO GO CRAZY.
GRRR
...
HE LOOKS JUST LIKE...
...IGNEEL...

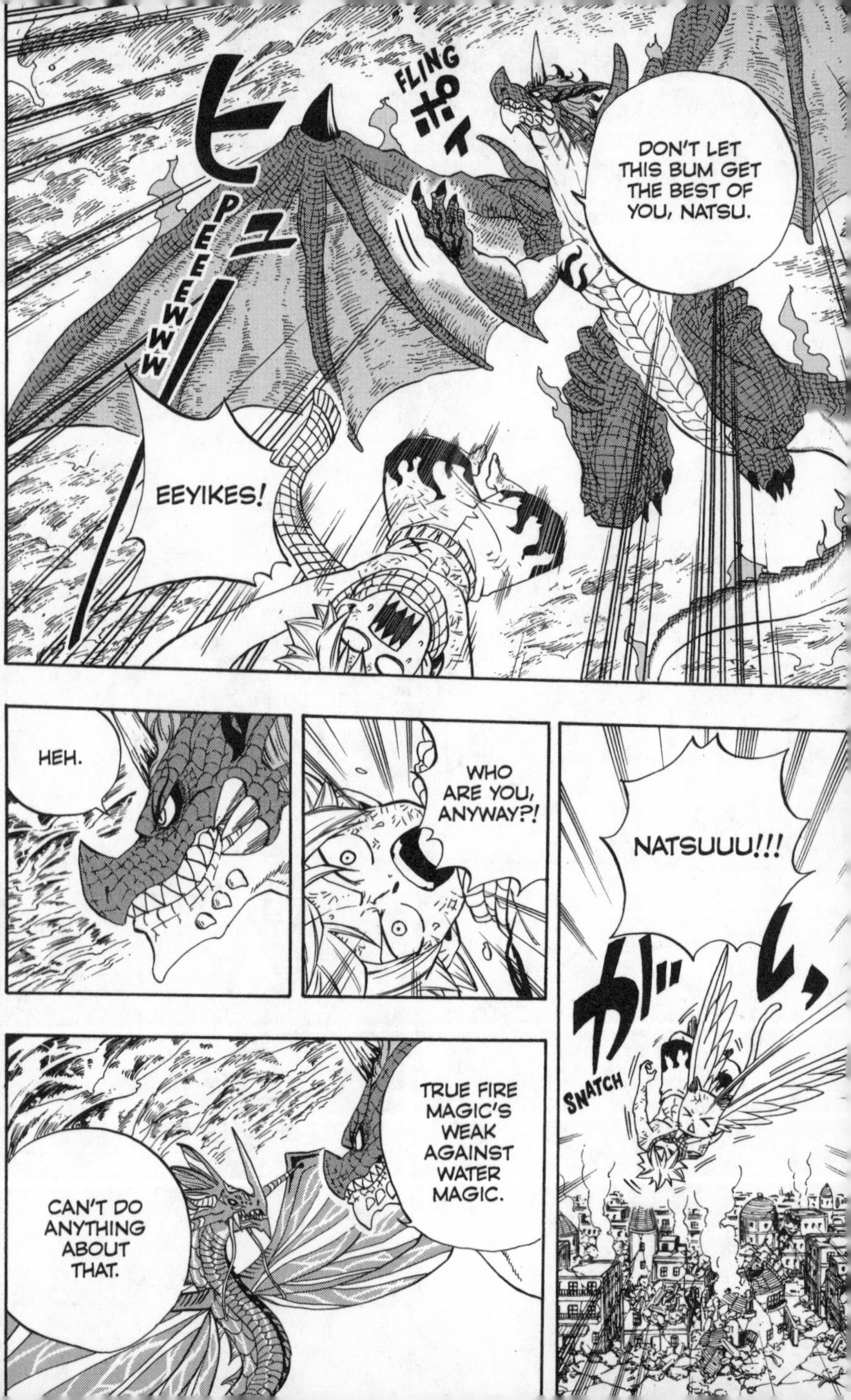
FLING
DON'T LET THIS BUM GET THE BEST OF YOU, NATSU.
PEEEEWWW
EEYIKES!
WHO ARE YOU, ANYWAY?!
HEH.
TRUE FIRE MAGIC'S WEAK AGAINST WATER MAGIC.
CAN'T DO ANYTHING ABOUT THAT.
NATSUUU!!!
SNATCH

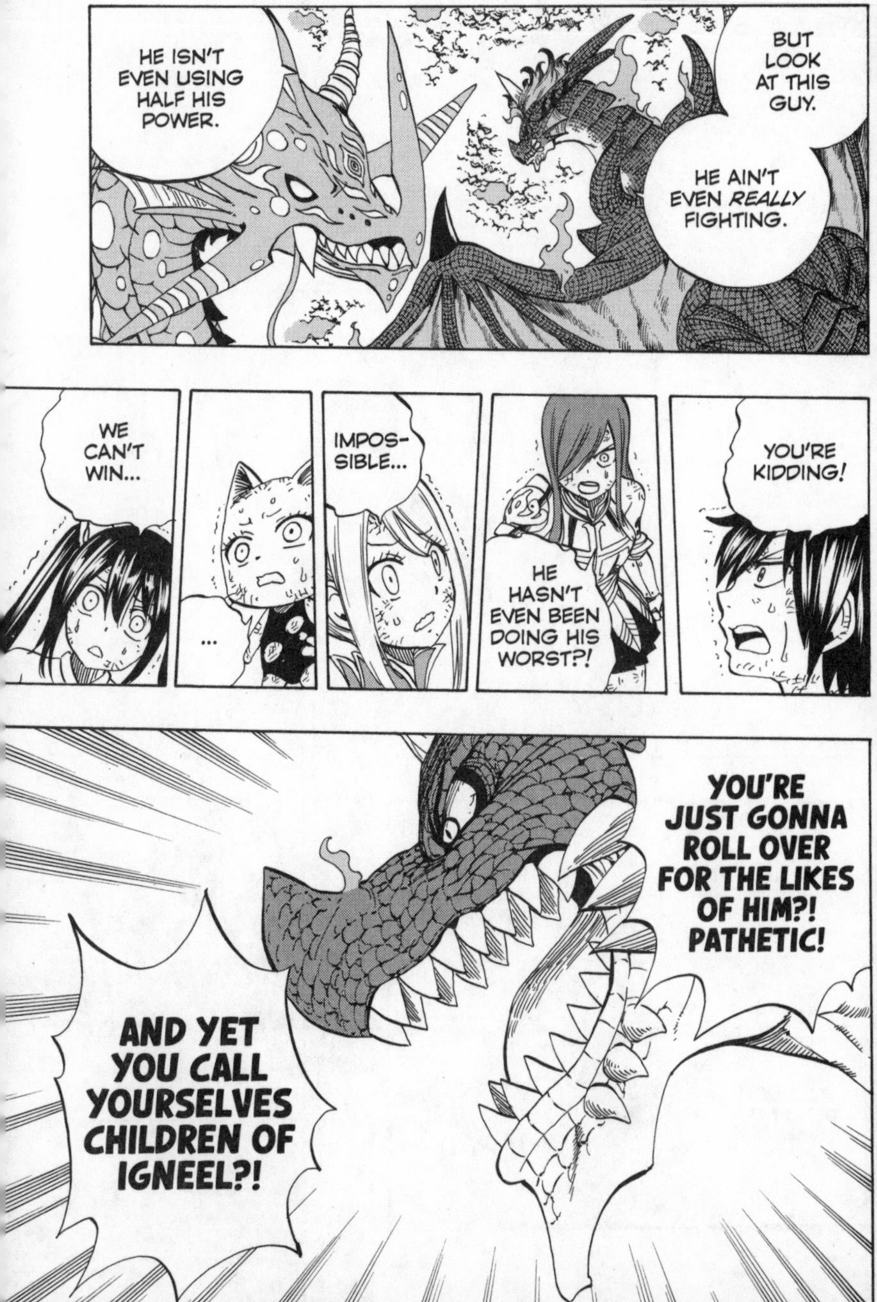
BUT LOOK AT THIS GUY.
HE AIN'T EVEN *REALLY* FIGHTING.
HE ISN'T EVEN USING HALF HIS POWER.
YOU'RE KIDDING!
HE HASN'T EVEN BEEN DOING HIS WORST?!
IMPOSSIBLE...
...
WE CAN'T WIN...
YOU'RE JUST GONNA ROLL OVER FOR THE LIKES OF HIM?! PATHETIC!
AND YET YOU CALL YOURSELVES CHILDREN OF IGNEEL?!

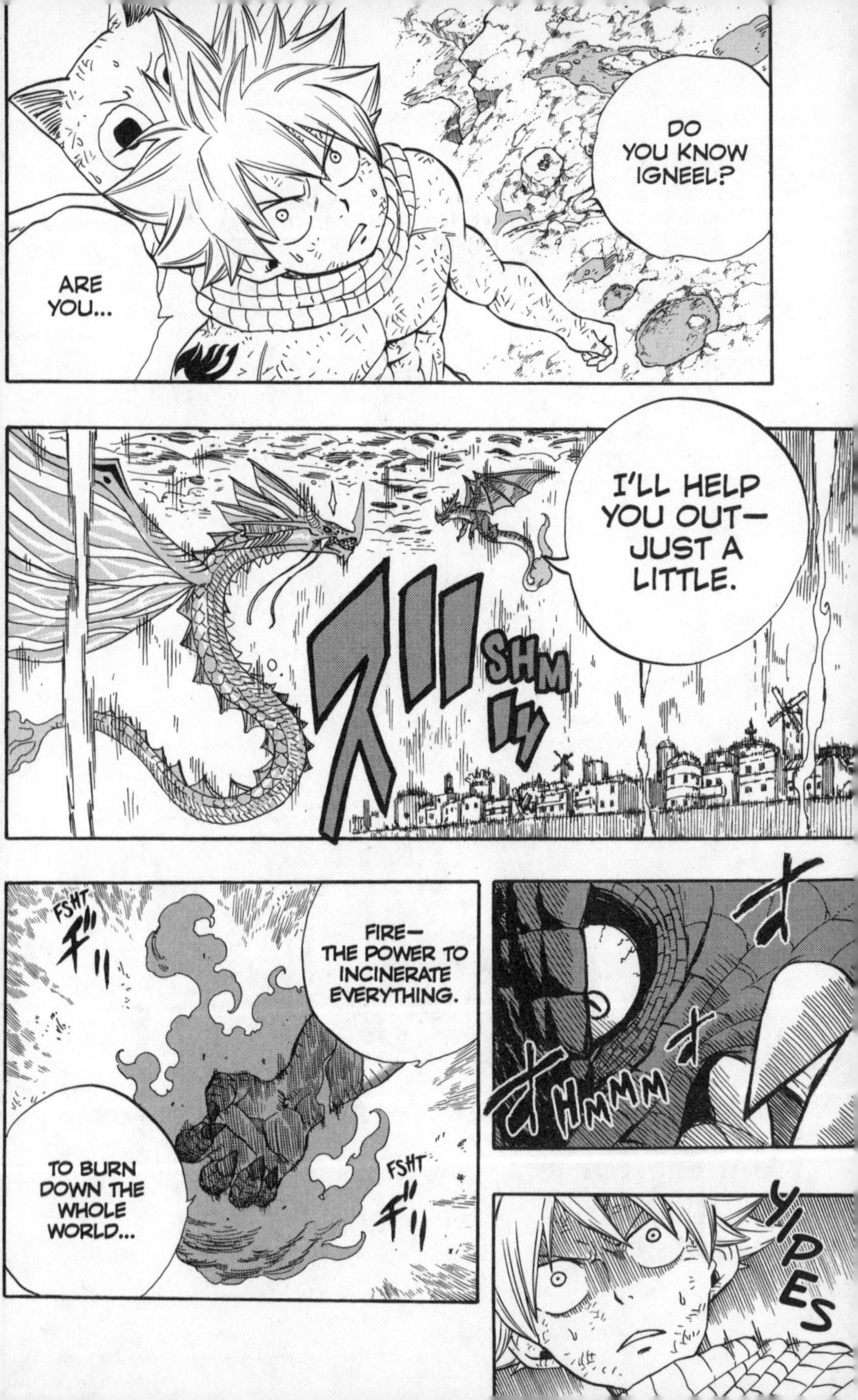
DO YOU KNOW IGNEEL?
ARE YOU...
I'LL HELP YOU OUT— JUST A LITTLE.
SHMM
HMMM
YIPES
FSHT
FIRE— THE POWER TO INCINERATE EVERYTHING.
TO BURN DOWN THE WHOLE WORLD...
FSHT

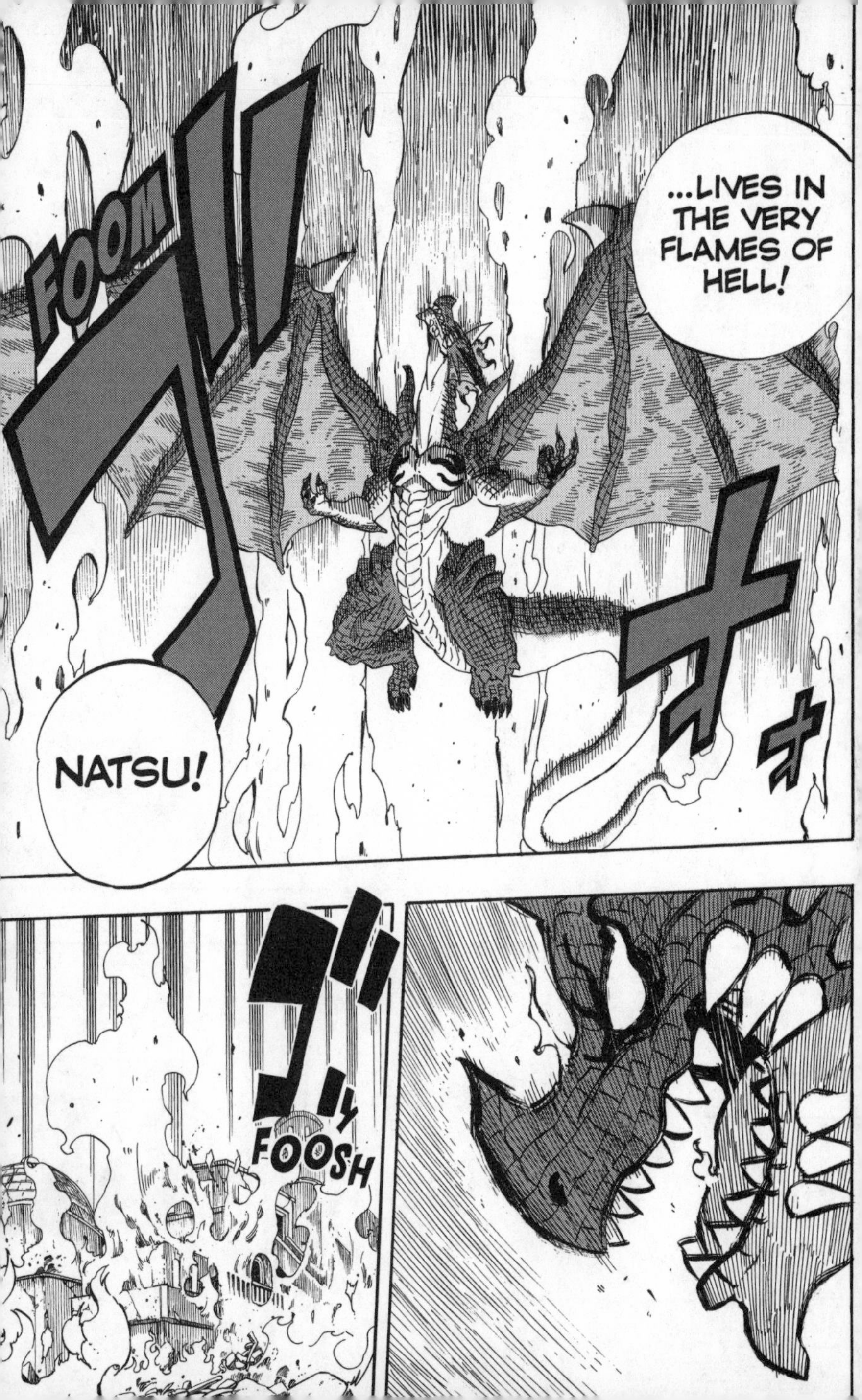
...LIVES IN THE VERY FLAMES OF HELL!
FOOM
NATSU!
FOOSH

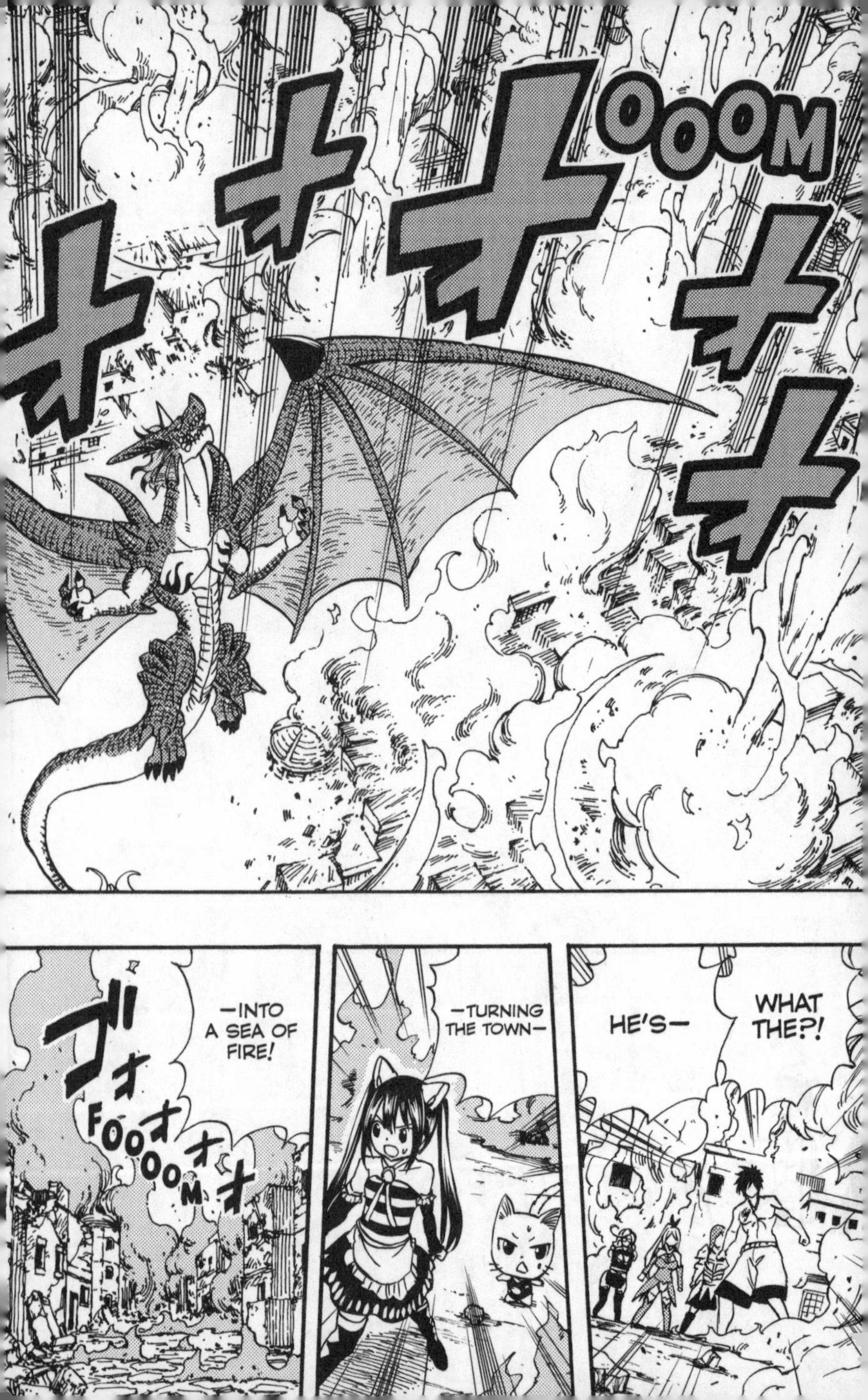
OOOM
WHAT THE?!
HE'S—
—TURNING THE TOWN—
—INTO A SEA OF FIRE!
ゴォ
FOOOOM

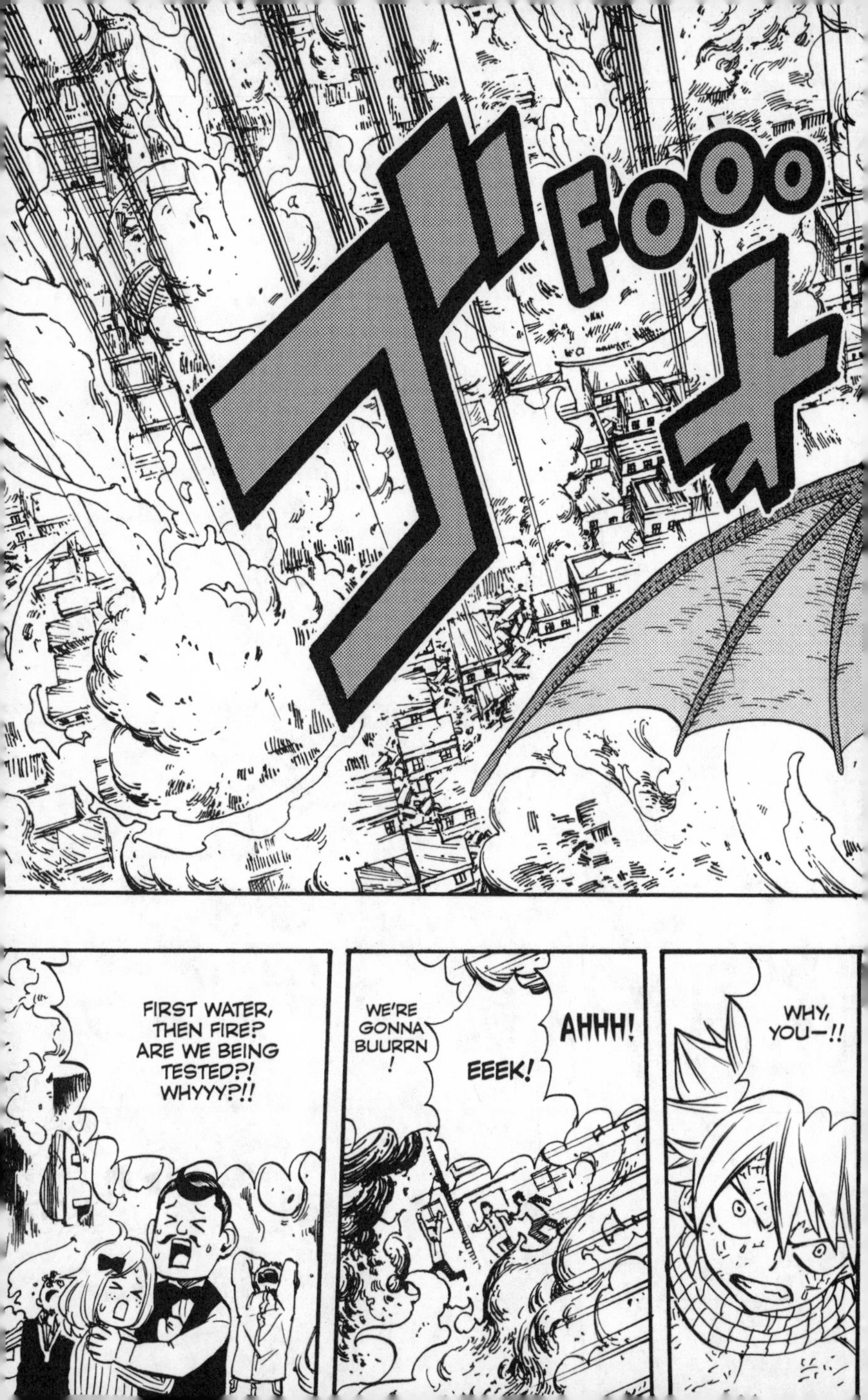
ゴォ
FOOO
WHY, YOU—!!
AHHH!
WE'RE GONNA BUURRN!
EEEK!
FIRST WATER, THEN FIRE? ARE WE BEING TESTED?! WHYYY?!!

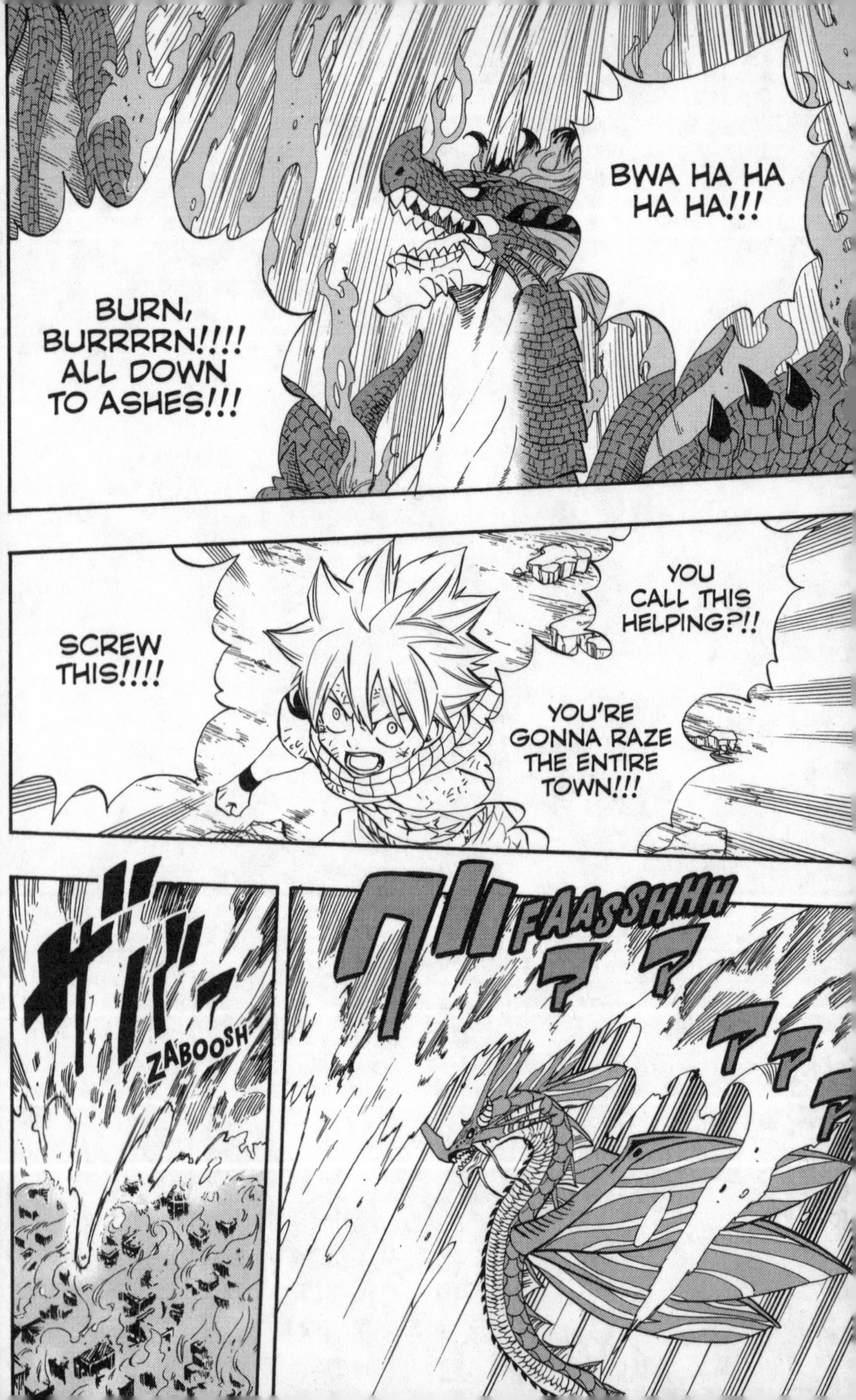
BWA HA HA HA HA!!!
BURN, BURRRRN!!!! ALL DOWN TO ASHES!!!
YOU CALL THIS HELPING?!!
YOU'RE GONNA RAZE THE ENTIRE TOWN!!!
SCREW THIS!!!!
FAASSHHH
ZABOOSH

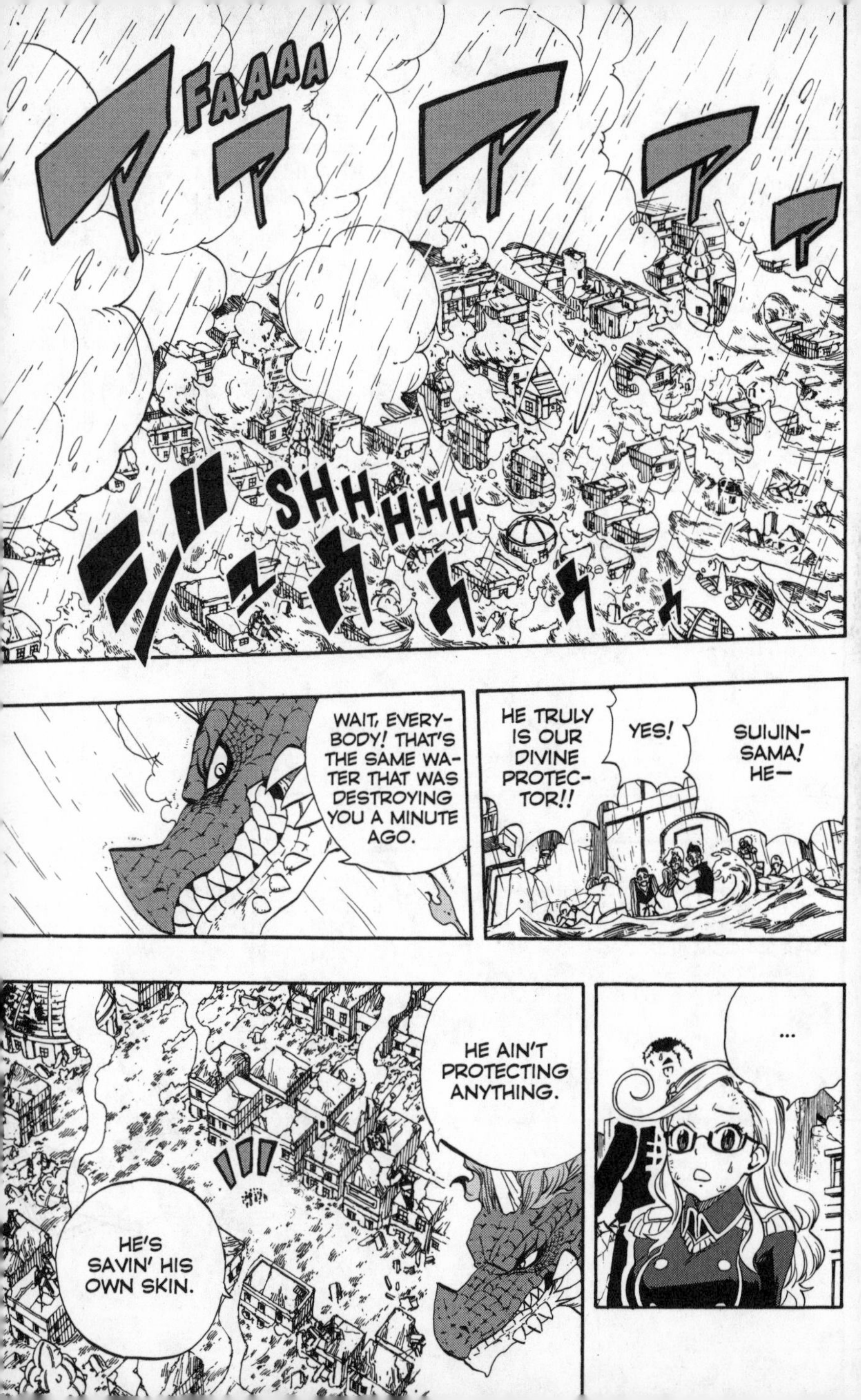
FAAAA
SHHHHHH
SUIJIN-SAMA! HE—
YES!
HE TRULY IS OUR DIVINE PROTECTOR!!
WAIT, EVERYBODY! THAT'S THE SAME WATER THAT WAS DESTROYING YOU A MINUTE AGO.
...
HE AIN'T PROTECTING ANYTHING.
HE'S SAVIN' HIS OWN SKIN.

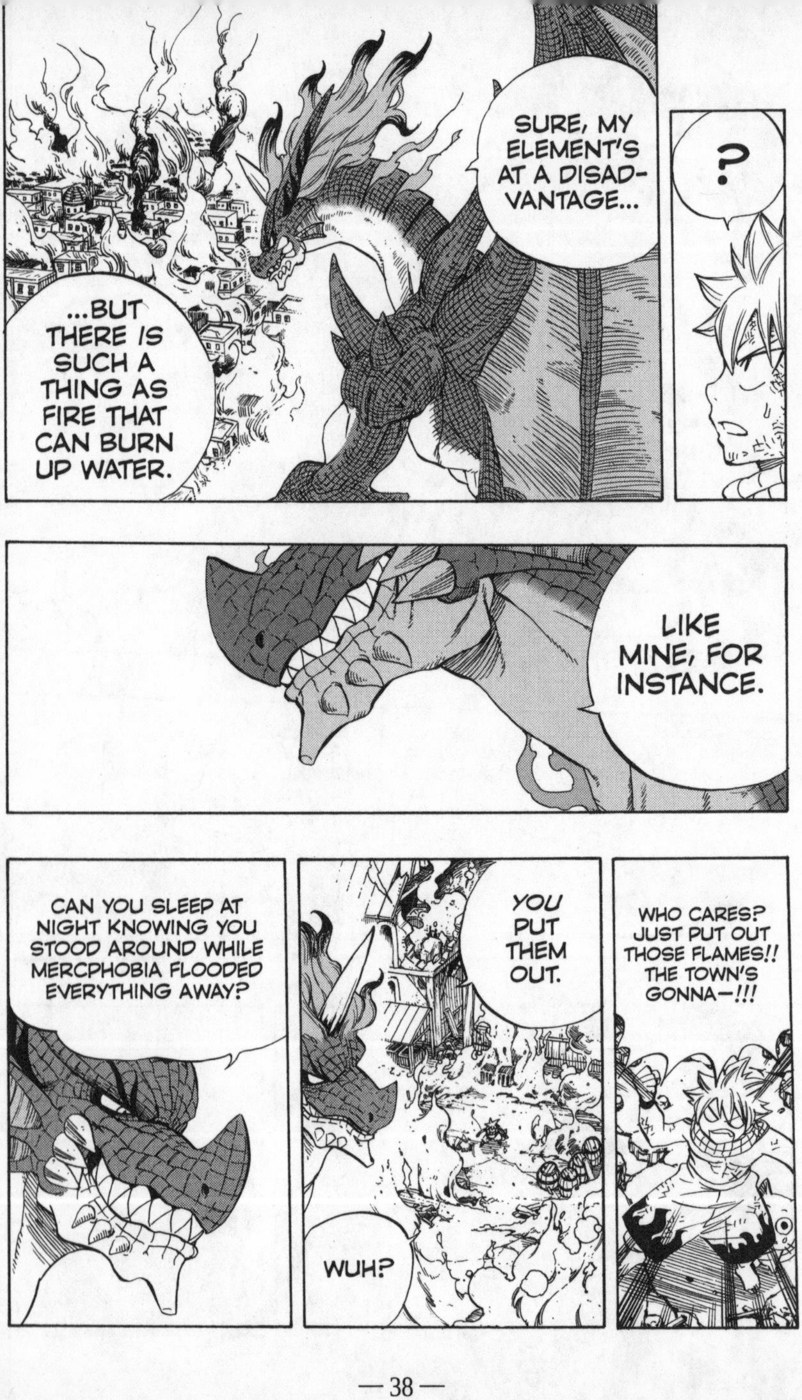
?
SURE, MY ELEMENT'S AT A DISADVANTAGE...
...BUT THERE IS SUCH A THING AS FIRE THAT CAN BURN UP WATER.
LIKE MINE, FOR INSTANCE.
WHO CARES? JUST PUT OUT THOSE FLAMES!! THE TOWN'S GONNA—!!!
YOU PUT THEM OUT.
WUH?
CAN YOU SLEEP AT NIGHT KNOWING YOU STOOD AROUND WHILE MERCPHOBIA FLOODED EVERYTHING AWAY?

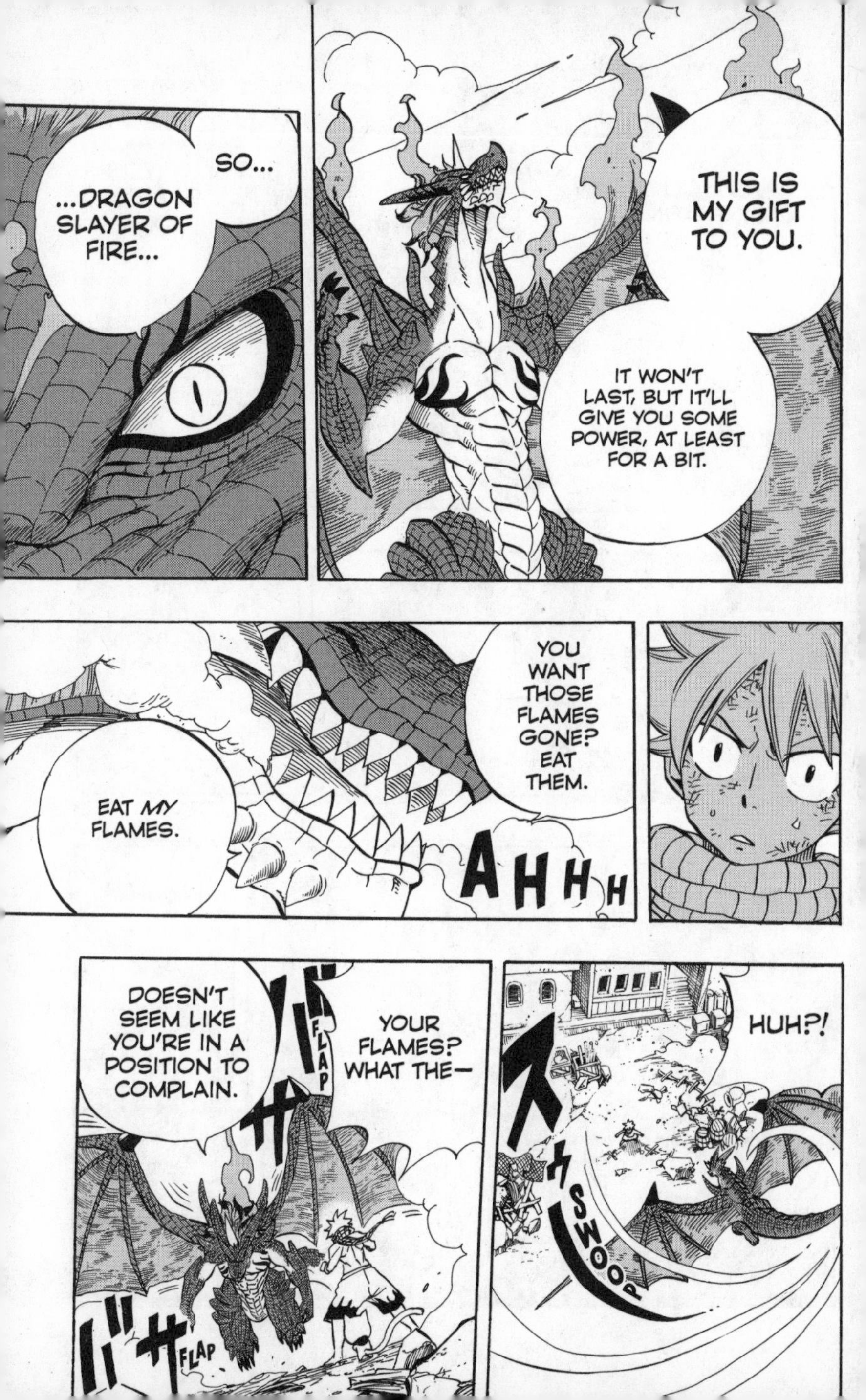
THIS IS MY GIFT TO YOU.
IT WON'T LAST, BUT IT'LL GIVE YOU SOME POWER, AT LEAST FOR A BIT.
SO...
...DRAGON SLAYER OF FIRE...
YOU WANT THOSE FLAMES GONE? EAT THEM.
EAT MY FLAMES.
AHHHH
HUH?!
SWOOP
YOUR FLAMES? WHAT THE—
DOESN'T SEEM LIKE YOU'RE IN A POSITION TO COMPLAIN.
FLAP
FLAP

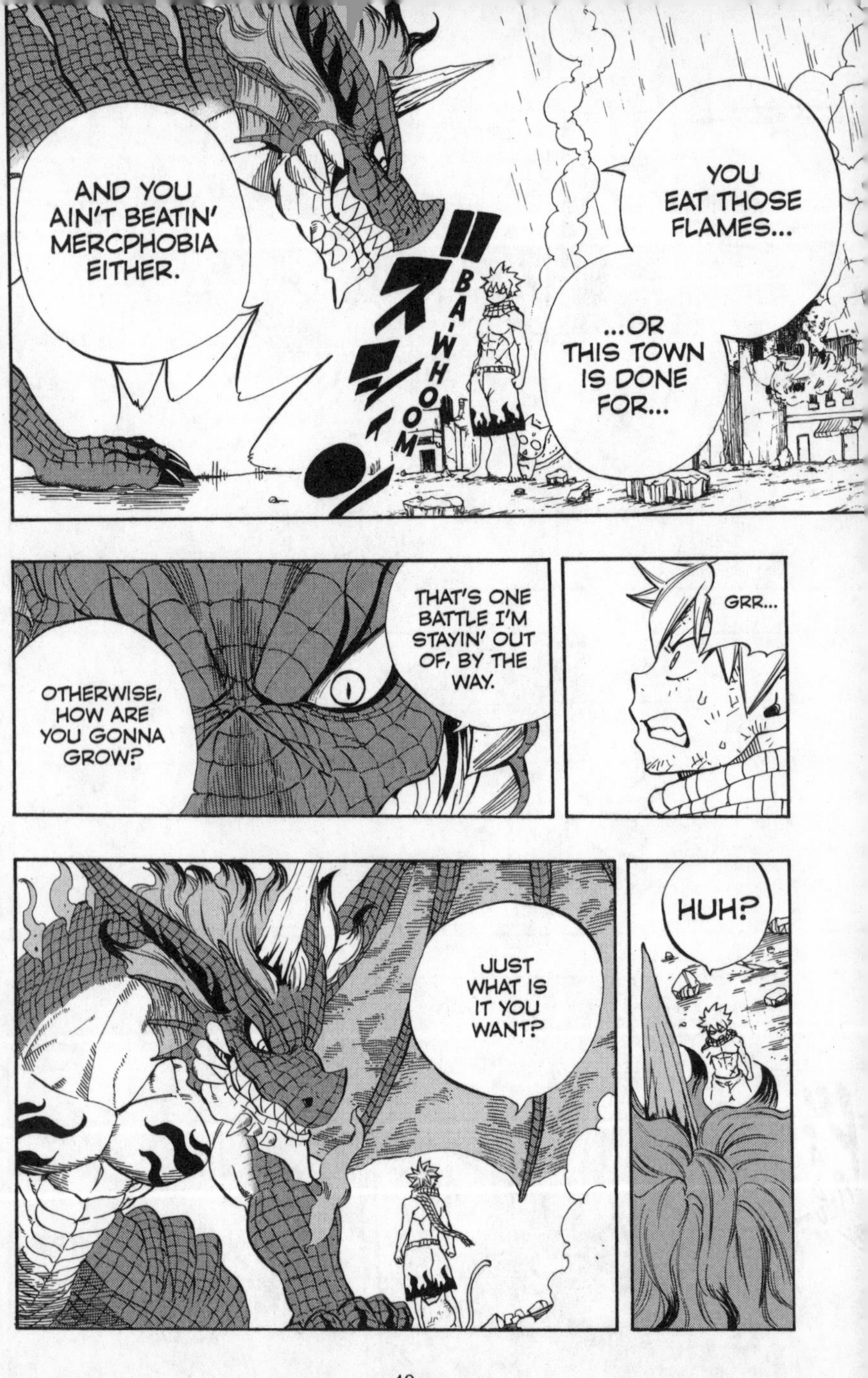
YOU EAT THOSE FLAMES...
...OR THIS TOWN IS DONE FOR...
BA-WHOOM
AND YOU AIN'T BEATIN' MERCPHOBIA EITHER.
GRR...
THAT'S ONE BATTLE I'M STAYIN' OUT OF, BY THE WAY.
OTHERWISE, HOW ARE YOU GONNA GROW?
HUH?
JUST WHAT IS IT YOU WANT?

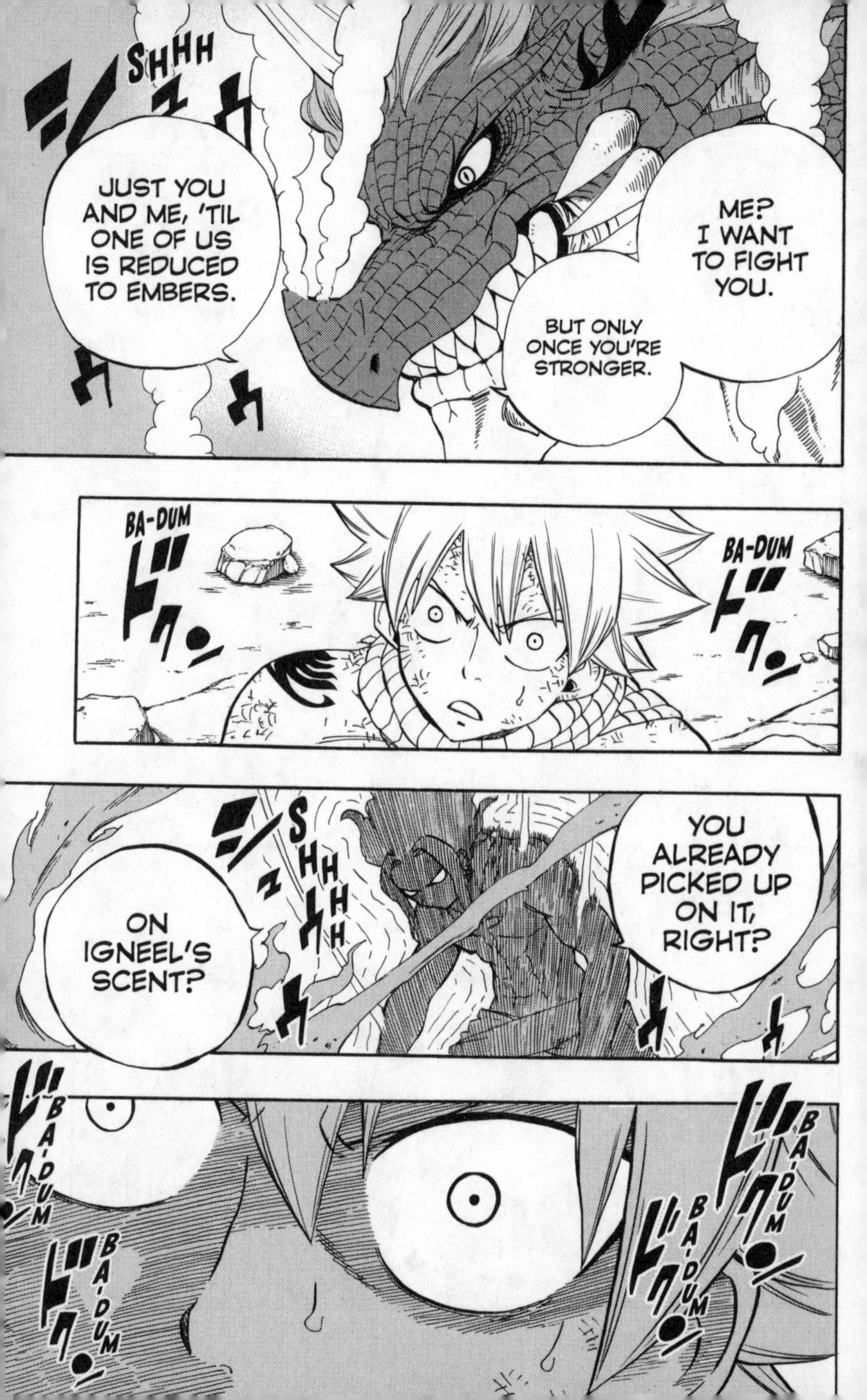
ME? I WANT TO FIGHT YOU.
BUT ONLY ONCE YOU'RE STRONGER.
SHHH
JUST YOU AND ME, 'TIL ONE OF US IS REDUCED TO EMBERS.
BA-DUM
BA-DUM
YOU ALREADY PICKED UP ON IT, RIGHT?
SHHHH
ON IGNEEL'S SCENT?
BA-DUM
BA-DUM
BA-DUM
BA-DUM

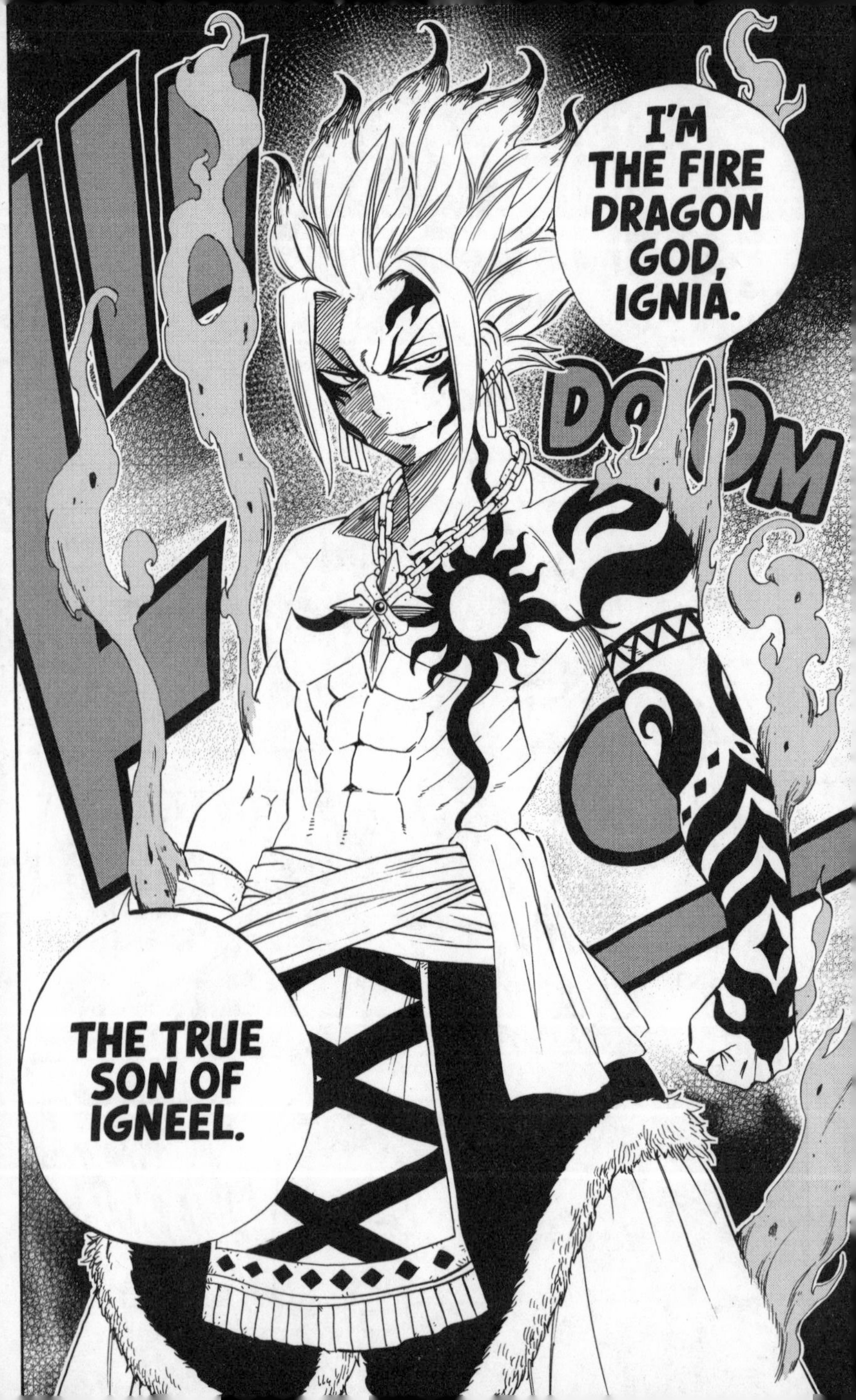
I'M THE FIRE DRAGON GOD, IGNIÁ.
THE TRUE SON OF IGNEEL.

FAIRY TAIL 100 YEARS QUEST

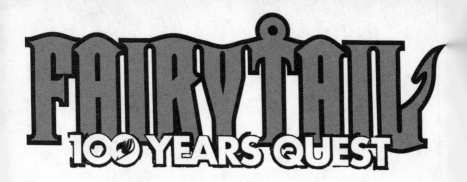

Chapter 21: Burn it All

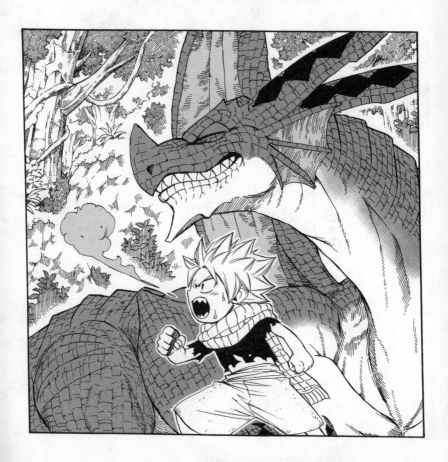

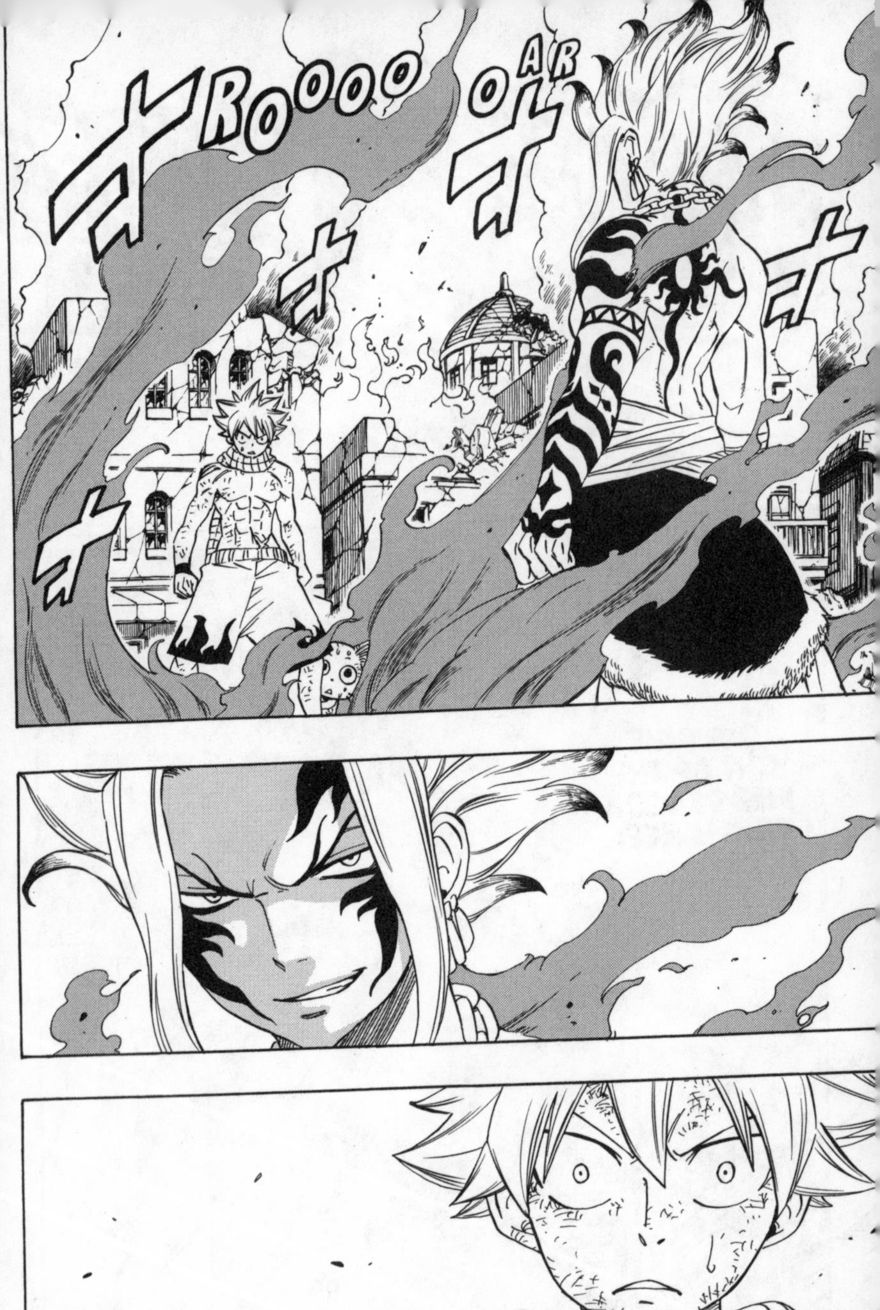
ROOOOOAR

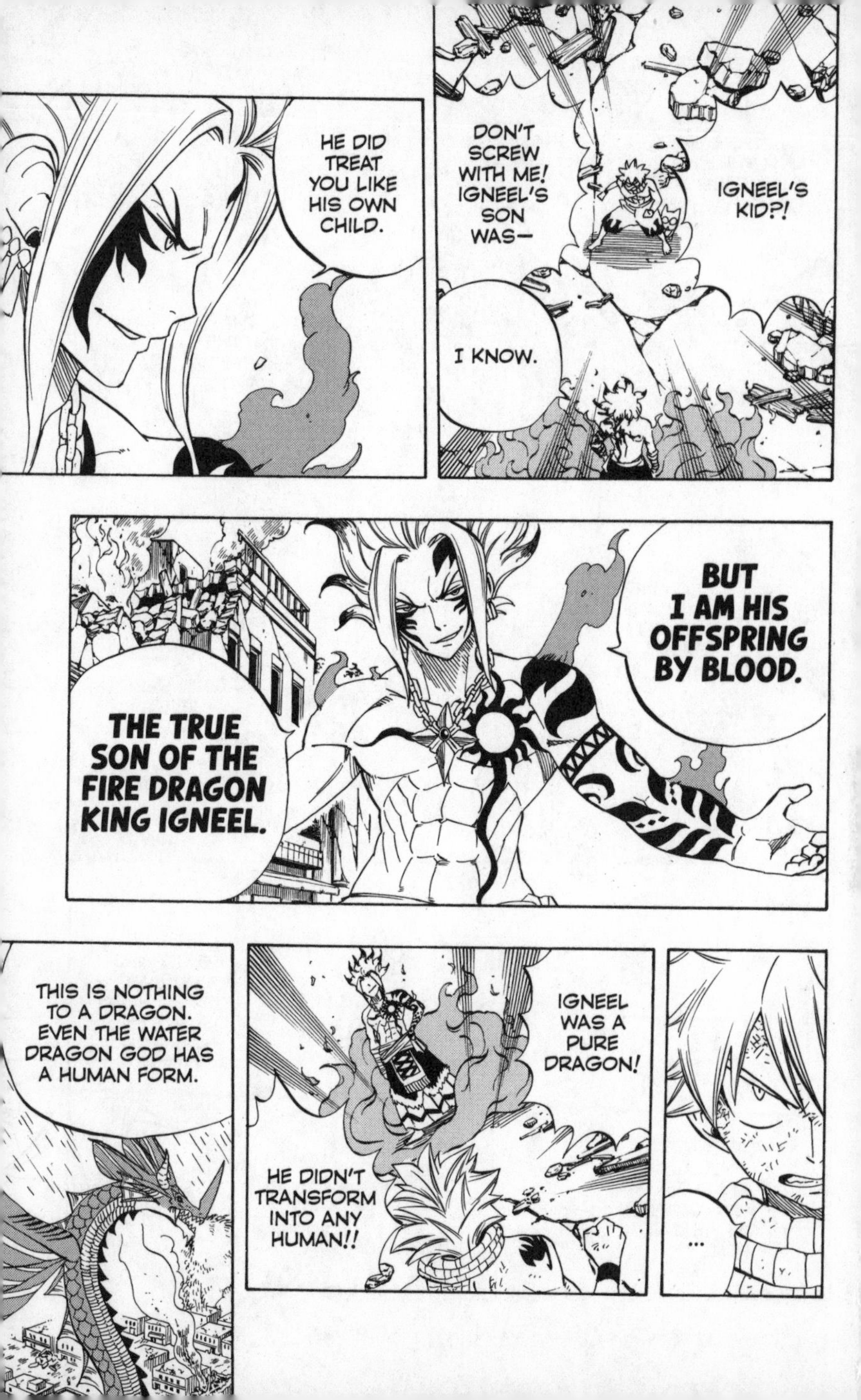
IGNEEL'S KID?!
DON'T SCREW WITH ME! IGNEEL'S SON WAS—
I KNOW.
HE DID TREAT YOU LIKE HIS OWN CHILD.
BUT I AM HIS OFFSPRING BY BLOOD.
THE TRUE SON OF THE FIRE DRAGON KING IGNEEL.
...
IGNEEL WAS A PURE DRAGON!
HE DIDN'T TRANSFORM INTO ANY HUMAN!!
THIS IS NOTHING TO A DRAGON. EVEN THE WATER DRAGON GOD HAS A HUMAN FORM.

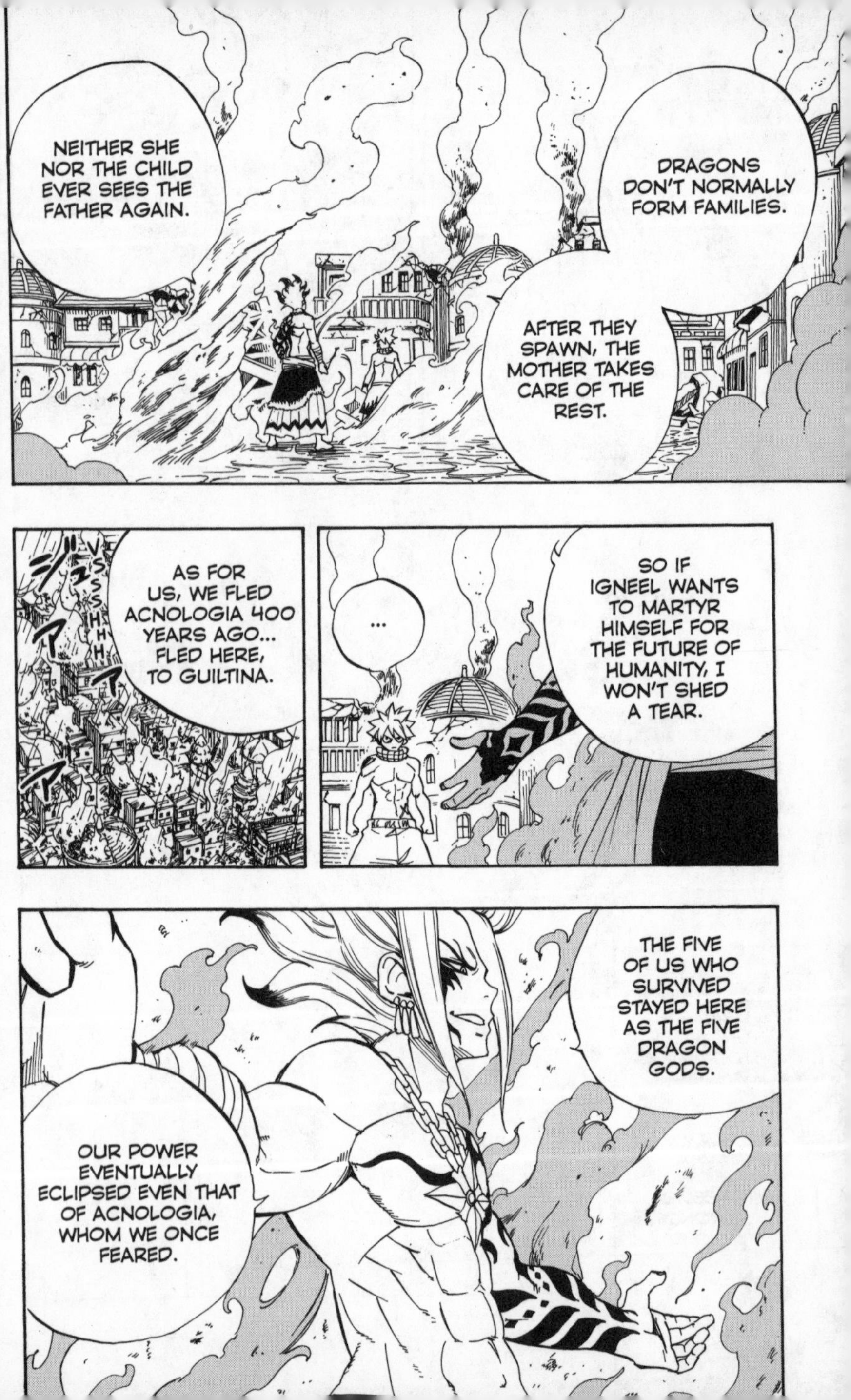
DRAGONS DON'T NORMALLY FORM FAMILIES.
AFTER THEY SPAWN, THE MOTHER TAKES CARE OF THE REST.
NEITHER SHE NOR THE CHILD EVER SEES THE FATHER AGAIN.
SO IF IGNEEL WANTS TO MARTYR HIMSELF FOR THE FUTURE OF HUMANITY, I WON'T SHED A TEAR.
...
VSSSHHH
AS FOR US, WE FLED ACNOLOGIA 400 YEARS AGO... FLED HERE, TO GUILTINA.
THE FIVE OF US WHO SURVIVED STAYED HERE AS THE FIVE DRAGON GODS.
OUR POWER EVENTUALLY ECLIPSED EVEN THAT OF ACNOLOGIA, WHOM WE ONCE FEARED.

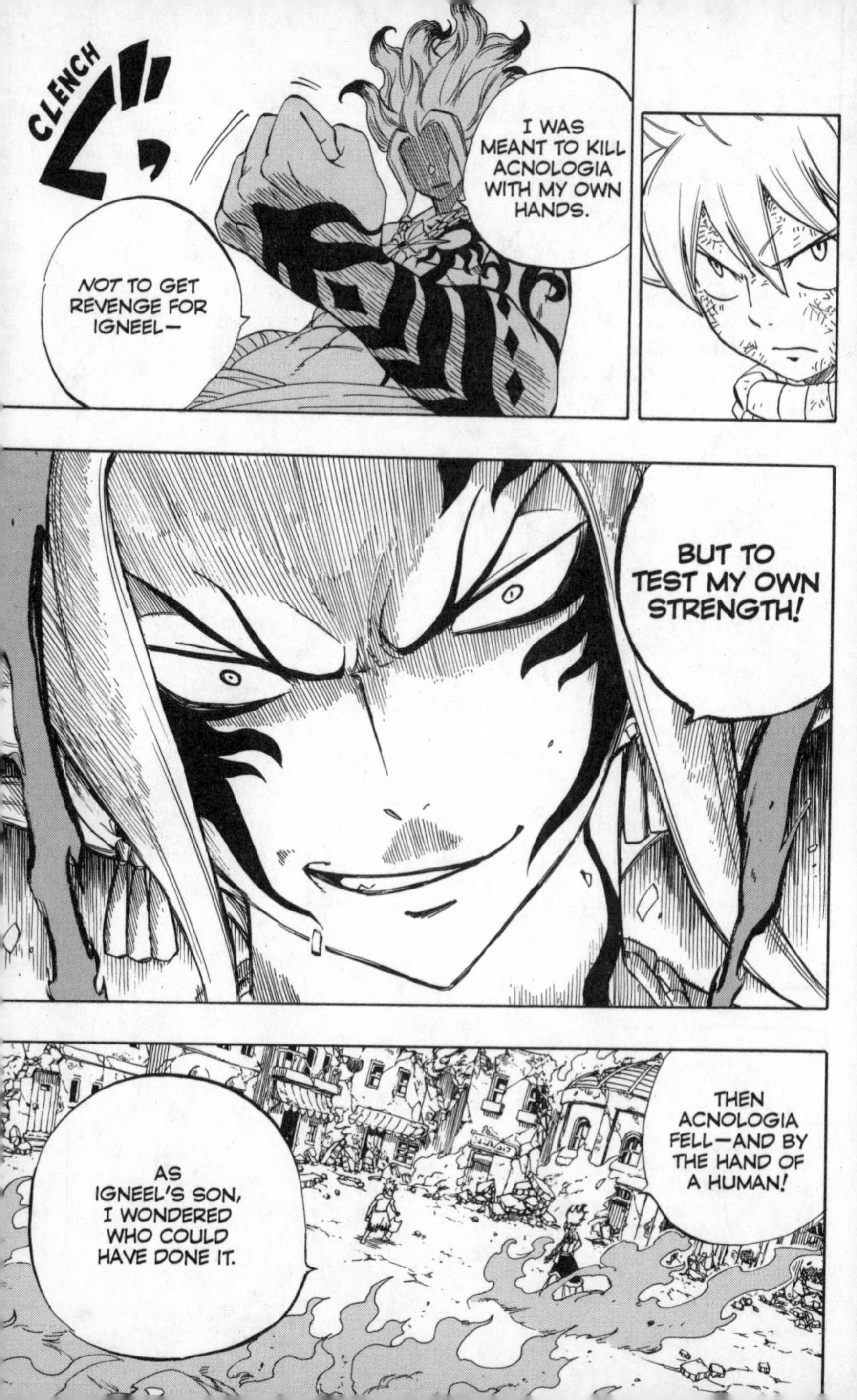
CLENCH
I WAS MEANT TO KILL ACNOLOGIA WITH MY OWN HANDS.
NOT TO GET REVENGE FOR IGNEEL—
BUT TO TEST MY OWN STRENGTH!
THEN ACNOLOGIA FELL—AND BY THE HAND OF A HUMAN!
AS IGNEEL'S SON, I WONDERED WHO COULD HAVE DONE IT.

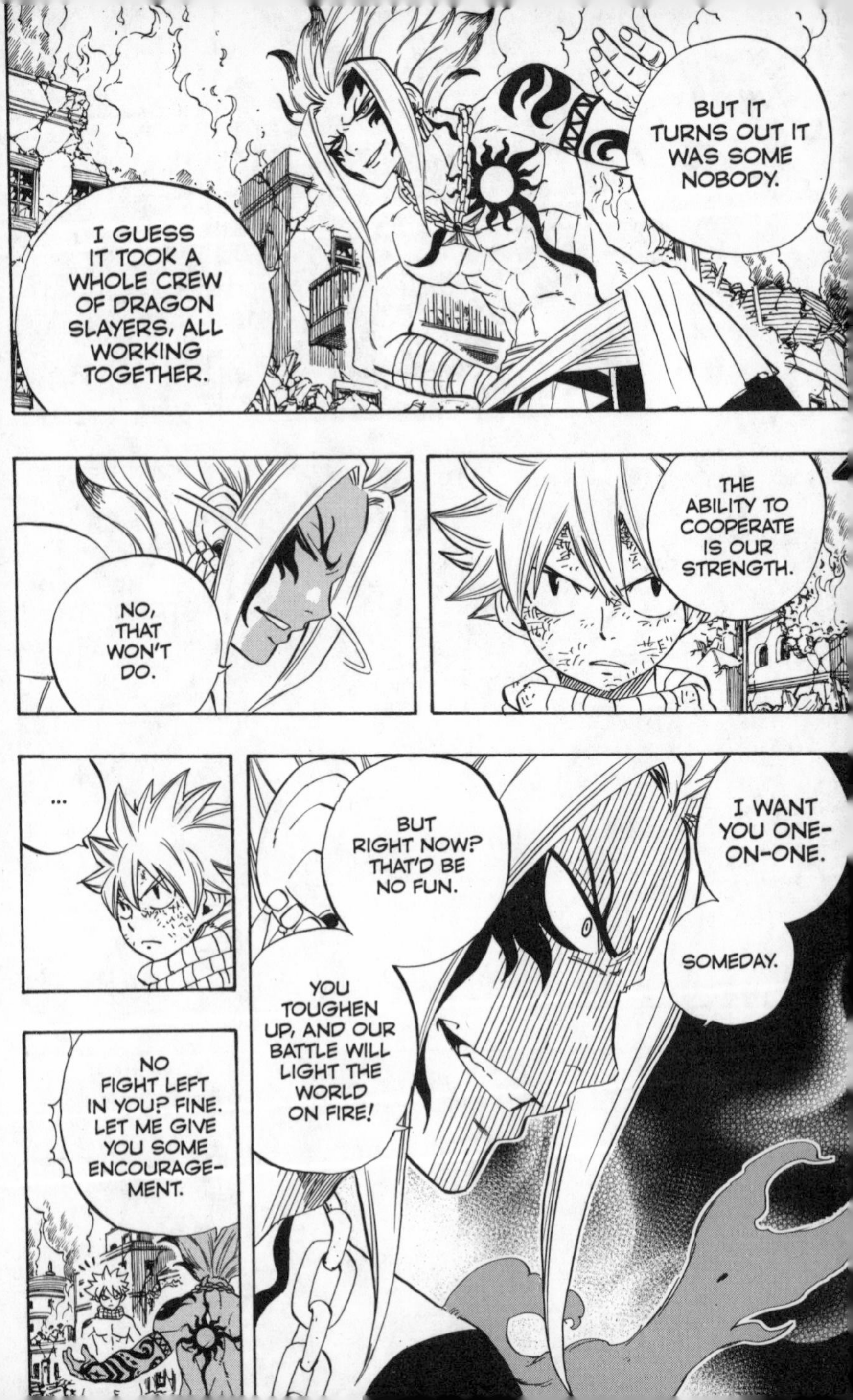
BUT IT TURNS OUT IT WAS SOME NOBODY.
I GUESS IT TOOK A WHOLE CREW OF DRAGON SLAYERS, ALL WORKING TOGETHER.
THE ABILITY TO COOPERATE IS OUR STRENGTH.
NO, THAT WON'T DO.
I WANT YOU ONE-ON-ONE.
SOMEDAY.
BUT RIGHT NOW? THAT'D BE NO FUN.
YOU TOUGHEN UP, AND OUR BATTLE WILL LIGHT THE WORLD ON FIRE!
...
NO FIGHT LEFT IN YOU? FINE. LET ME GIVE YOU SOME ENCOURAGE-MENT.

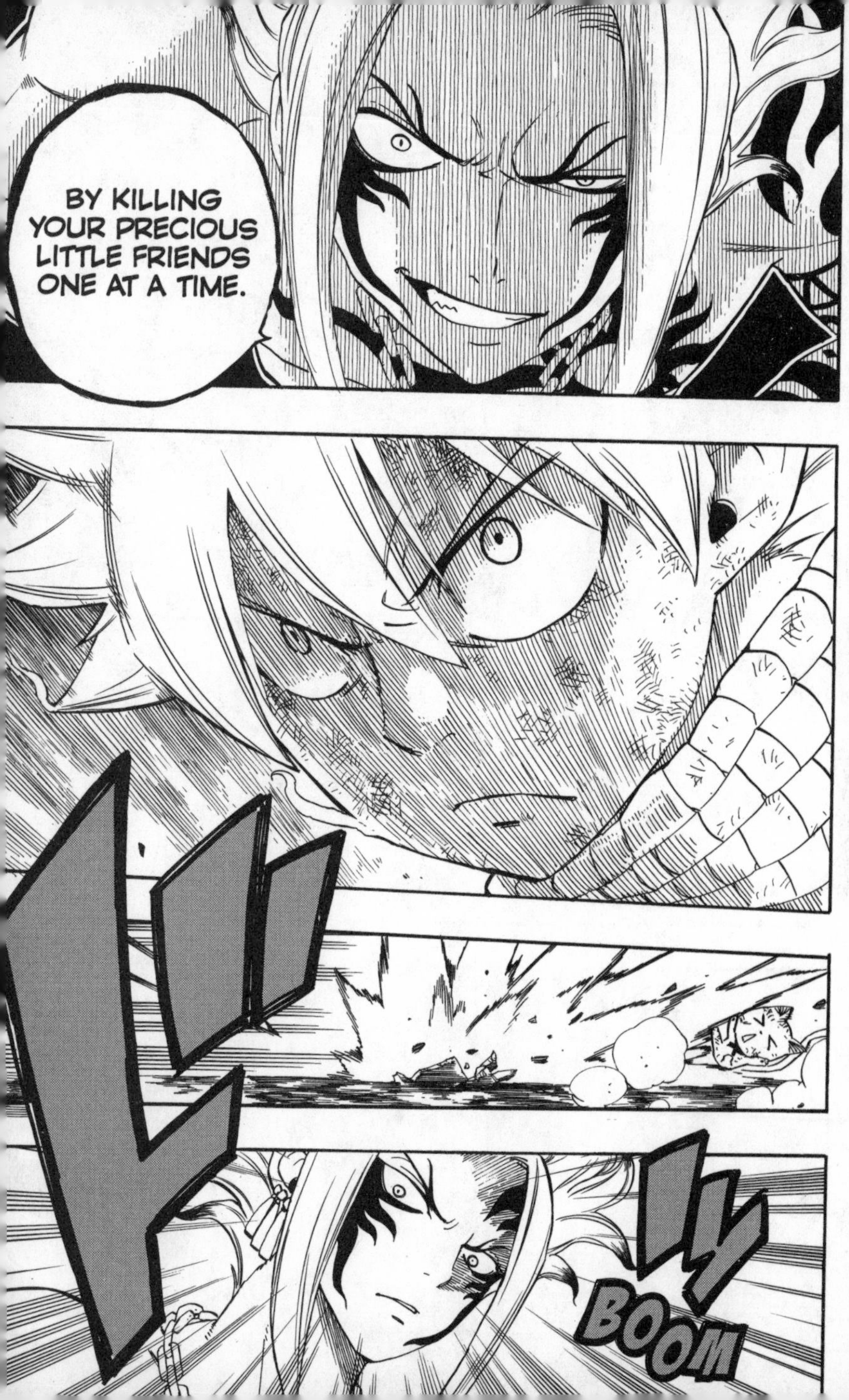
BY KILLING YOUR PRECIOUS LITTLE FRIENDS ONE AT A TIME.
BOOM

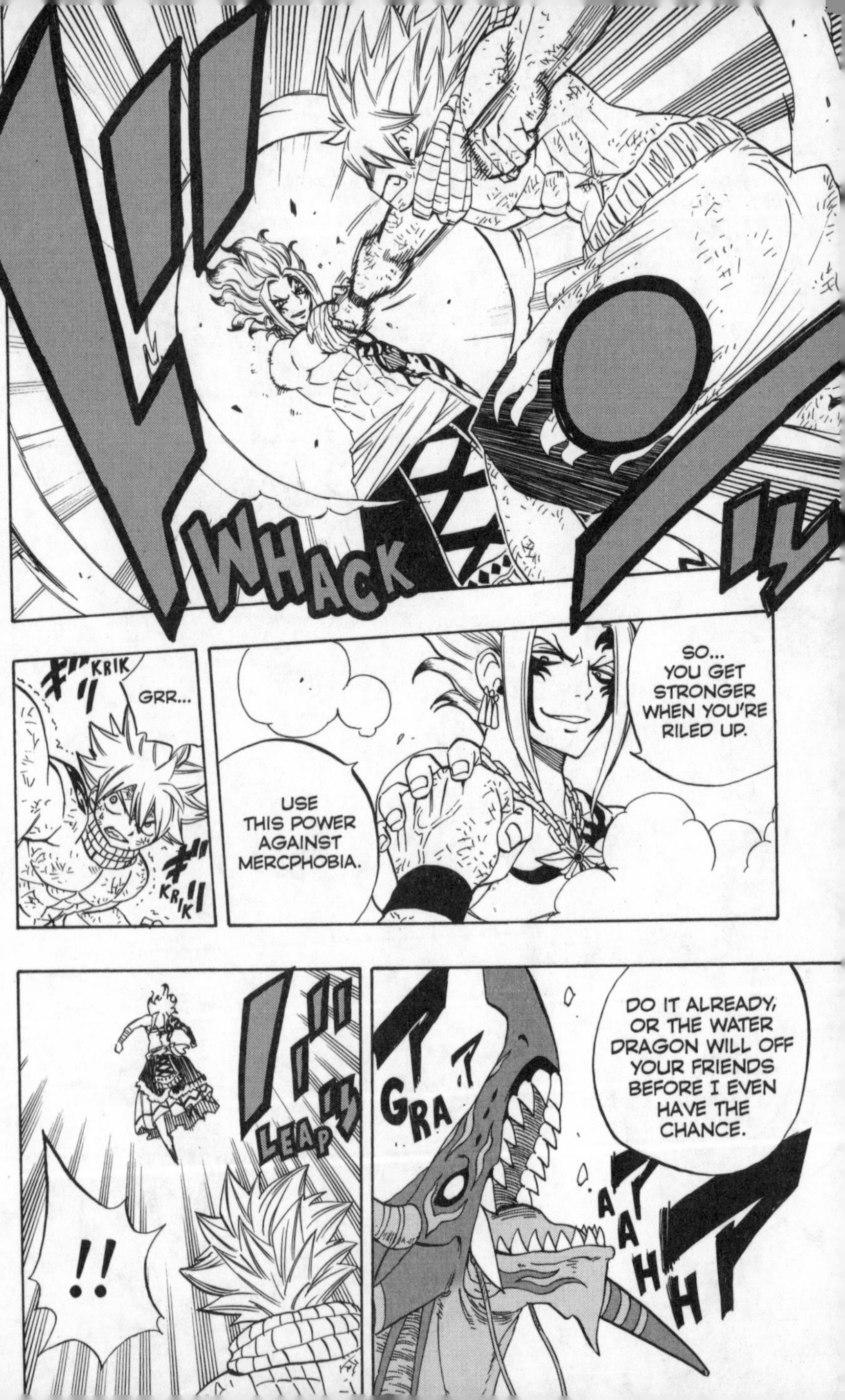
WHACK
SO... YOU GET STRONGER WHEN YOU'RE RILED UP.
USE THIS POWER AGAINST MERCPHOBIA.
KRIK
GRR...
KRIK
DO IT ALREADY, OR THE WATER DRAGON WILL OFF YOUR FRIENDS BEFORE I EVEN HAVE THE CHANCE.
AAAHH
GRA
LEAP
!!

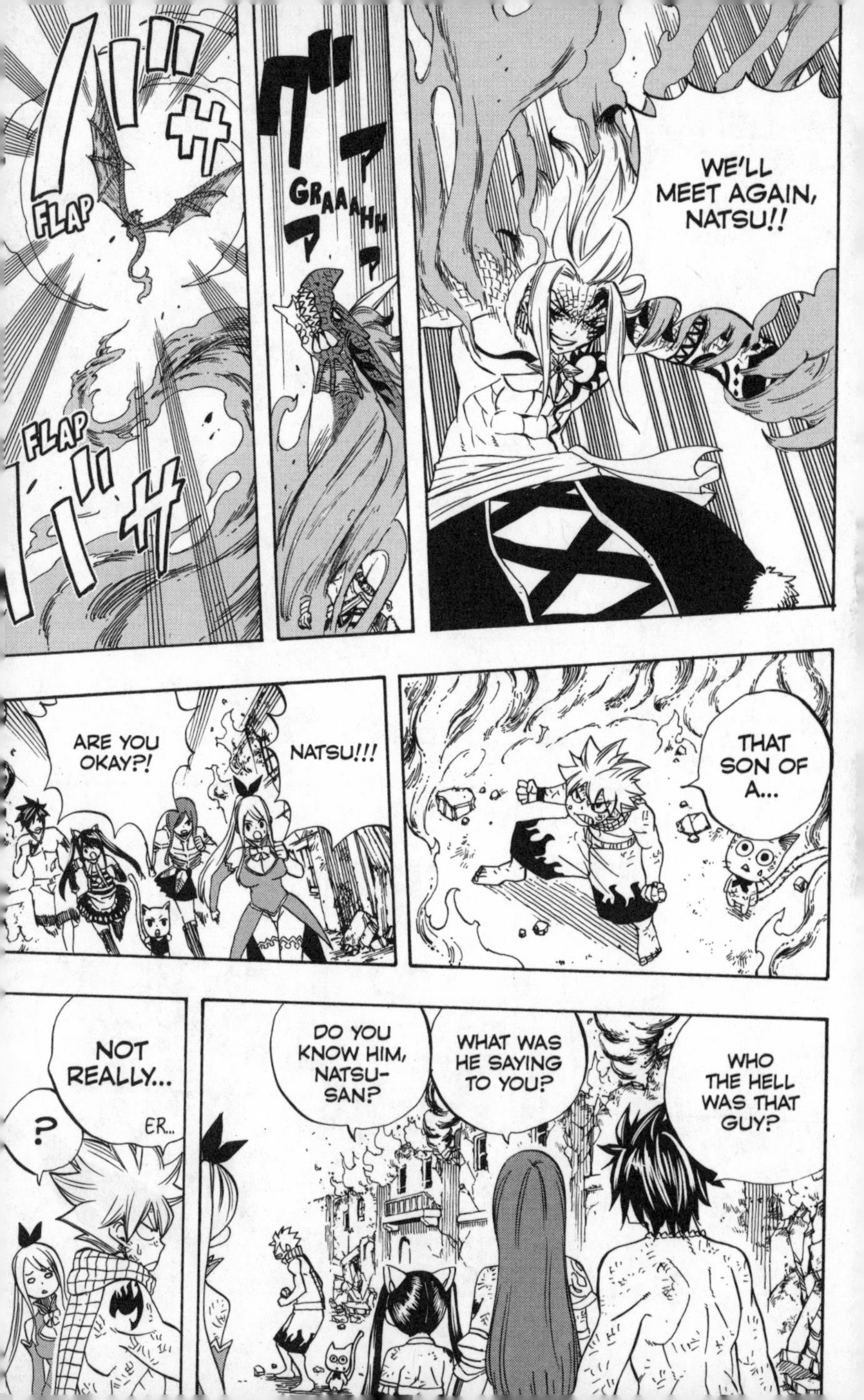
WE'LL MEET AGAIN, NATSU!!
GRAAAHHH
FLAP
FLAP
THAT SON OF A...
NATSU!!!
ARE YOU OKAY?!
WHO THE HELL WAS THAT GUY?
WHAT WAS HE SAYING TO YOU?
DO YOU KNOW HIM, NATSU-SAN?
NOT REALLY...
ER...
?

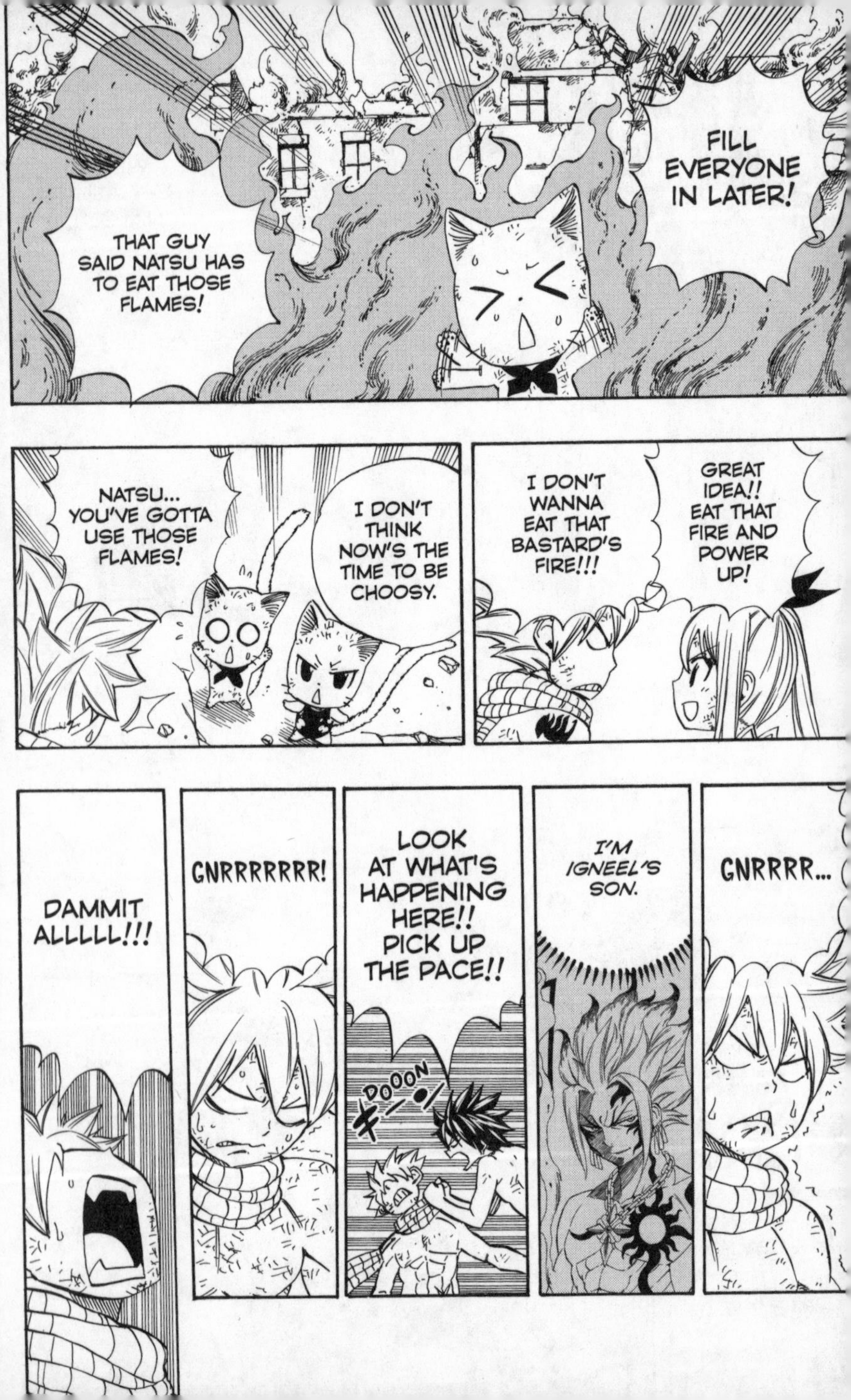
FILL EVERYONE IN LATER!
THAT GUY SAID NATSU HAS TO EAT THOSE FLAMES!
GREAT IDEA!! EAT THAT FIRE AND POWER UP!
I DON'T WANNA EAT THAT BASTARD'S FIRE!!!
NATSU... YOU'VE GOTTA USE THOSE FLAMES!
I DON'T THINK NOW'S THE TIME TO BE CHOOSY.
GNRRRR...
I'M IGNEEL'S SON.
LOOK AT WHAT'S HAPPENING HERE!! PICK UP THE PACE!!
DOOON
GNRRRRRRR!
DAMMIT ALLLLL!!!

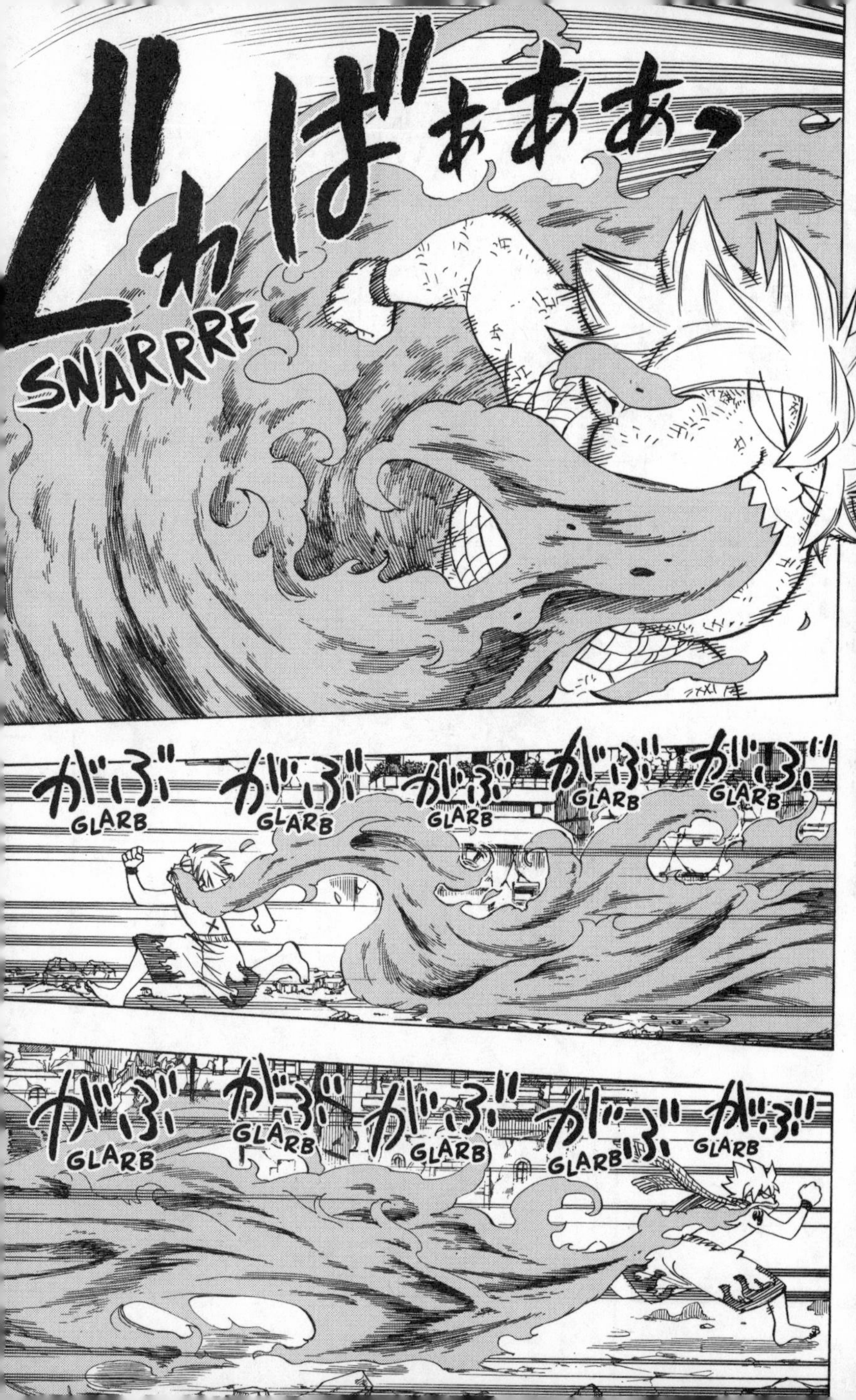
SNARRRF
がぶ
GLARB
がぶ
GLARB
がぶ
GLARB
がぶ
GLARB
がぶ
GLARB
がぶ
GLARB
がぶ
GLARB
がぶ
GLARB
がぶ
GLARB
がぶ
GLARB

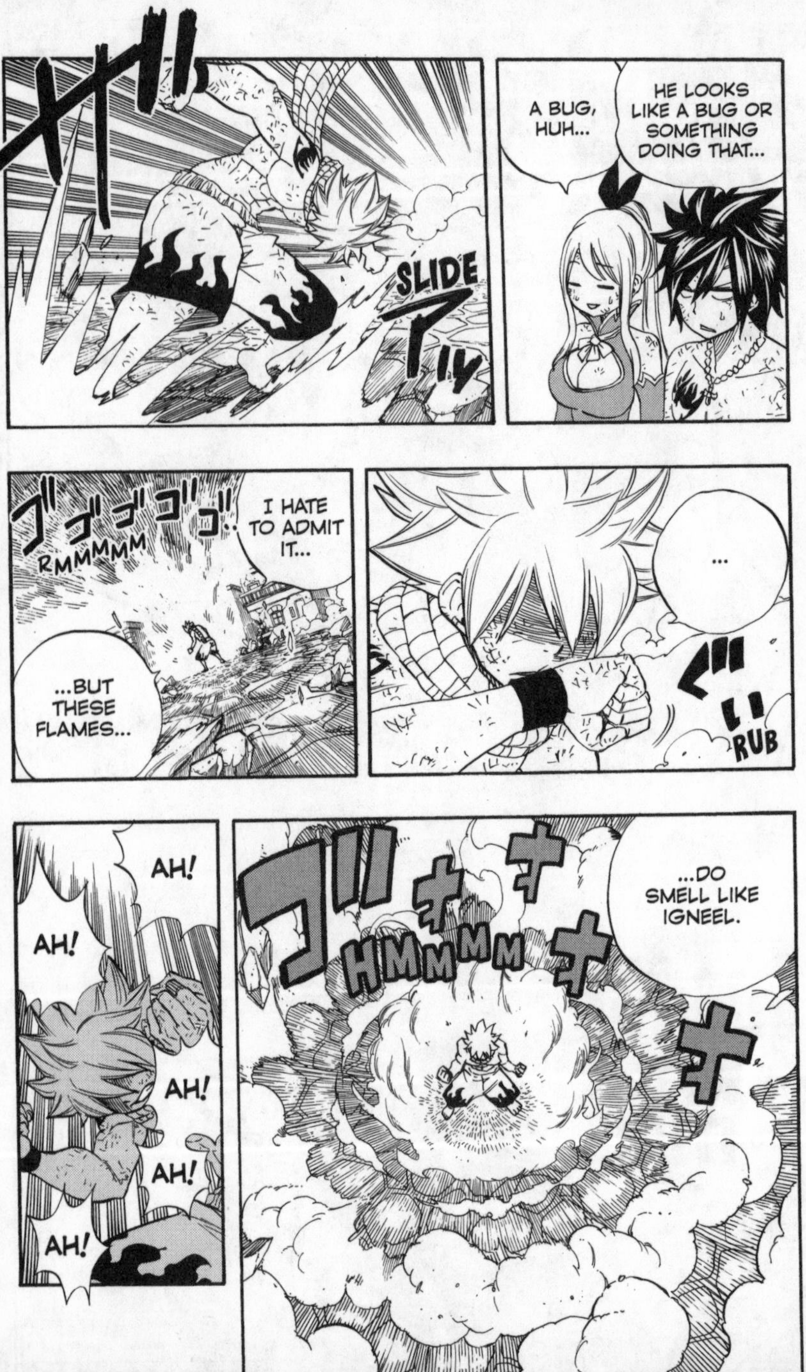
HE LOOKS LIKE A BUG OR SOMETHING DOING THAT...
A BUG, HUH...
SLIDE
...
RUB
I HATE TO ADMIT IT...
...BUT THESE FLAMES...
RMMMMM
...DO SMELL LIKE IGNEEL.
HMMMMM
AH!
AH!
AH!
AH!
AH!

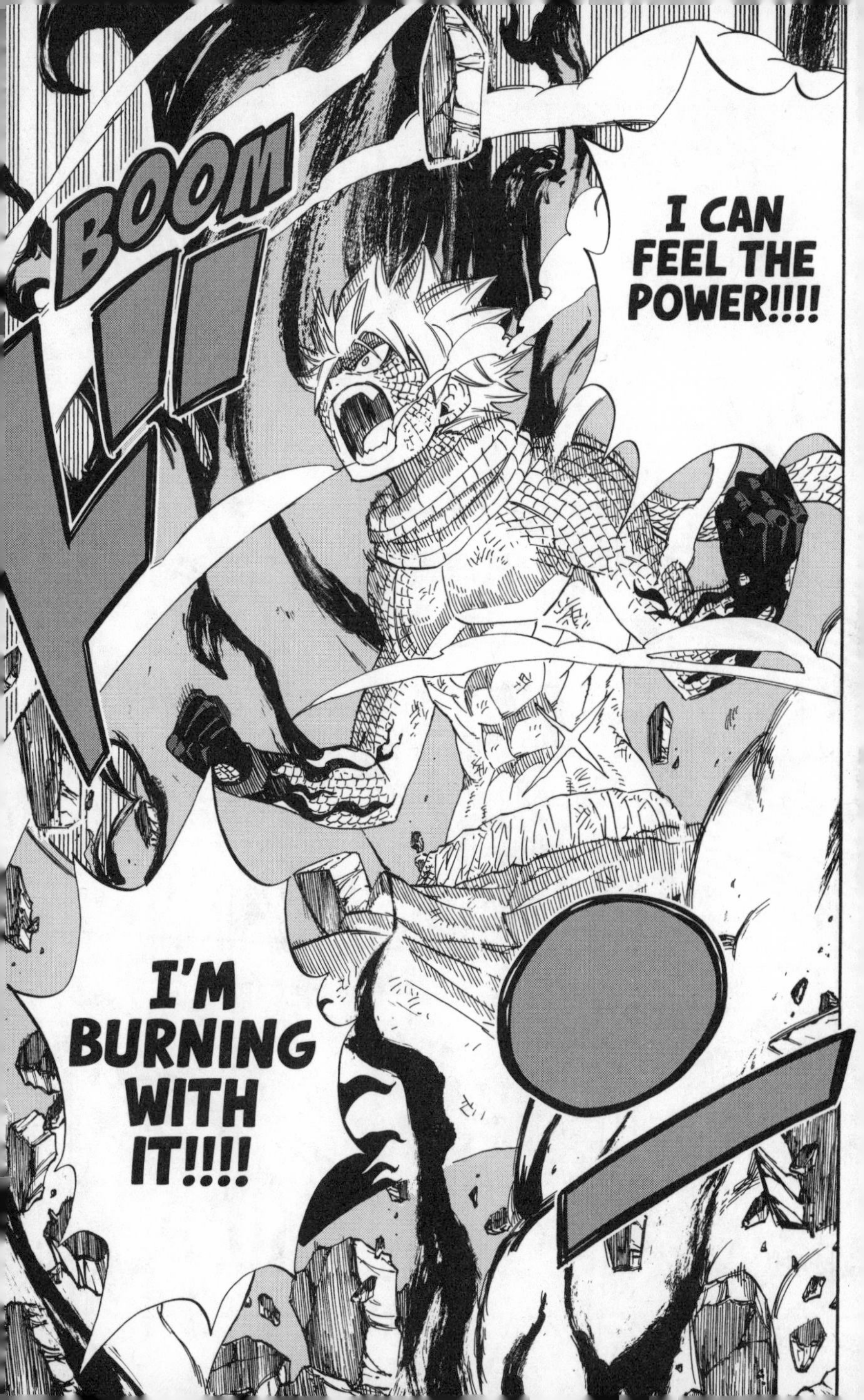
I CAN FEEL THE POWER!!!!
BOOM
I'M BURNING WITH IT!!!!

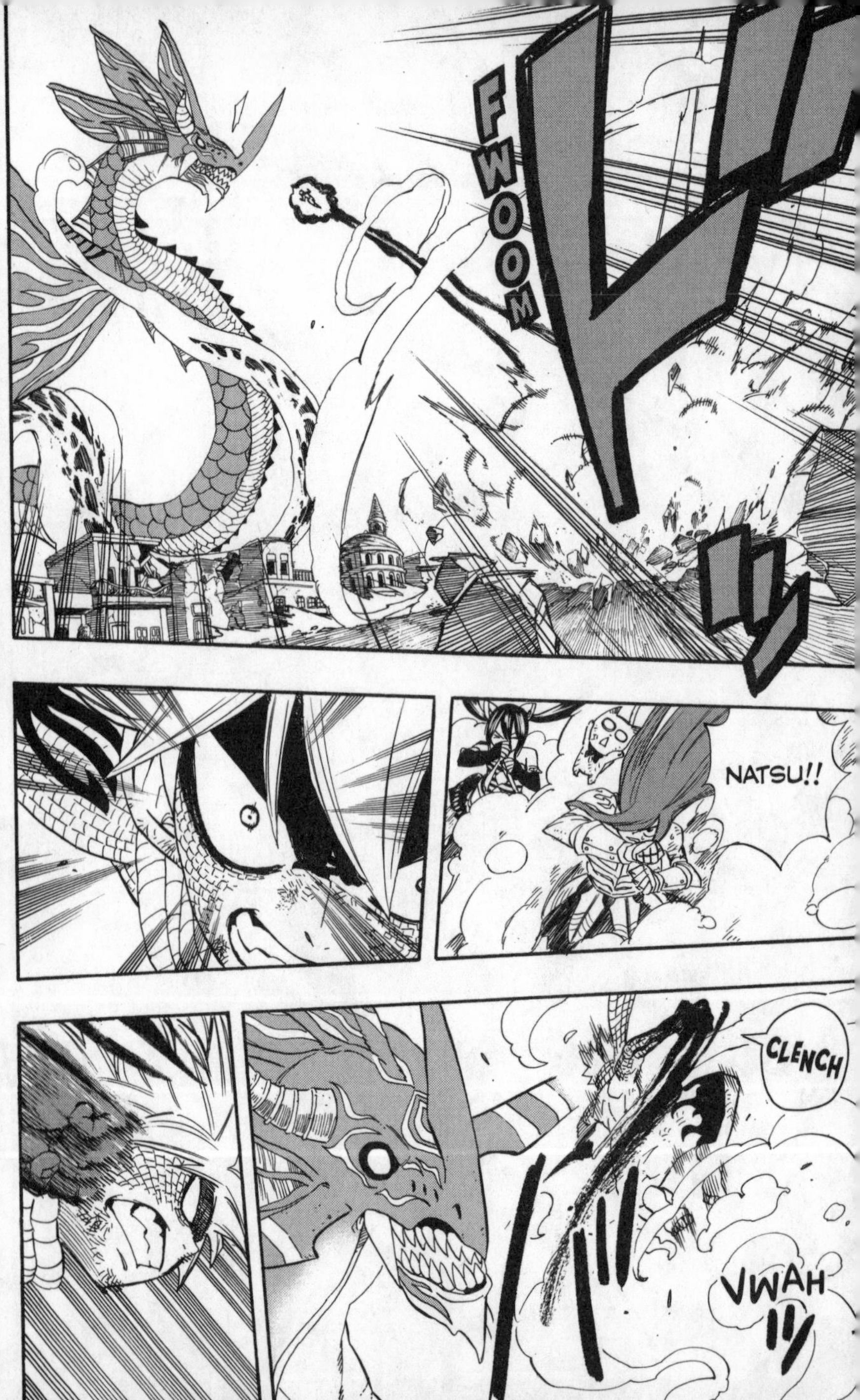
FWOOM
NATSU!!
CLENCH
VWAH

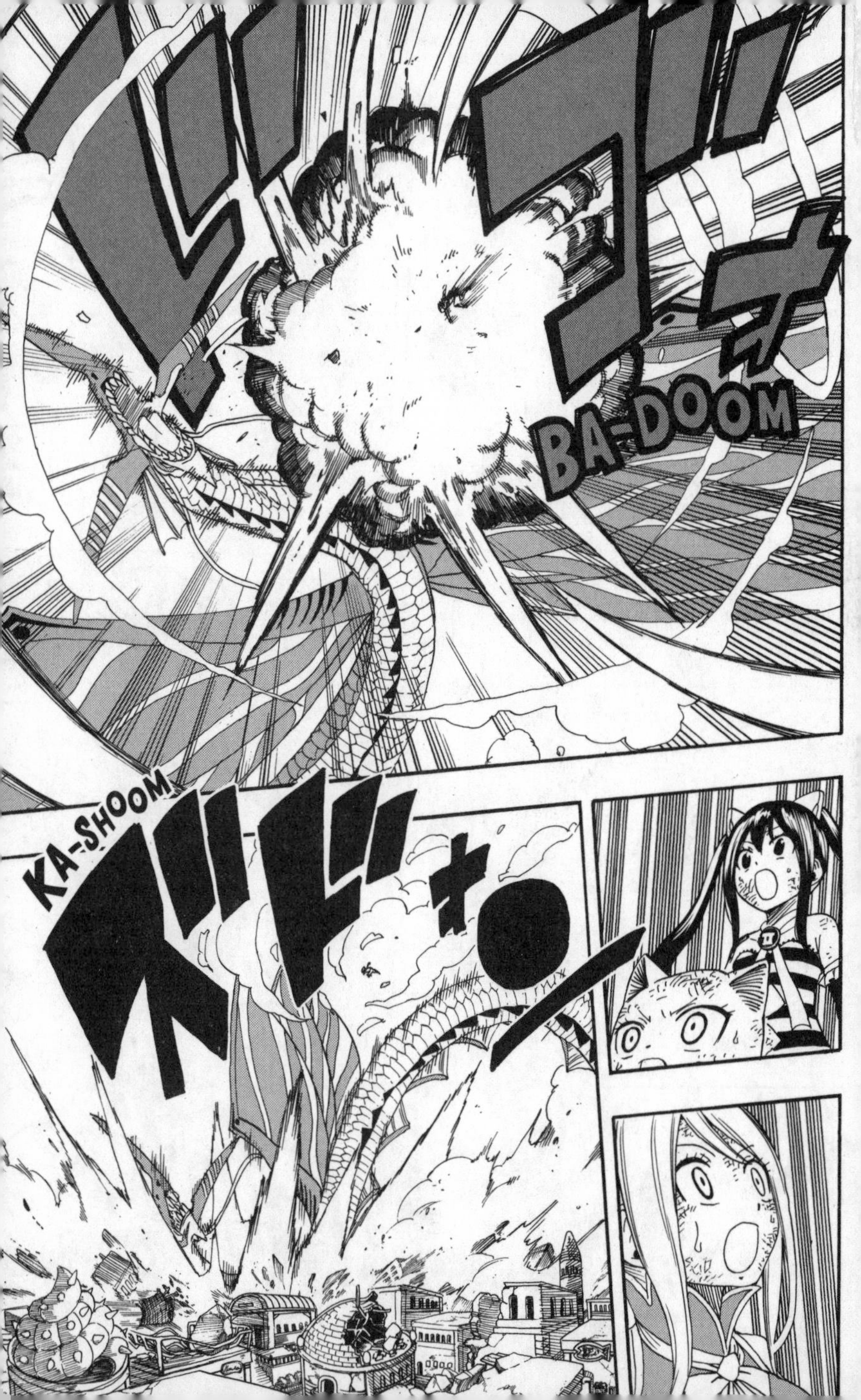
BA-DOOM
KA-SHOOM

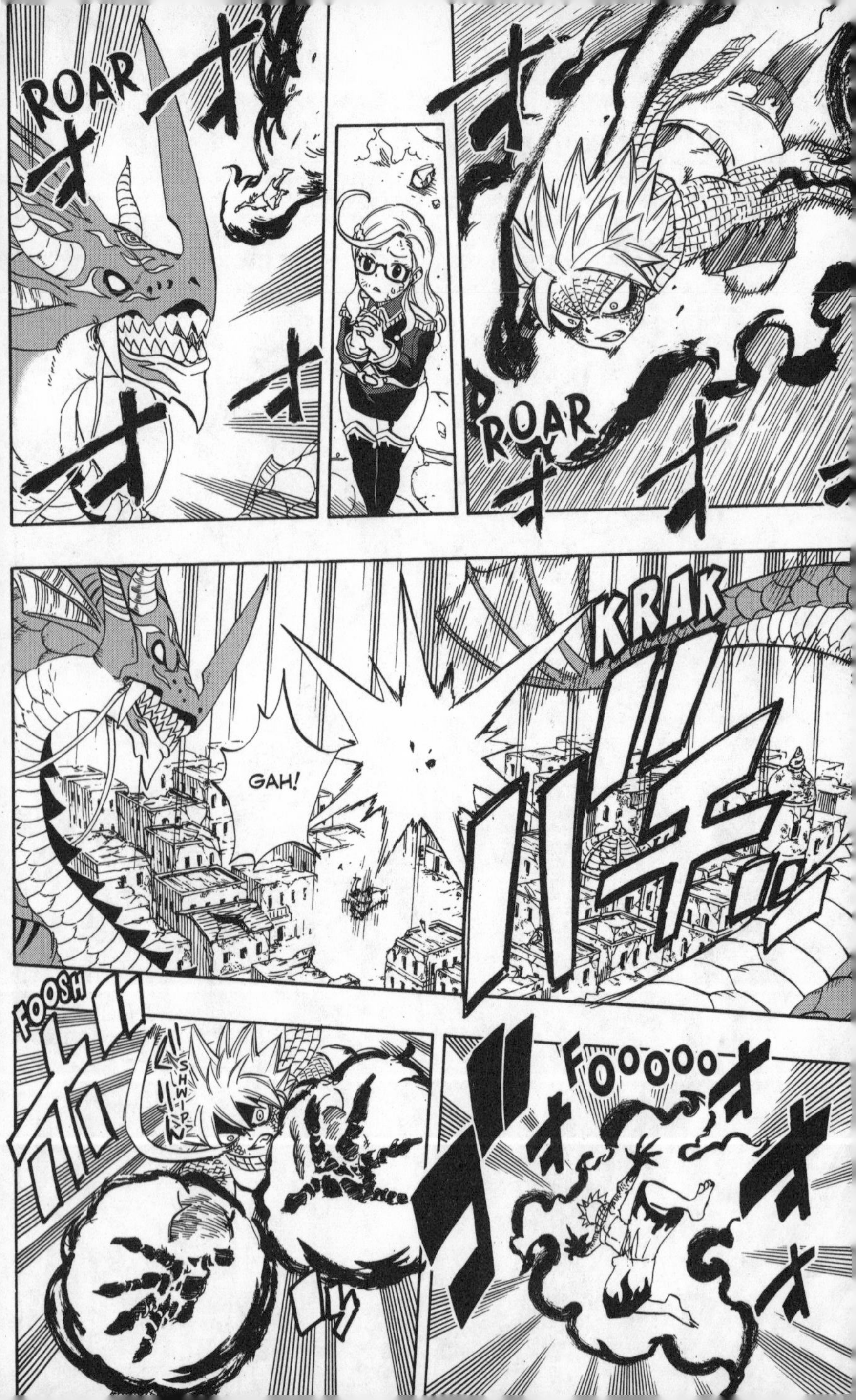
ROAR
ROAR
KRAK
GAH!
FOOOOO
FOOSH
SHWIP

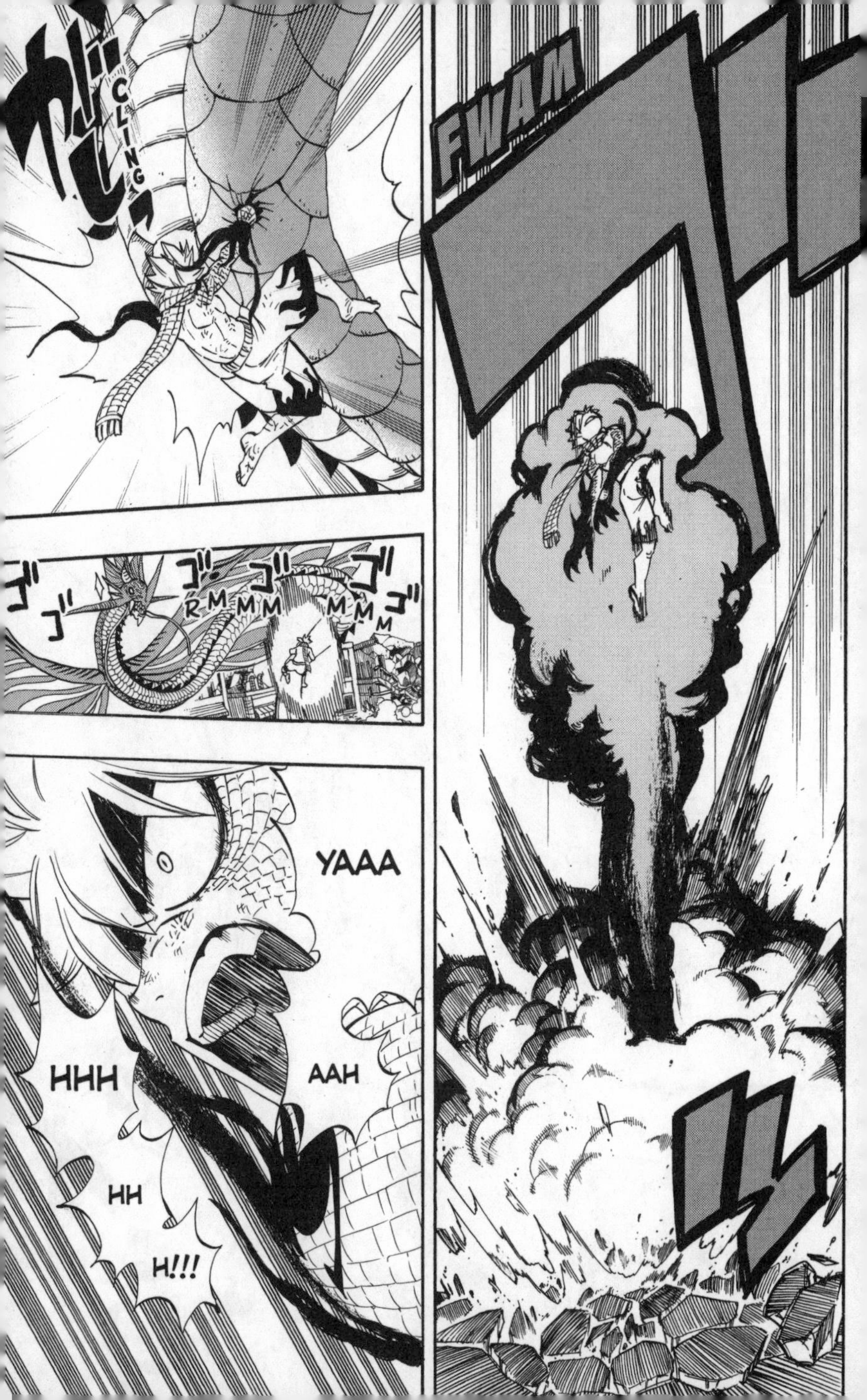
FWAM
CLING
RMMMMMMM
YAAA
AAH
HHH
HH
H!!!

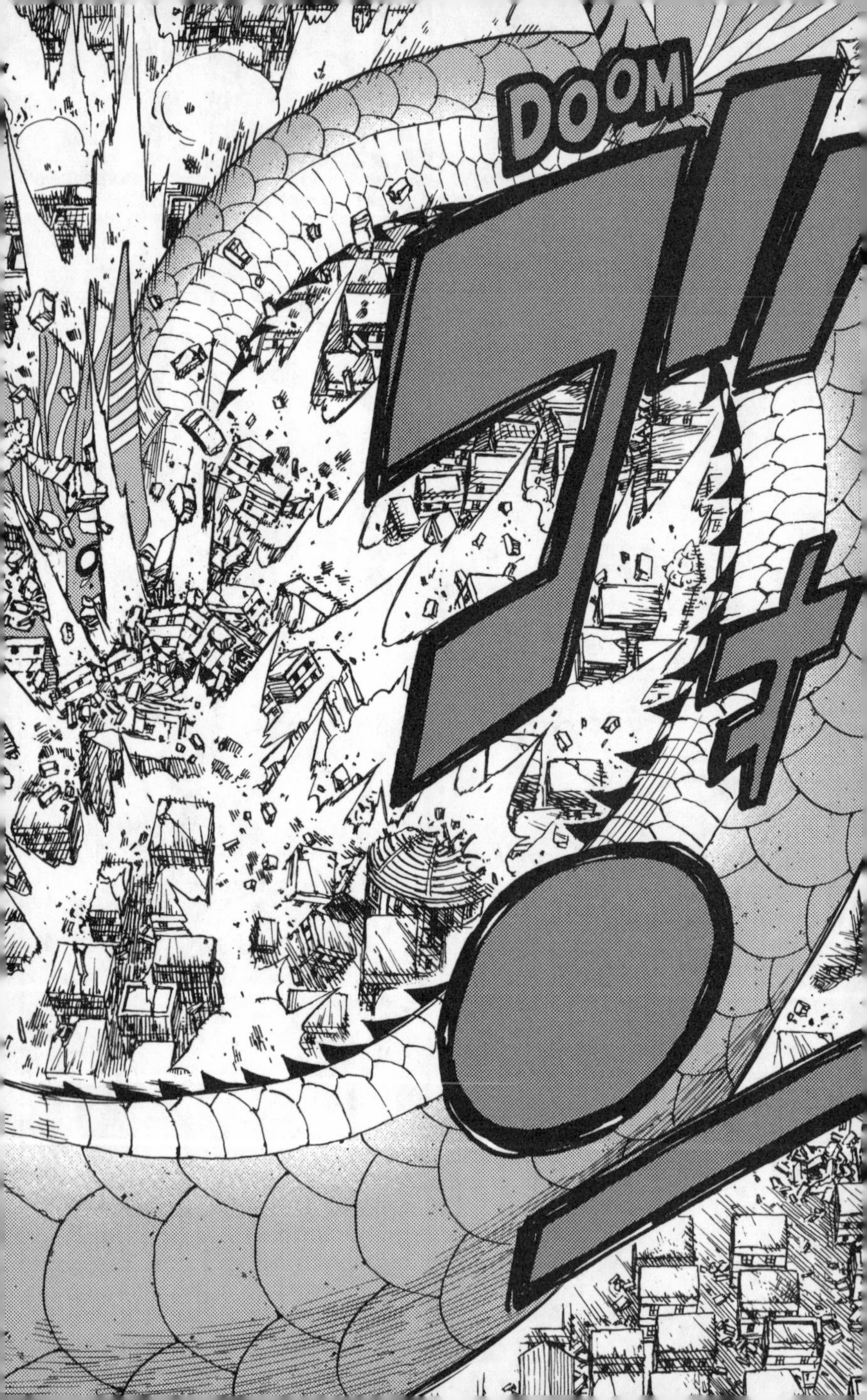
DOOM

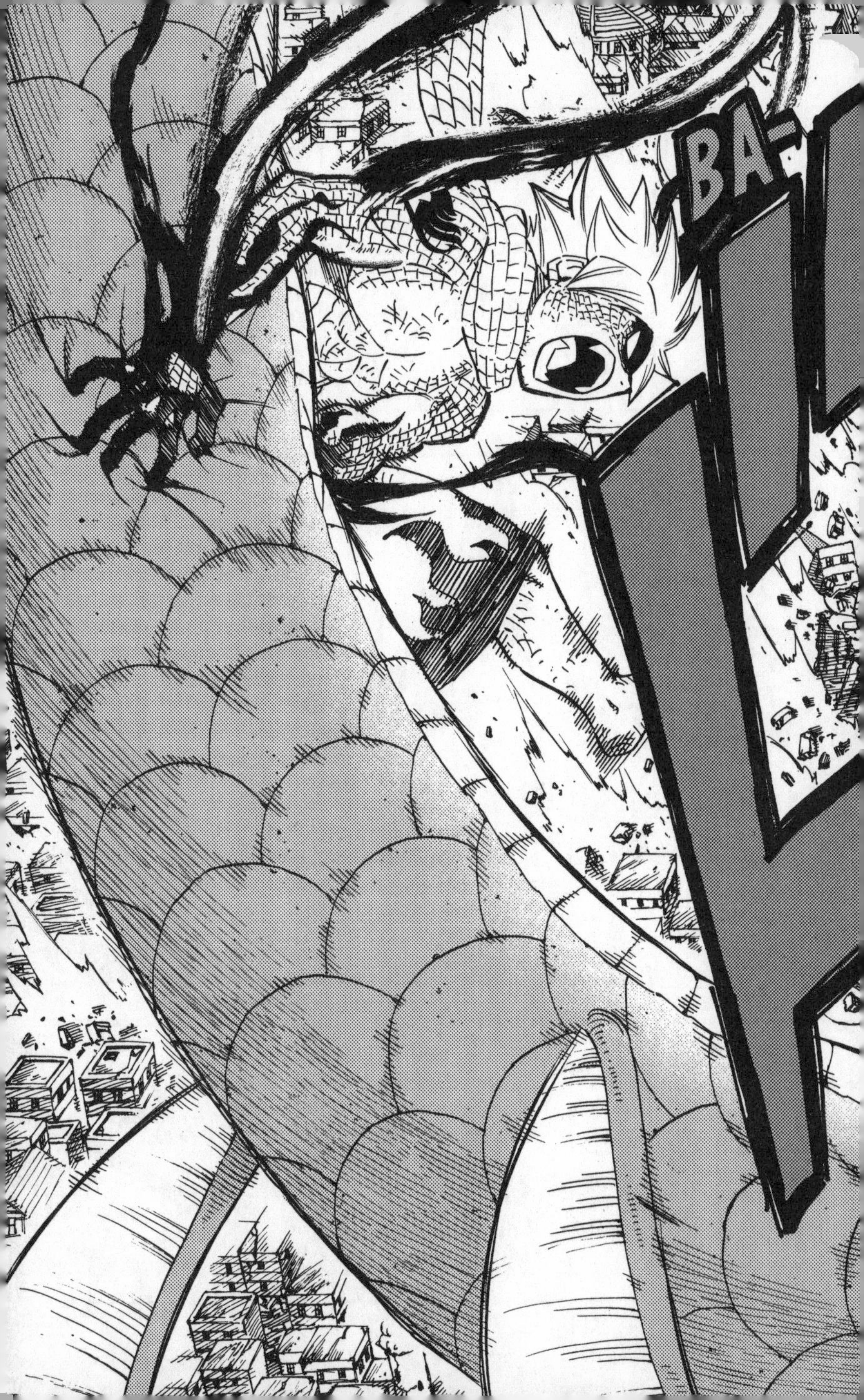
BA-

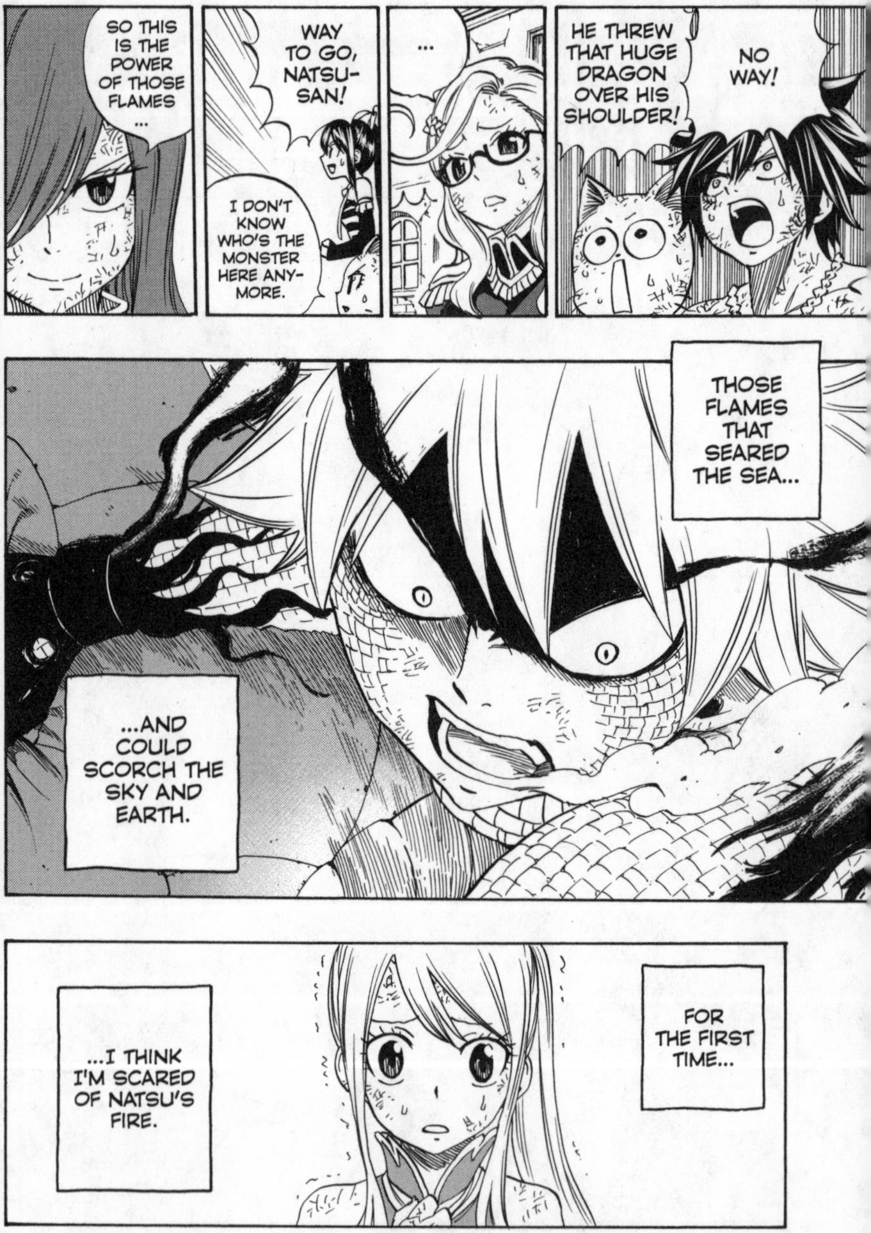
NO WAY!
HE THREW THAT HUGE DRAGON OVER HIS SHOULDER!
...
WAY TO GO, NATSU-SAN!
I DON'T KNOW WHO'S THE MONSTER HERE ANY-MORE.
SO THIS IS THE POWER OF THOSE FLAMES ...
THOSE FLAMES THAT SEARED THE SEA...
...AND COULD SCORCH THE SKY AND EARTH.
FOR THE FIRST TIME...
...I THINK I'M SCARED OF NATSU'S FIRE.

FAIRY TAIL
100 YEARS QUEST

CHAPTER 22: A TEAM EFFORT

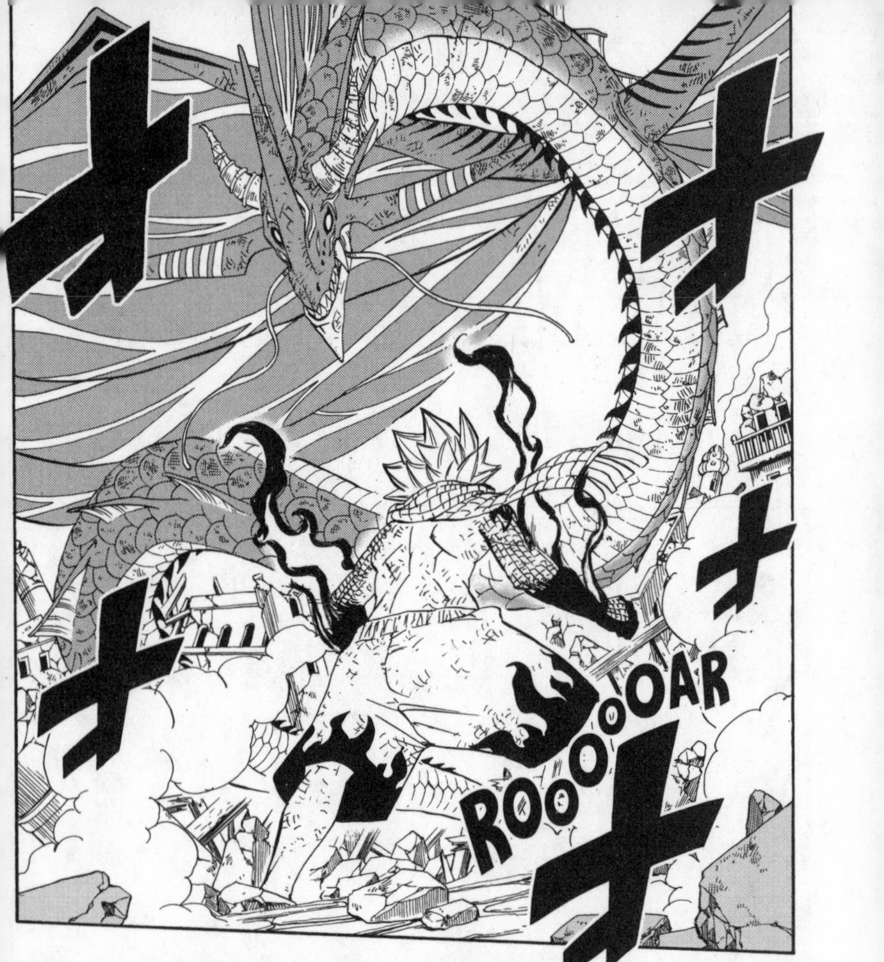
ROOOOOOAR
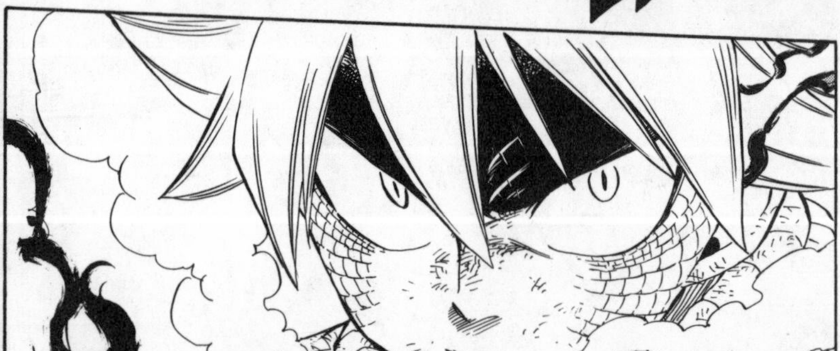

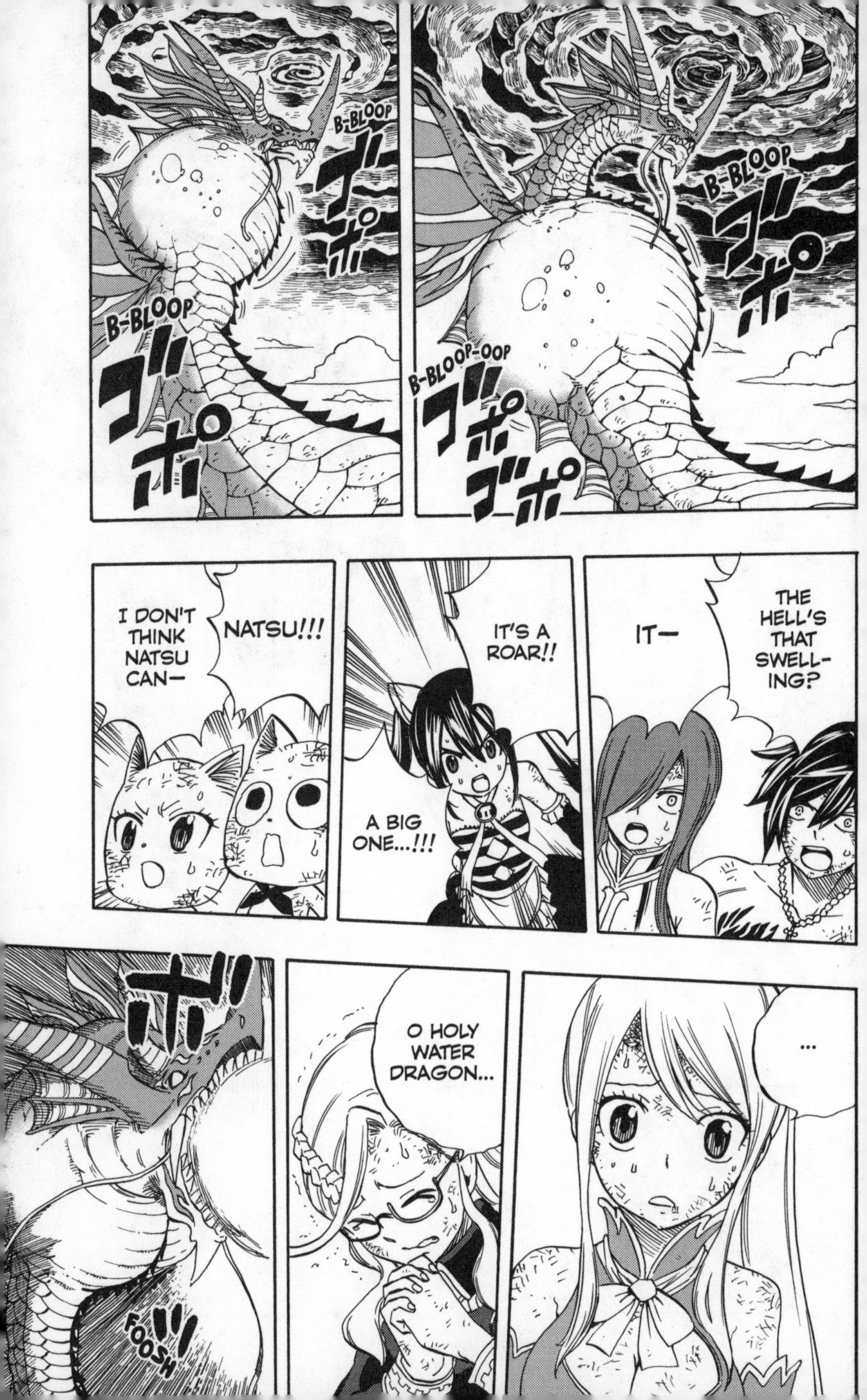
B-BLOOP
B-BLOOP-OOP
B-BLOOP
B-BLOOP
THE HELL'S THAT SWELL-ING?
IT—
IT'S A ROAR!!
A BIG ONE...!!!
NATSU!!!
I DON'T THINK NATSU CAN—
...
O HOLY WATER DRAGON...
FOOSH

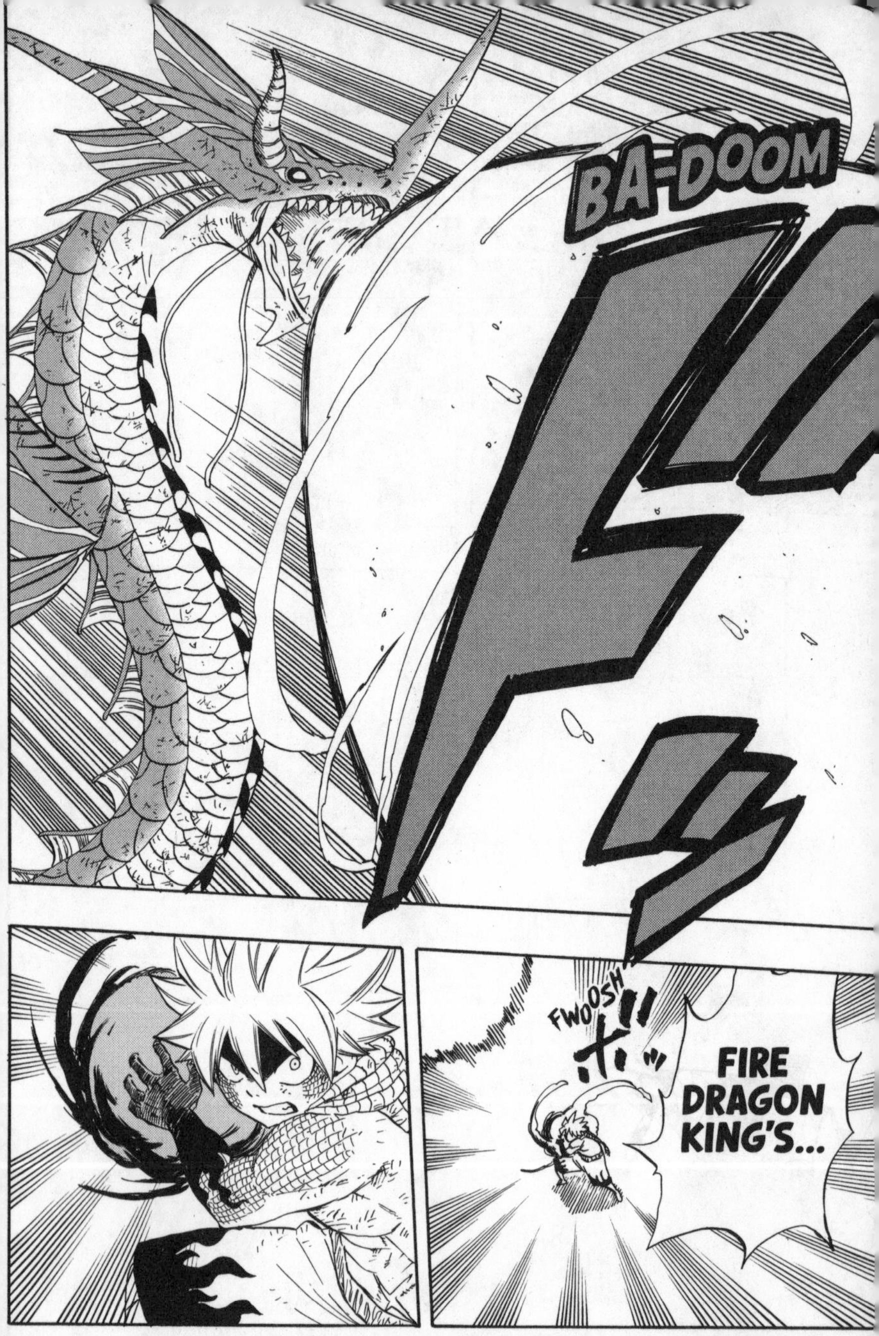
BA-DOOM
FWOOSH
FIRE DRAGON KING'S...

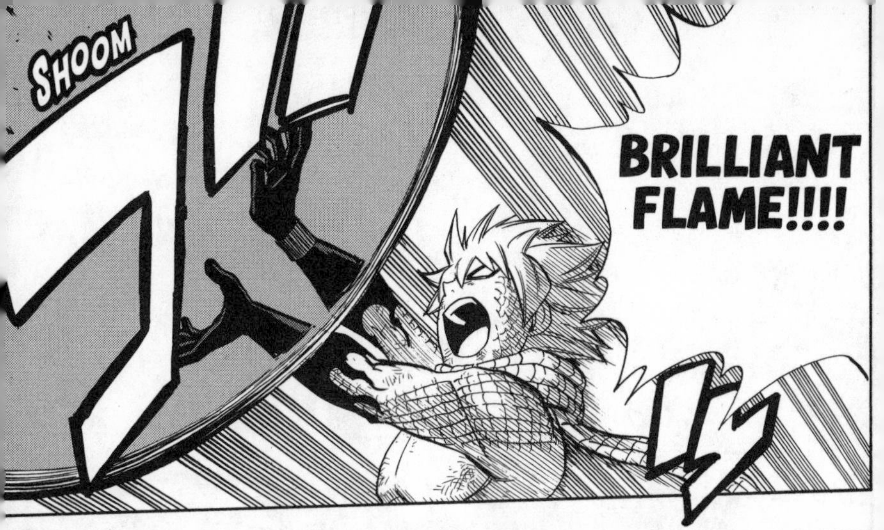
BRILLIANT
FLAME!!!!
SHOOM

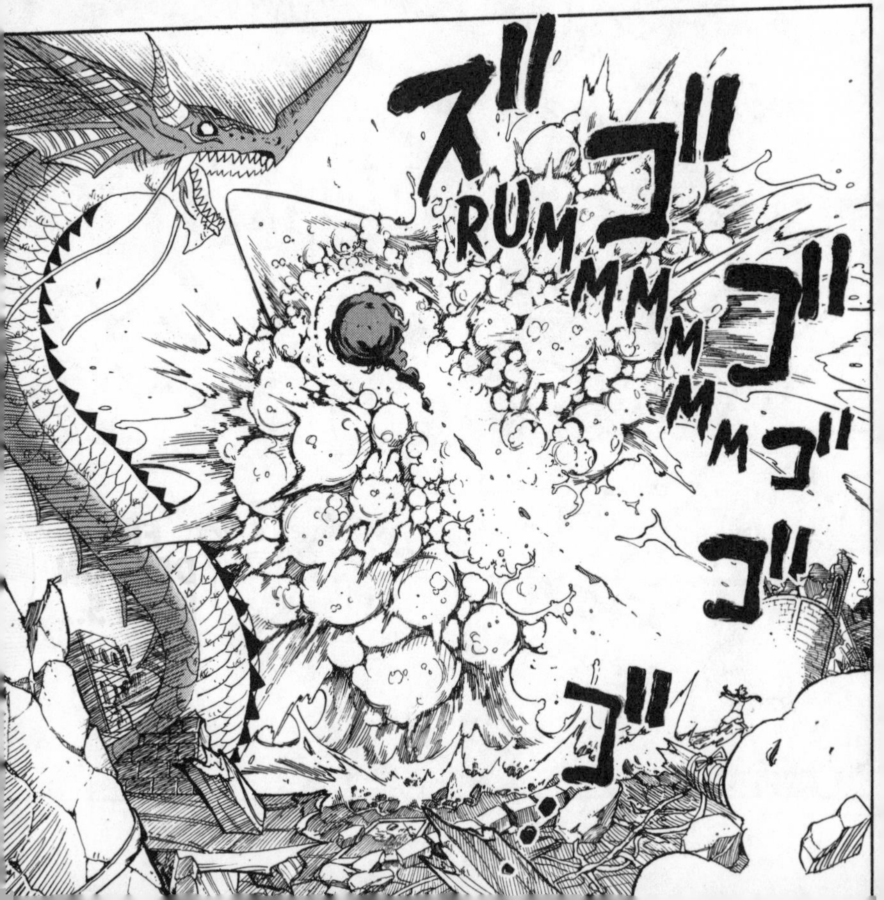
RUMMMMMM

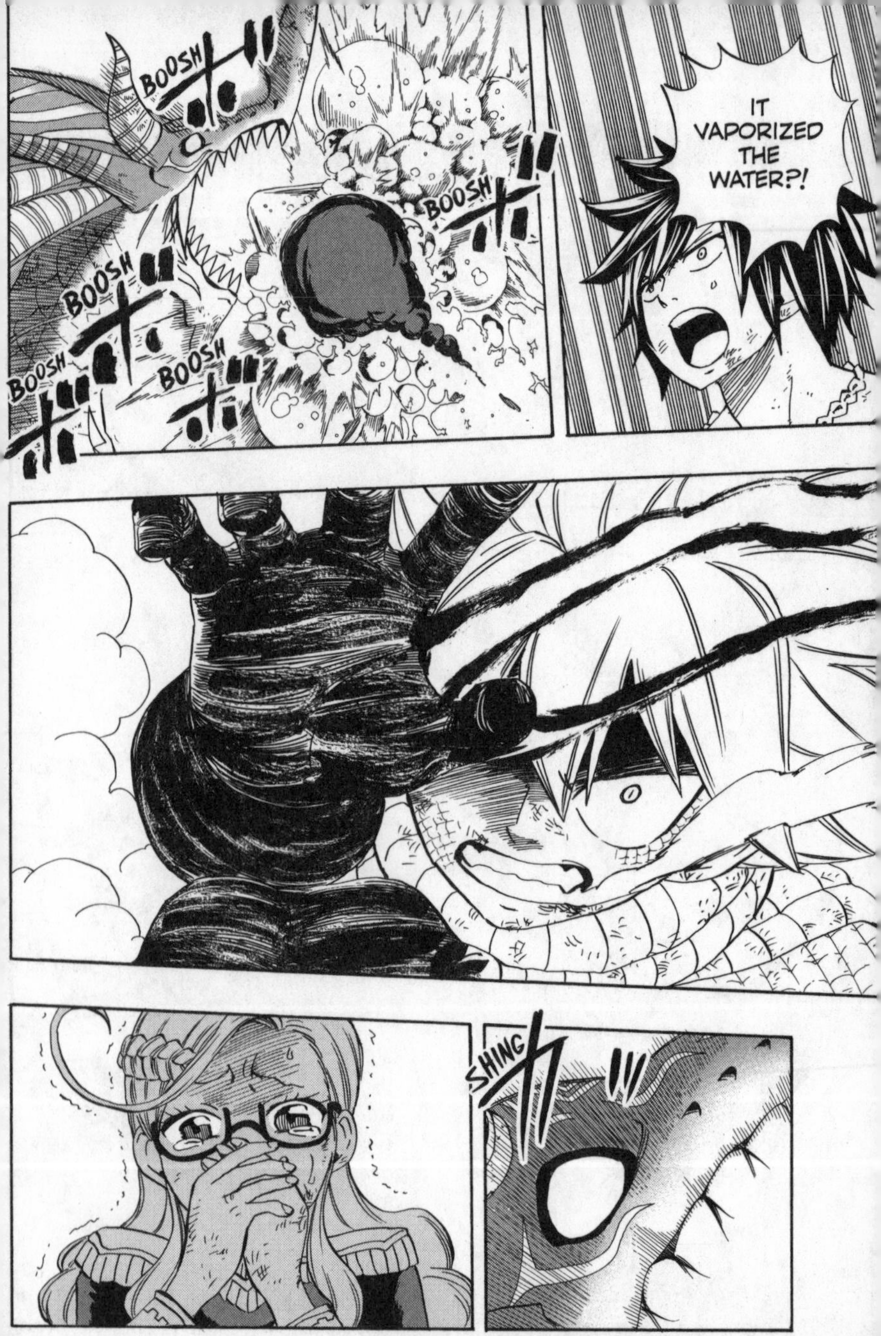
IT VAPORIZED THE WATER?!
BOOSH
BOOSH
BOOSH
BOOSH
BOOSH
BOOSH
SHING

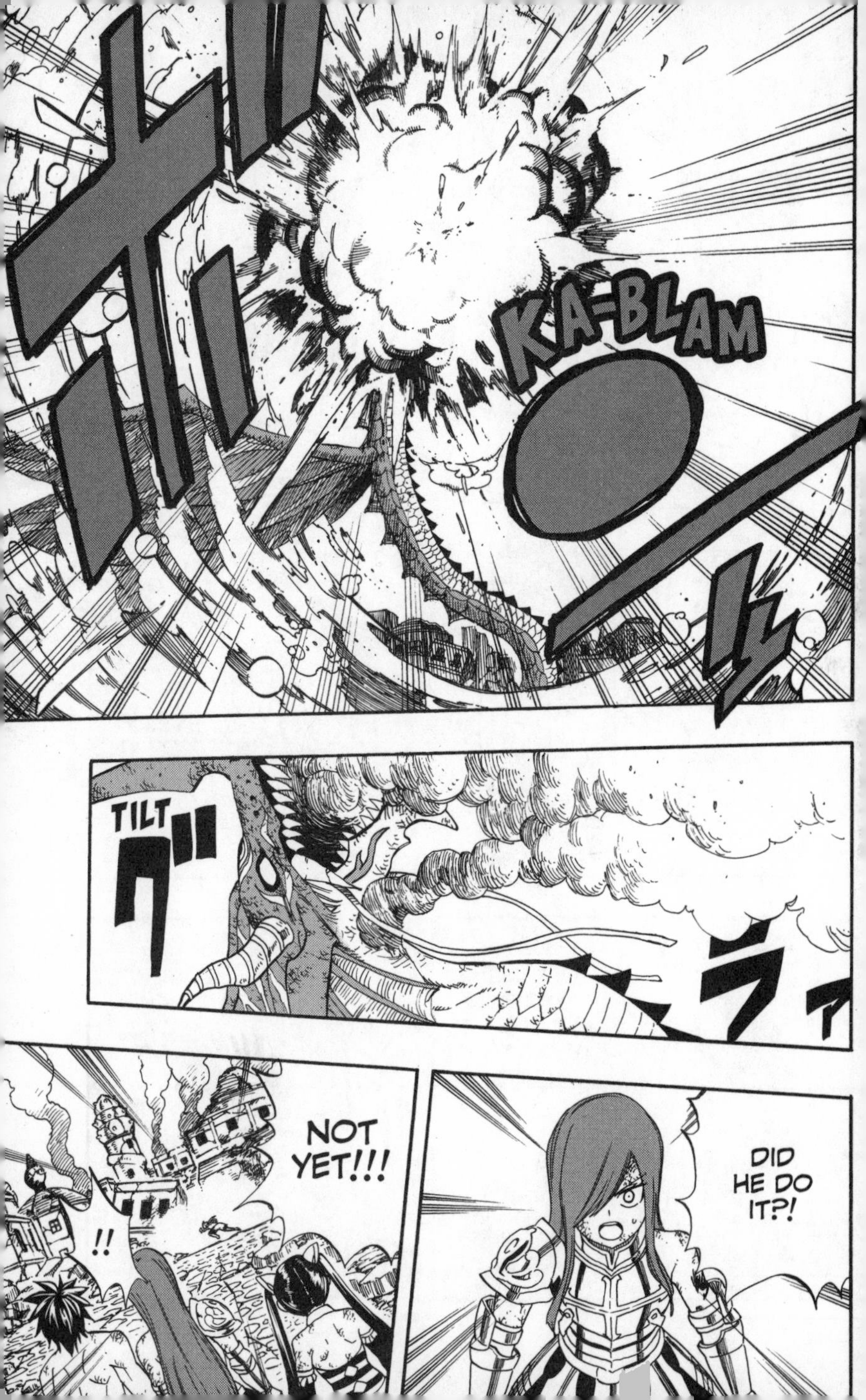
KA-BLAM
TILT
DID HE DO IT?!
NOT YET!!!
!!

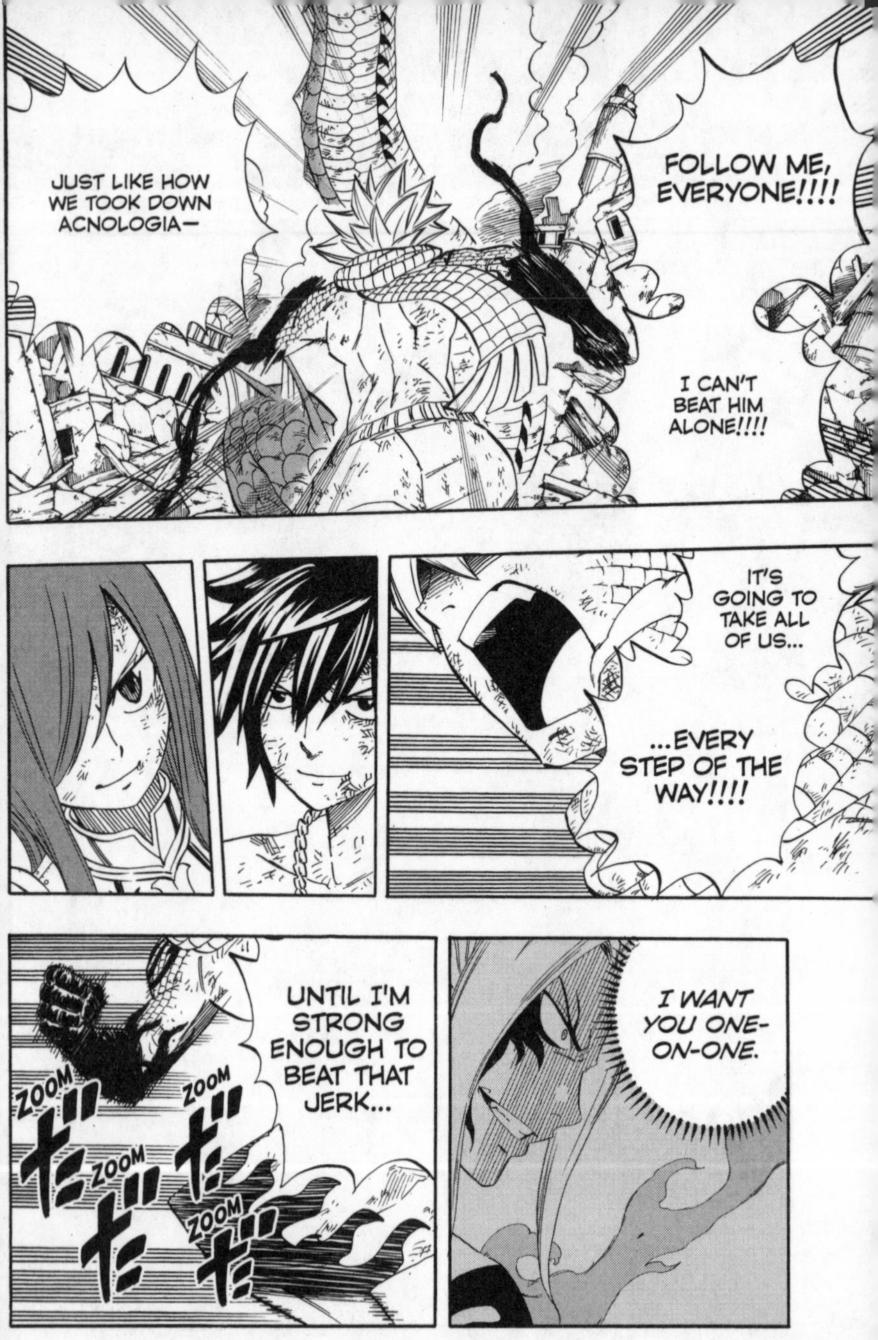
FOLLOW ME, EVERYONE!!!!
I CAN'T BEAT HIM ALONE!!!!
JUST LIKE HOW WE TOOK DOWN ACNOLOGIA—
IT'S GOING TO TAKE ALL OF US...
...EVERY STEP OF THE WAY!!!!
I WANT YOU ONE-ON-ONE.
UNTIL I'M STRONG ENOUGH TO BEAT THAT JERK...
ZOOM
ZOOM
ZOOM
ZOOM

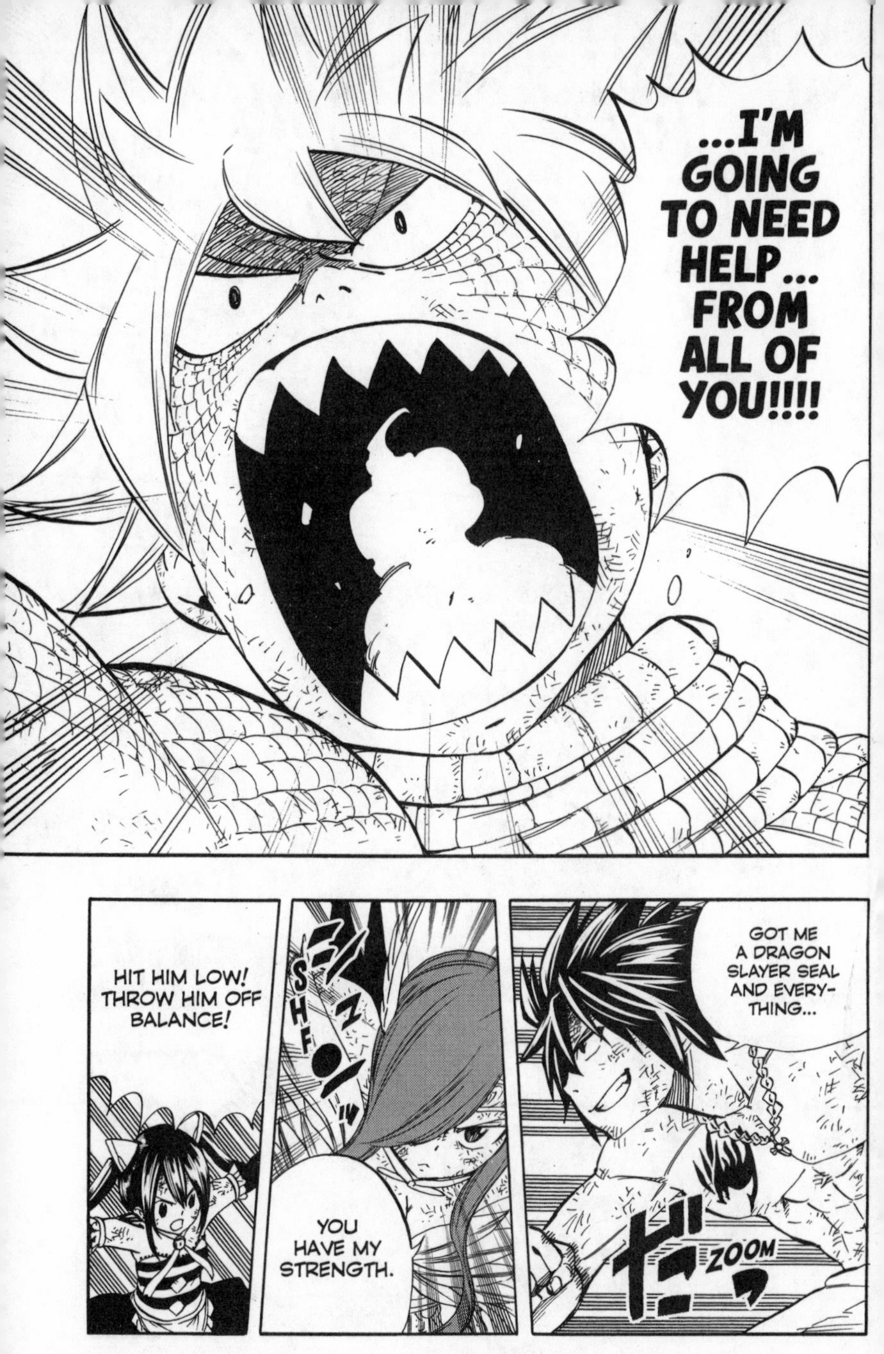
...I'M GOING TO NEED HELP... FROM ALL OF YOU!!!!
GOT ME A DRAGON SLAYER SEAL AND EVERY-THING...
ZOOM
SHF
YOU HAVE MY STRENGTH.
HIT HIM LOW! THROW HIM OFF BALANCE!

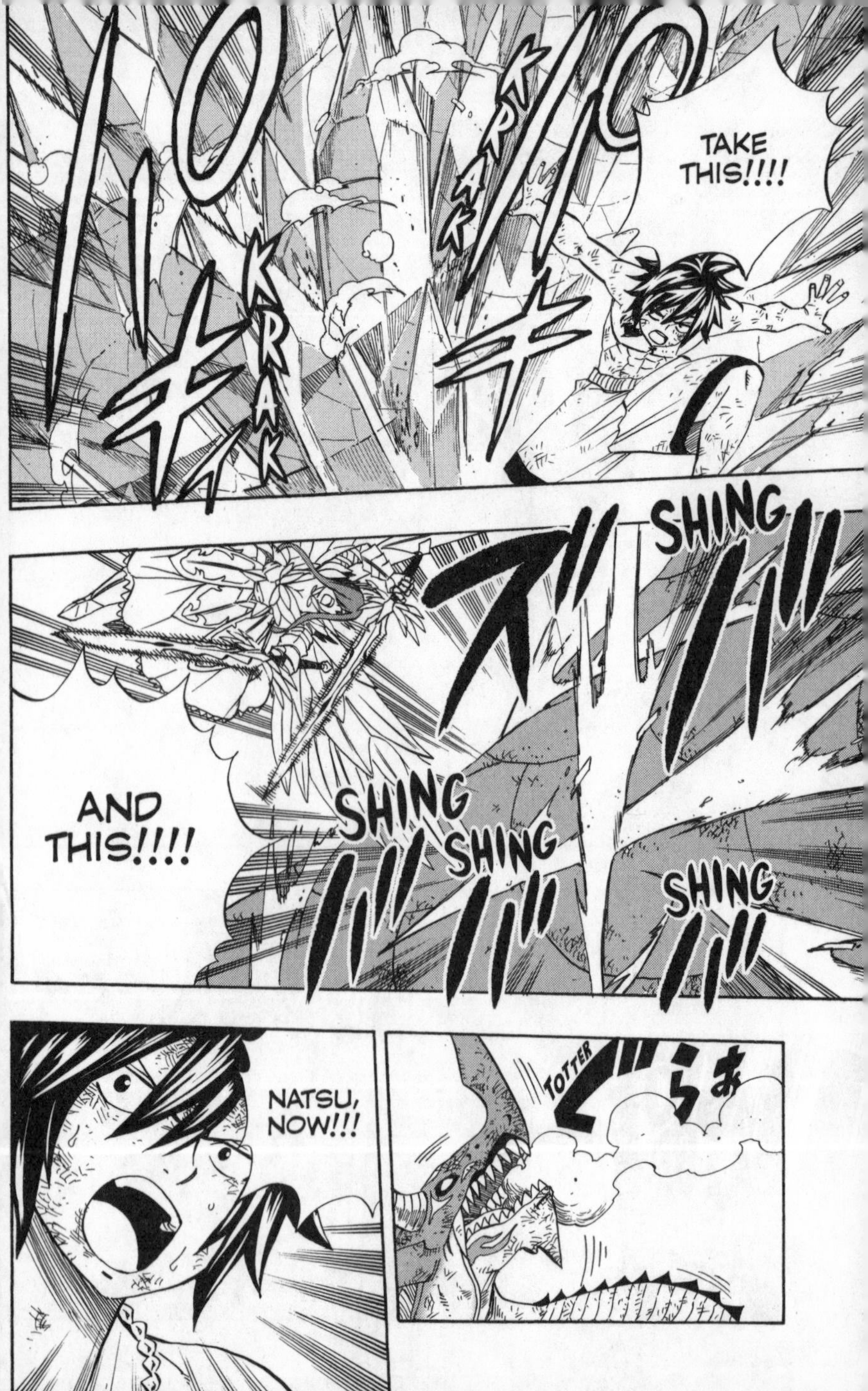
TAKE THIS!!!!
KRAK
KRAK
SHING
AND THIS!!!!
SHING
SHING
SHING
TOTTER
NATSU, NOW!!!

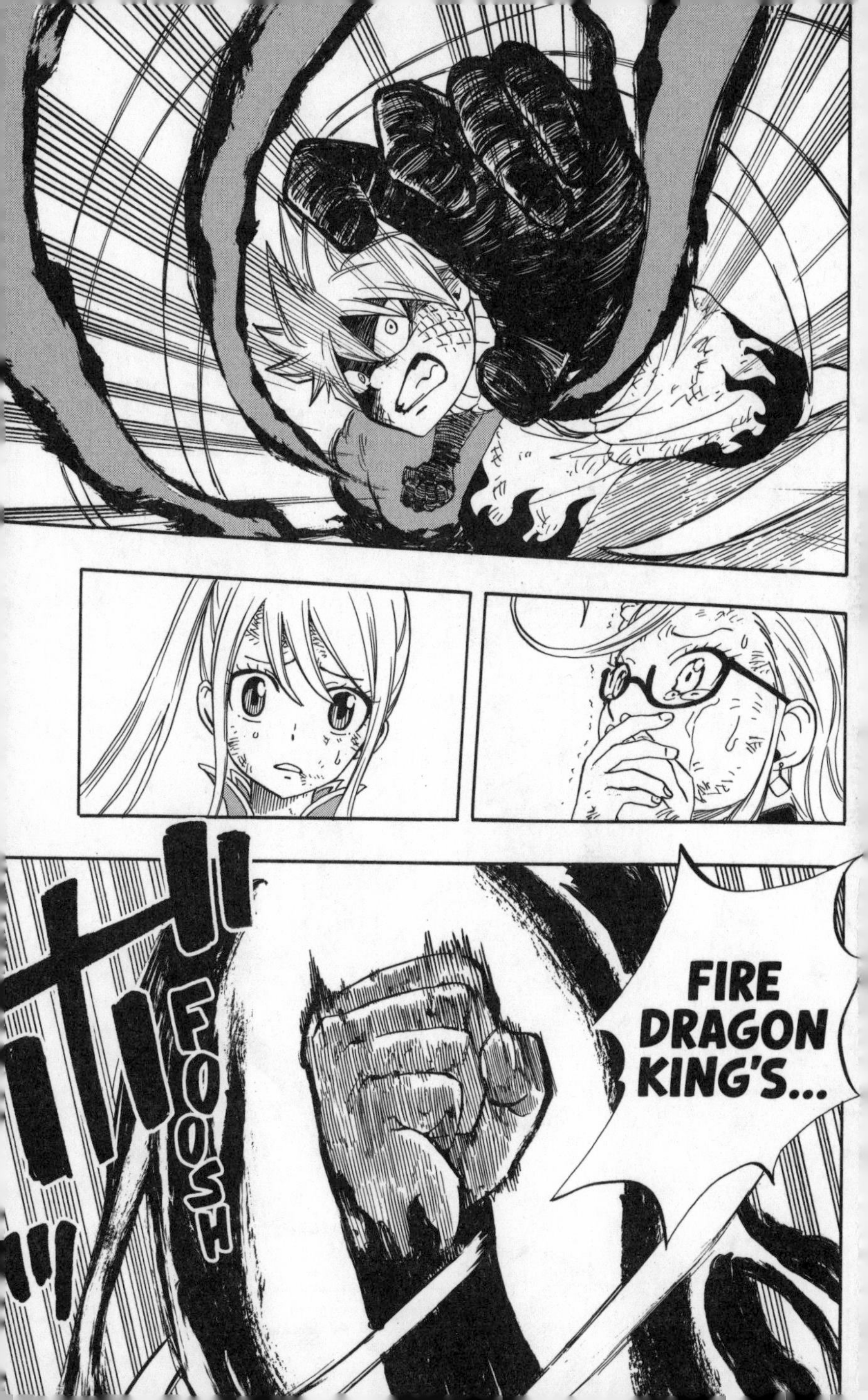
FIRE DRAGON KING'S...
FOOSH

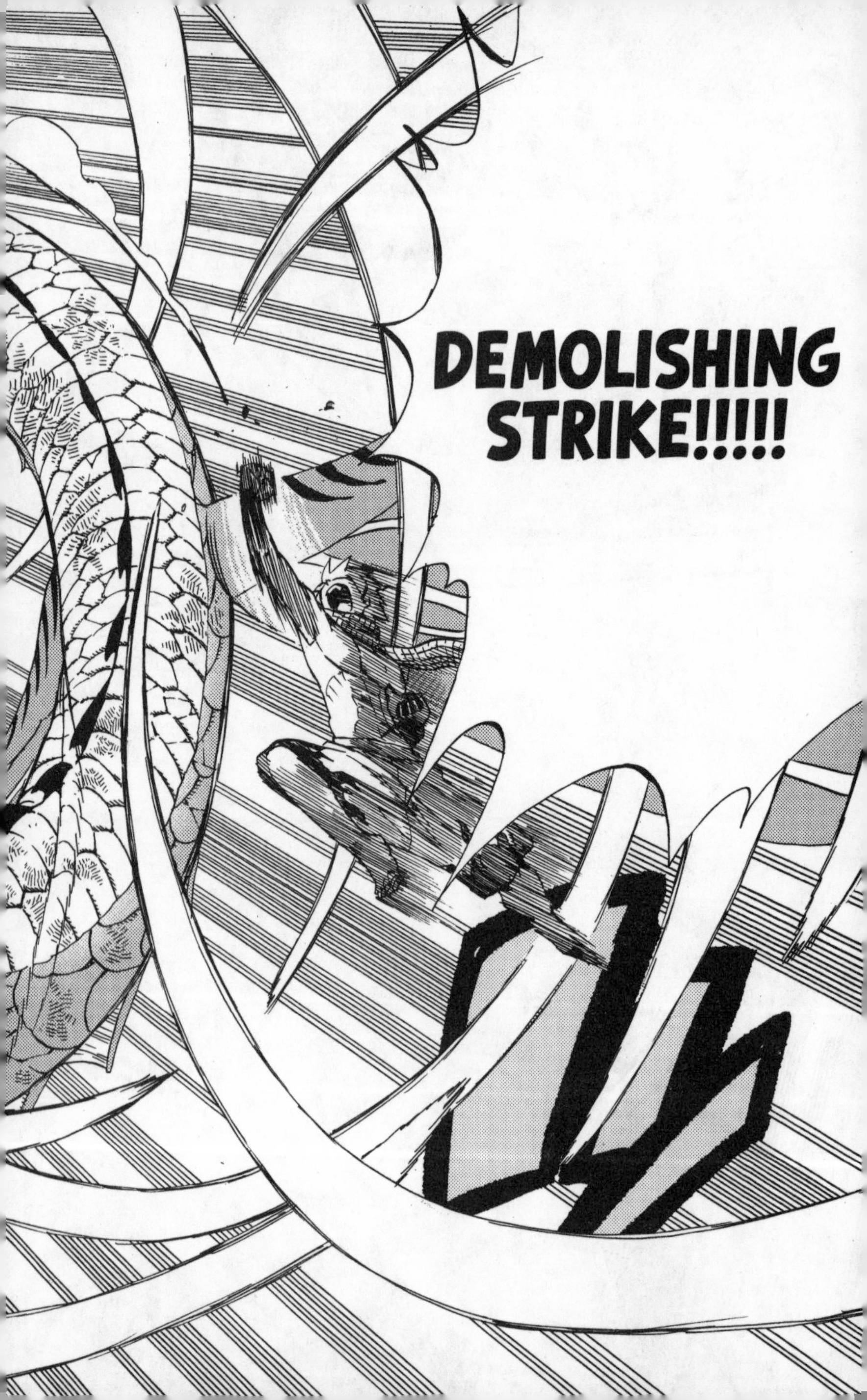
DEMOLISHING STRIKE!!!!!

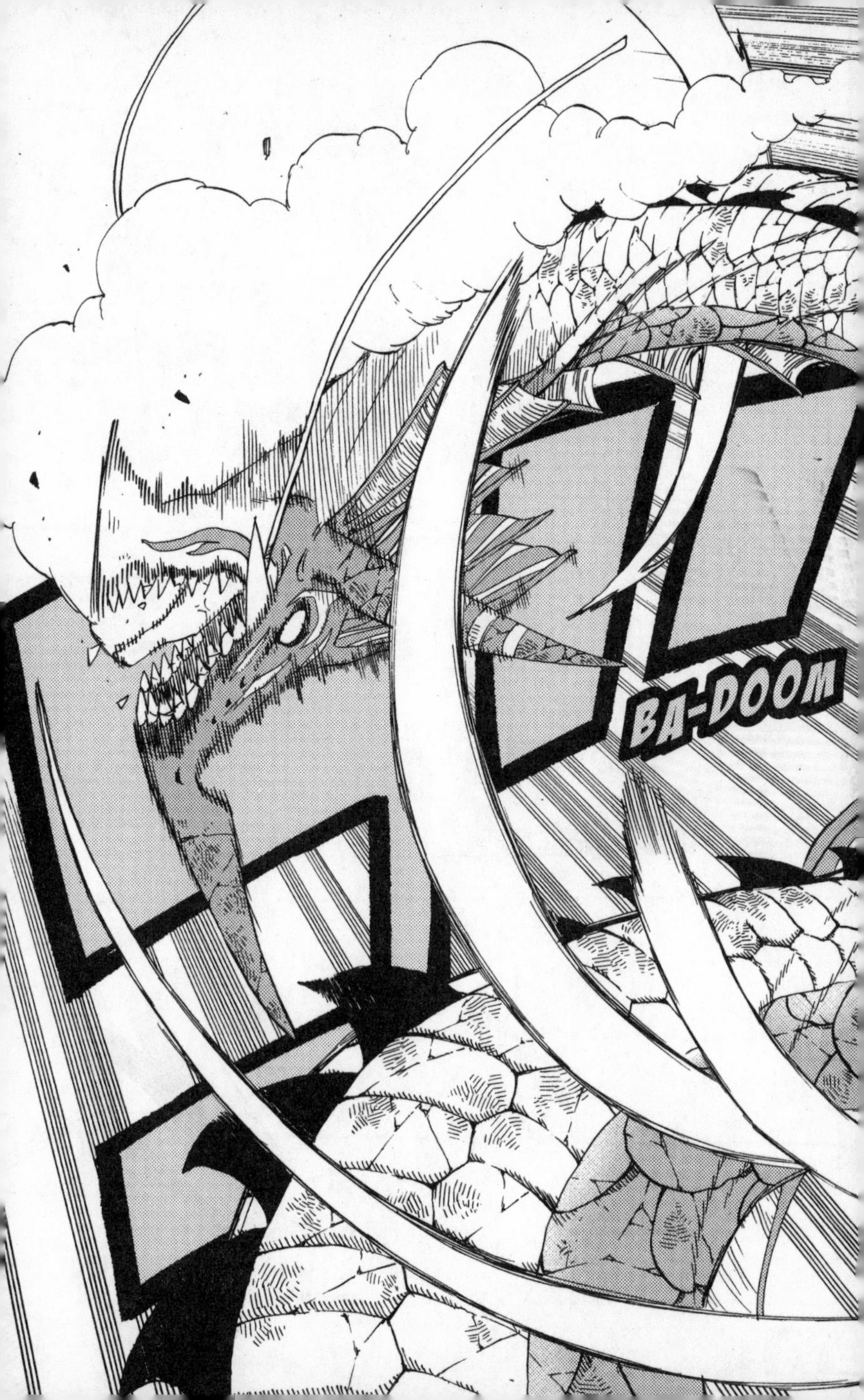
BA-DOOM

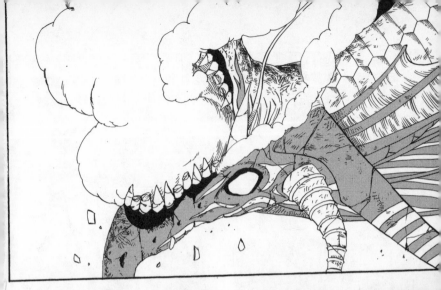

O HONORED WATER DRAGON ...

THIS...

...WAS FOR THE BEST...

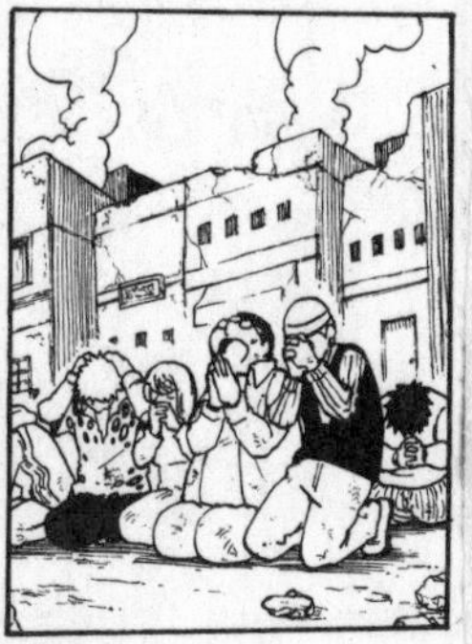
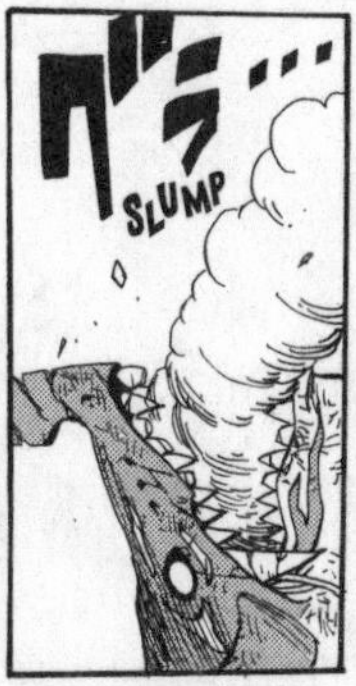
SLUMP
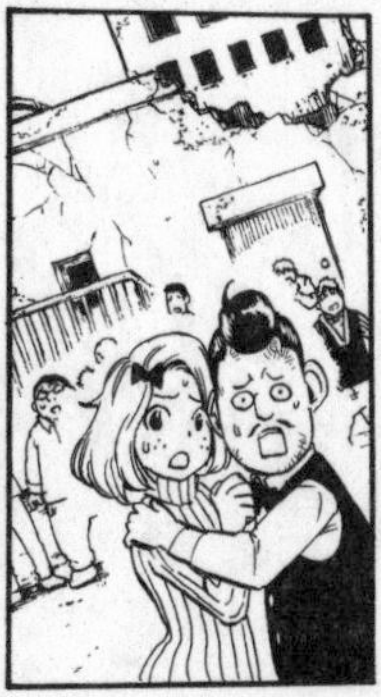
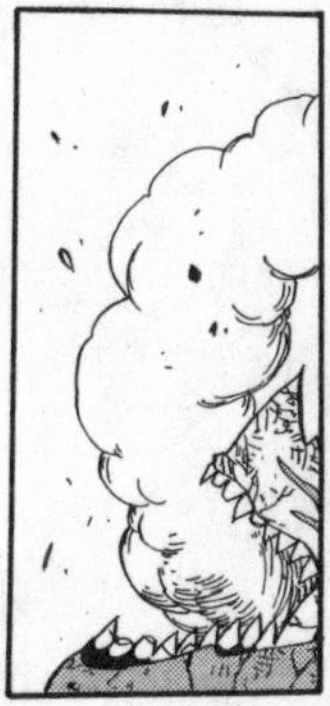
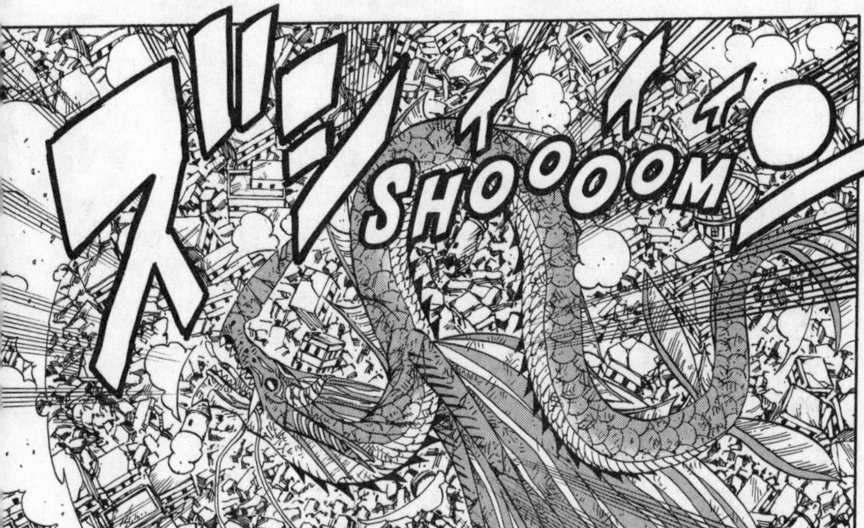
SHOOOOM
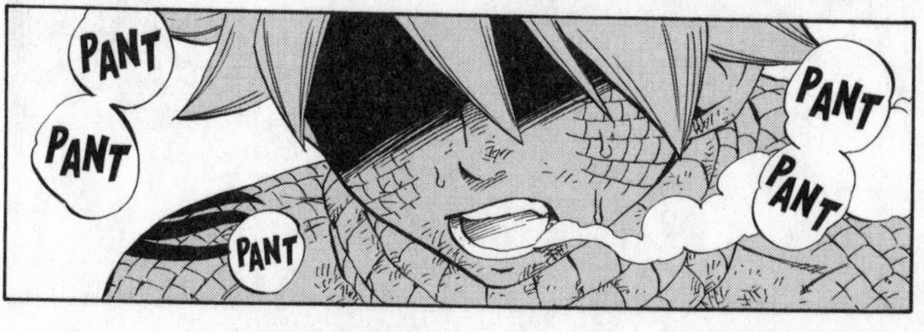
PANT
PANT
PANT
PANT
PANT

PANT PANT PANT PANT PANT

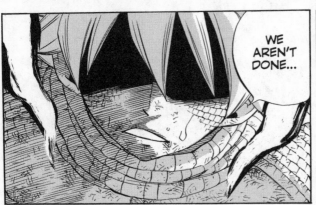

WE AREN'T DONE...

SHF

NATSU?

THE BODY'S... STILL HERE...

KRAKL KRAKL

!

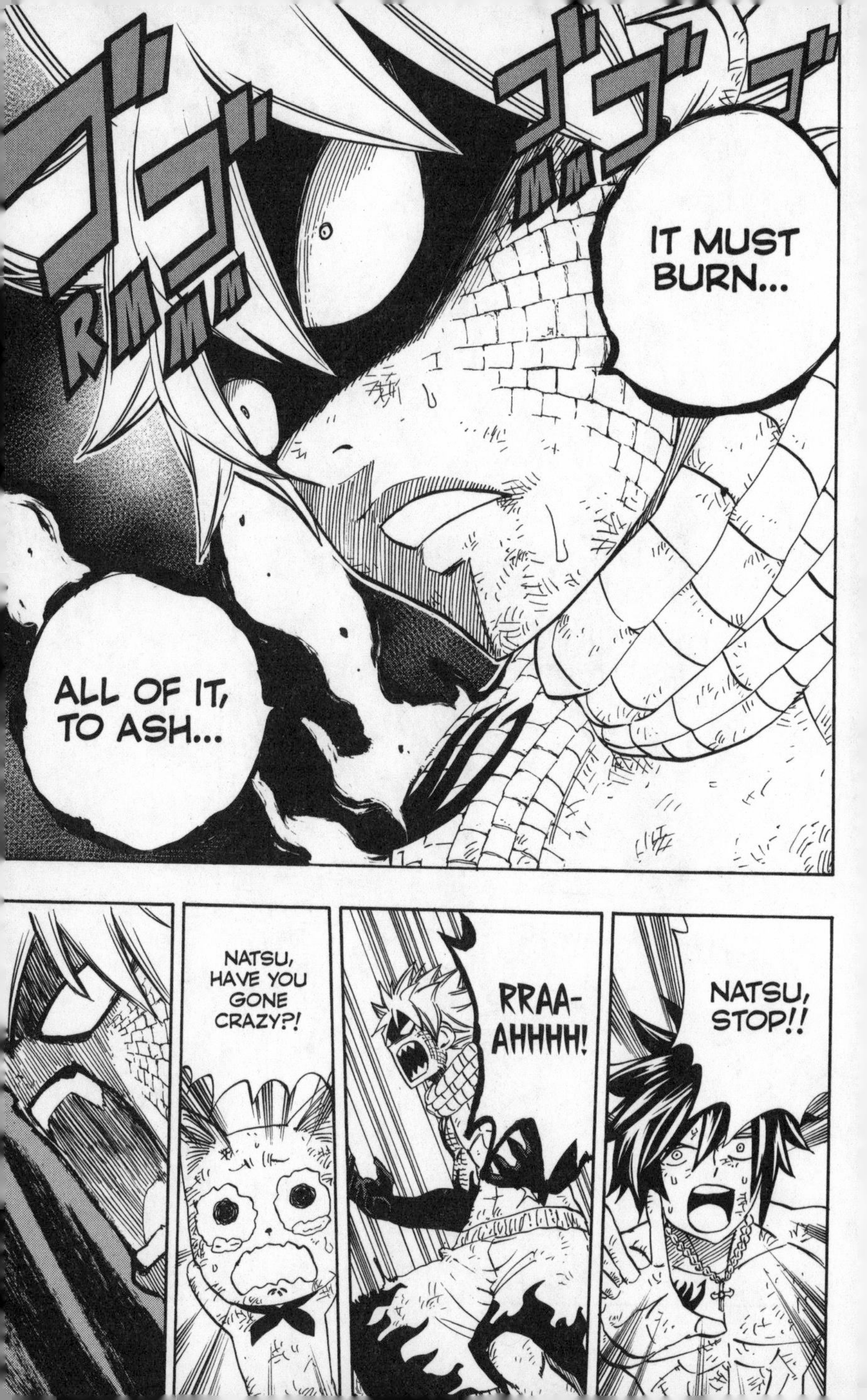
MM
IT MUST BURN...
RMMM
ALL OF IT, TO ASH...
NATSU, STOP!!
RRAA-AHHHH!
NATSU, HAVE YOU GONE CRAZY?!

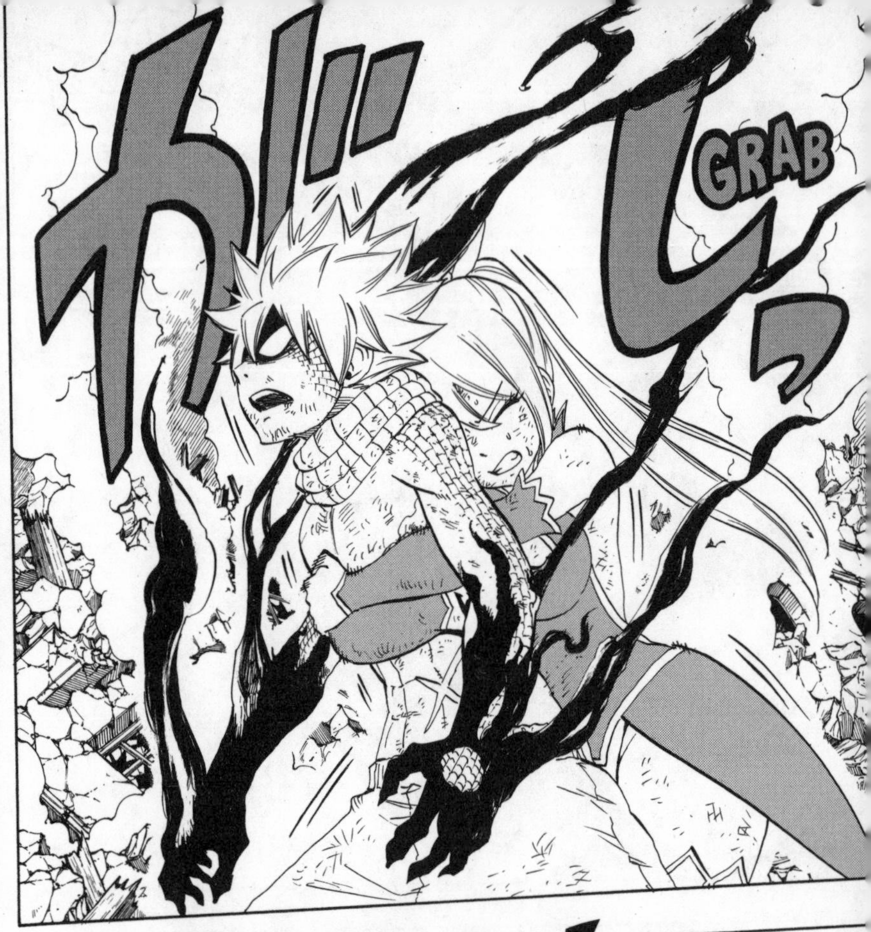
GRAB

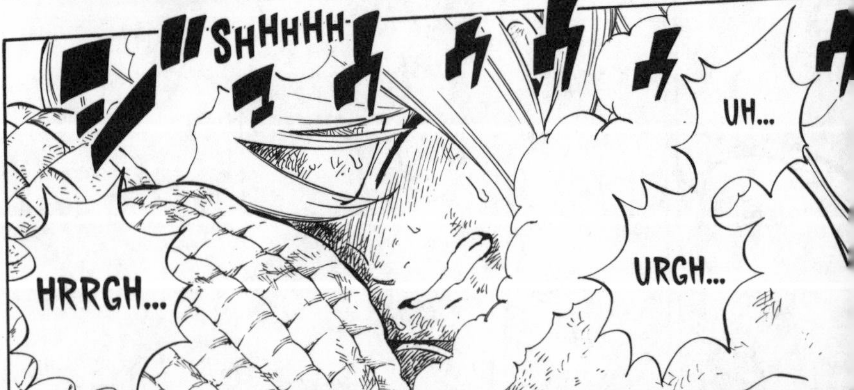
SHHHHH
UH...
URGH...
HRRGH...

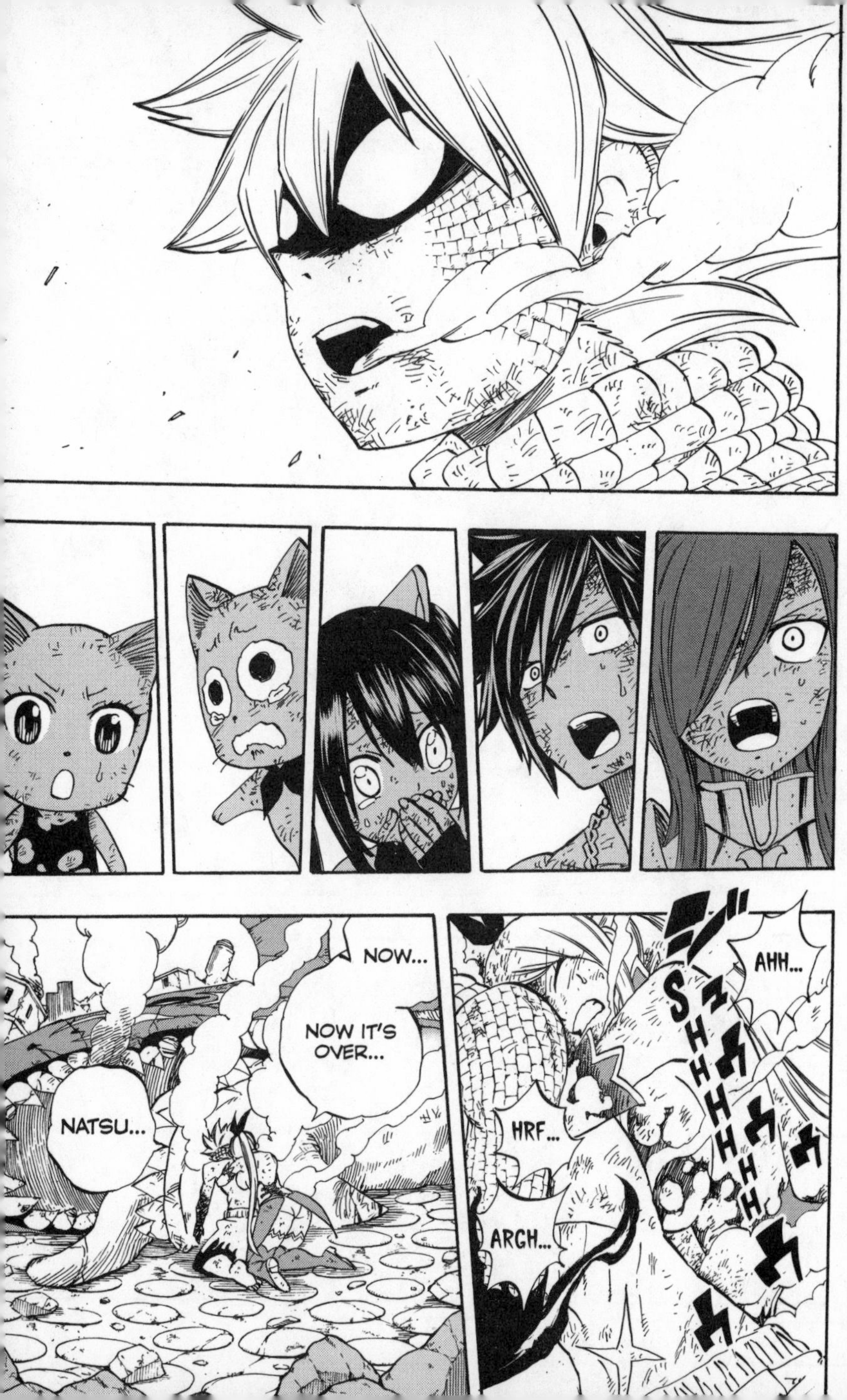
AHH...
SHHHHHH
HRF...
ARGH...
NOW...
NOW IT'S OVER...
NATSU...

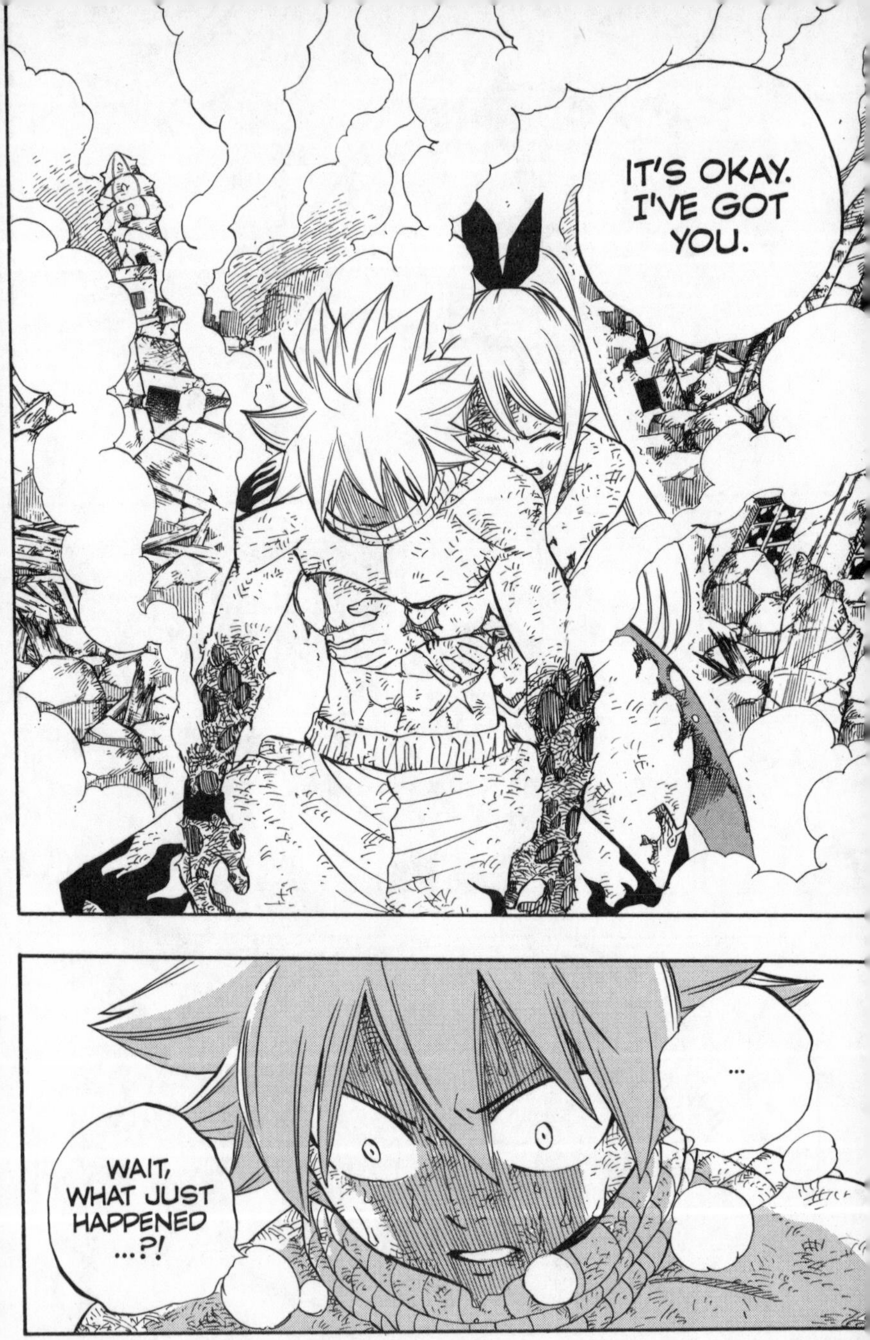
IT'S OKAY. I'VE GOT YOU.
...
WAIT, WHAT JUST HAPPENED ...?!

FAIRY TAIL 100 YEARS QUEST

Chapter 23: The Blessed Harbor Town

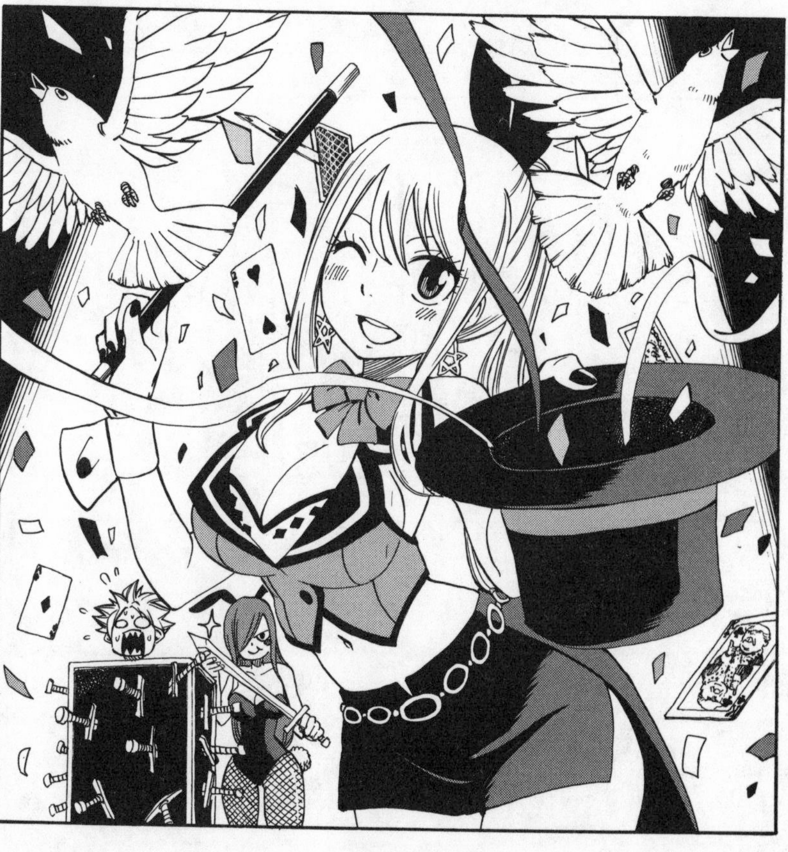

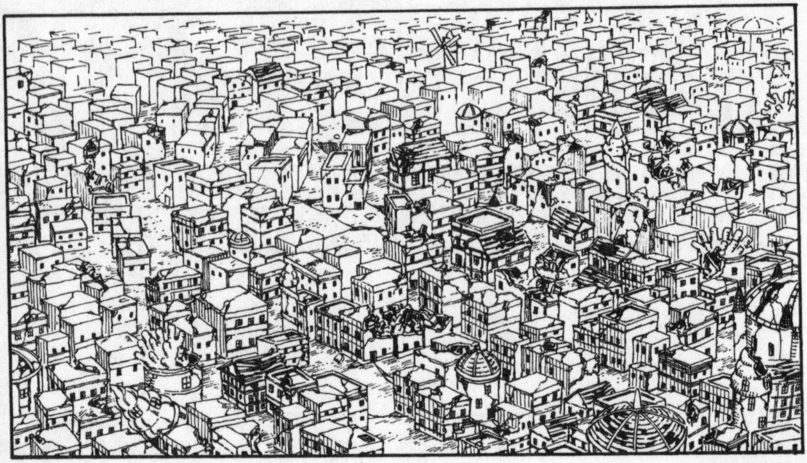
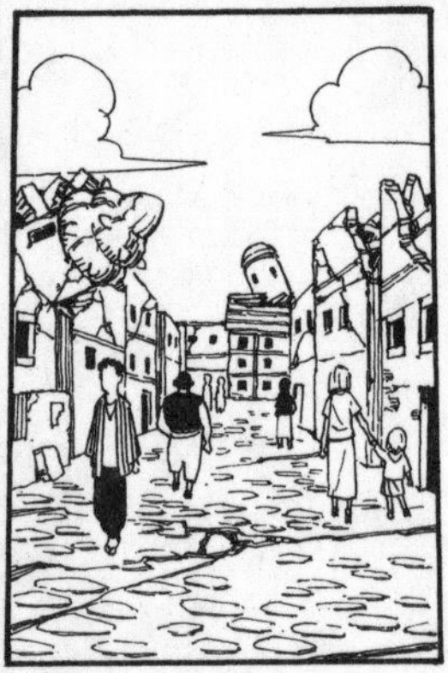
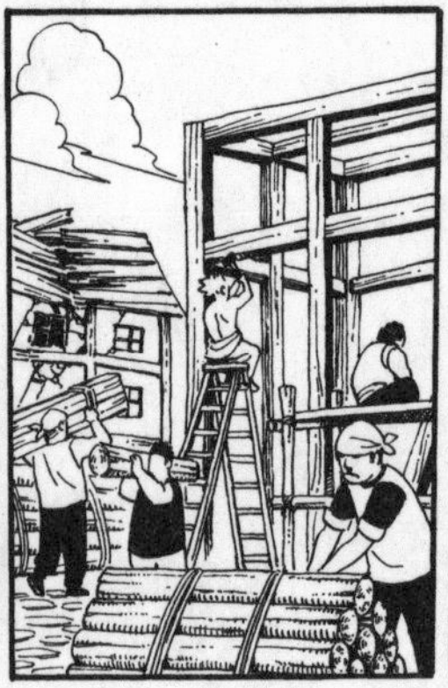
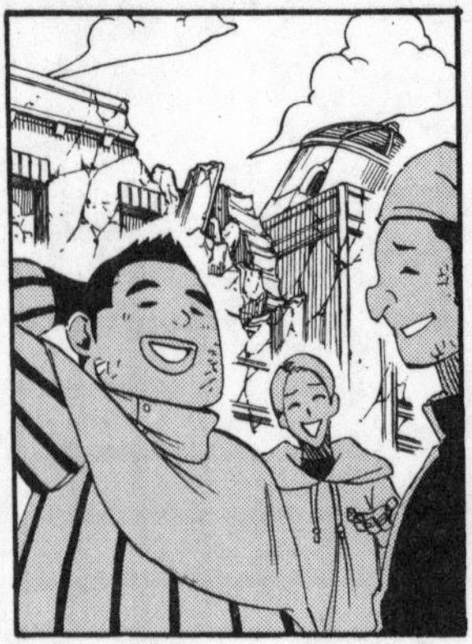
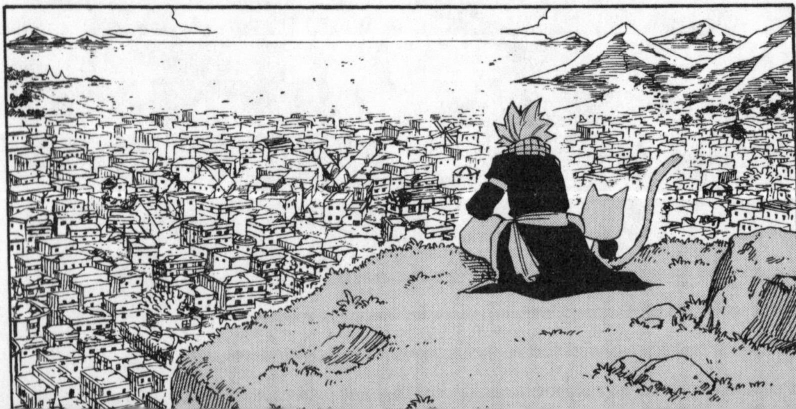

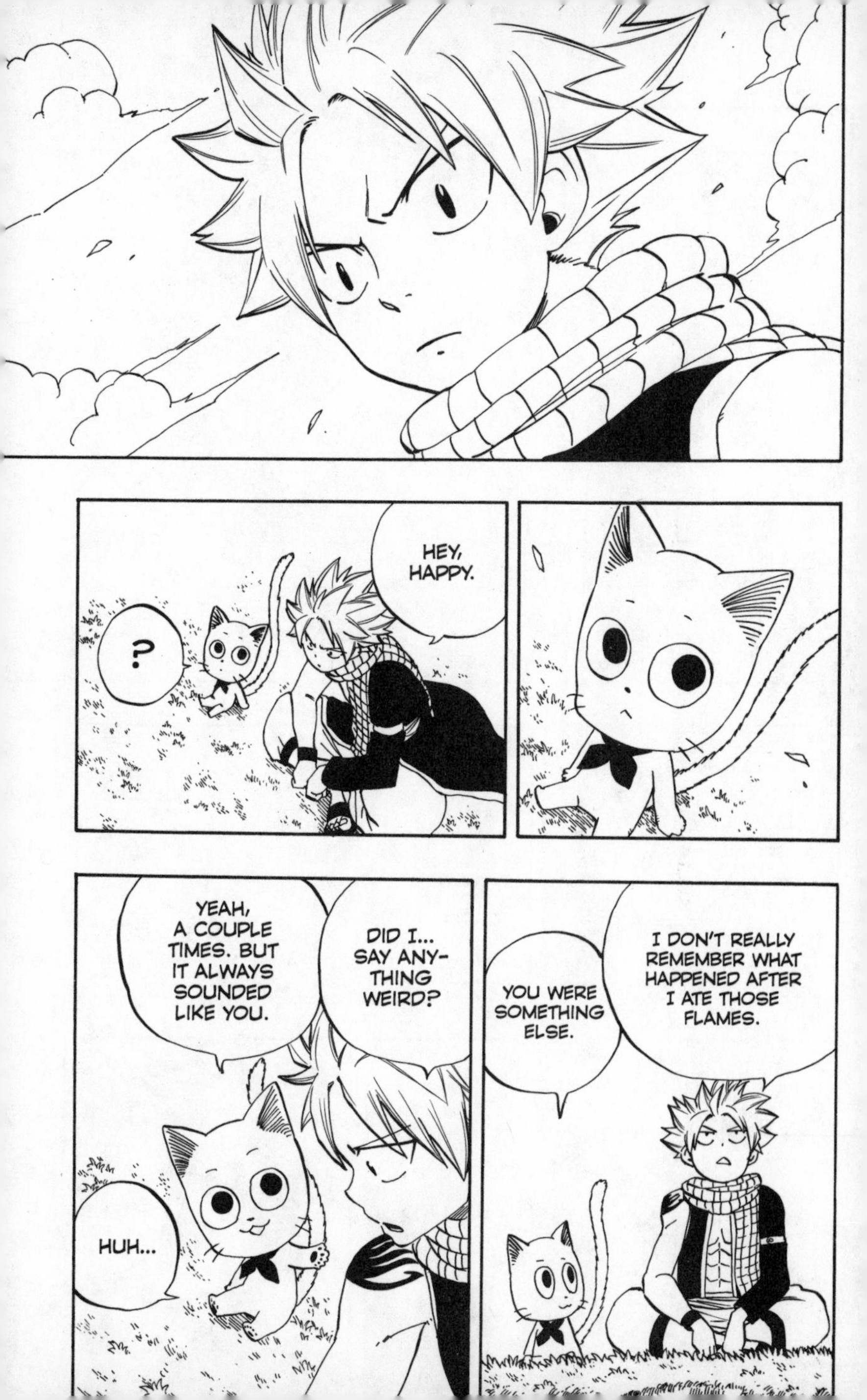
HEY, HAPPY.
?
I DON'T REALLY REMEMBER WHAT HAPPENED AFTER I ATE THOSE FLAMES.
YOU WERE SOMETHING ELSE.
DID I... SAY ANY-THING WEIRD?
YEAH, A COUPLE TIMES. BUT IT ALWAYS SOUNDED LIKE YOU.
HUH...

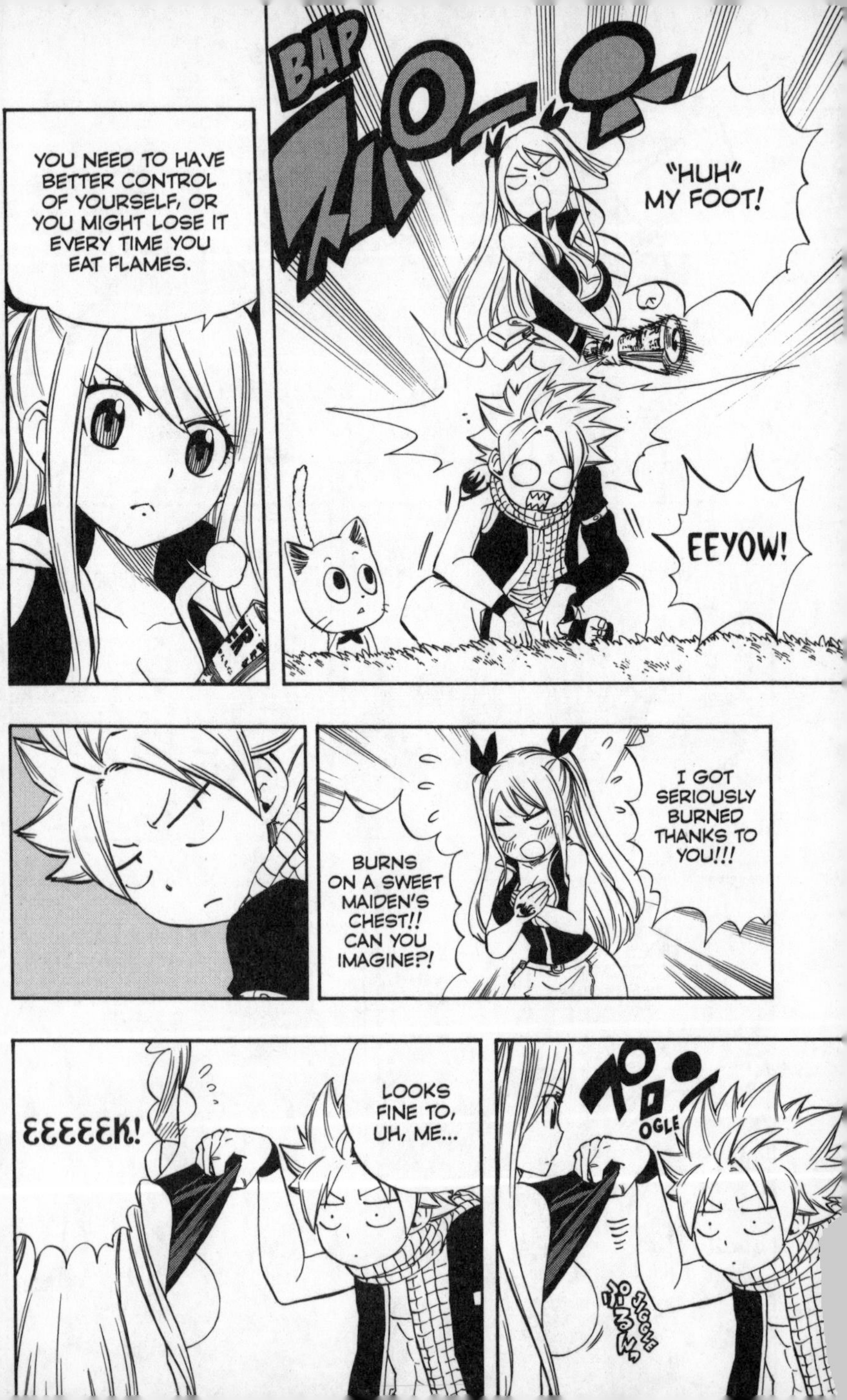
BAP
"HUH" MY FOOT!
EEYOW!
YOU NEED TO HAVE BETTER CONTROL OF YOURSELF, OR YOU MIGHT LOSE IT EVERY TIME YOU EAT FLAMES.
I GOT SERIOUSLY BURNED THANKS TO YOU!!!
BURNS ON A SWEET MAIDEN'S CHEST!! CAN YOU IMAGINE?!
OGLE
JIGGLE
LOOKS FINE TO, UH, ME...
EEEEEK!

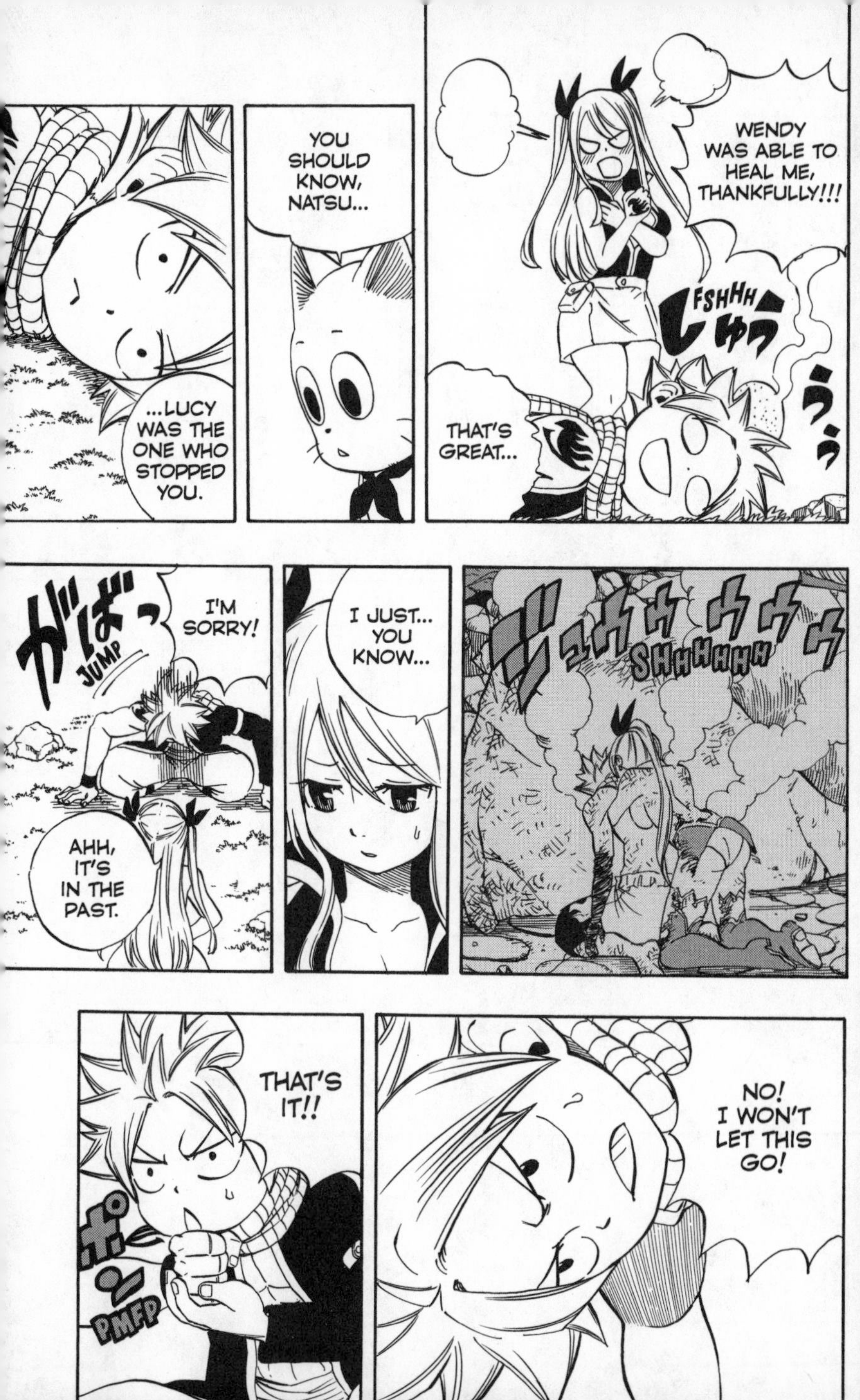
WENDY WAS ABLE TO HEAL ME, THANKFULLY!!!
FSHHH
THAT'S GREAT...
YOU SHOULD KNOW, NATSU...
...LUCY WAS THE ONE WHO STOPPED YOU.
SHHHHHH
I JUST... YOU KNOW...
I'M SORRY!
JUMP
AHH, IT'S IN THE PAST.
NO! I WON'T LET THIS GO!
THAT'S IT!!
PMFP

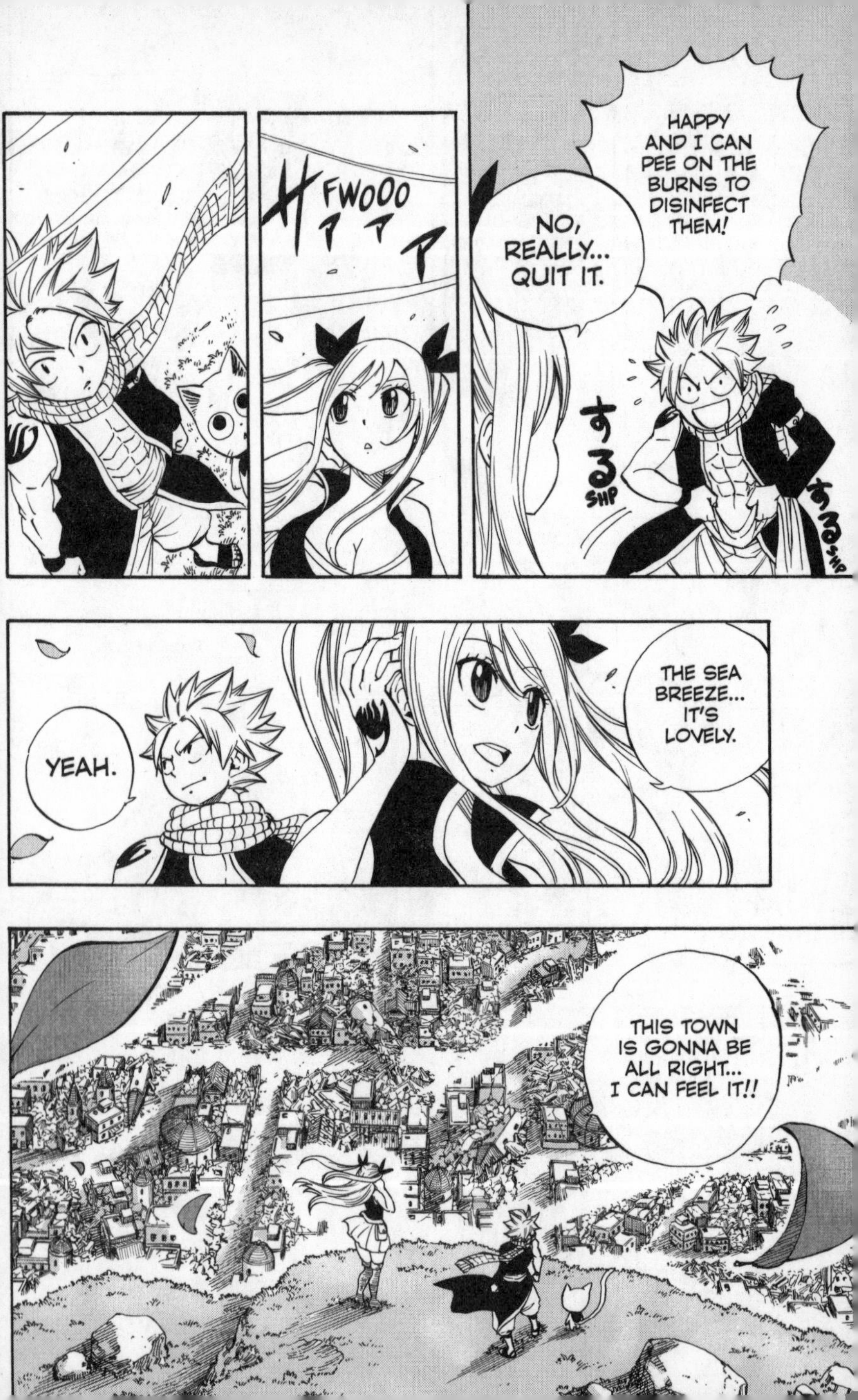
HAPPY AND I CAN PEE ON THE BURNS TO DISINFECT THEM!
NO, REALLY... QUIT IT.
する SHP
する SHP
FWOOO
THE SEA BREEZE... IT'S LOVELY.
YEAH.
THIS TOWN IS GONNA BE ALL RIGHT... I CAN FEEL IT!!

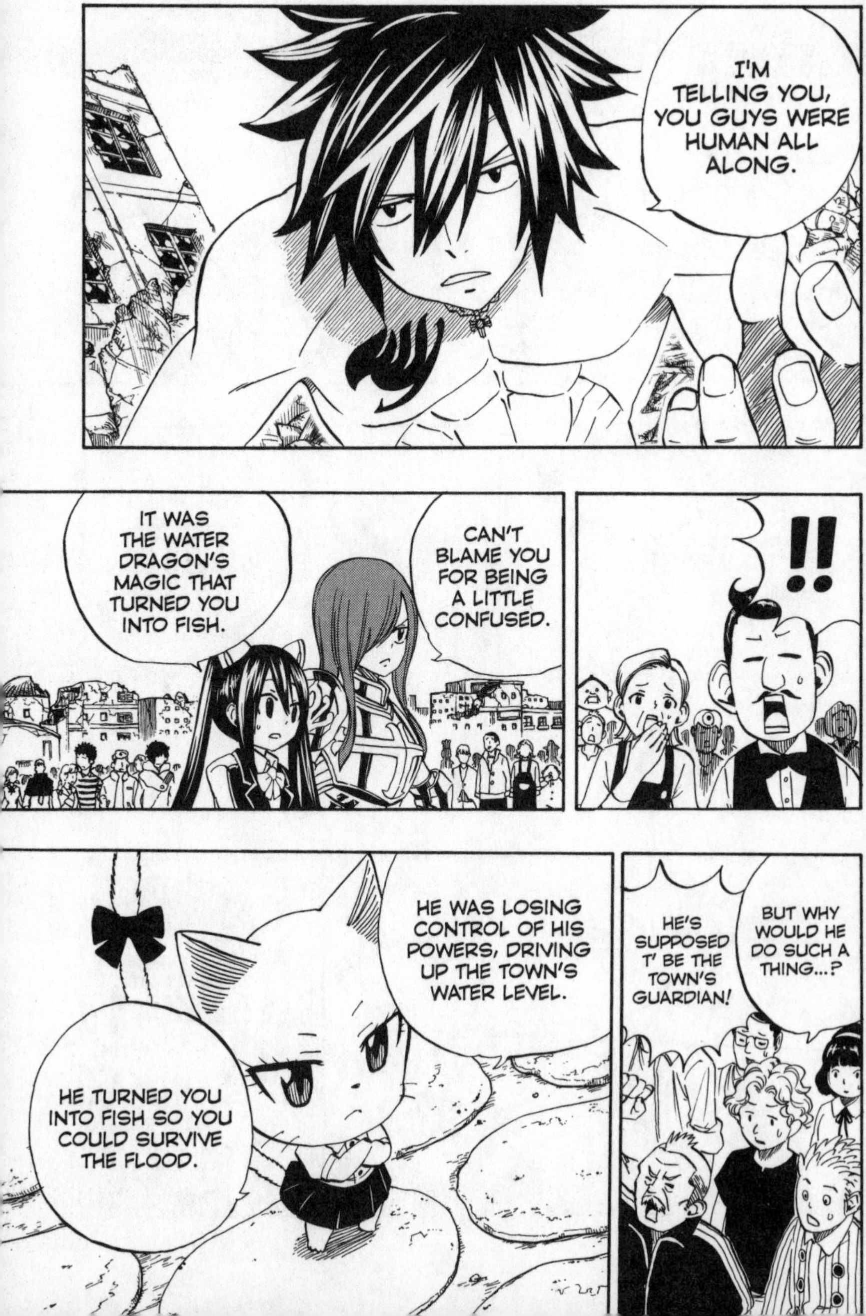
I'M TELLING YOU, YOU GUYS WERE HUMAN ALL ALONG.
!!
CAN'T BLAME YOU FOR BEING A LITTLE CONFUSED.
IT WAS THE WATER DRAGON'S MAGIC THAT TURNED YOU INTO FISH.
BUT WHY WOULD HE DO SUCH A THING...?
HE'S SUPPOSED T' BE THE TOWN'S GUARDIAN!
HE WAS LOSING CONTROL OF HIS POWERS, DRIVING UP THE TOWN'S WATER LEVEL.
HE TURNED YOU INTO FISH SO YOU COULD SURVIVE THE FLOOD.

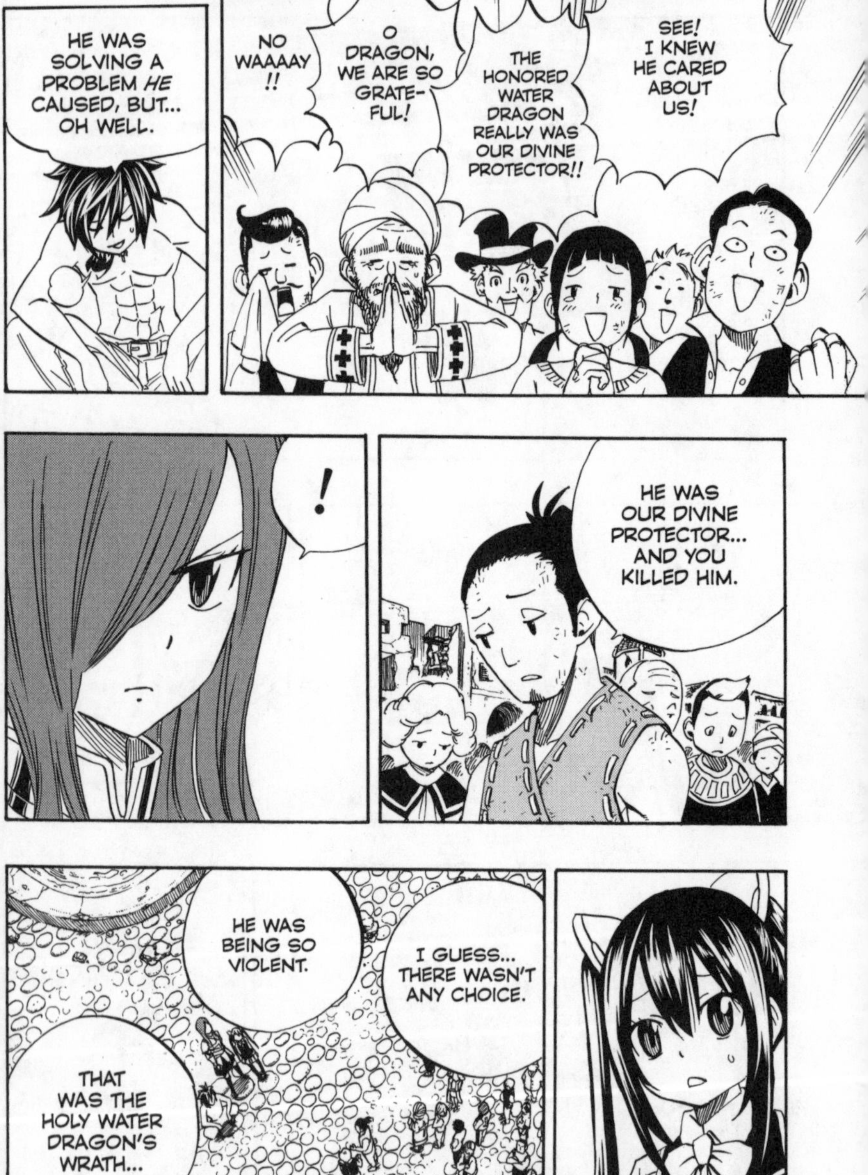
SEE! I KNEW HE CARED ABOUT US!
THE HONORED WATER DRAGON REALLY WAS OUR DIVINE PROTECTOR!!
O DRAGON, WE ARE SO GRATE-FUL!
NO WAAAAY!!
HE WAS SOLVING A PROBLEM *HE* CAUSED, BUT... OH WELL.
HE WAS OUR DIVINE PROTECTOR... AND YOU KILLED HIM.
!
HE WAS BEING SO VIOLENT.
I GUESS... THERE WASN'T ANY CHOICE.
THAT WAS THE HOLY WATER DRAGON'S WRATH...

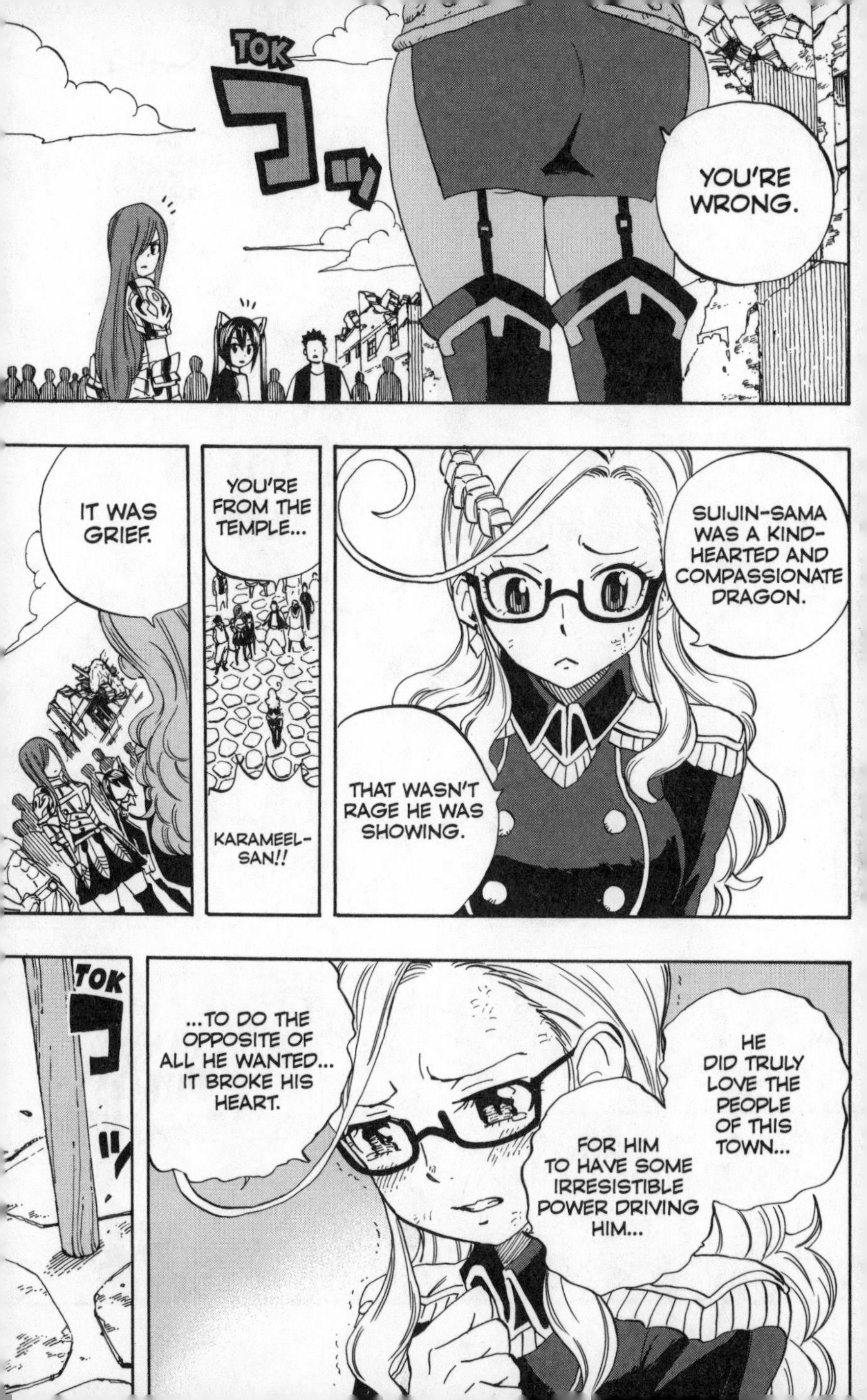
TOK
YOU'RE WRONG.
SUIJIN-SAMA WAS A KIND-HEARTED AND COMPASSIONATE DRAGON.
THAT WASN'T RAGE HE WAS SHOWING.
YOU'RE FROM THE TEMPLE...
KARAMEEL-SAN!!
IT WAS GRIEF.
HE DID TRULY LOVE THE PEOPLE OF THIS TOWN...
FOR HIM TO HAVE SOME IRRESISTIBLE POWER DRIVING HIM...
...TO DO THE OPPOSITE OF ALL HE WANTED... IT BROKE HIS HEART.
TOK

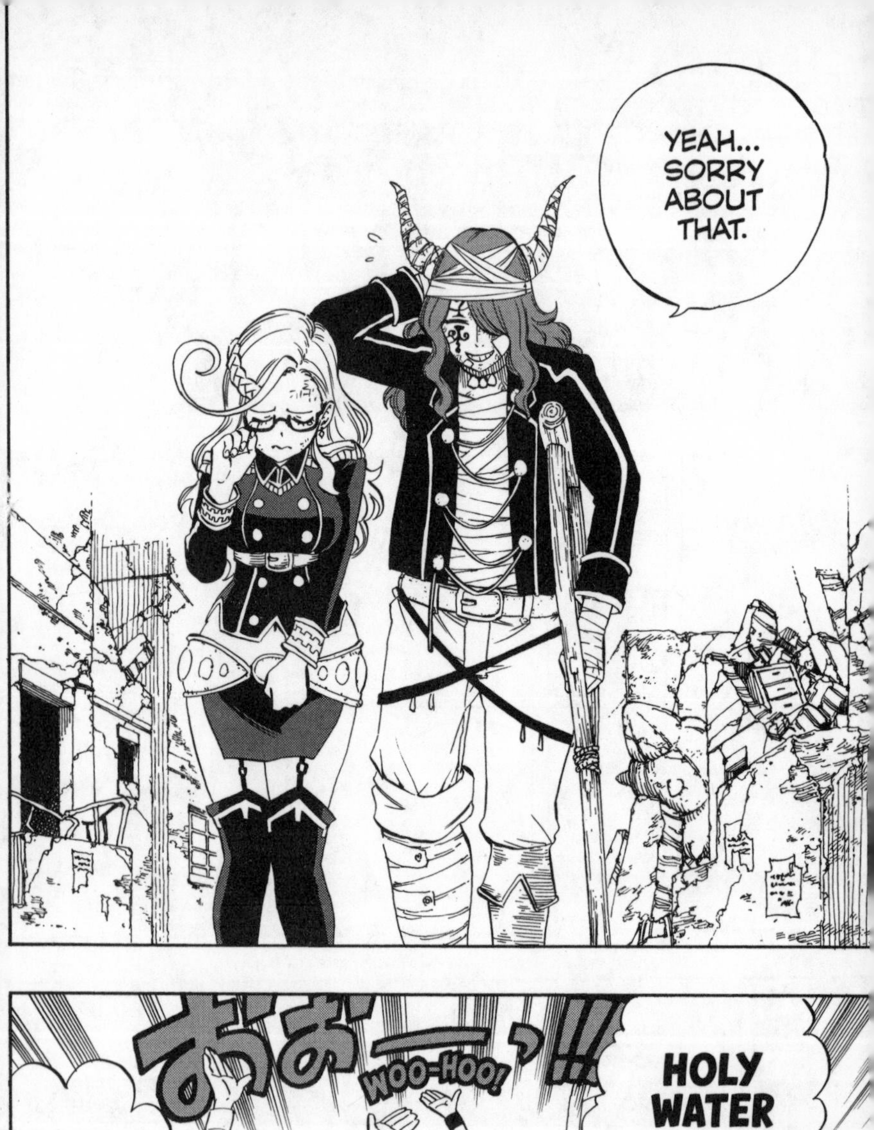
YEAH... SORRY ABOUT THAT.

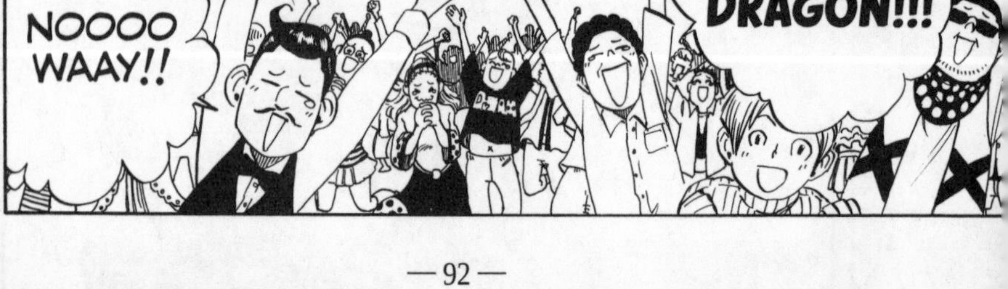
HOLY WATER DRAGON!!!
おおーー!!
WOO-HOO!
NOOOO WAAY!!

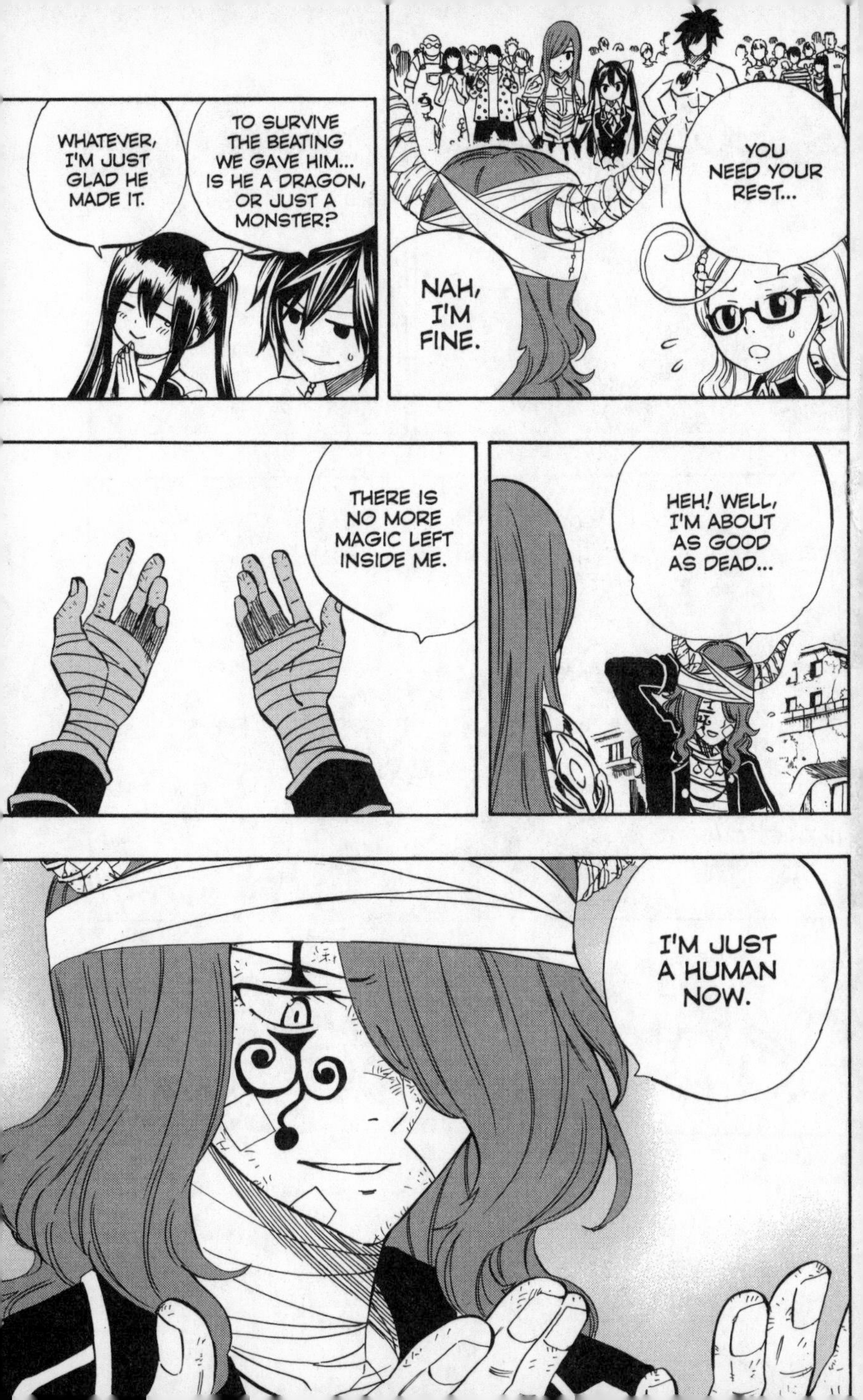
YOU NEED YOUR REST...
NAH, I'M FINE.
TO SURVIVE THE BEATING WE GAVE HIM... IS HE A DRAGON, OR JUST A MONSTER?
WHATEVER, I'M JUST GLAD HE MADE IT.
HEH! WELL, I'M ABOUT AS GOOD AS DEAD...
THERE IS NO MORE MAGIC LEFT INSIDE ME.
I'M JUST A HUMAN NOW.

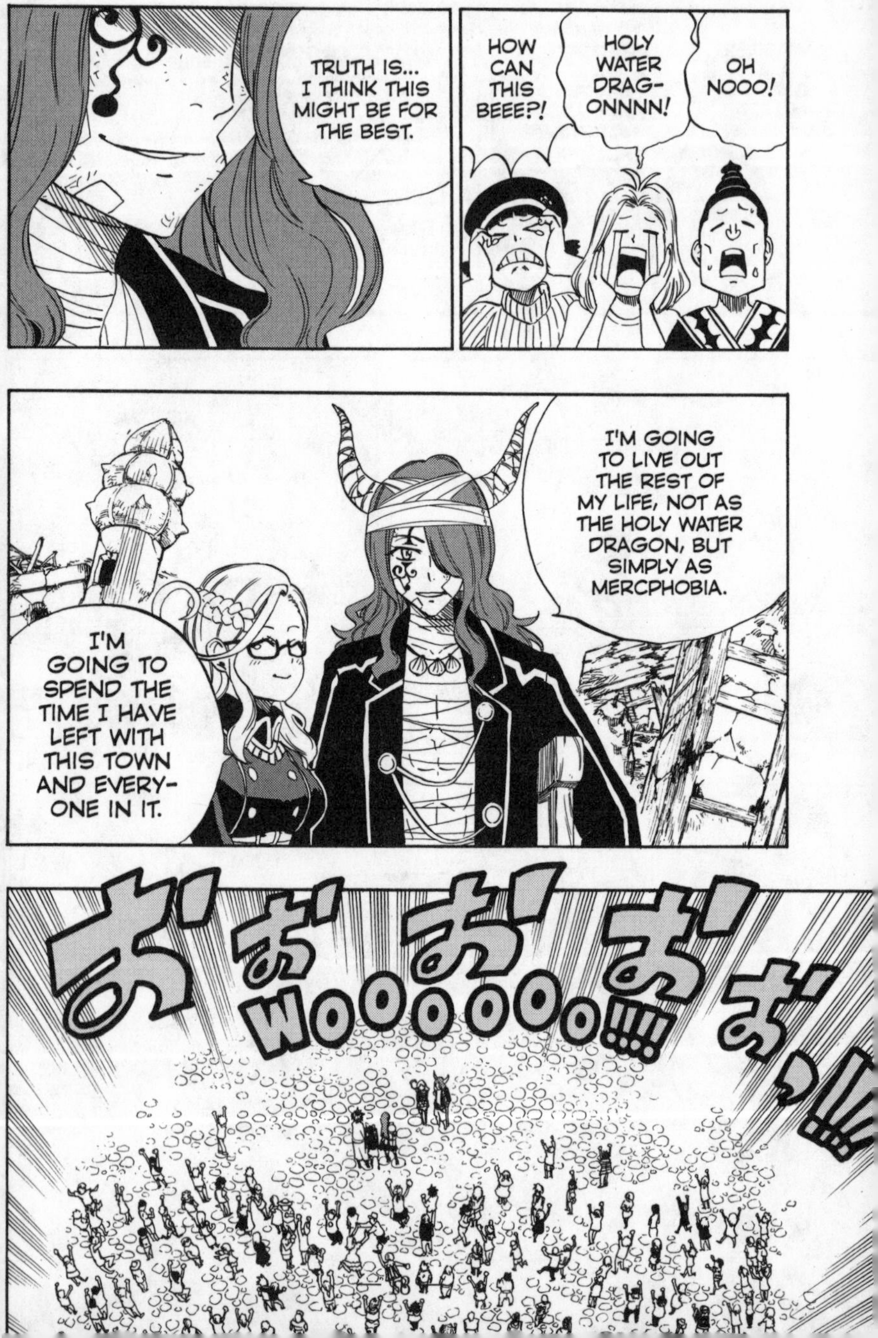
OH NOOO!
HOLY WATER DRAG-ONNNN!
HOW CAN THIS BEEE?!
TRUTH IS... I THINK THIS MIGHT BE FOR THE BEST.
I'M GOING TO LIVE OUT THE REST OF MY LIFE, NOT AS THE HOLY WATER DRAGON, BUT SIMPLY AS MERCPHOBIA.
I'M GOING TO SPEND THE TIME I HAVE LEFT WITH THIS TOWN AND EVERY-ONE IN IT.
WOOOOOOO!!!!

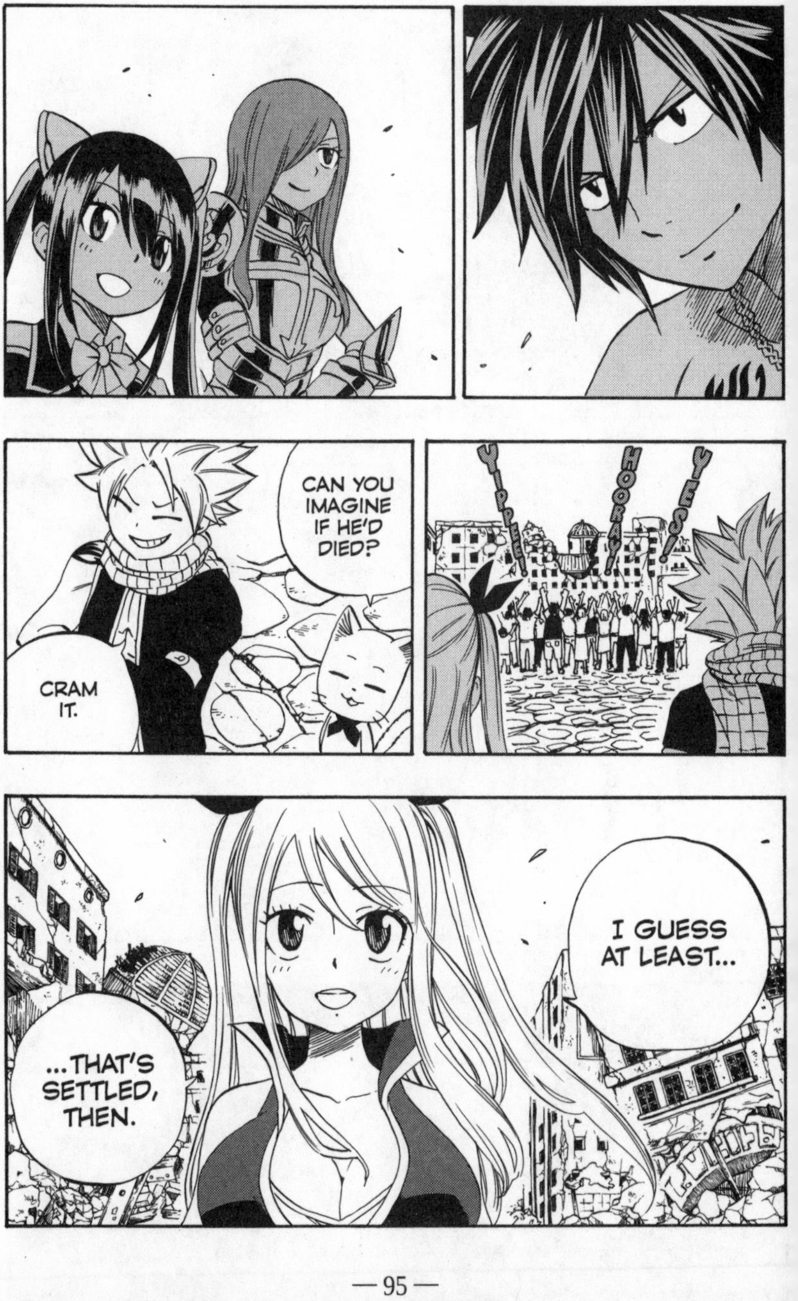
YES!
HOORAY!
YIPPEE!
CAN YOU IMAGINE IF HE'D DIED?
CRAM IT.
I GUESS AT LEAST...
...THAT'S SETTLED, THEN.

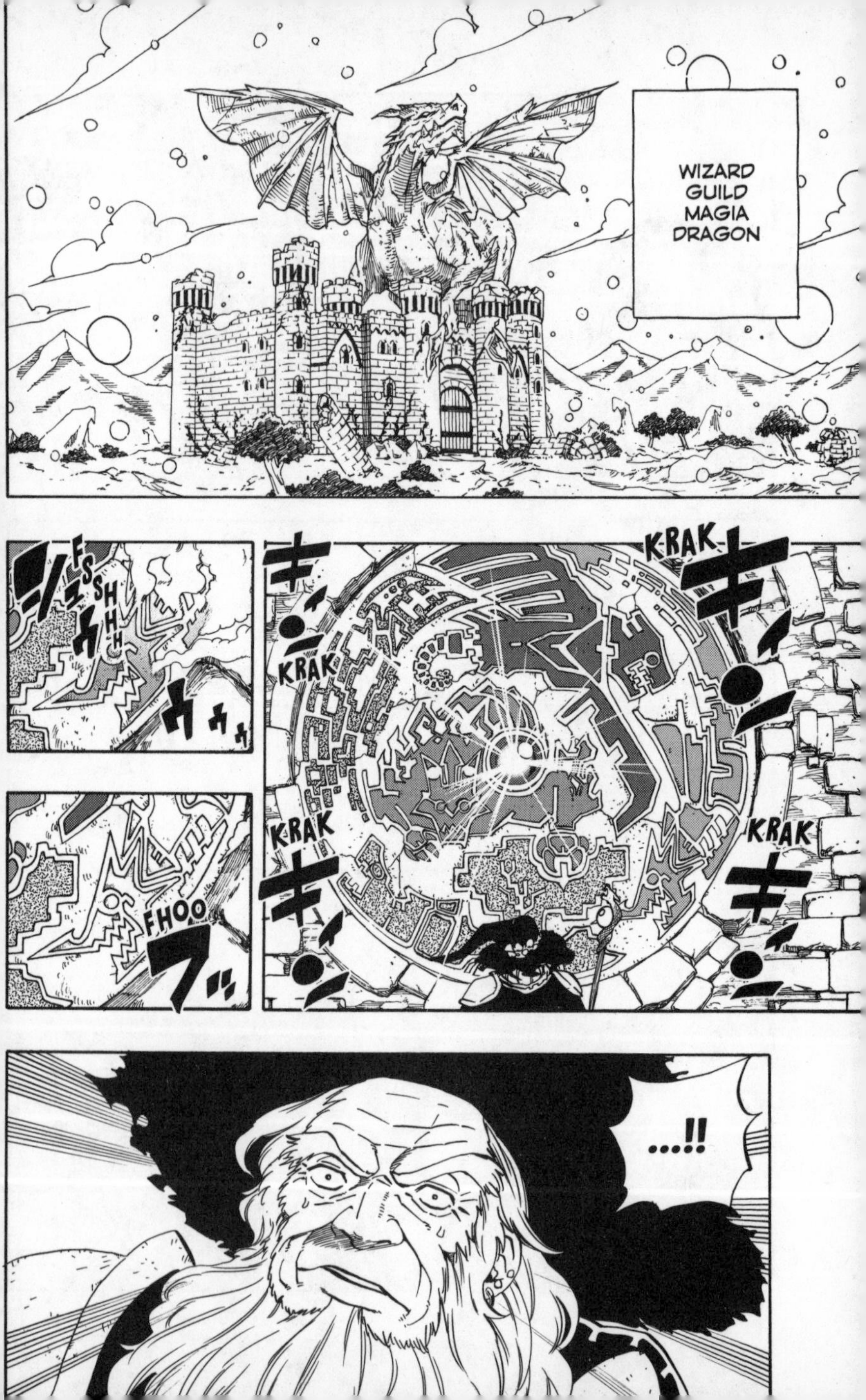
WIZARD GUILD MAGIA DRAGON
KRAK
KRAK
KRAK
KRAK
FSSHHH
FHOO
...!!

ONE OF THE FIVE DRAGON GODS HAS FALLEN...

NO ONE HAS MANAGED THAT IN A HUNDRED YEARS.

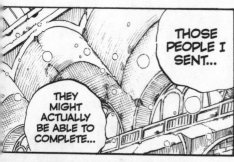

THOSE PEOPLE I SENT...

THEY MIGHT ACTUALLY BE ABLE TO COMPLETE...

AHH...!

...THE 100 YEARS QUEST...

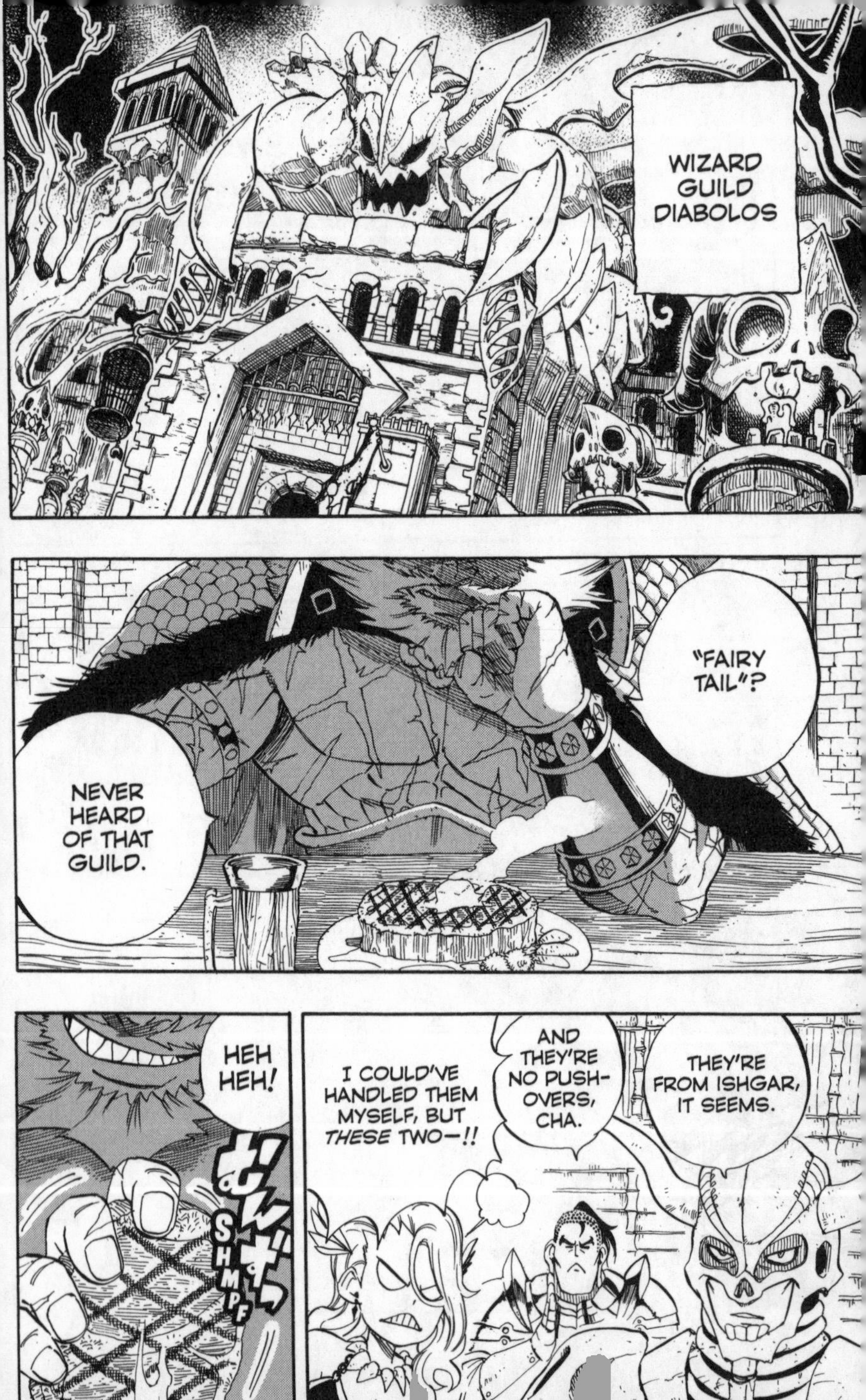
WIZARD GUILD DIABOLOS
"FAIRY TAIL"?
NEVER HEARD OF THAT GUILD.
THEY'RE FROM ISHGAR, IT SEEMS.
AND THEY'RE NO PUSH-OVERS, CHA.
I COULD'VE HANDLED THEM MYSELF, BUT *THESE* TWO—!!
HEH HEH!
SHMPF

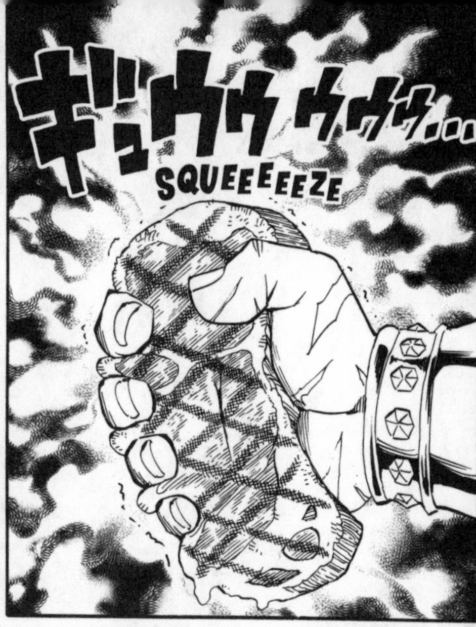
SQUEEEEEEZE

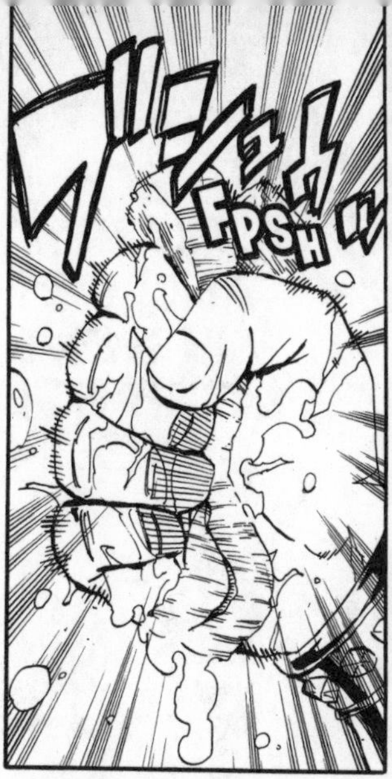
FPSH

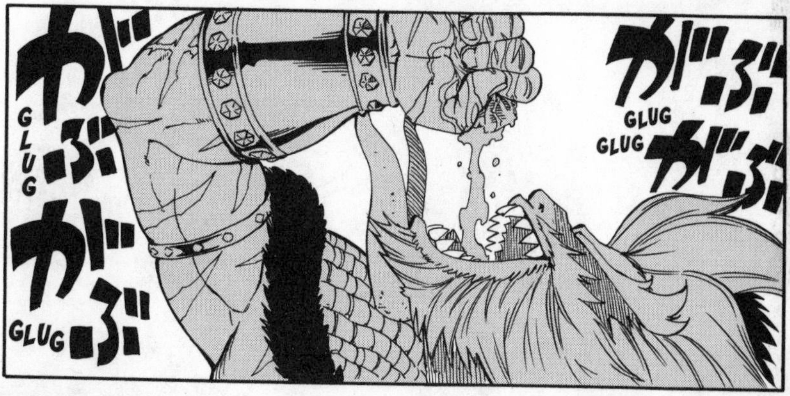
GLUG
GLUG
GLUG
GLUG
GLUG

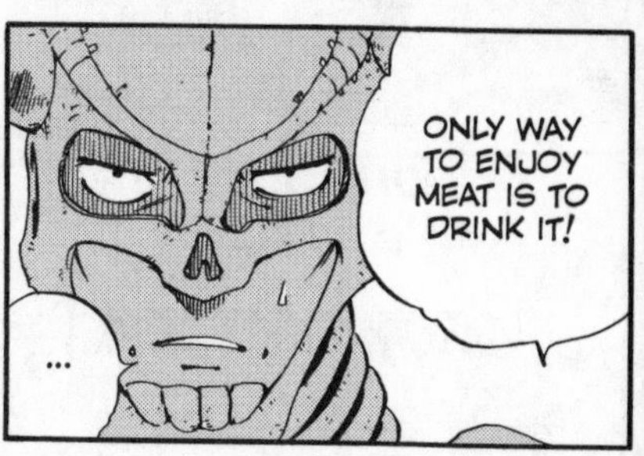
ONLY WAY TO ENJOY MEAT IS TO DRINK IT!
...

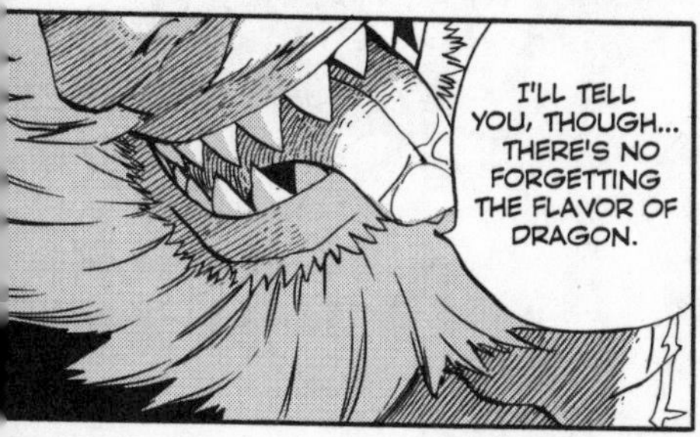
I'LL TELL YOU, THOUGH... THERE'S NO FORGETTING THE FLAVOR OF DRAGON.

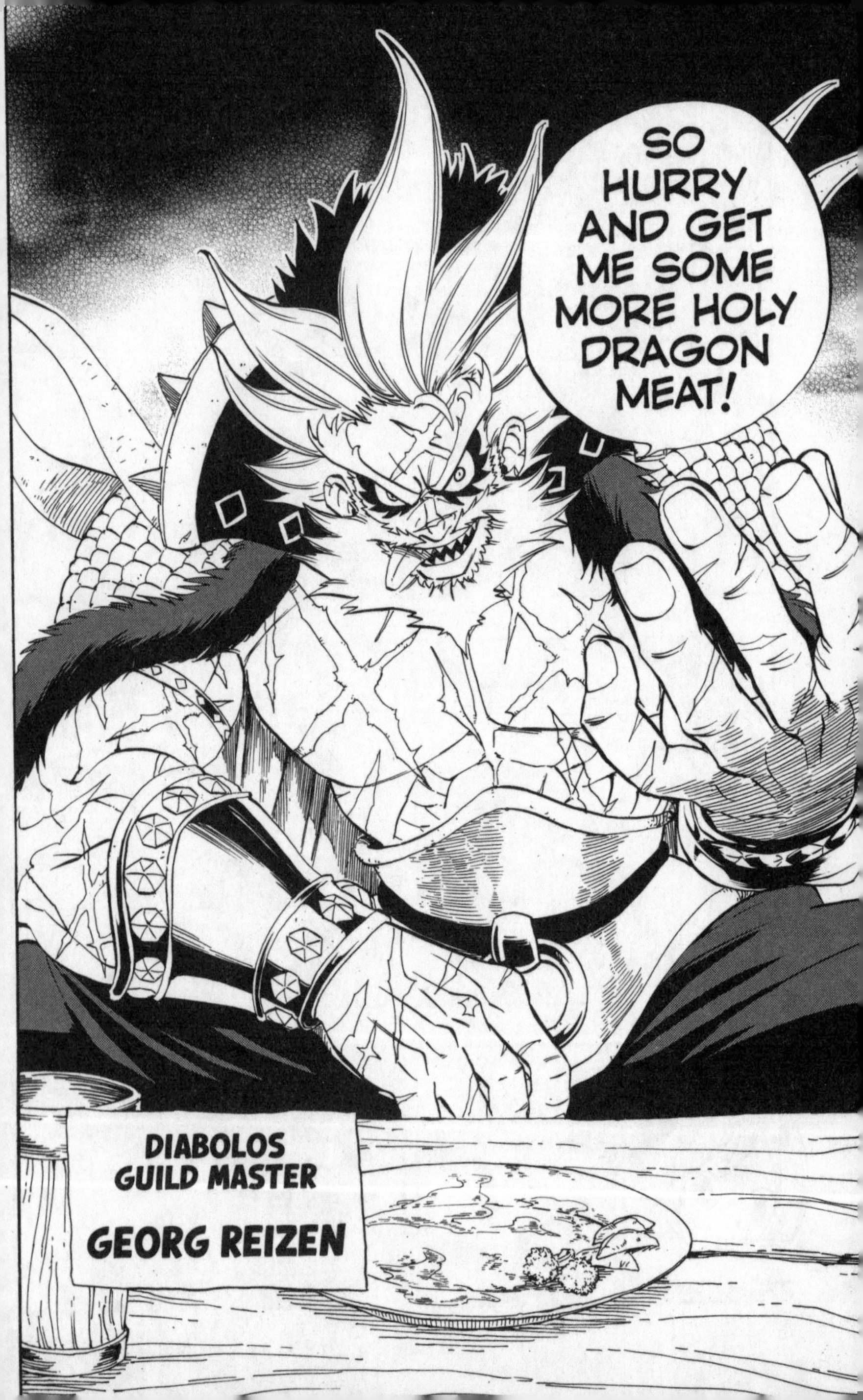
SO HURRY AND GET ME SOME MORE HOLY DRAGON MEAT!
DIABOLOS GUILD MASTER
GEORG REIZEN

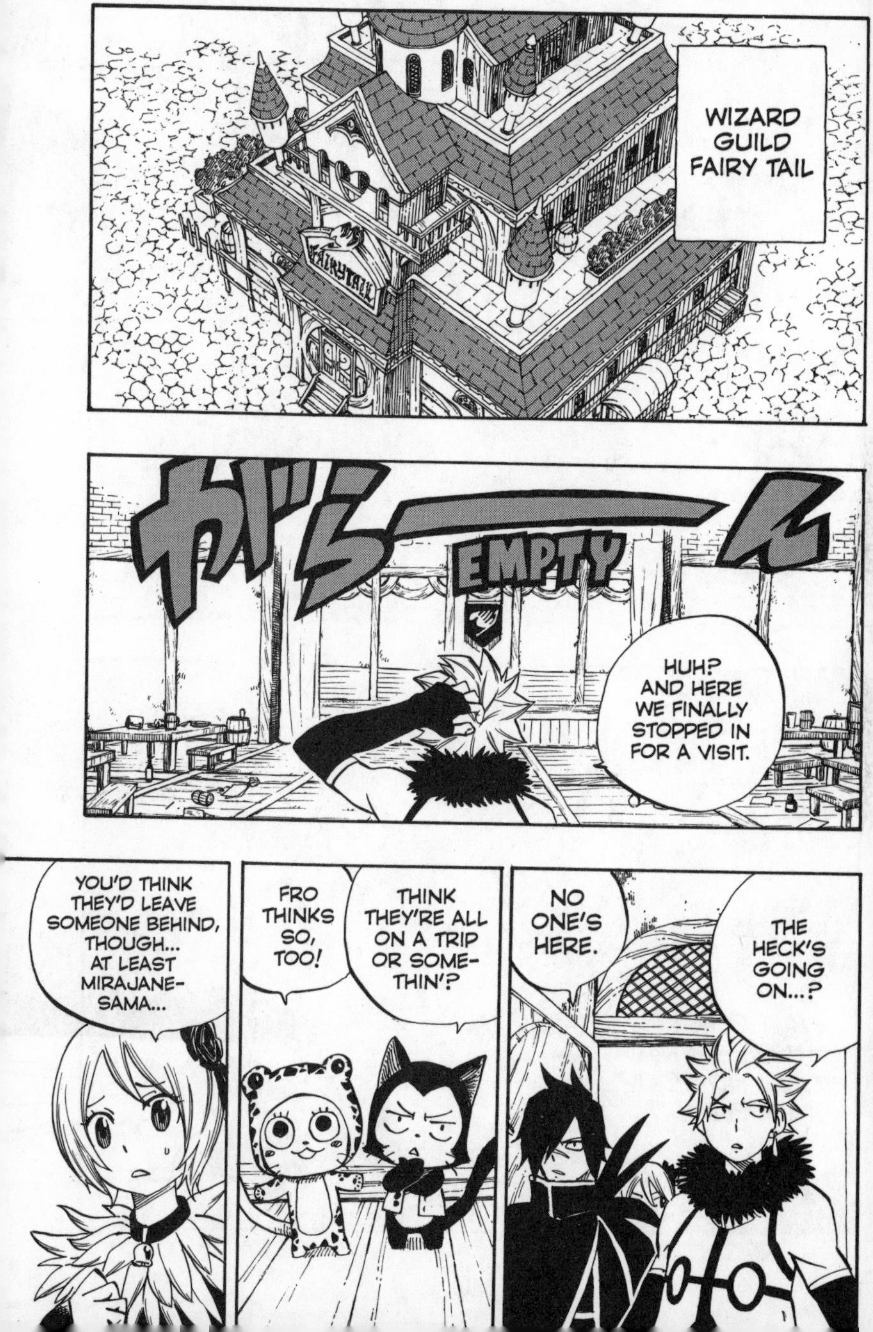
WIZARD GUILD FAIRY TAIL
FAIRY TAIL
がら──ん
EMPTY
HUH? AND HERE WE FINALLY STOPPED IN FOR A VISIT.
THE HECK'S GOING ON...?
NO ONE'S HERE.
THINK THEY'RE ALL ON A TRIP OR SOME-THIN'?
FRO THINKS SO, TOO!
YOU'D THINK THEY'D LEAVE SOMEONE BEHIND, THOUGH... AT LEAST MIRAJANE-SAMA...

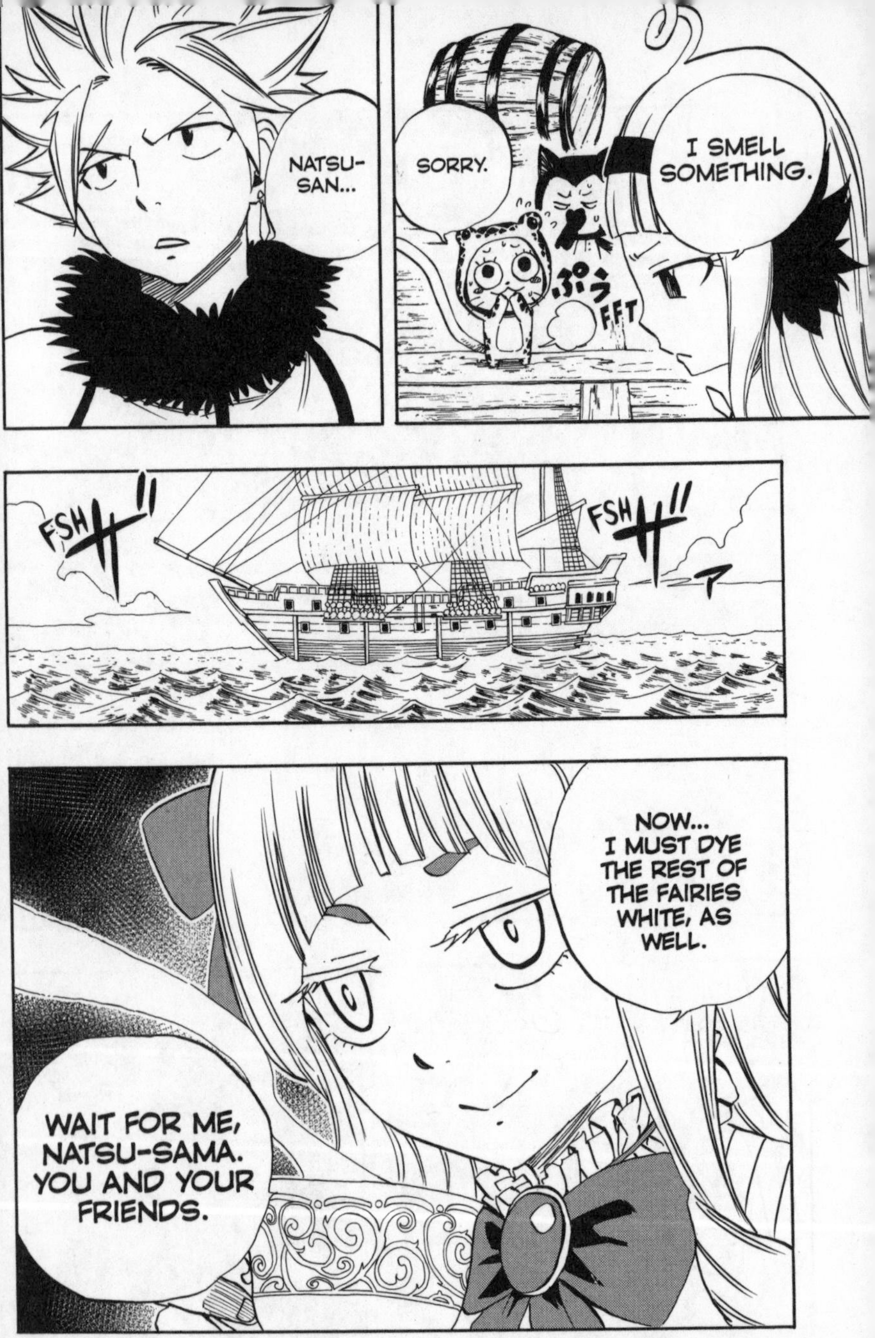
I SMELL SOMETHING.
SORRY.
FFT
NATSU-SAN...
FSH
FSH
NOW... I MUST DYE THE REST OF THE FAIRIES WHITE, AS WELL.
WAIT FOR ME, NATSU-SAMA. YOU AND YOUR FRIENDS.

FAIRY TAIL 100 YEARS QUEST

CHAPTER 24: ALL'S WELL THAT ENDS WELL

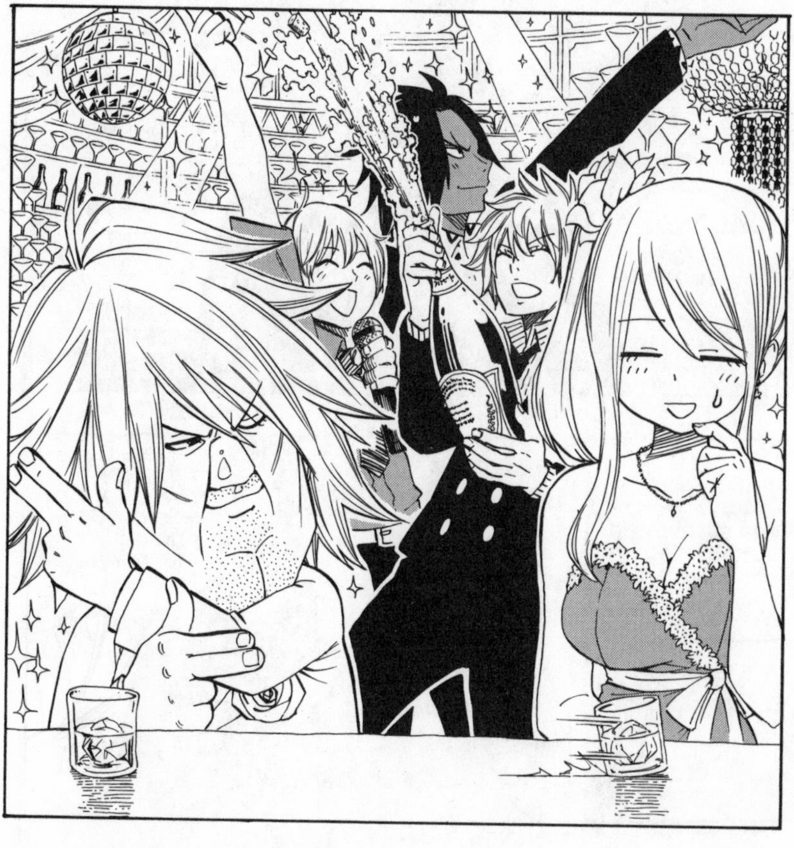

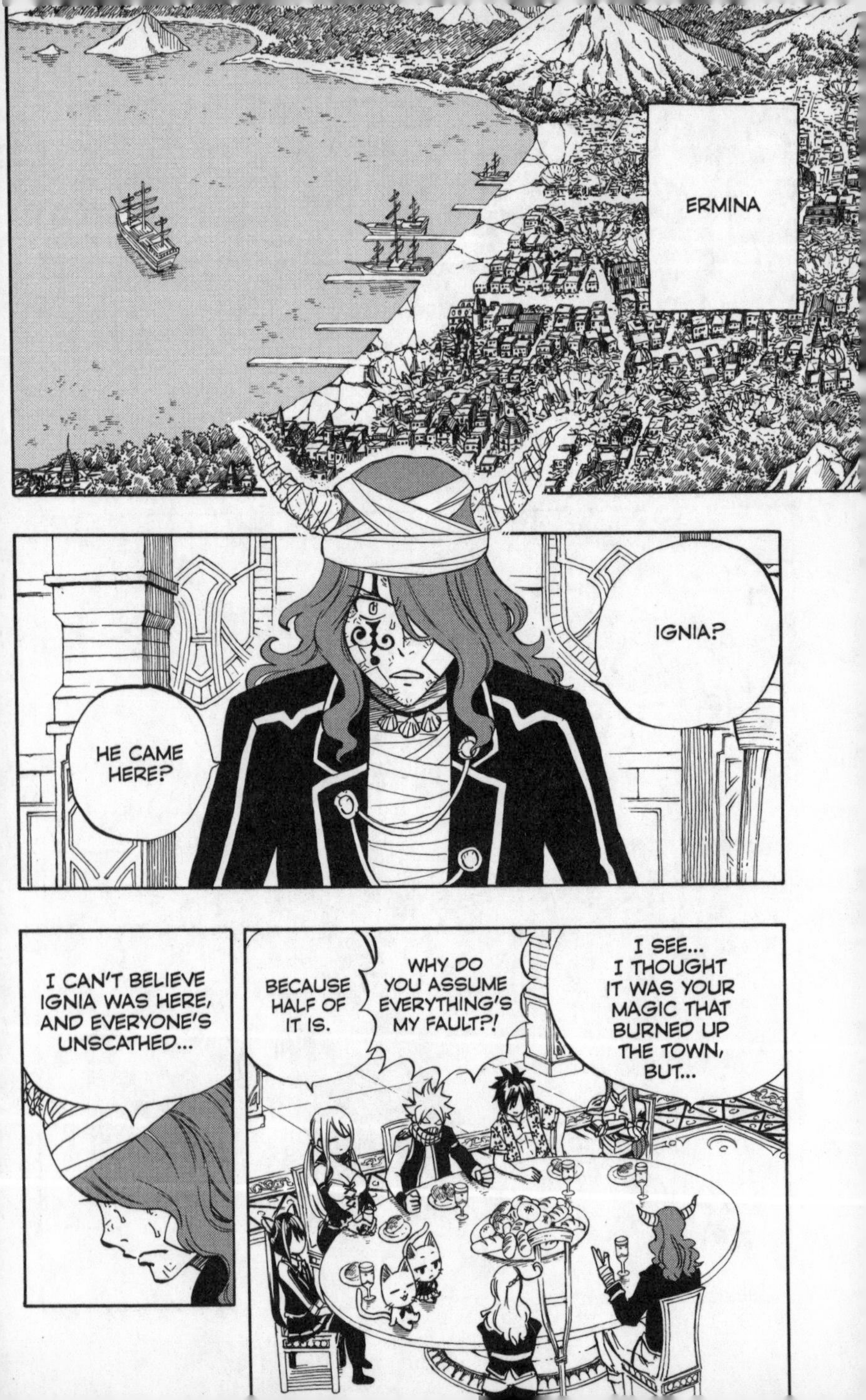
ERMINA
IGNIA?
HE CAME HERE?
I SEE... I THOUGHT IT WAS YOUR MAGIC THAT BURNED UP THE TOWN, BUT...
WHY DO YOU ASSUME EVERYTHING'S MY FAULT?!
BECAUSE HALF OF IT IS.
I CAN'T BELIEVE IGNIA WAS HERE, AND EVERYONE'S UNSCATHED...

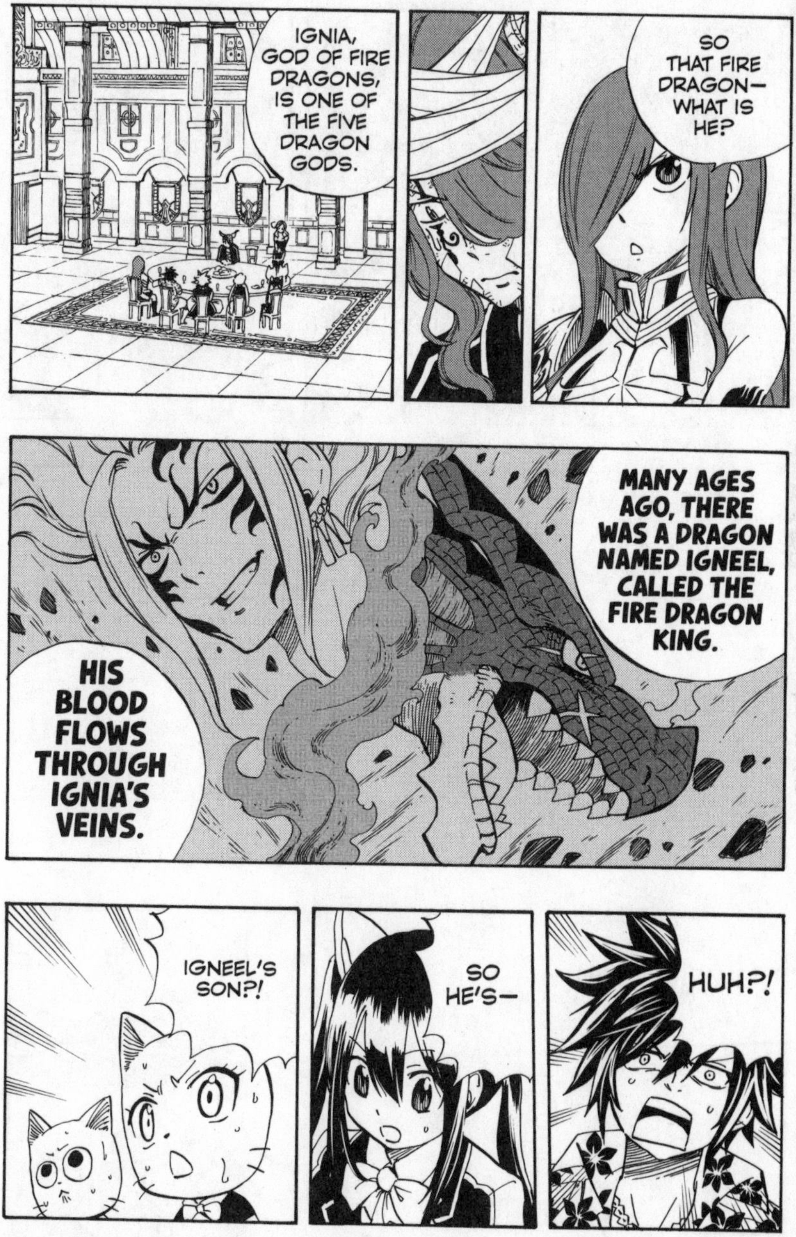
SO THAT FIRE DRAGON— WHAT IS HE?
IGNIA, GOD OF FIRE DRAGONS, IS ONE OF THE FIVE DRAGON GODS.
MANY AGES AGO, THERE WAS A DRAGON NAMED IGNEEL, CALLED THE FIRE DRAGON KING.
HIS BLOOD FLOWS THROUGH IGNIA'S VEINS.
HUH?!
SO HE'S—
IGNEEL'S SON?!

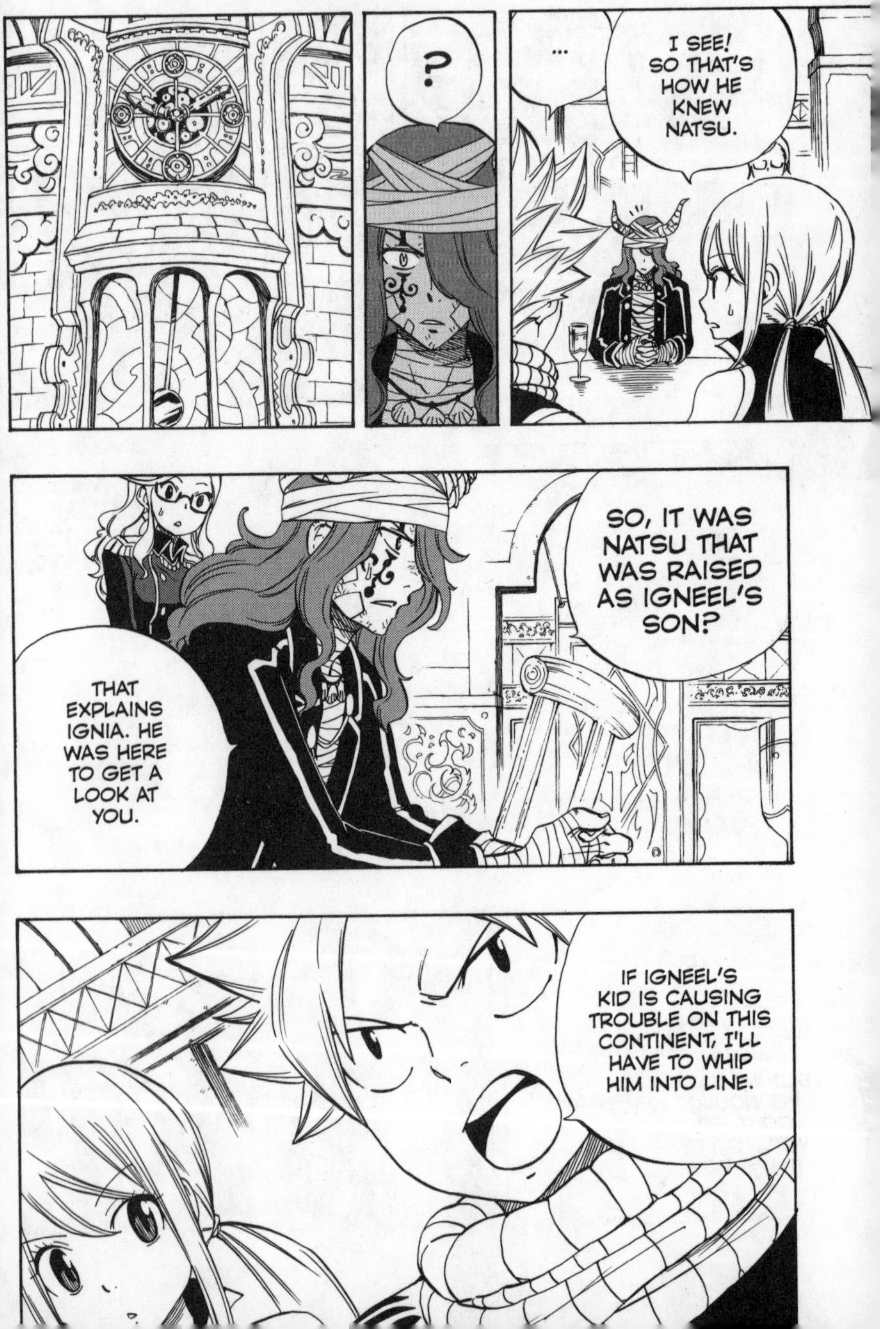
I SEE! SO THAT'S HOW HE KNEW NATSU.
...
?
SO, IT WAS NATSU THAT WAS RAISED AS IGNEEL'S SON?
THAT EXPLAINS IGNIA. HE WAS HERE TO GET A LOOK AT YOU.
IF IGNEEL'S KID IS CAUSING TROUBLE ON THIS CONTINENT, I'LL HAVE TO WHIP HIM INTO LINE.

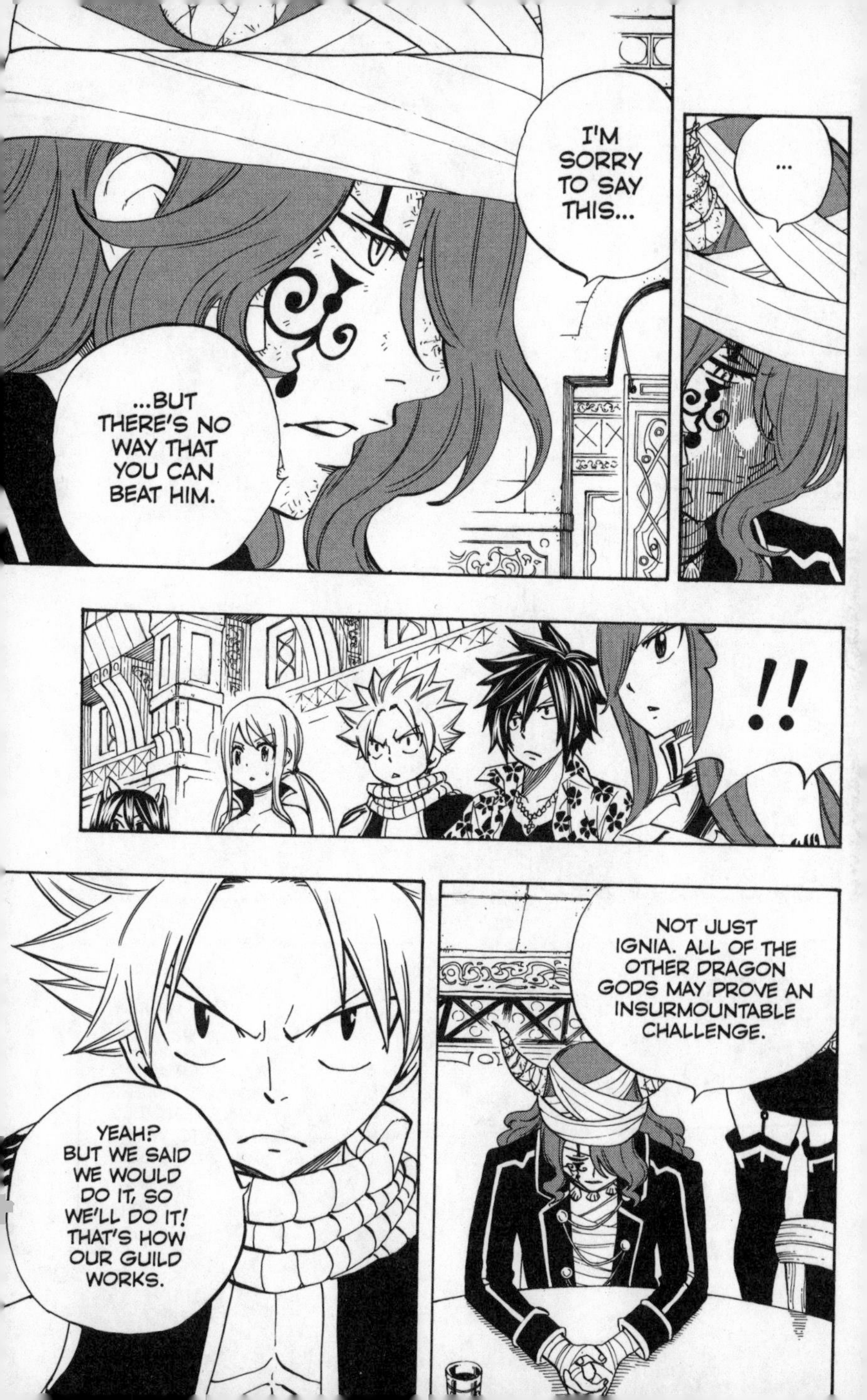
...
I'M SORRY TO SAY THIS...
...BUT THERE'S NO WAY THAT YOU CAN BEAT HIM.
!!
NOT JUST IGNIA. ALL OF THE OTHER DRAGON GODS MAY PROVE AN INSURMOUNTABLE CHALLENGE.
YEAH? BUT WE SAID WE WOULD DO IT, SO WE'LL DO IT! THAT'S HOW OUR GUILD WORKS.

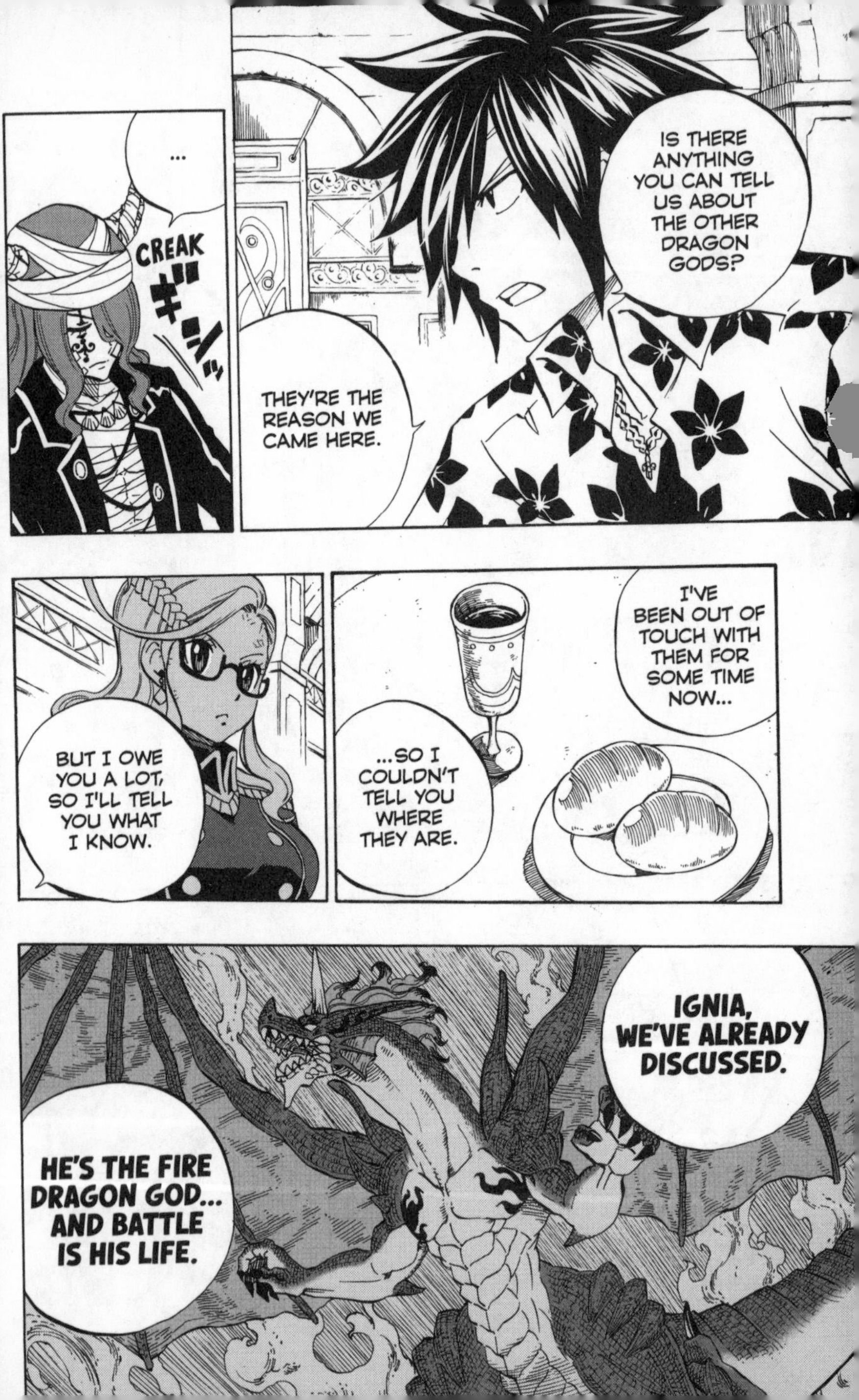
IS THERE ANYTHING YOU CAN TELL US ABOUT THE OTHER DRAGON GODS?
THEY'RE THE REASON WE CAME HERE.
...
CREAK
I'VE BEEN OUT OF TOUCH WITH THEM FOR SOME TIME NOW...
...SO I COULDN'T TELL YOU WHERE THEY ARE.
BUT I OWE YOU A LOT, SO I'LL TELL YOU WHAT I KNOW.
IGNIA, WE'VE ALREADY DISCUSSED.
HE'S THE FIRE DRAGON GOD... AND BATTLE IS HIS LIFE.

HE'S DEVASTATED COUNTLESS LANDS.

IT'S SOMETHING OF A MIRACLE ERMINA IS EVEN STILL HERE.

NEXT IS THE WOOD DRAGON GOD, ALDORON.

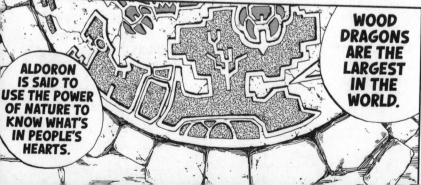

WOOD DRAGONS ARE THE LARGEST IN THE WORLD.

ALDORON IS SAID TO USE THE POWER OF NATURE TO KNOW WHAT'S IN PEOPLE'S HEARTS.

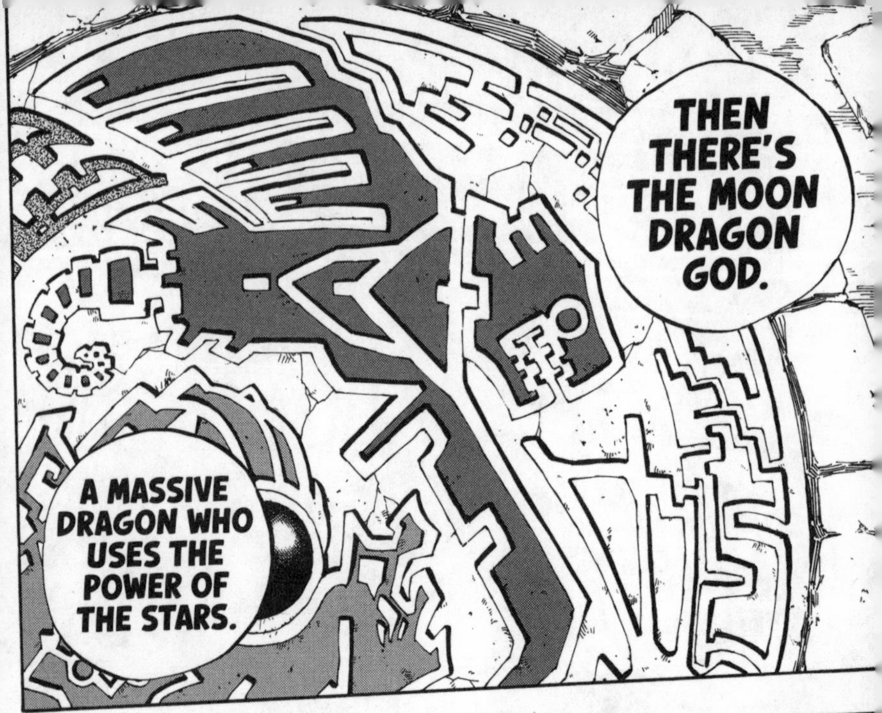
THEN THERE'S THE MOON DRAGON GOD.
A MASSIVE DRAGON WHO USES THE POWER OF THE STARS.

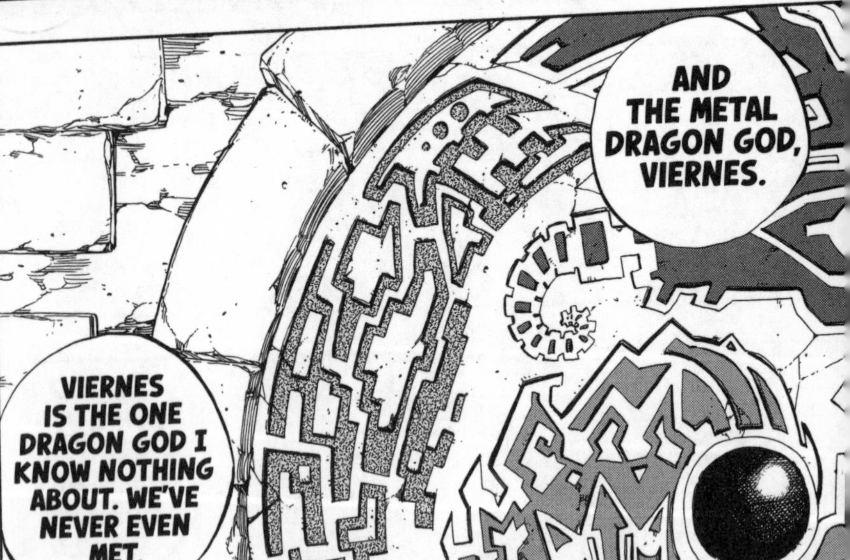
AND THE METAL DRAGON GOD, VIERNES.
VIERNES IS THE ONE DRAGON GOD I KNOW NOTHING ABOUT. WE'VE NEVER EVEN MET.

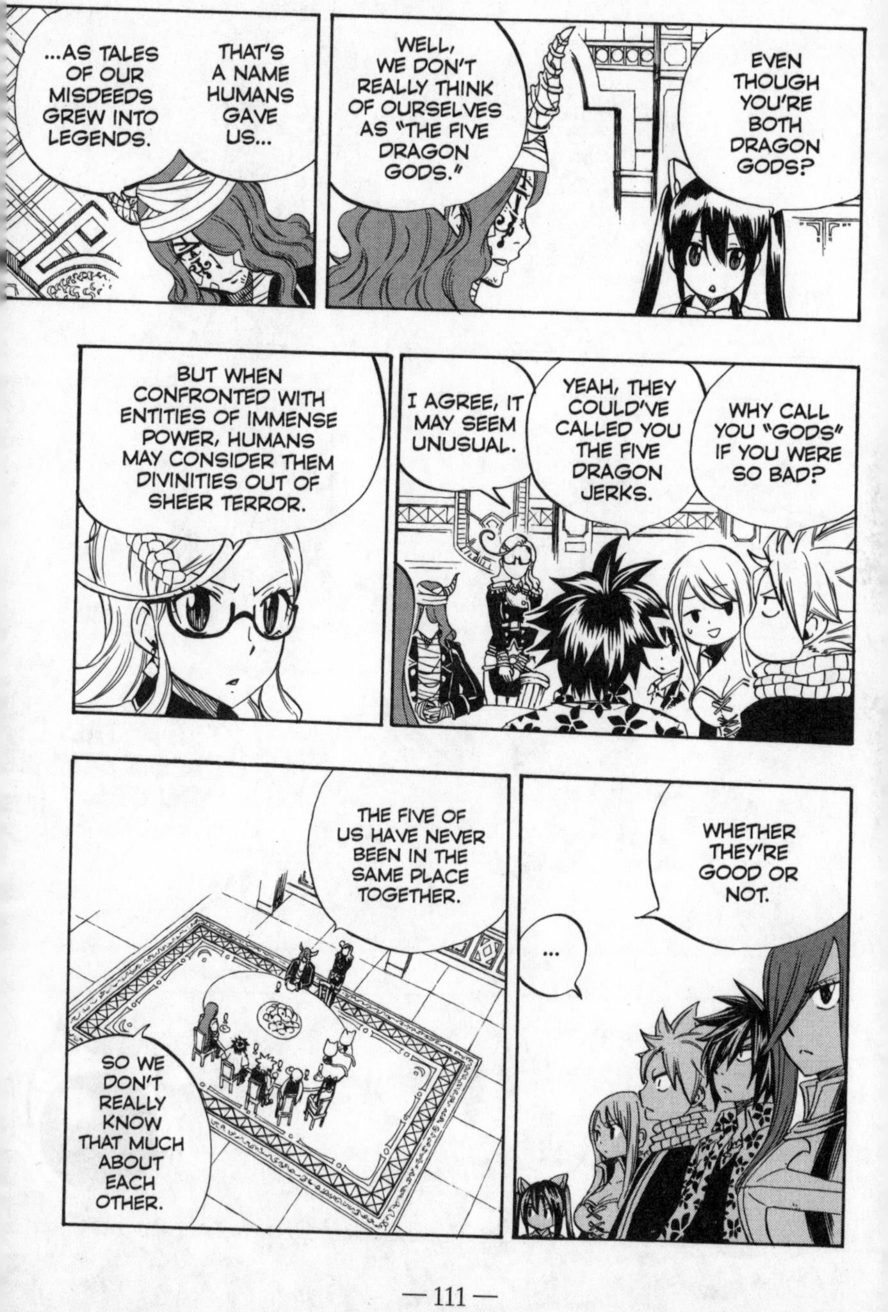
EVEN THOUGH YOU'RE BOTH DRAGON GODS?
WELL, WE DON'T REALLY THINK OF OURSELVES AS "THE FIVE DRAGON GODS."
THAT'S A NAME HUMANS GAVE US...
...AS TALES OF OUR MISDEEDS GREW INTO LEGENDS.
WHY CALL YOU "GODS" IF YOU WERE SO BAD?
YEAH, THEY COULD'VE CALLED YOU THE FIVE DRAGON JERKS.
I AGREE, IT MAY SEEM UNUSUAL.
BUT WHEN CONFRONTED WITH ENTITIES OF IMMENSE POWER, HUMANS MAY CONSIDER THEM DIVINITIES OUT OF SHEER TERROR.
WHETHER THEY'RE GOOD OR NOT.
...
THE FIVE OF US HAVE NEVER BEEN IN THE SAME PLACE TOGETHER.
SO WE DON'T REALLY KNOW THAT MUCH ABOUT EACH OTHER.

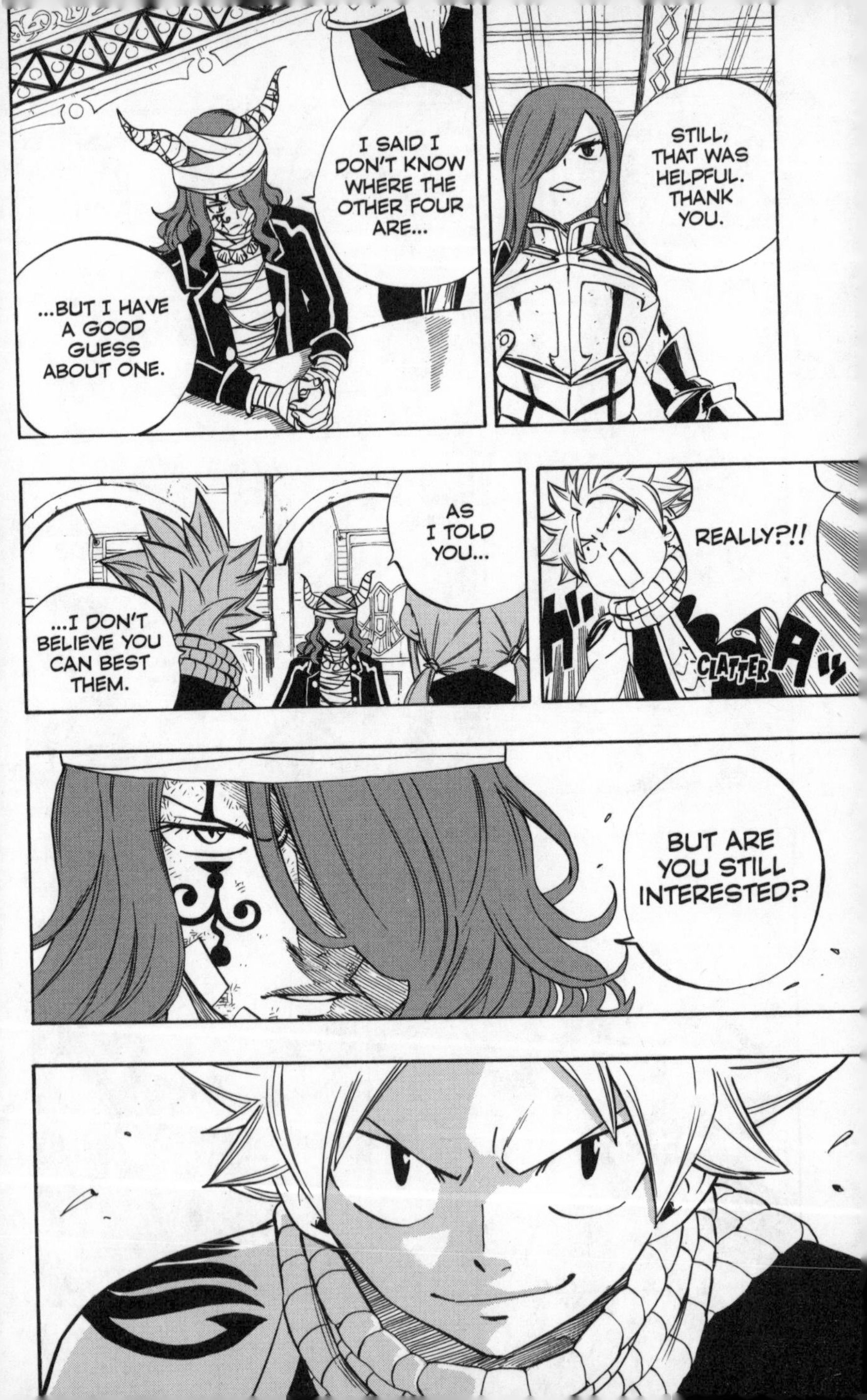
STILL, THAT WAS HELPFUL. THANK YOU.
I SAID I DON'T KNOW WHERE THE OTHER FOUR ARE...
...BUT I HAVE A GOOD GUESS ABOUT ONE.
REALLY?!!
CLATTER
AS I TOLD YOU...
...I DON'T BELIEVE YOU CAN BEST THEM.
BUT ARE YOU STILL INTERESTED?

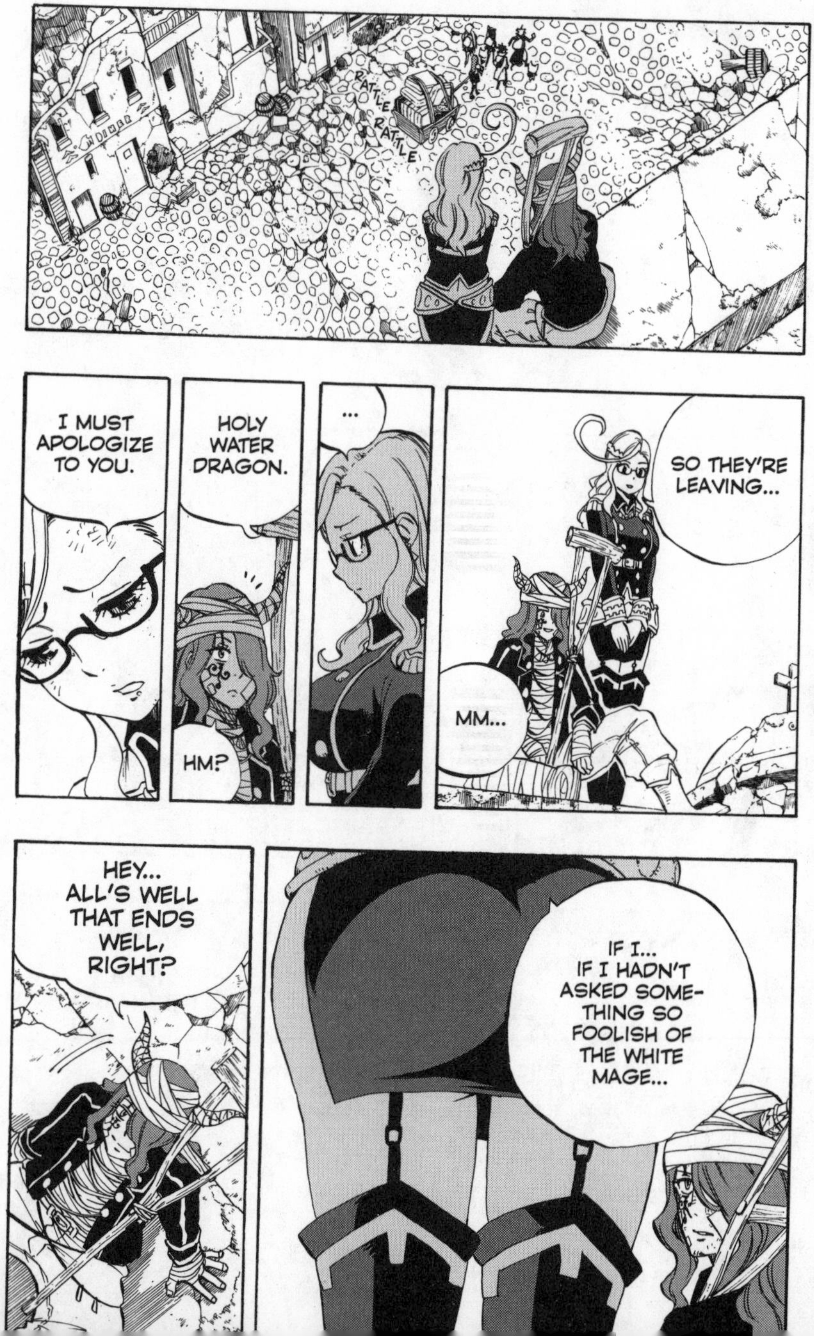
RATTLE RATTLE
SO THEY'RE LEAVING...
MM...
...
HOLY WATER DRAGON.
HM?
I MUST APOLOGIZE TO YOU.
IF I... IF I HADN'T ASKED SOME-THING SO FOOLISH OF THE WHITE MAGE...
HEY... ALL'S WELL THAT ENDS WELL, RIGHT?

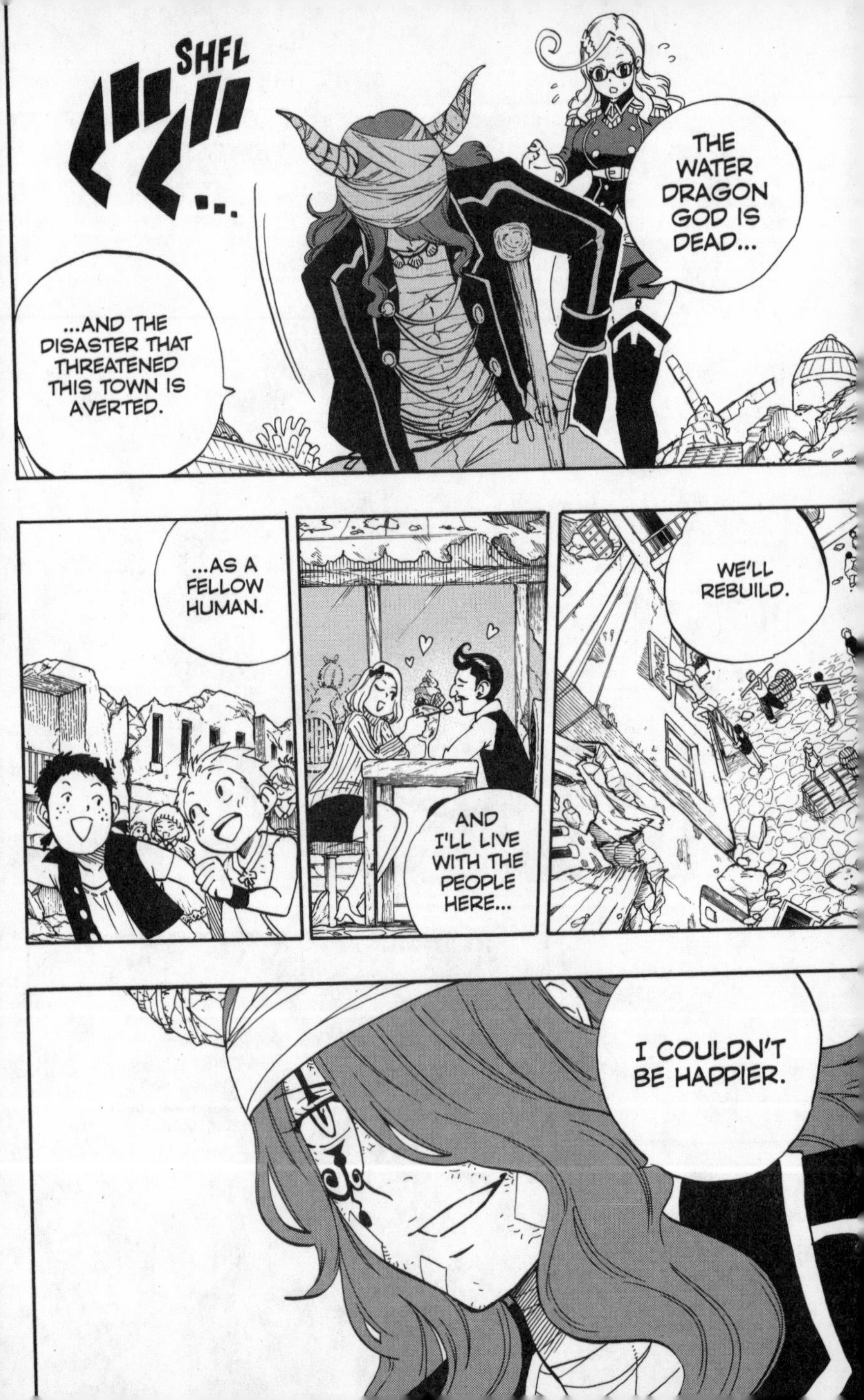
THE WATER DRAGON GOD IS DEAD...
SHFL
...AND THE DISASTER THAT THREATENED THIS TOWN IS AVERTED.
WE'LL REBUILD.
AND I'LL LIVE WITH THE PEOPLE HERE...
...AS A FELLOW HUMAN.
I COULDN'T BE HAPPIER.

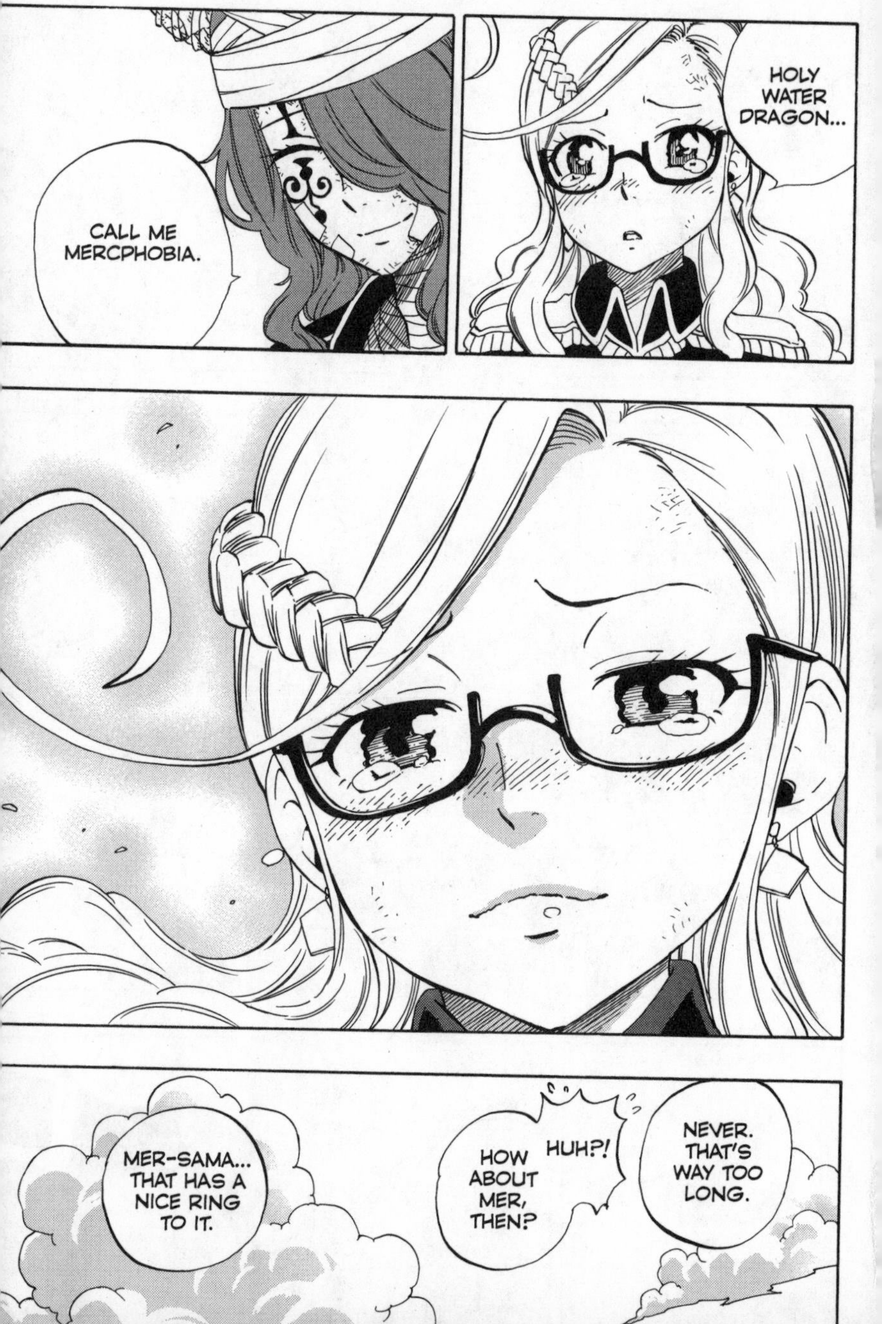
HOLY WATER DRAGON...
CALL ME MERCPHOBIA.
NEVER. THAT'S WAY TOO LONG.
HUH?!
HOW ABOUT MER, THEN?
MER-SAMA... THAT HAS A NICE RING TO IT.

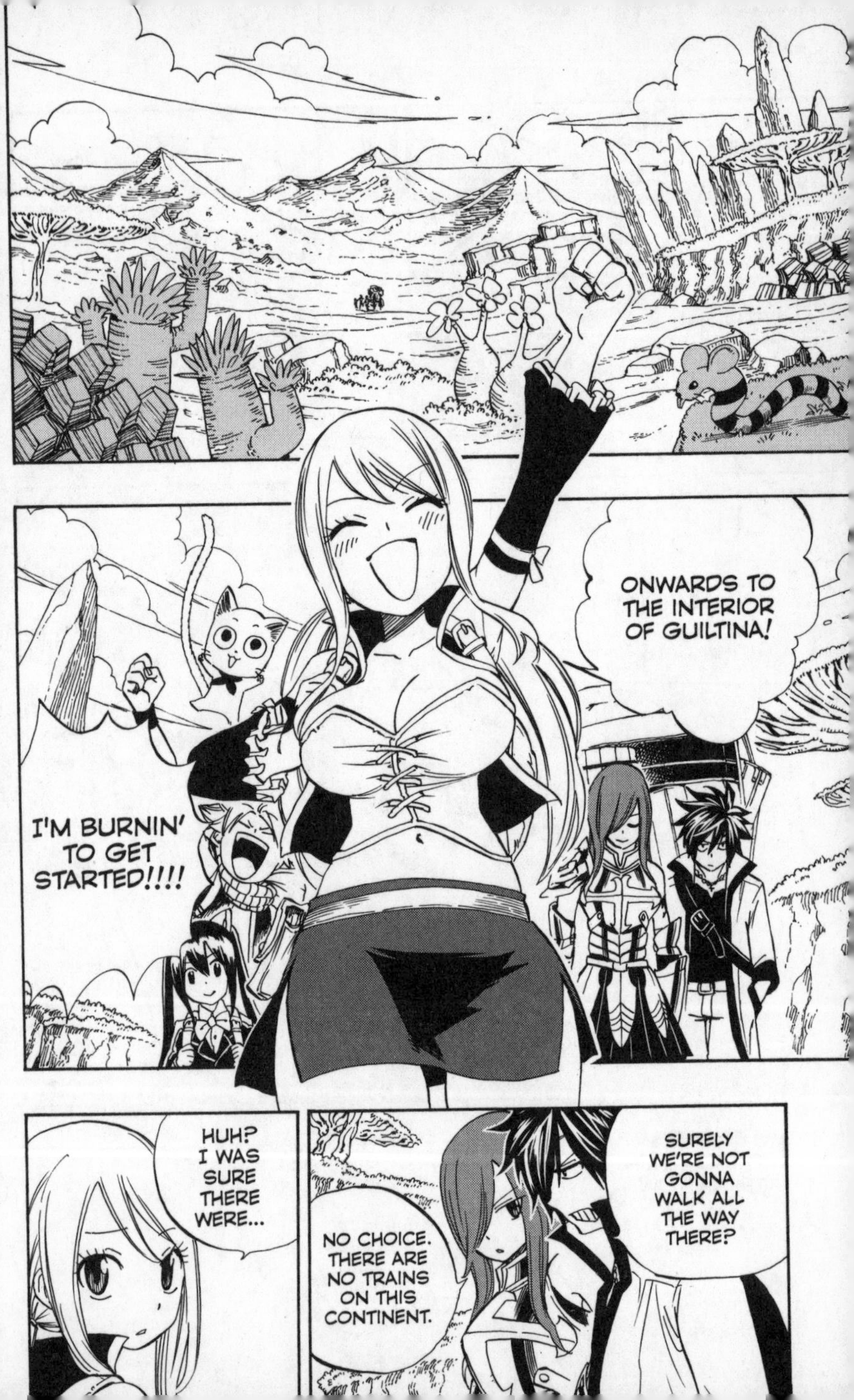
ONWARDS TO THE INTERIOR OF GUILTINA!
I'M BURNIN' TO GET STARTED!!!!
SURELY WE'RE NOT GONNA WALK ALL THE WAY THERE?
NO CHOICE. THERE ARE NO TRAINS ON THIS CONTINENT.
HUH? I WAS SURE THERE WERE...

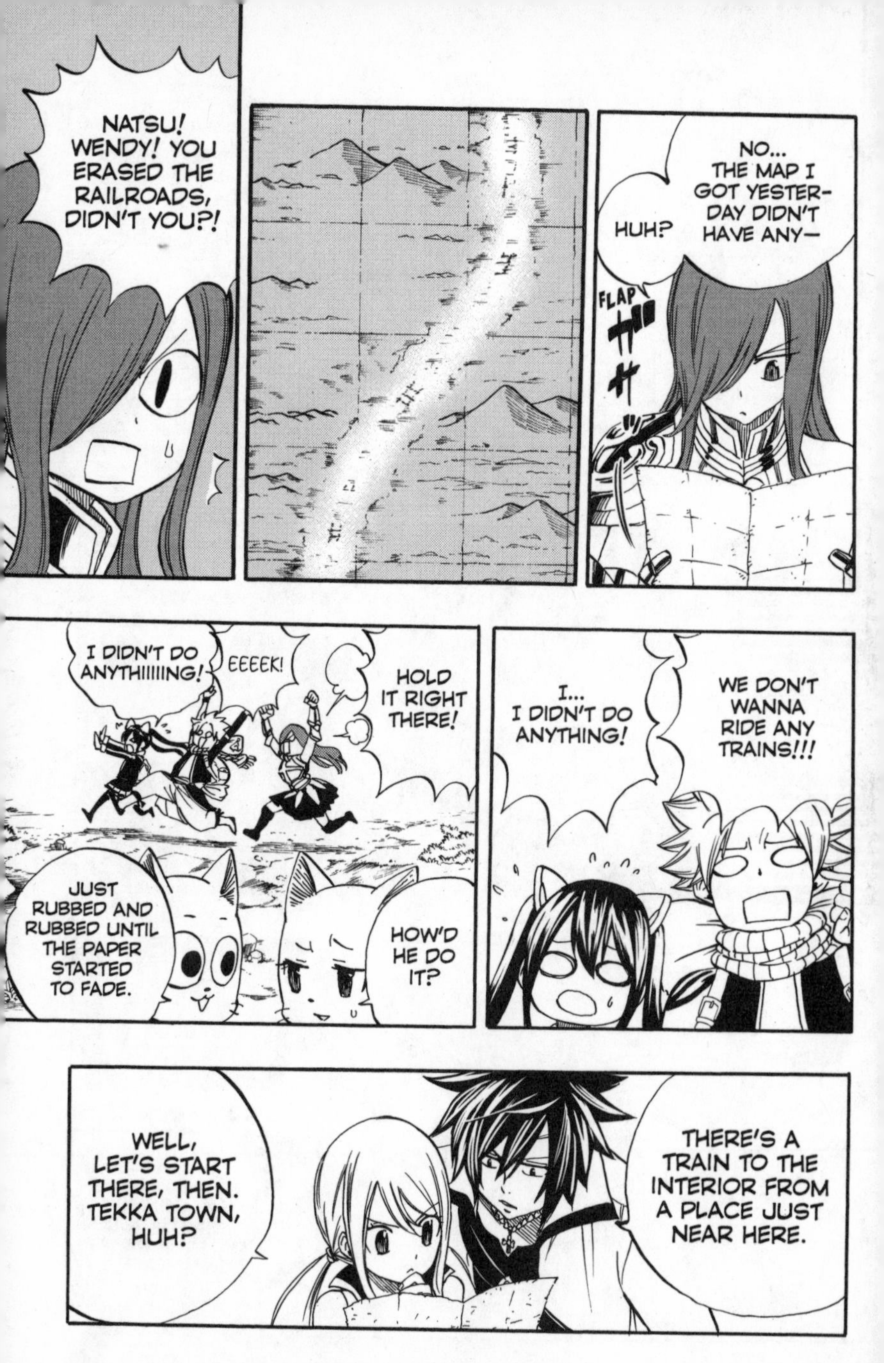
HUH?
NO... THE MAP I GOT YESTER-DAY DIDN'T HAVE ANY—
FLAP
NATSU! WENDY! YOU ERASED THE RAILROADS, DIDN'T YOU?!
WE DON'T WANNA RIDE ANY TRAINS!!!
I... I DIDN'T DO ANYTHING!
HOLD IT RIGHT THERE!
EEEEK!
I DIDN'T DO ANYTHIIIIING!
HOW'D HE DO IT?
JUST RUBBED AND RUBBED UNTIL THE PAPER STARTED TO FADE.
THERE'S A TRAIN TO THE INTERIOR FROM A PLACE JUST NEAR HERE.
WELL, LET'S START THERE, THEN. TEKKA TOWN, HUH?

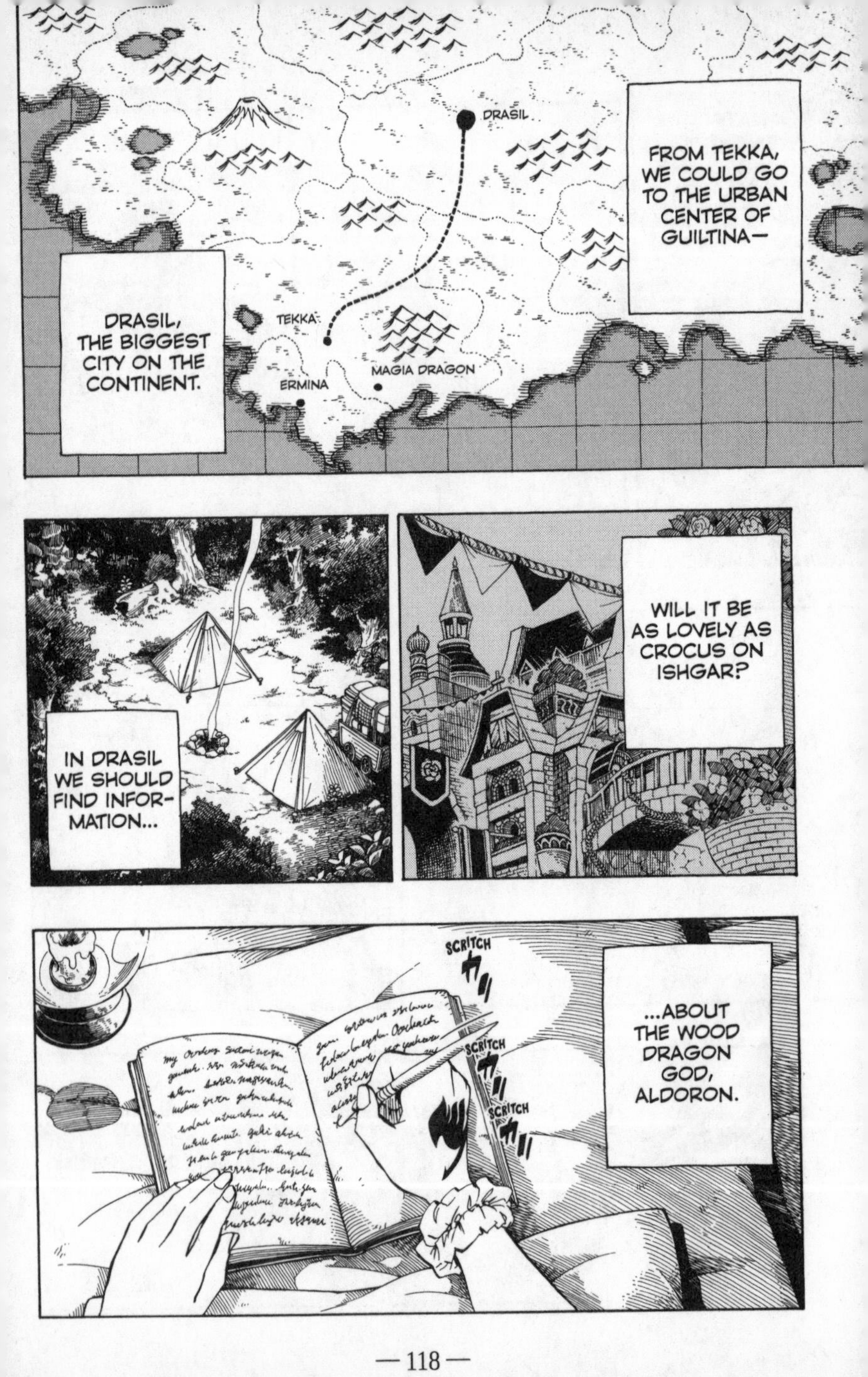
FROM TEKKA, WE COULD GO TO THE URBAN CENTER OF GUILTINA—
DRASIL
TEKKA
MAGIA DRAGON
ERMINA
DRASIL, THE BIGGEST CITY ON THE CONTINENT.
WILL IT BE AS LOVELY AS CROCUS ON ISHGAR?
IN DRASIL WE SHOULD FIND INFORMATION...
SCRITCH
SCRITCH
SCRITCH
...ABOUT THE WOOD DRAGON GOD, ALDORON.

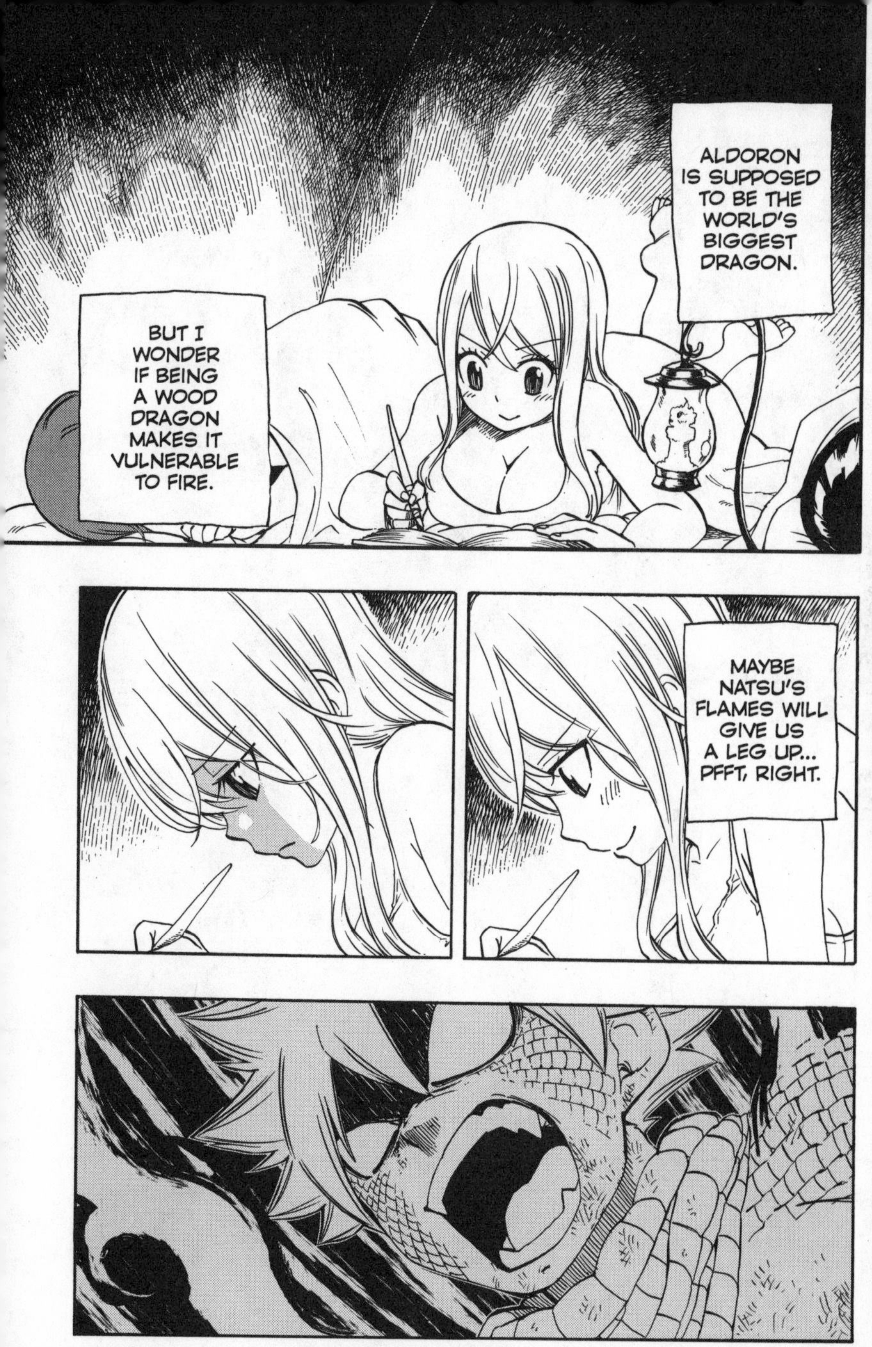
ALDORON IS SUPPOSED TO BE THE WORLD'S BIGGEST DRAGON.
BUT I WONDER IF BEING A WOOD DRAGON MAKES IT VULNERABLE TO FIRE.
MAYBE NATSU'S FLAMES WILL GIVE US A LEG UP... PFFT, RIGHT.

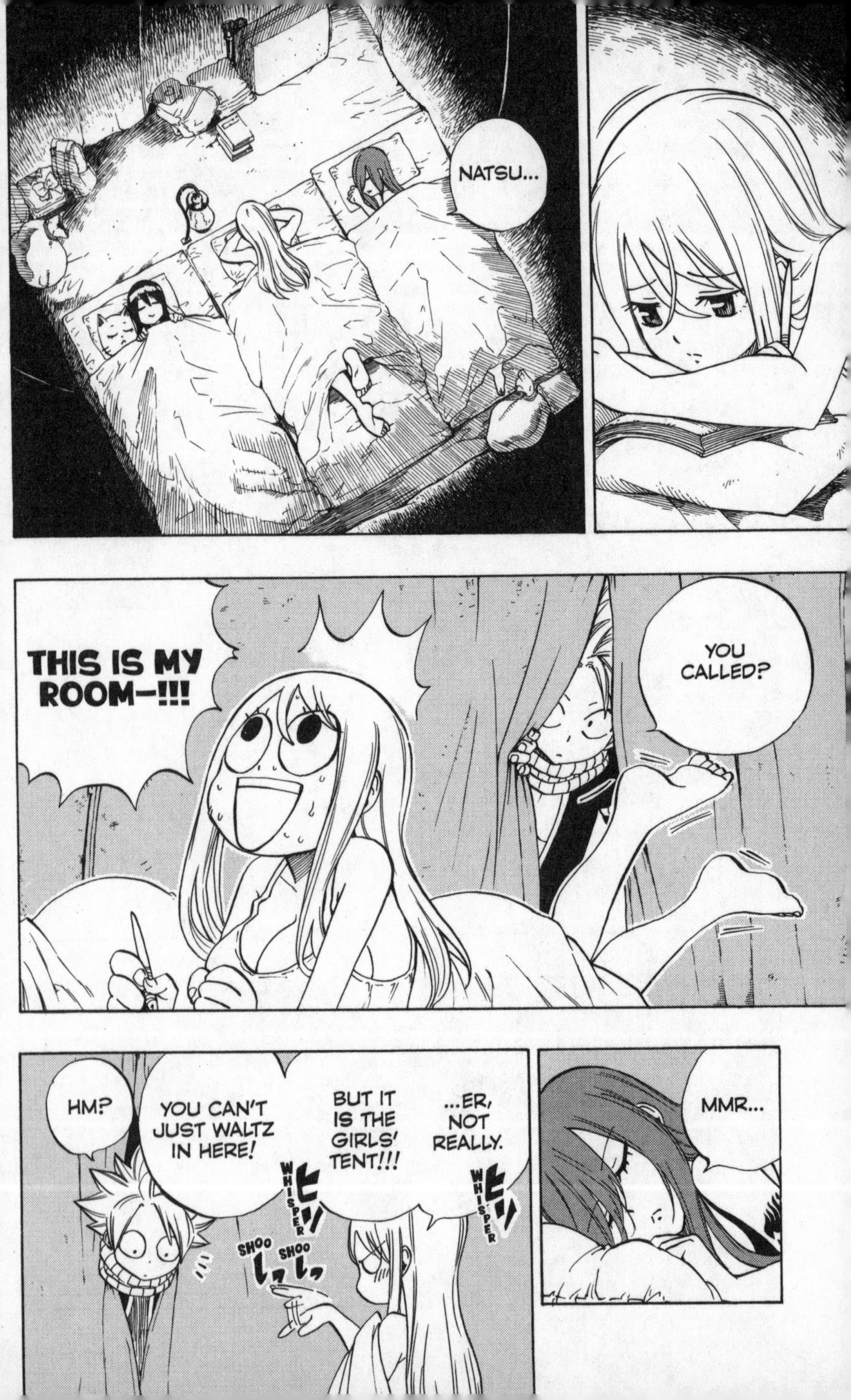
NATSU...
THIS IS MY ROOM—!!!
YOU CALLED?
HM?
YOU CAN'T JUST WALTZ IN HERE!
BUT IT IS THE GIRLS' TENT!!!
WHISPER
SHOO SHOO
...ER, NOT REALLY.
WHISPER
MMR...

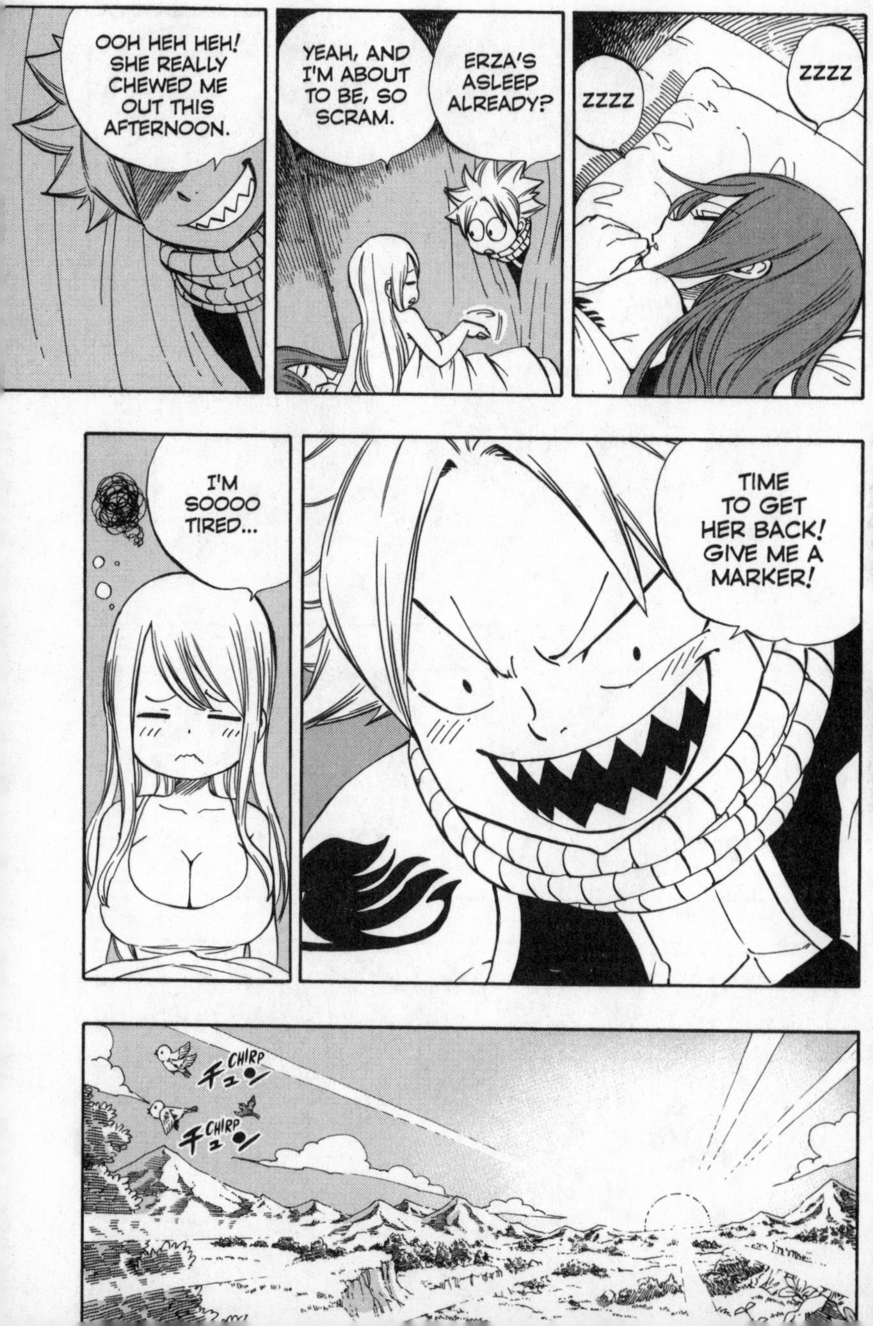
ZZZZ
ZZZZ
ERZA'S ASLEEP ALREADY?
YEAH, AND I'M ABOUT TO BE, SO SCRAM.
OOH HEH HEH! SHE REALLY CHEWED ME OUT THIS AFTERNOON.
TIME TO GET HER BACK! GIVE ME A MARKER!
I'M SOOOO TIRED...
CHIRP
チュン
CHIRP
チュン

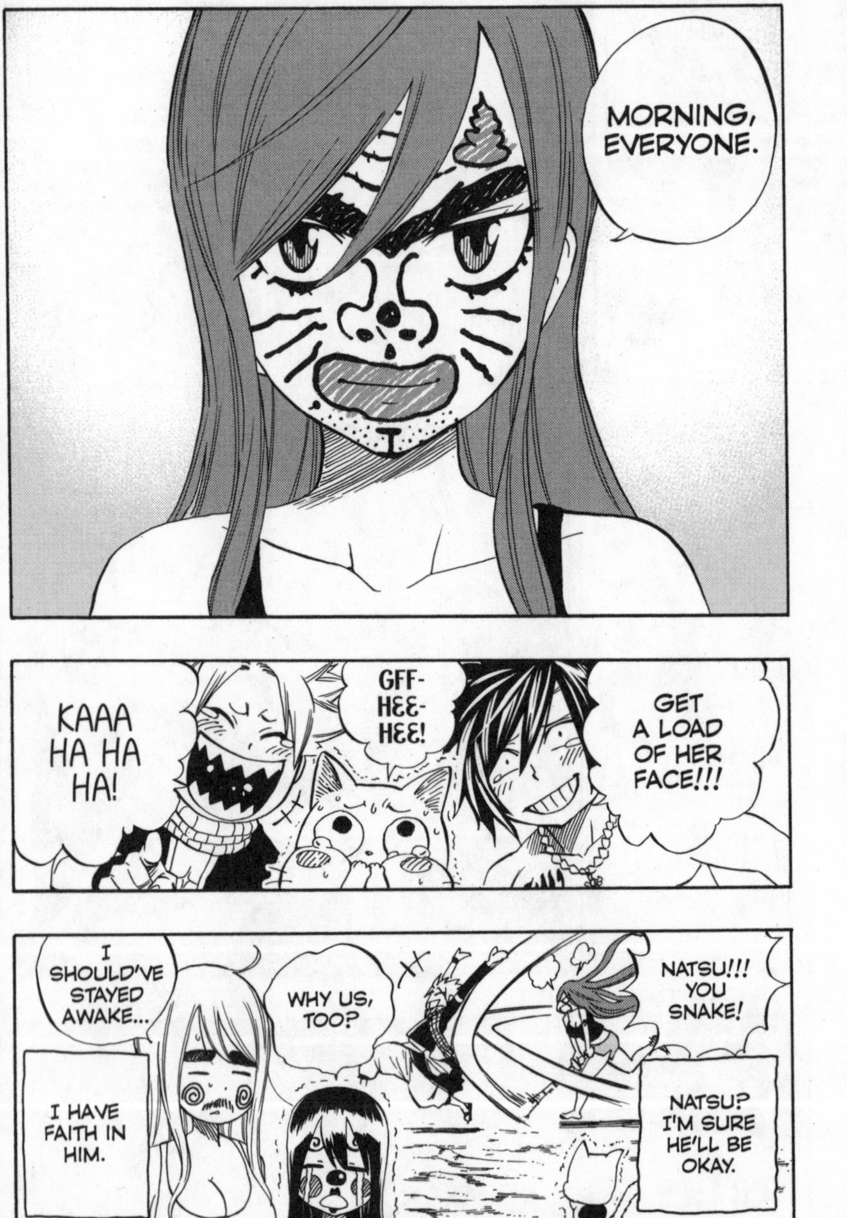
MORNING, EVERYONE.
GET A LOAD OF HER FACE!!!
GFF-HEE-HEE!
KAAA HA HA HA!
NATSU!!! YOU SNAKE!
NATSU? I'M SURE HE'LL BE OKAY.
WHY US, TOO?
I SHOULD'VE STAYED AWAKE...
I HAVE FAITH IN HIM.

FAIRY TAIL
100 YEARS QUEST

Chapter 25: Fairy Nail

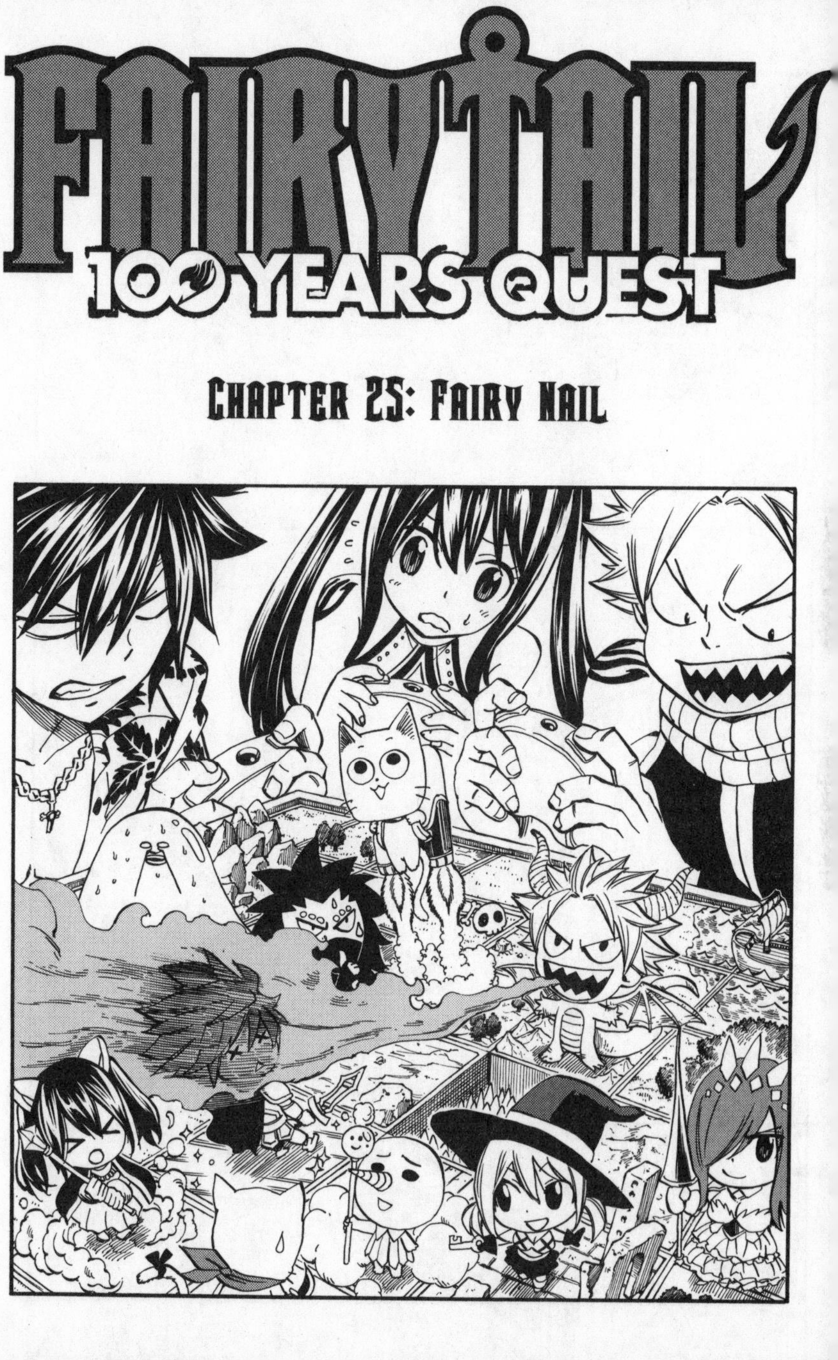

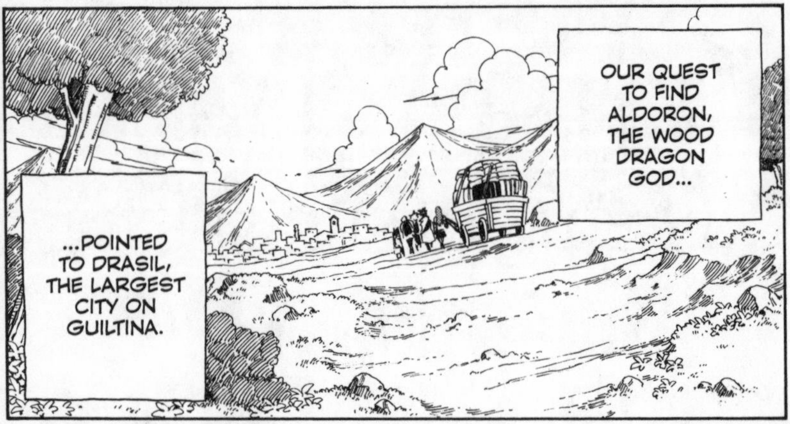
OUR QUEST TO FIND ALDORON, THE WOOD DRAGON GOD...
...POINTED TO DRASIL, THE LARGEST CITY ON GUILTINA.

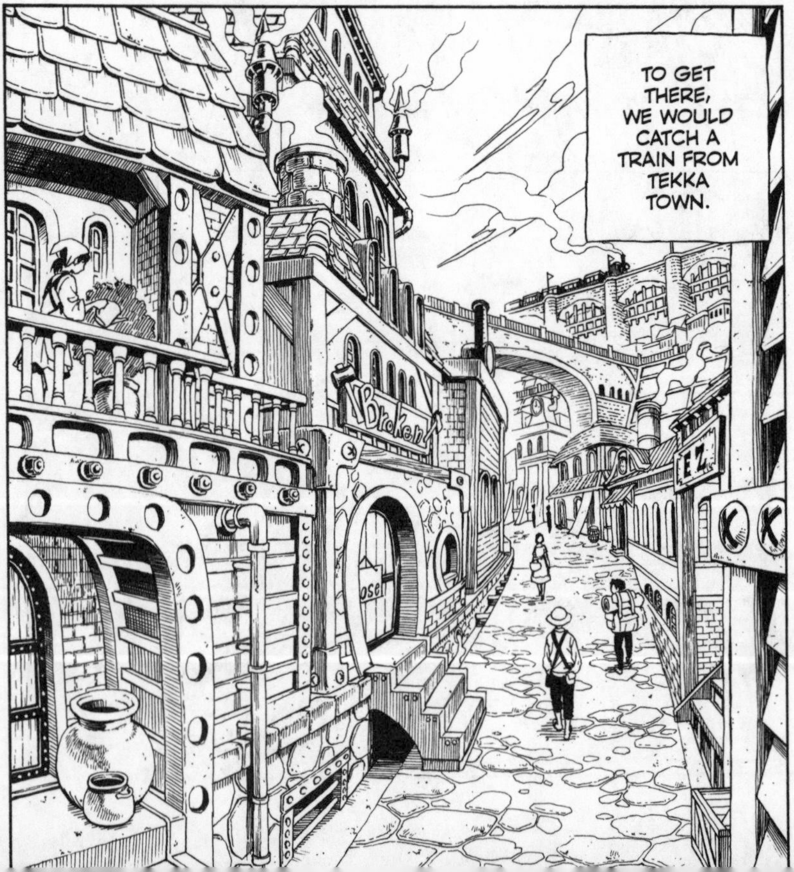
TO GET THERE, WE WOULD CATCH A TRAIN FROM TEKKA TOWN.
Broken
E.Z.

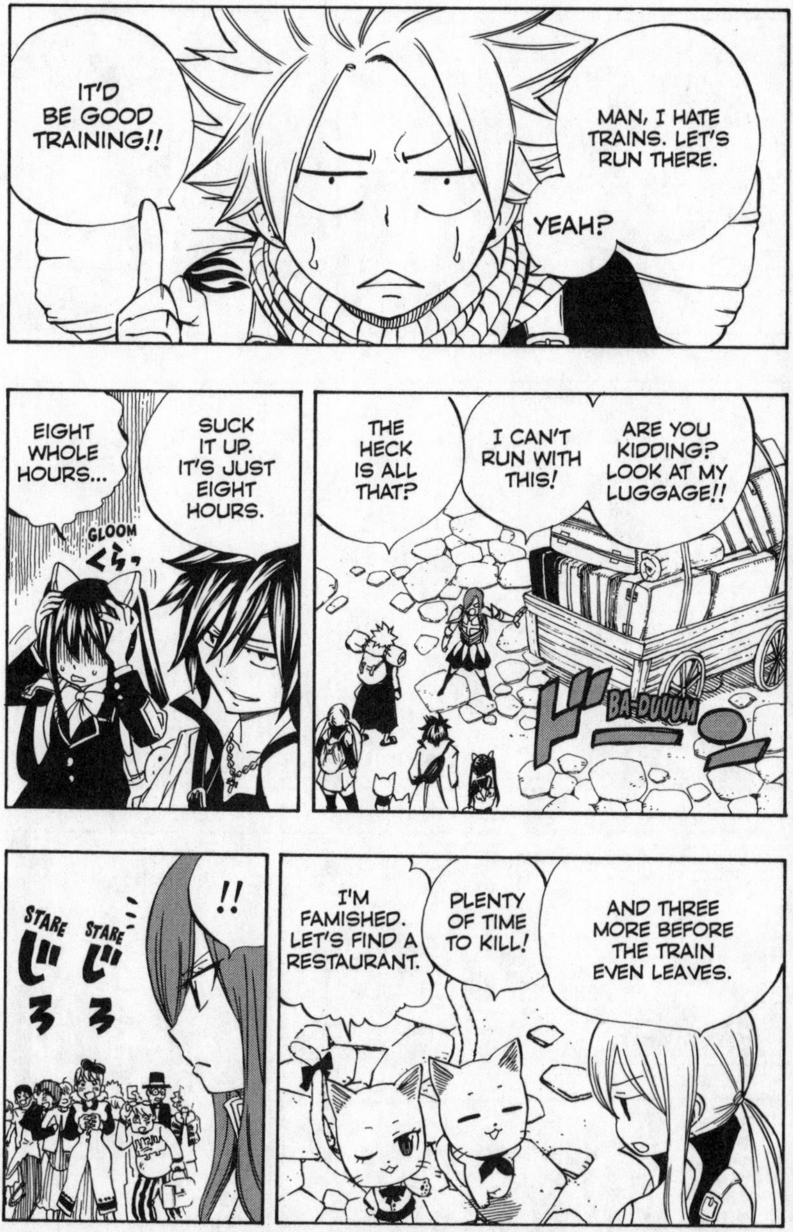
MAN, I HATE TRAINS. LET'S RUN THERE.
YEAH?
IT'D BE GOOD TRAINING!!
ARE YOU KIDDING? LOOK AT MY LUGGAGE!!
I CAN'T RUN WITH THIS!
THE HECK IS ALL THAT?
BA-DUUUM
EIGHT WHOLE HOURS...
SUCK IT UP. IT'S JUST EIGHT HOURS.
GLOOM
AND THREE MORE BEFORE THE TRAIN EVEN LEAVES.
PLENTY OF TIME TO KILL!
I'M FAMISHED. LET'S FIND A RESTAURANT.
!!
STARE
STARE

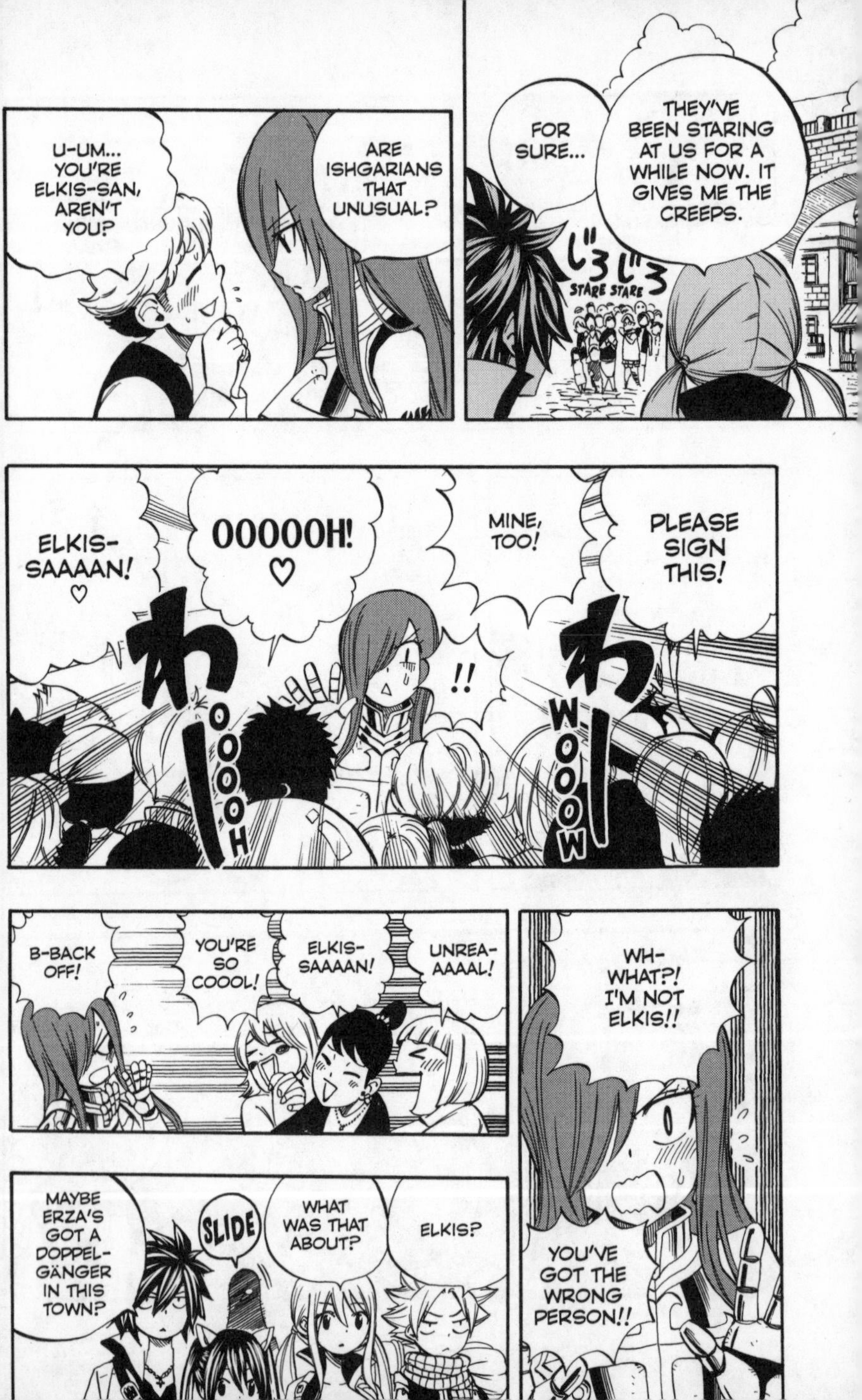
THEY'VE BEEN STARING AT US FOR A WHILE NOW. IT GIVES ME THE CREEPS.
FOR SURE...
じろじろ
STARE STARE
ARE ISHGARIANS THAT UNUSUAL?
U-UM... YOU'RE ELKIS-SAN, AREN'T YOU?
PLEASE SIGN THIS!
MINE, TOO!
わー
WOOOOW
!!
OOOOOH! ♡
ELKIS-SAAAAN! ♡
わー
OOOOOH
WH-WHAT?! I'M NOT ELKIS!!
YOU'VE GOT THE WRONG PERSON!!
UNREA-AAAAL!
ELKIS-SAAAAN!
YOU'RE SO COOOL!
B-BACK OFF!
ELKIS?
WHAT WAS THAT ABOUT?
SLIDE
MAYBE ERZA'S GOT A DOPPEL-GÄNGER IN THIS TOWN?

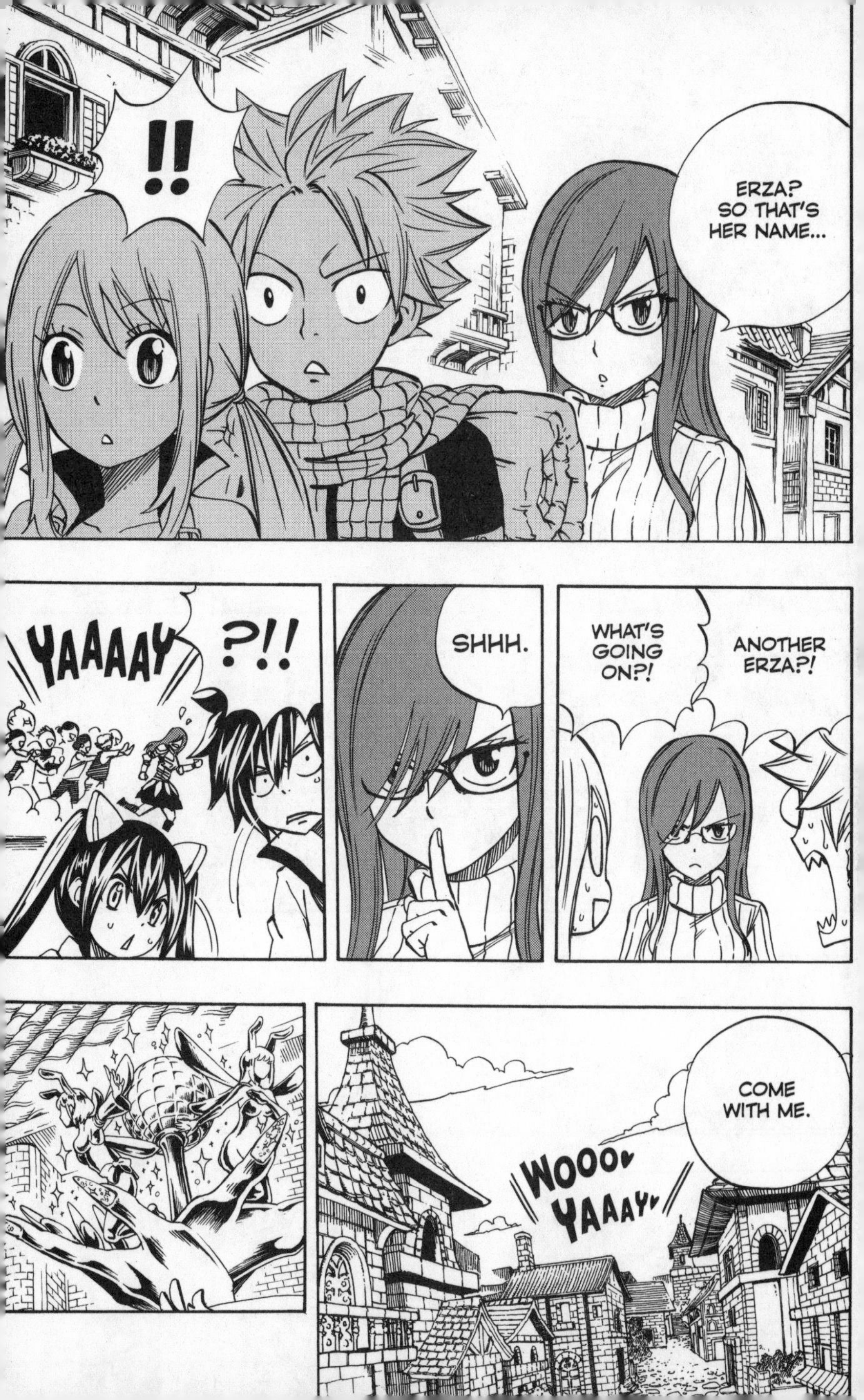
ERZA? SO THAT'S HER NAME...
!!
ANOTHER ERZA?!
WHAT'S GOING ON?!
SHHH.
?!!
YAAAAY
COME WITH ME.
WOOO♥ YAAAY♥

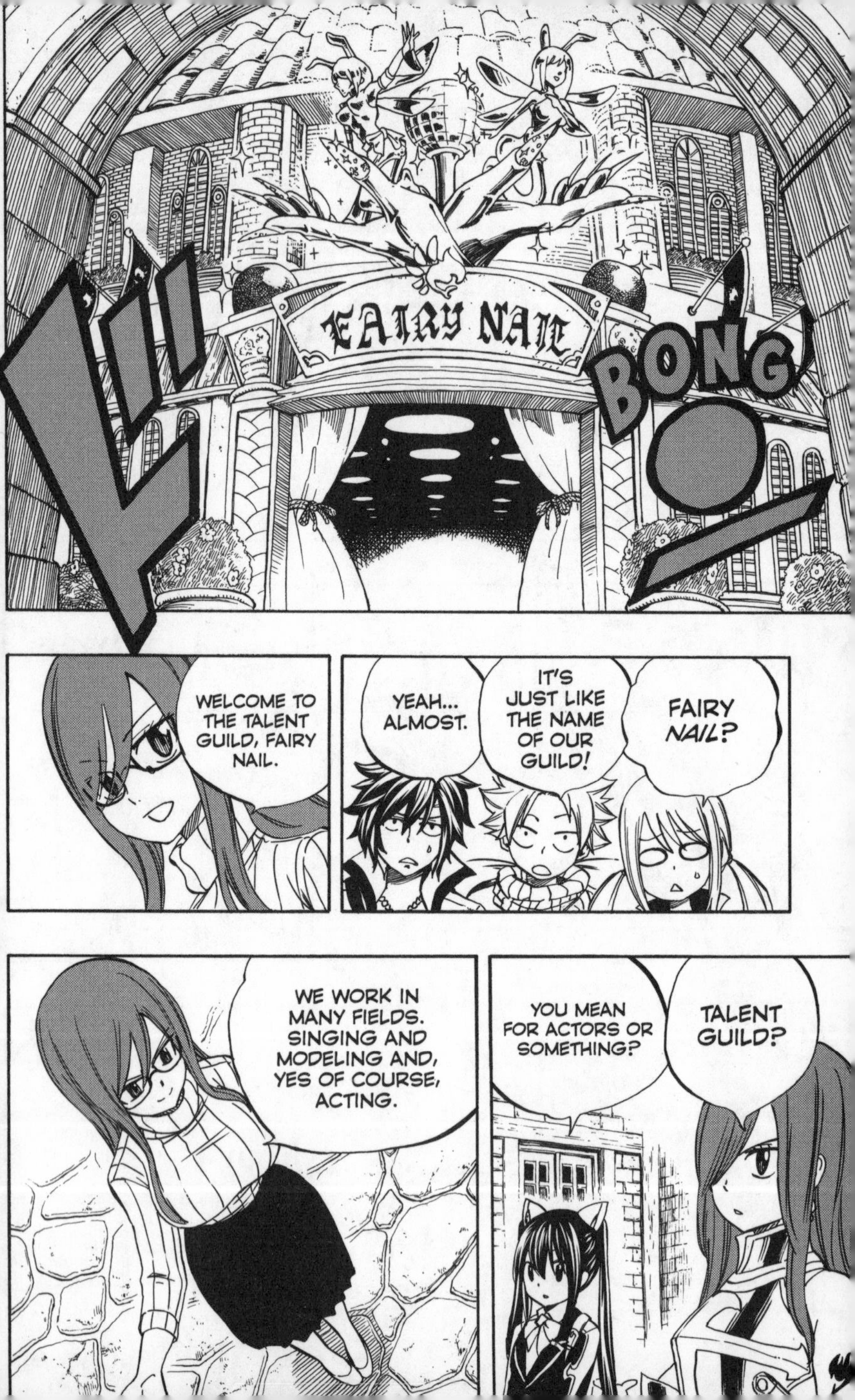
FAIRY NAIL
BONG
FAIRY NAIL?
IT'S JUST LIKE THE NAME OF OUR GUILD!
YEAH... ALMOST.
WELCOME TO THE TALENT GUILD, FAIRY NAIL.
TALENT GUILD?
YOU MEAN FOR ACTORS OR SOMETHING?
WE WORK IN MANY FIELDS. SINGING AND MODELING AND, YES OF COURSE, ACTING.

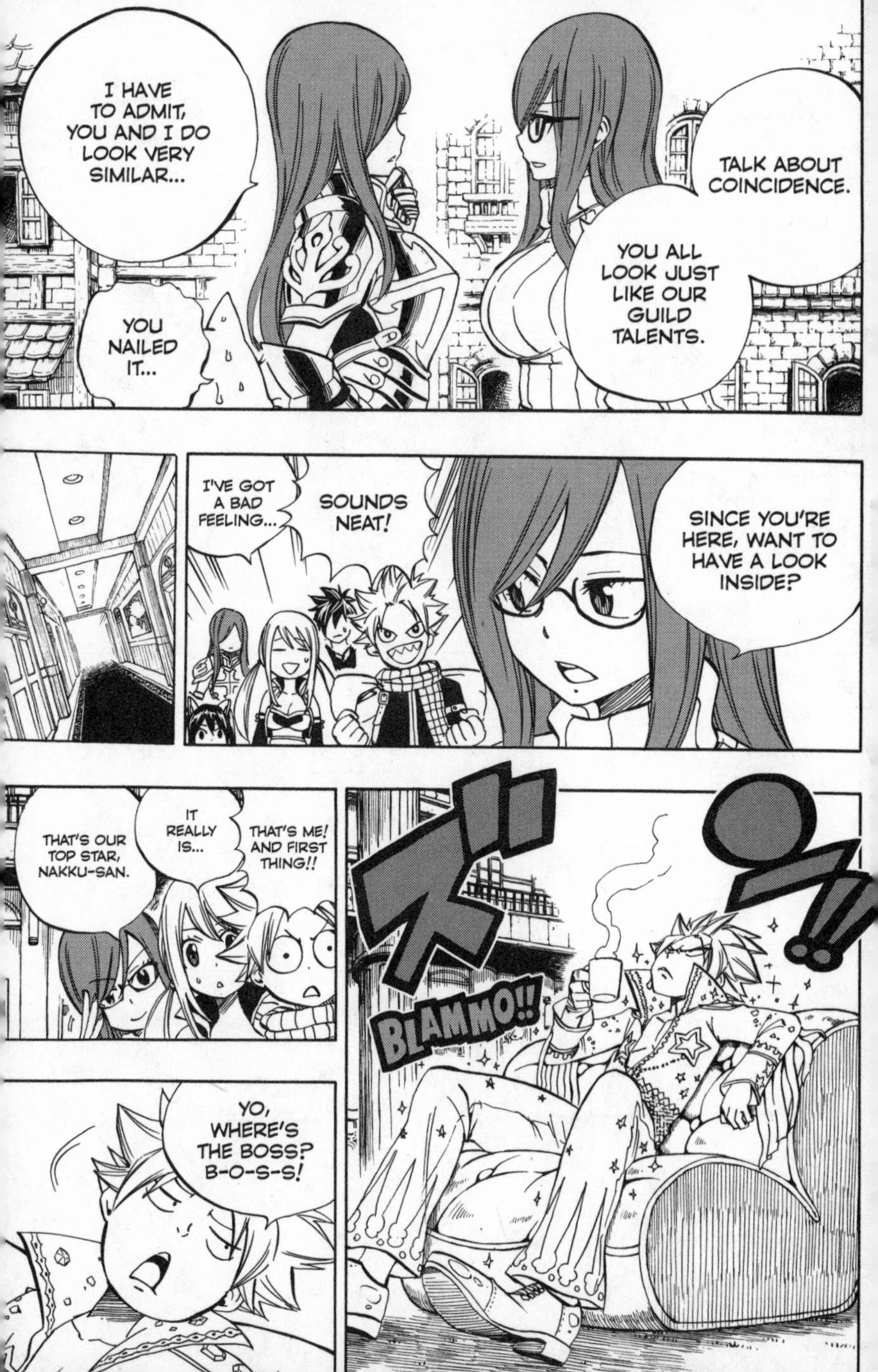
TALK ABOUT COINCIDENCE.
YOU ALL LOOK JUST LIKE OUR GUILD TALENTS.
I HAVE TO ADMIT, YOU AND I DO LOOK VERY SIMILAR...
YOU NAILED IT...
SINCE YOU'RE HERE, WANT TO HAVE A LOOK INSIDE?
SOUNDS NEAT!
I'VE GOT A BAD FEELING...
ズ
BLAMMO!!
THAT'S OUR TOP STAR, NAKKU-SAN.
THAT'S ME! AND FIRST THING!!
IT REALLY IS...
YO, WHERE'S THE BOSS? B-O-S-S!

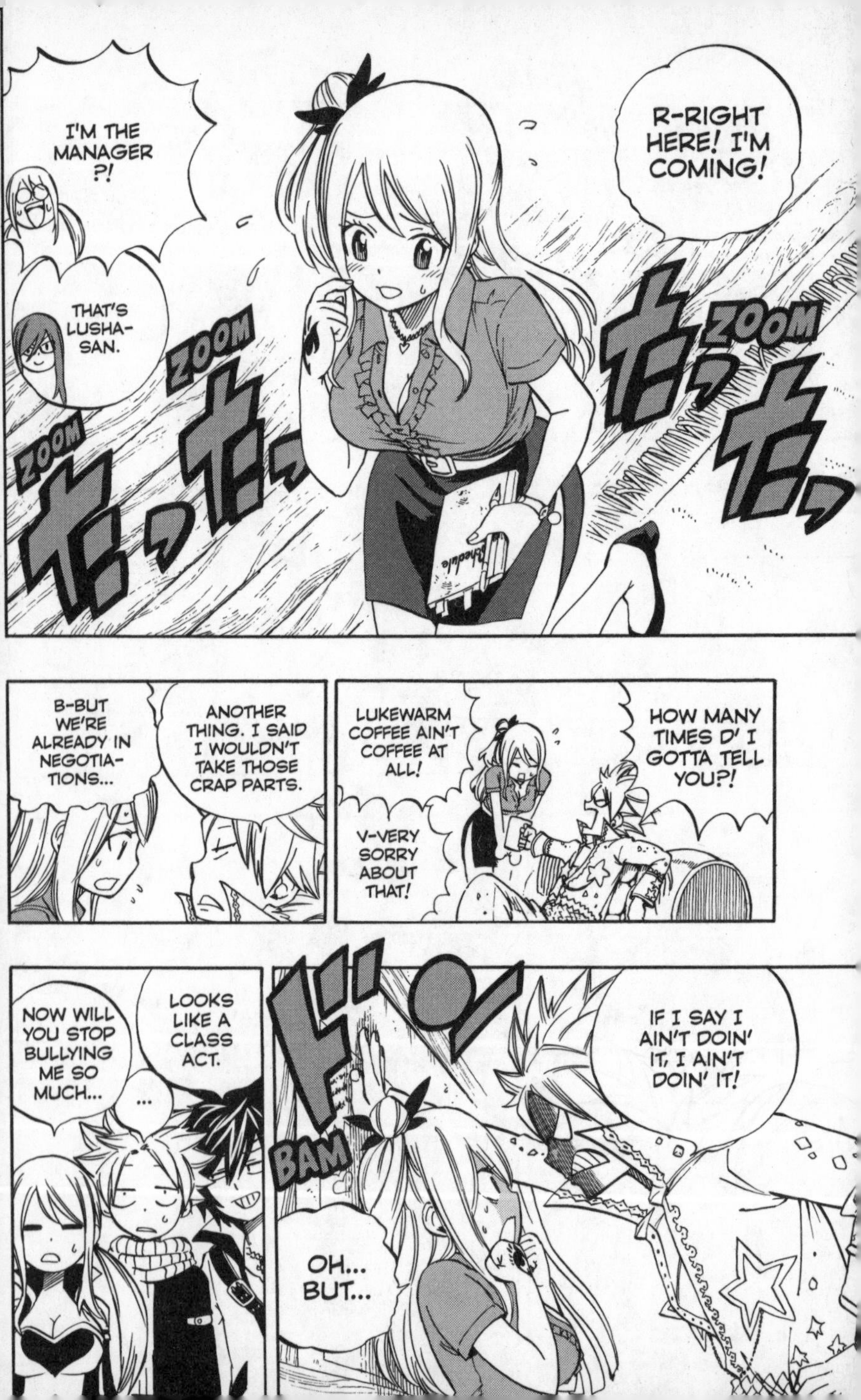
R-RIGHT HERE! I'M COMING!
I'M THE MANAGER ?!
THAT'S LUSHA-SAN.
ZOOM
ZOOM
ZOOM
HOW MANY TIMES D' I GOTTA TELL YOU?!
LUKEWARM COFFEE AIN'T COFFEE AT ALL!
V-VERY SORRY ABOUT THAT!
ANOTHER THING. I SAID I WOULDN'T TAKE THOSE CRAP PARTS.
B-BUT WE'RE ALREADY IN NEGOTIA-TIONS...
IF I SAY I AIN'T DOIN' IT, I AIN'T DOIN' IT!
BAM
OH... BUT...
LOOKS LIKE A CLASS ACT.
NOW WILL YOU STOP BULLYING ME SO MUCH...
...

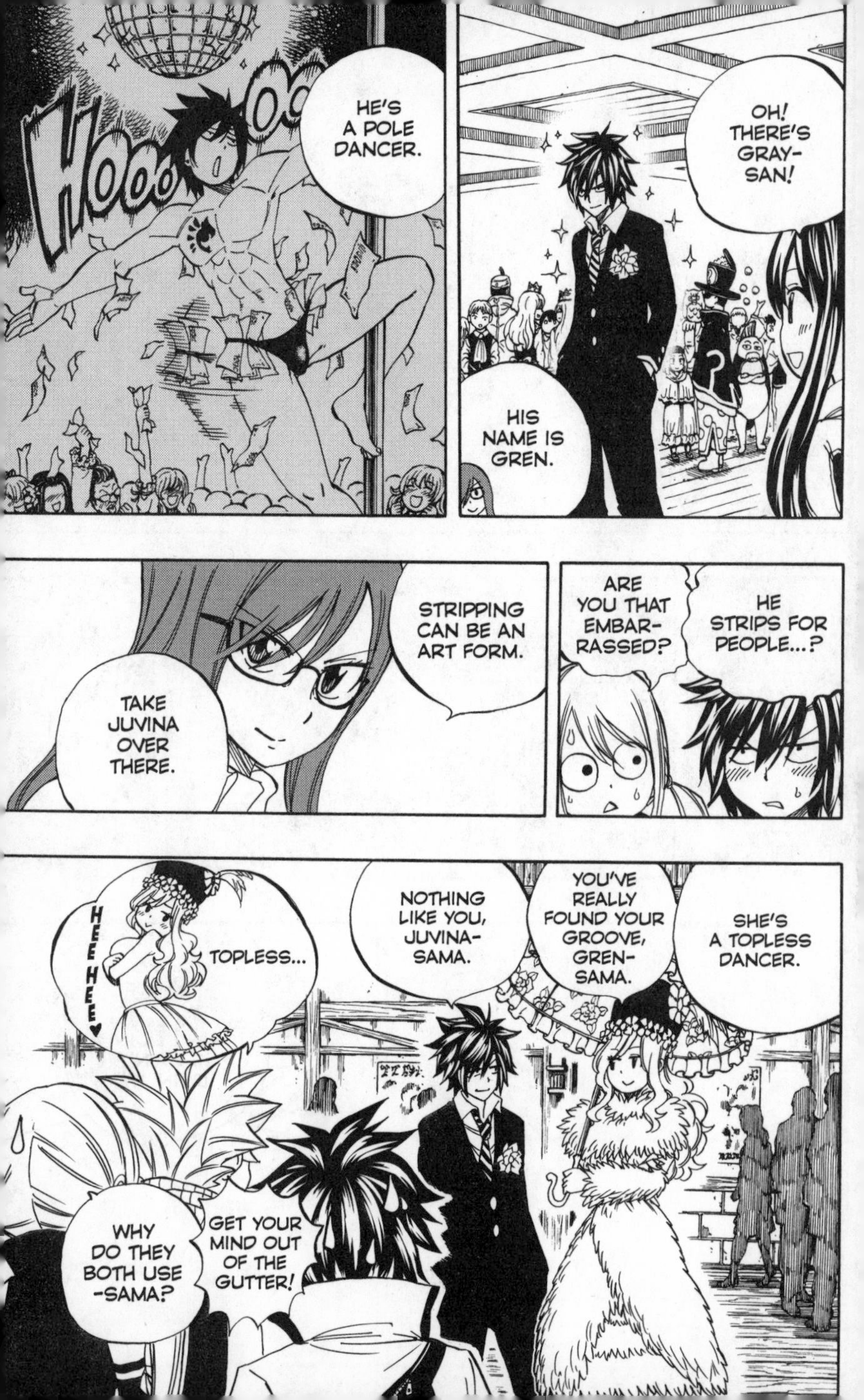
OH! THERE'S GRAY-SAN!
HIS NAME IS GREN.
HE'S A POLE DANCER.
HE STRIPS FOR PEOPLE...?
ARE YOU THAT EMBAR-RASSED?
STRIPPING CAN BE AN ART FORM.
TAKE JUVINA OVER THERE.
SHE'S A TOPLESS DANCER.
YOU'VE REALLY FOUND YOUR GROOVE, GREN-SAMA.
NOTHING LIKE YOU, JUVINA-SAMA.
TOPLESS...
HEE HEE♥
GET YOUR MIND OUT OF THE GUTTER!
WHY DO THEY BOTH USE -SAMA?

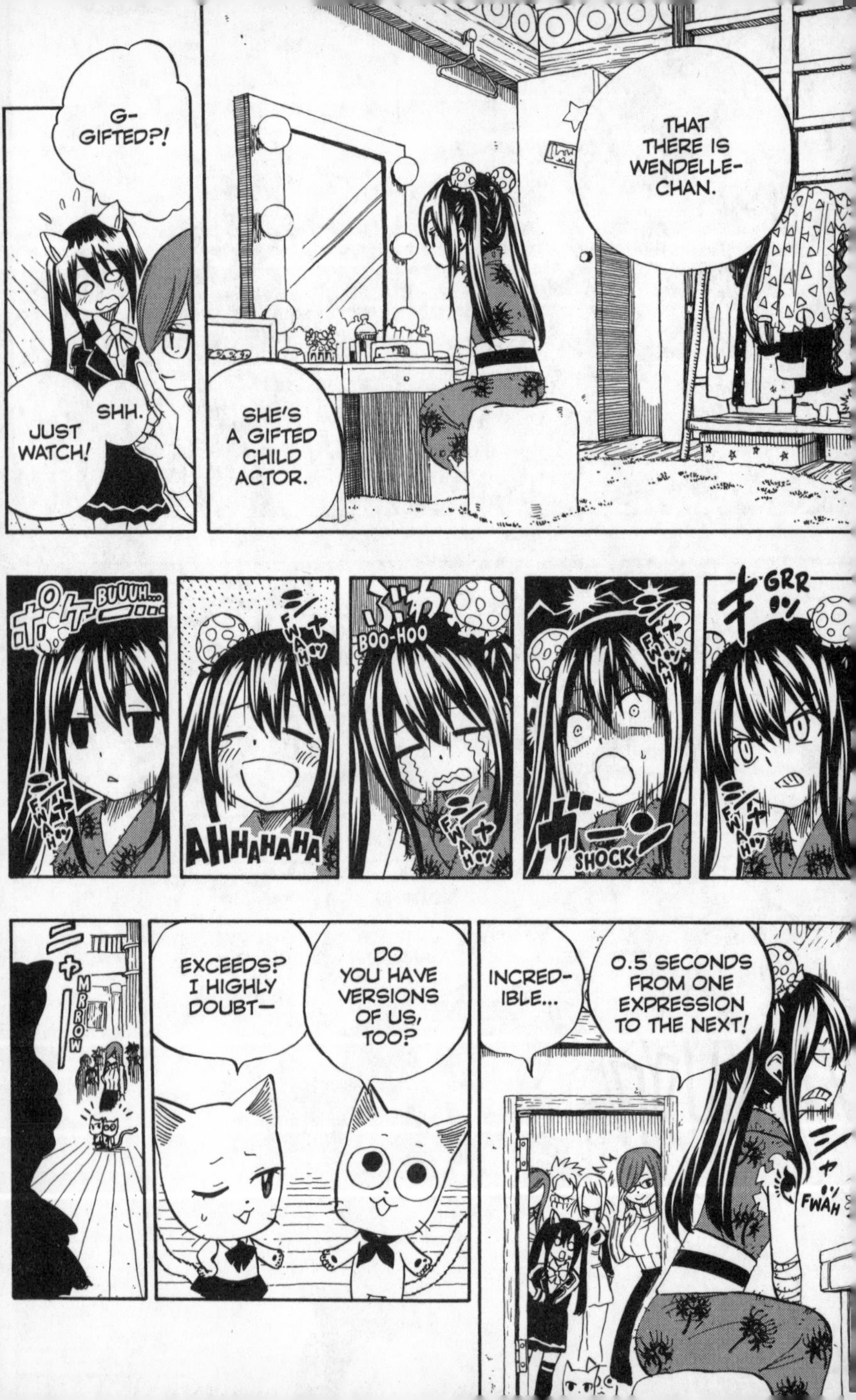
THAT THERE IS WENDELLE-CHAN.
SHE'S A GIFTED CHILD ACTOR.
G-GIFTED?!
SHH.
JUST WATCH!
GRR
FWAH
SHOCK
FWAH
BOO-HOO
FWAH
AHHAHAHA
FWAH
BUUUH...
FWAH
0.5 SECONDS FROM ONE EXPRESSION TO THE NEXT!
INCREDIBLE...
FWAH
DO YOU HAVE VERSIONS OF US, TOO?
EXCEEDS? I HIGHLY DOUBT—
MRROW

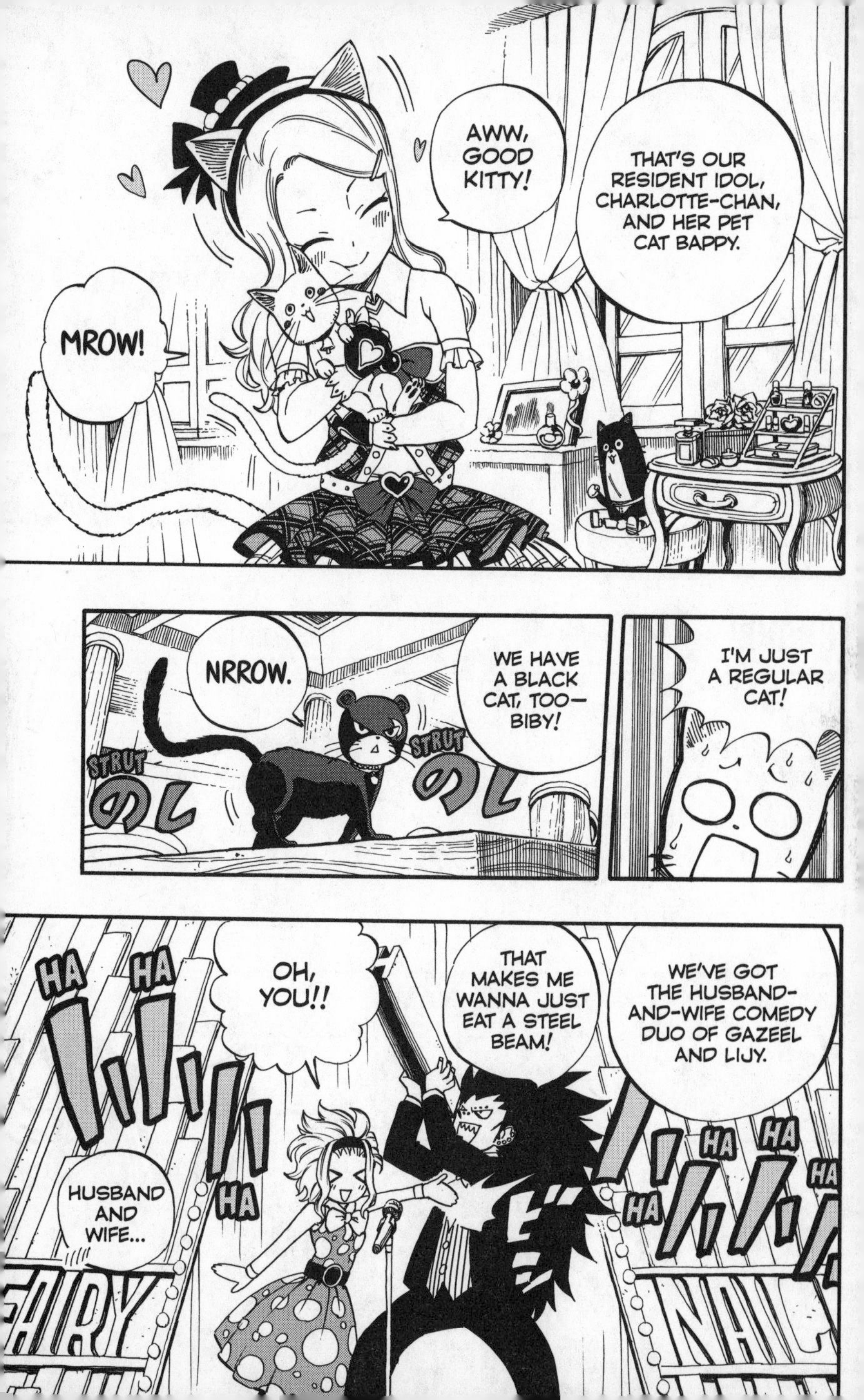
THAT'S OUR RESIDENT IDOL, CHARLOTTE-CHAN, AND HER PET CAT BAPPY.
AWW, GOOD KITTY!
MROW!
I'M JUST A REGULAR CAT!
WE HAVE A BLACK CAT, TOO— BIBY!
NRROW.
STRUT のし
STRUT のし
WE'VE GOT THE HUSBAND-AND-WIFE COMEDY DUO OF GAZEEL AND LIJY.
HA HA HA HA
THAT MAKES ME WANNA JUST EAT A STEEL BEAM!
OH, YOU!!
HA HA
HA
HUSBAND AND WIFE...
FAIRY

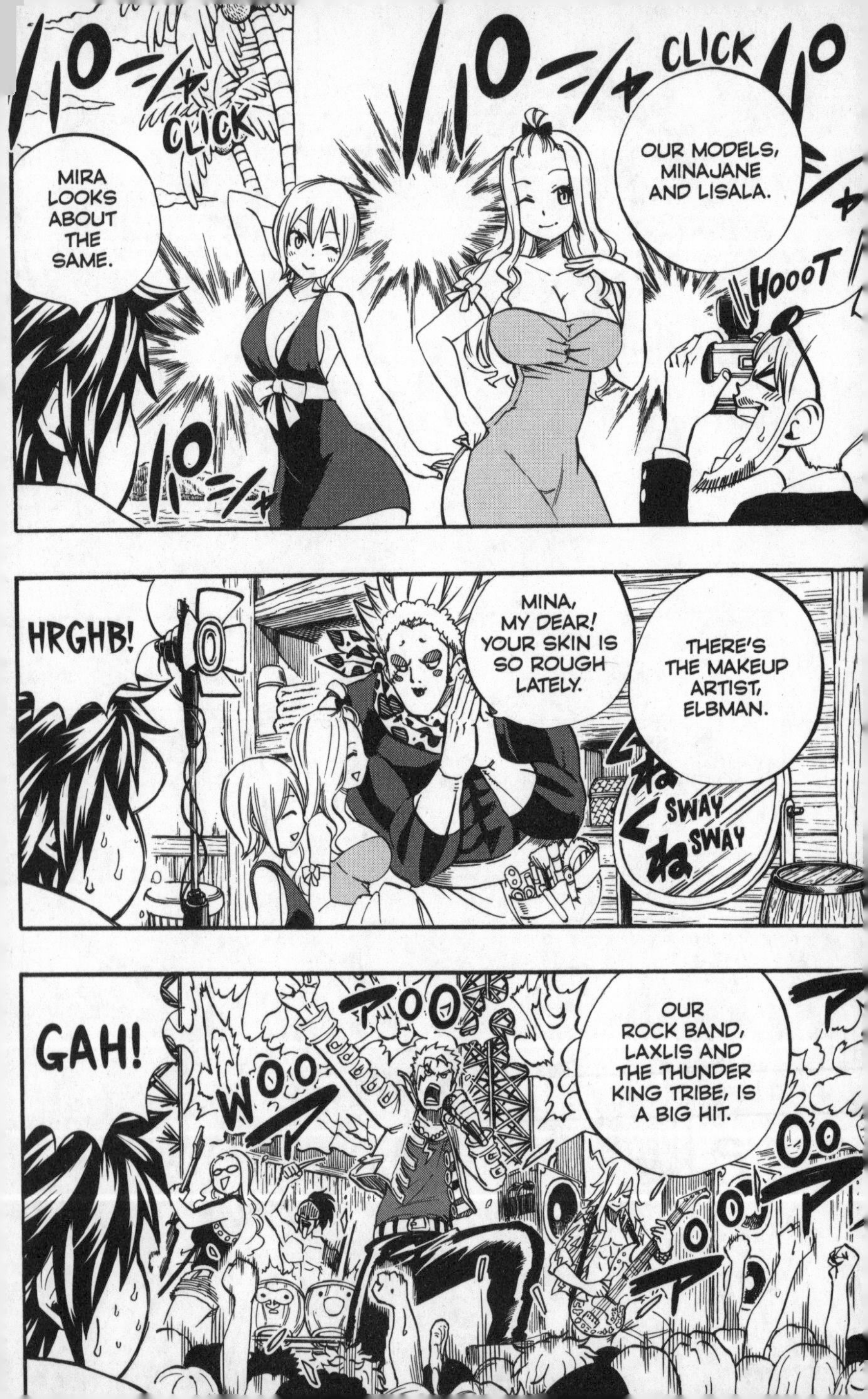
CLICK
OUR MODELS, MINAJANE AND LISALA.
HOOOT
CLICK
MIRA LOOKS ABOUT THE SAME.
THERE'S THE MAKEUP ARTIST, ELBMAN.
MINA, MY DEAR! YOUR SKIN IS SO ROUGH LATELY.
SWAY SWAY
HRGHB!
OUR ROCK BAND, LAXLIS AND THE THUNDER KING TRIBE, IS A BIG HIT.
WOO
GAH!

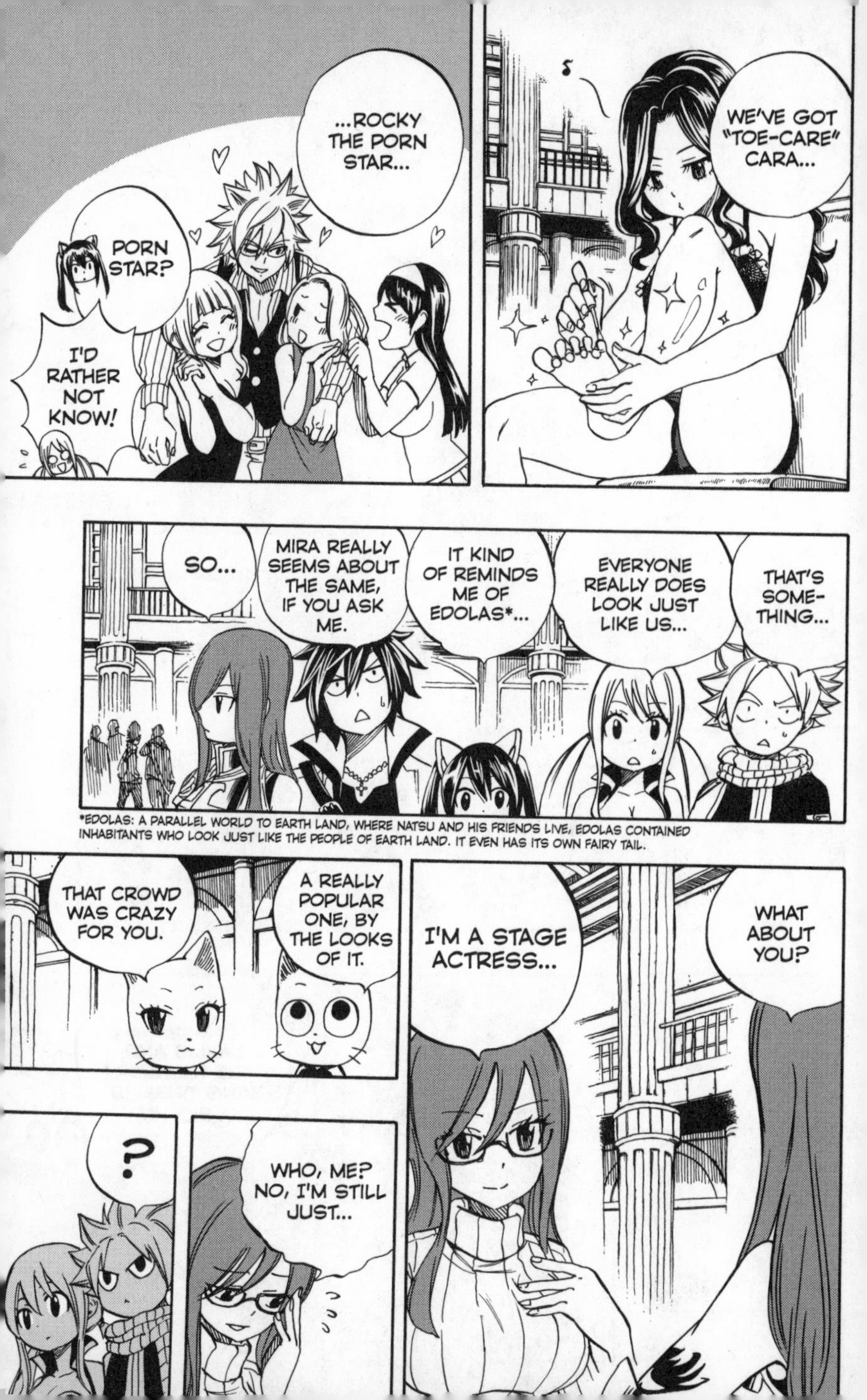
WE'VE GOT "TOE-CARE" CARA...
...ROCKY THE PORN STAR...
PORN STAR?
I'D RATHER NOT KNOW!
THAT'S SOME-THING...
EVERYONE REALLY DOES LOOK JUST LIKE US...
IT KIND OF REMINDS ME OF EDOLAS*...
MIRA REALLY SEEMS ABOUT THE SAME, IF YOU ASK ME.
SO...
WHAT ABOUT YOU?
I'M A STAGE ACTRESS...
A REALLY POPULAR ONE, BY THE LOOKS OF IT.
THAT CROWD WAS CRAZY FOR YOU.
WHO, ME? NO, I'M STILL JUST...
?

*EDOLAS: A PARALLEL WORLD TO EARTH LAND, WHERE NATSU AND HIS FRIENDS LIVE. EDOLAS CONTAINED INHABITANTS WHO LOOK JUST LIKE THE PEOPLE OF EARTH LAND. IT EVEN HAS ITS OWN FAIRY TAIL.

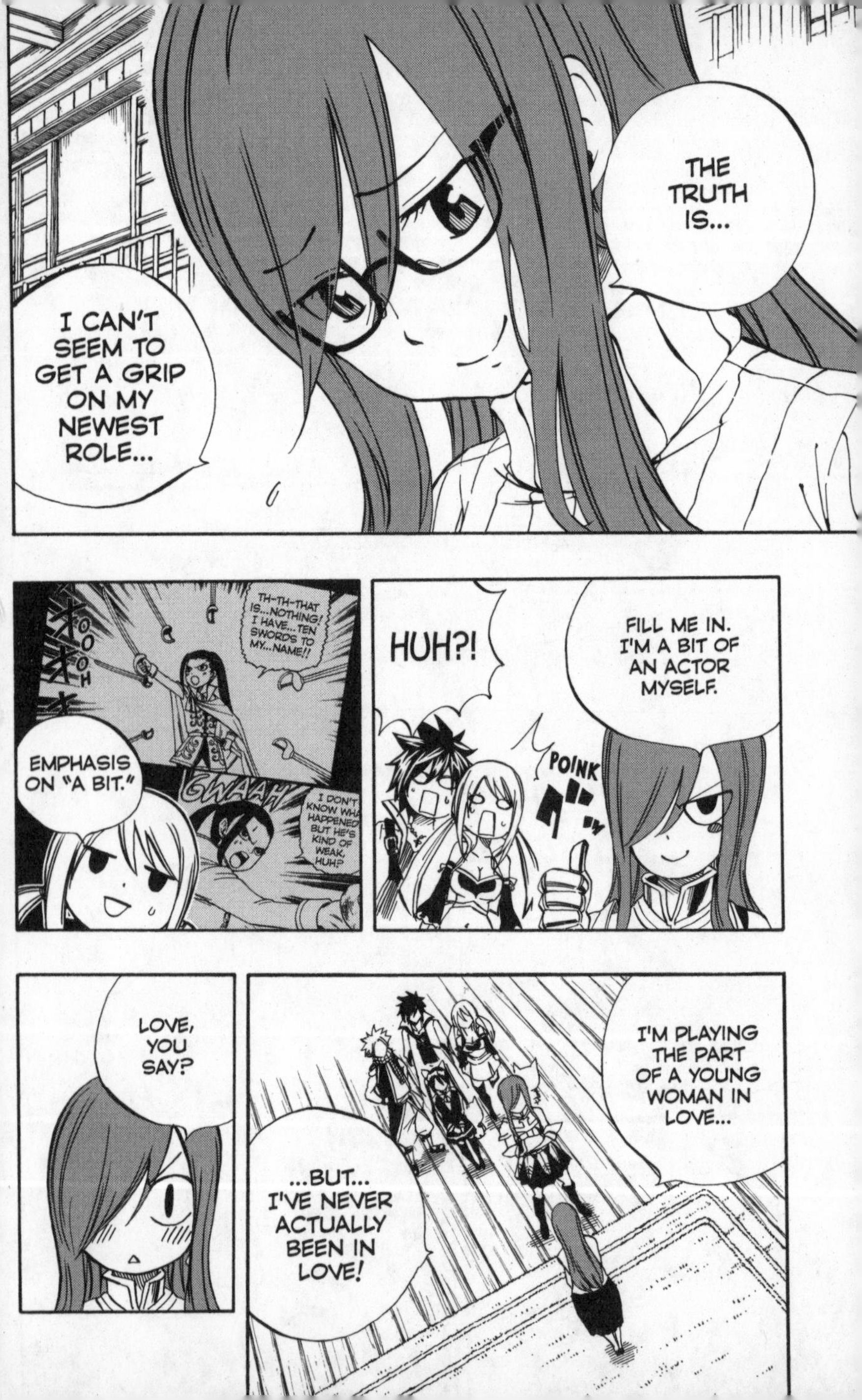
THE TRUTH IS...
I CAN'T SEEM TO GET A GRIP ON MY NEWEST ROLE...
FILL ME IN. I'M A BIT OF AN ACTOR MYSELF.
HUH?!
POINK
TH-TH-THAT IS...NOTHING! I HAVE...TEN SWORDS TO MY...NAME!!
OOOH
GWAAH
I DON'T KNOW WHA HAPPENED BUT HE'S KIND OF WEAK, HUH?
EMPHASIS ON "A BIT."
I'M PLAYING THE PART OF A YOUNG WOMAN IN LOVE...
...BUT... I'VE NEVER ACTUALLY BEEN IN LOVE!
LOVE, YOU SAY?

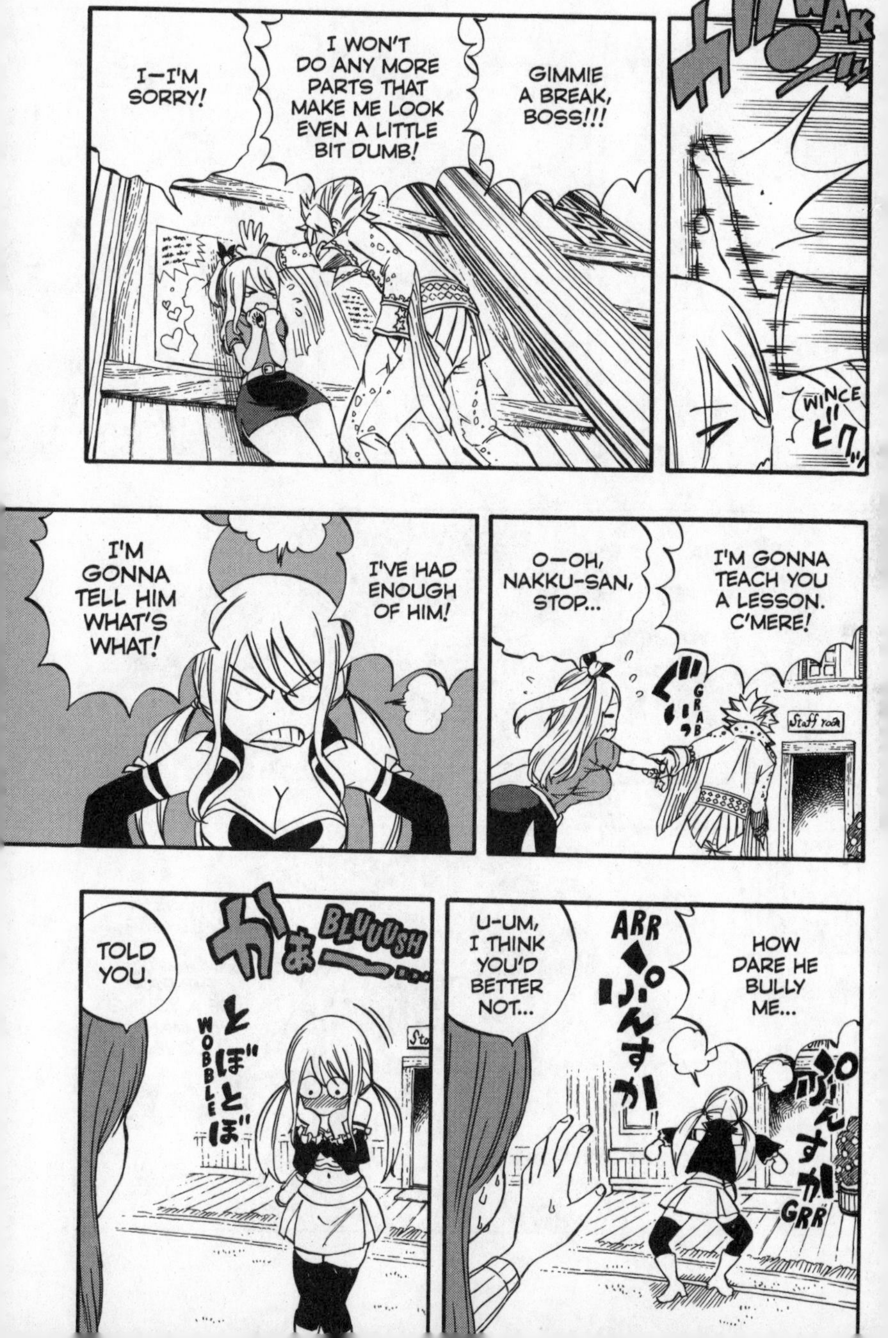
WAK
WINCE
GIMMIE A BREAK, BOSS!!!
I WON'T DO ANY MORE PARTS THAT MAKE ME LOOK EVEN A LITTLE BIT DUMB!
I–I'M SORRY!
I'M GONNA TEACH YOU A LESSON. C'MERE!
O–OH, NAKKU-SAN, STOP...
GRAB
Staff room
I'VE HAD ENOUGH OF HIM!
I'M GONNA TELL HIM WHAT'S WHAT!
HOW DARE HE BULLY ME...
GRR
ARR
U-UM, I THINK YOU'D BETTER NOT...
BLUUUSH
TOLD YOU.
WOBBLE

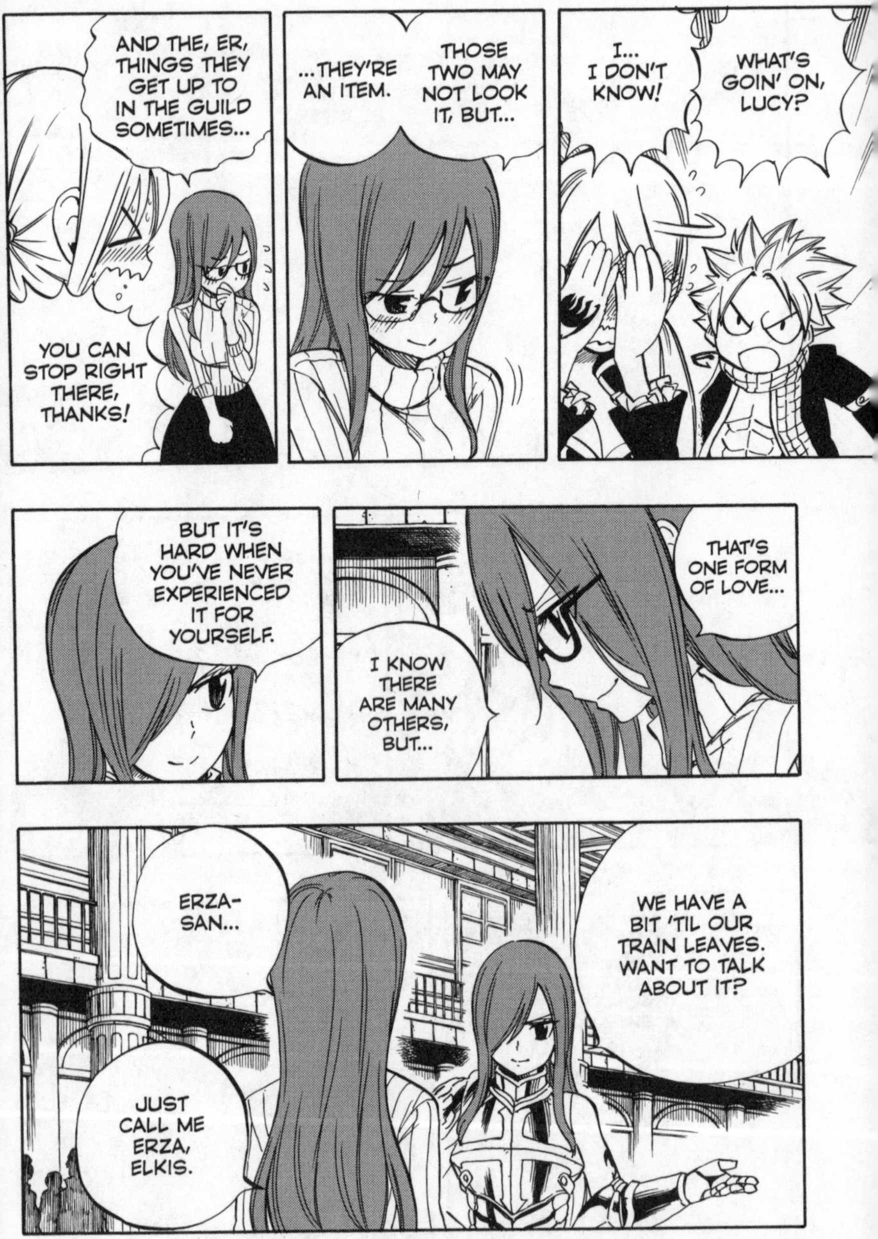
WHAT'S GOIN' ON, LUCY?
I... I DON'T KNOW!
THOSE TWO MAY NOT LOOK IT, BUT...
...THEY'RE AN ITEM.
AND THE, ER, THINGS THEY GET UP TO IN THE GUILD SOMETIMES...
YOU CAN STOP RIGHT THERE, THANKS!
THAT'S ONE FORM OF LOVE...
I KNOW THERE ARE MANY OTHERS, BUT...
BUT IT'S HARD WHEN YOU'VE NEVER EXPERIENCED IT FOR YOURSELF.
WE HAVE A BIT 'TIL OUR TRAIN LEAVES. WANT TO TALK ABOUT IT?
ERZA-SAN...
JUST CALL ME ERZA, ELKIS.

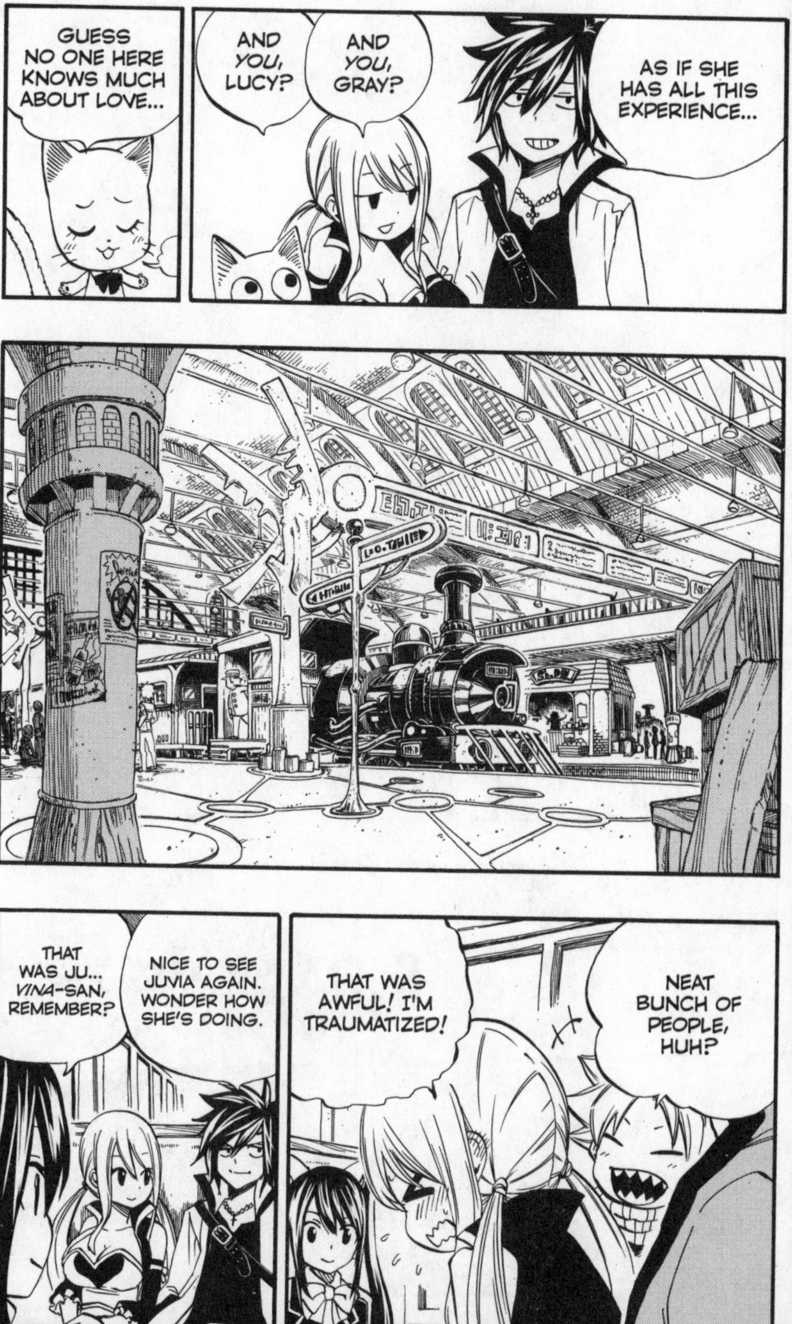
AS IF SHE HAS ALL THIS EXPERIENCE...
AND YOU, GRAY?
AND YOU, LUCY?
GUESS NO ONE HERE KNOWS MUCH ABOUT LOVE...
NEAT BUNCH OF PEOPLE, HUH?
THAT WAS AWFUL! I'M TRAUMATIZED!
NICE TO SEE JUVIA AGAIN. WONDER HOW SHE'S DOING.
THAT WAS JU... VINA-SAN, REMEMBER?

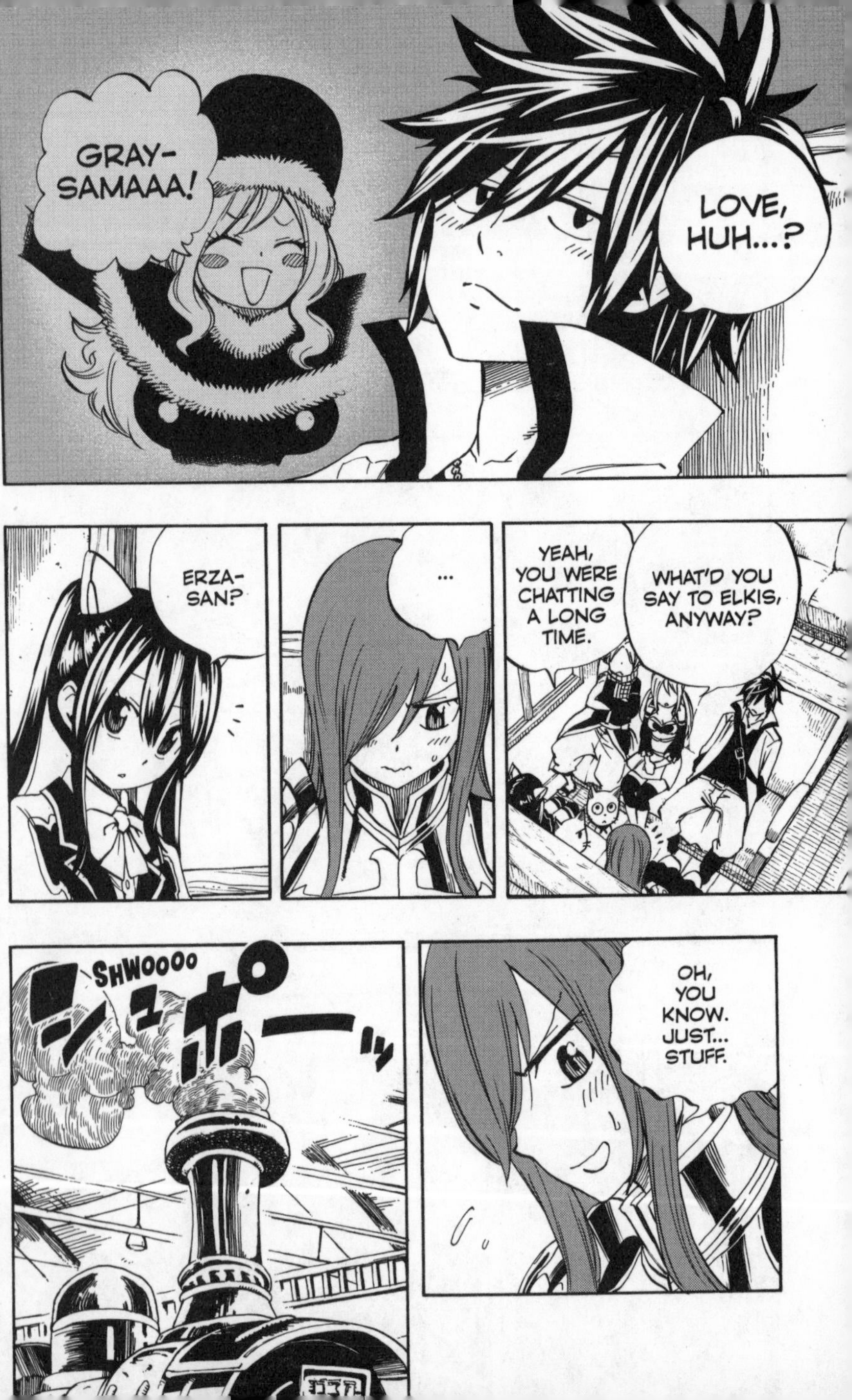
LOVE, HUH...?
GRAY-SAMAAA!
WHAT'D YOU SAY TO ELKIS, ANYWAY?
YEAH, YOU WERE CHATTING A LONG TIME.
...
ERZA-SAN?
OH, YOU KNOW. JUST... STUFF.
SHWOOOO

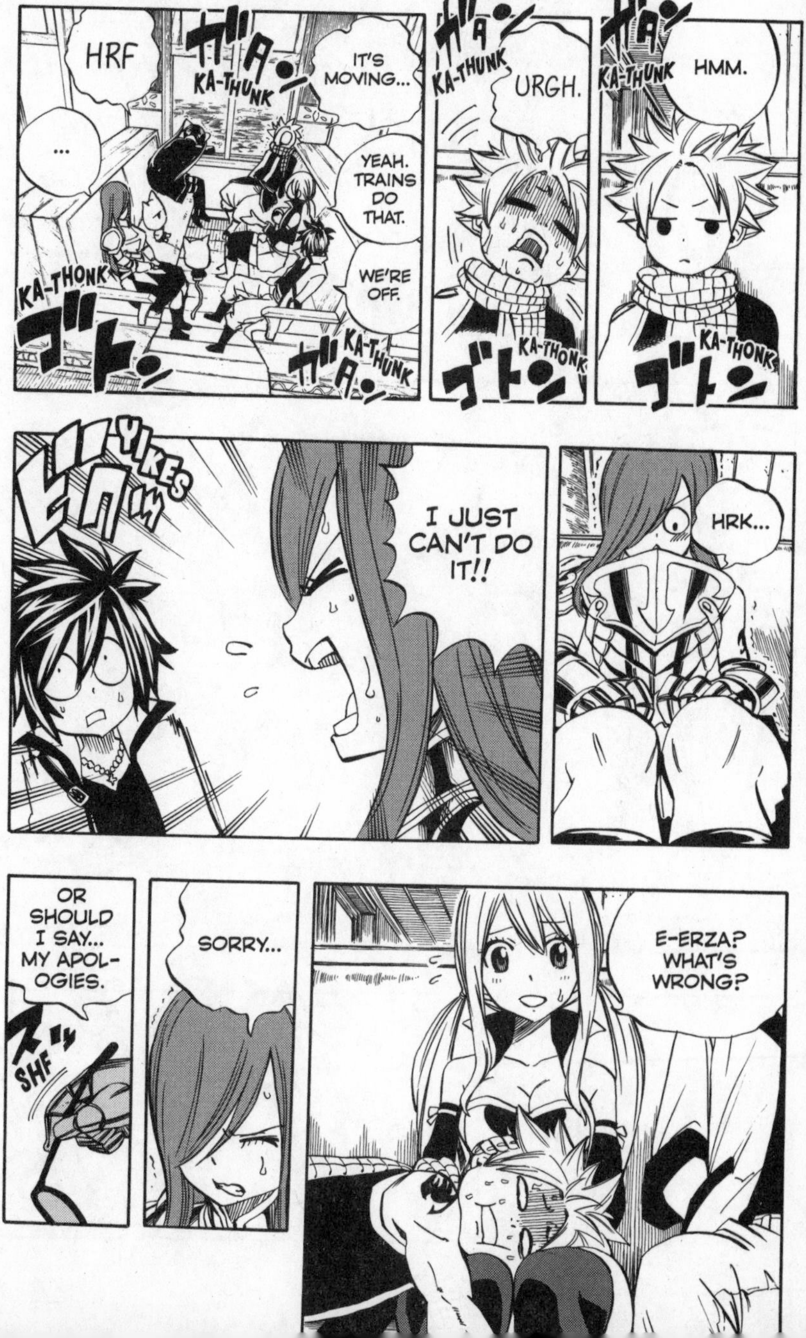
KA-THUNK
HMM.
KA-THONK
KA-THUNK
URGH.
KA-THONK
KA-THUNK
IT'S MOVING...
HRF
...
YEAH. TRAINS DO THAT.
WE'RE OFF.
KA-THONK
KA-THUNK
HRK...
I JUST CAN'T DO IT!!
YIKES
E-ERZA? WHAT'S WRONG?
SORRY...
OR SHOULD I SAY... MY APOLOGIES.
SHF

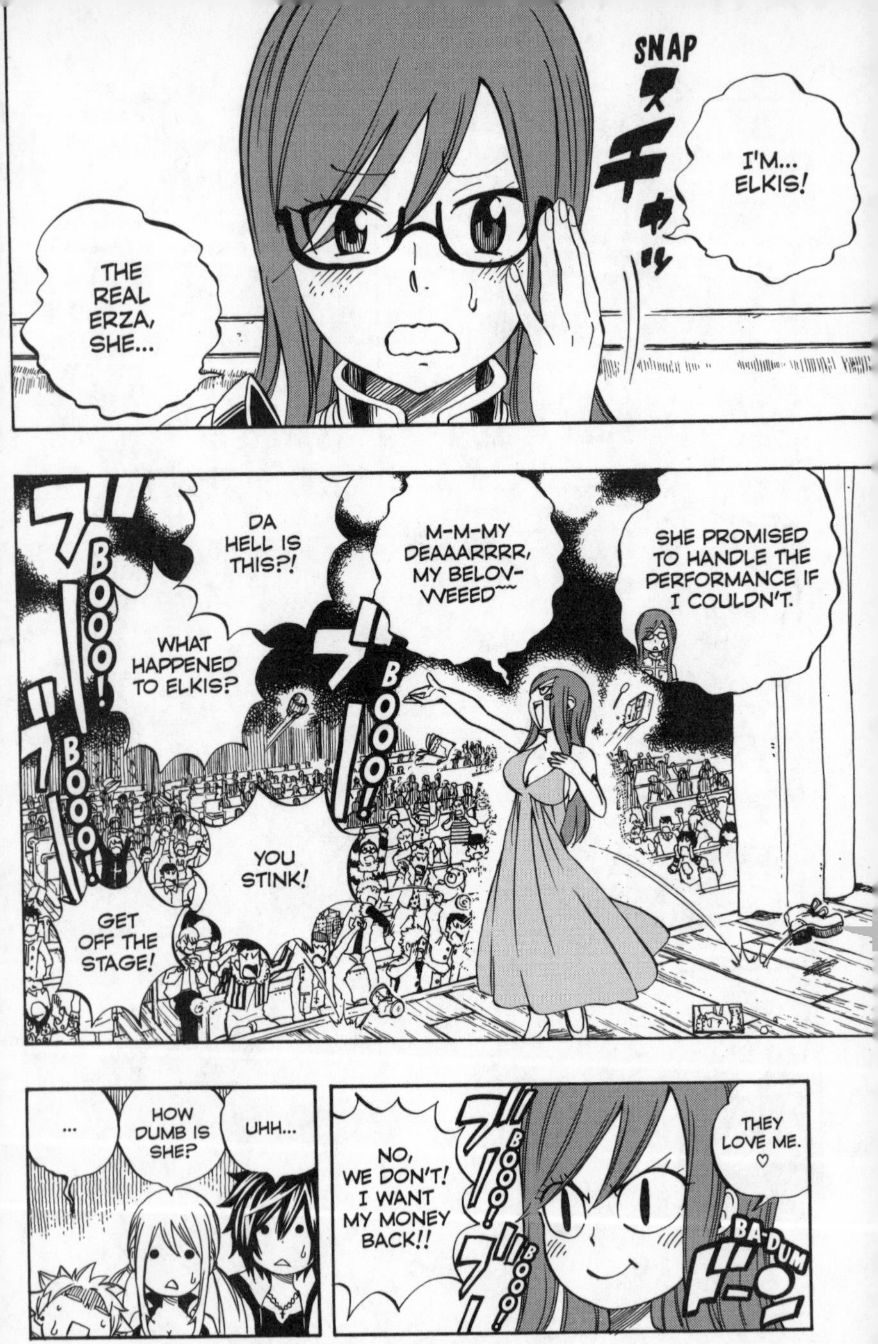
SNAP
I'M... ELKIS!
THE REAL ERZA, SHE...
SHE PROMISED TO HANDLE THE PERFORMANCE IF I COULDN'T.
M-M-MY DEAAARRRR, MY BELOV-WEEED~~~
DA HELL IS THIS?!
WHAT HAPPENED TO ELKIS?
BOOO!
BOOO!
BOOO!
YOU STINK!
GET OFF THE STAGE!
THEY LOVE ME. ♡
BA-DUM
BOOO!
BOOO!
NO, WE DON'T! I WANT MY MONEY BACK!!
UHH...
HOW DUMB IS SHE?
...

FAIRY TAIL 100 YEARS QUEST

Chapter 26: At Rainhill

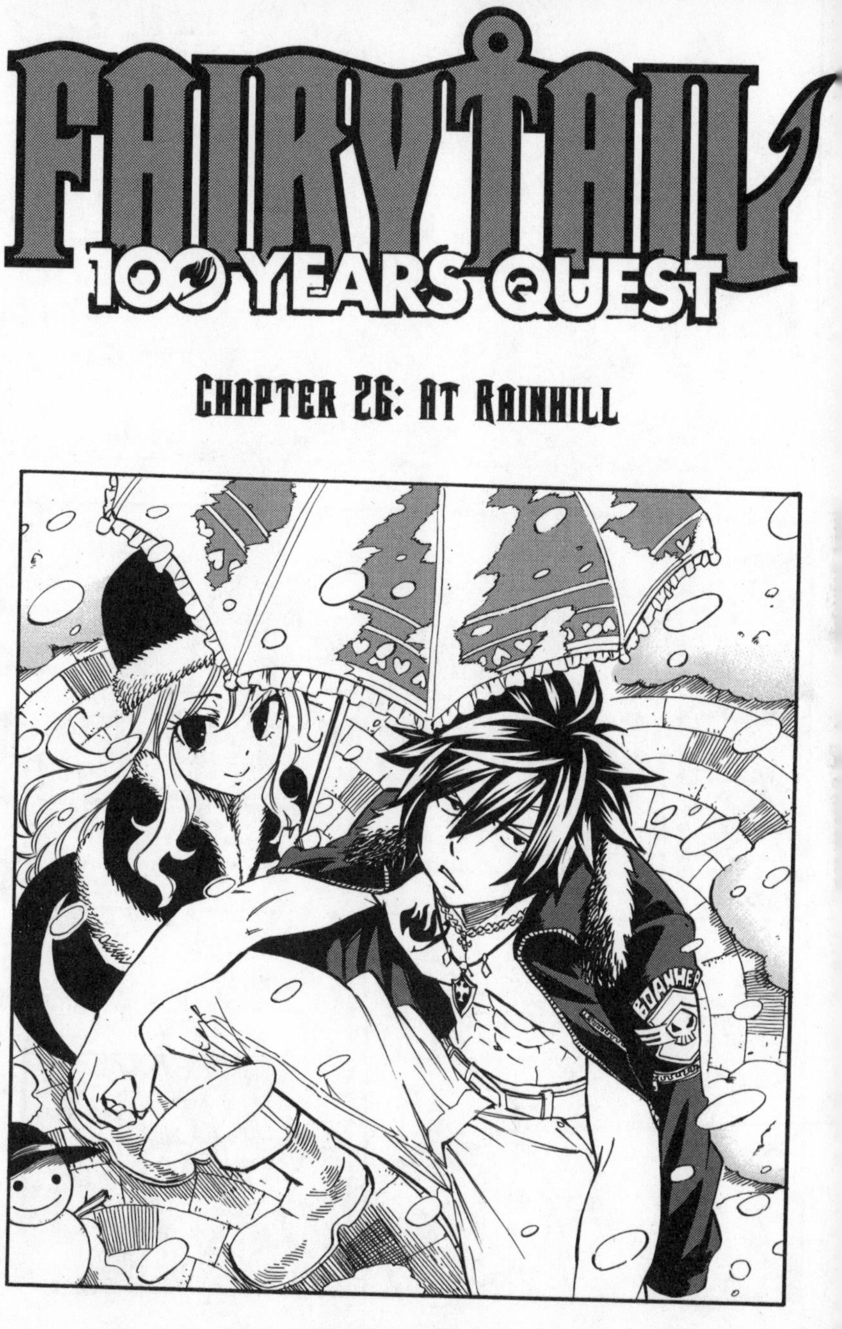

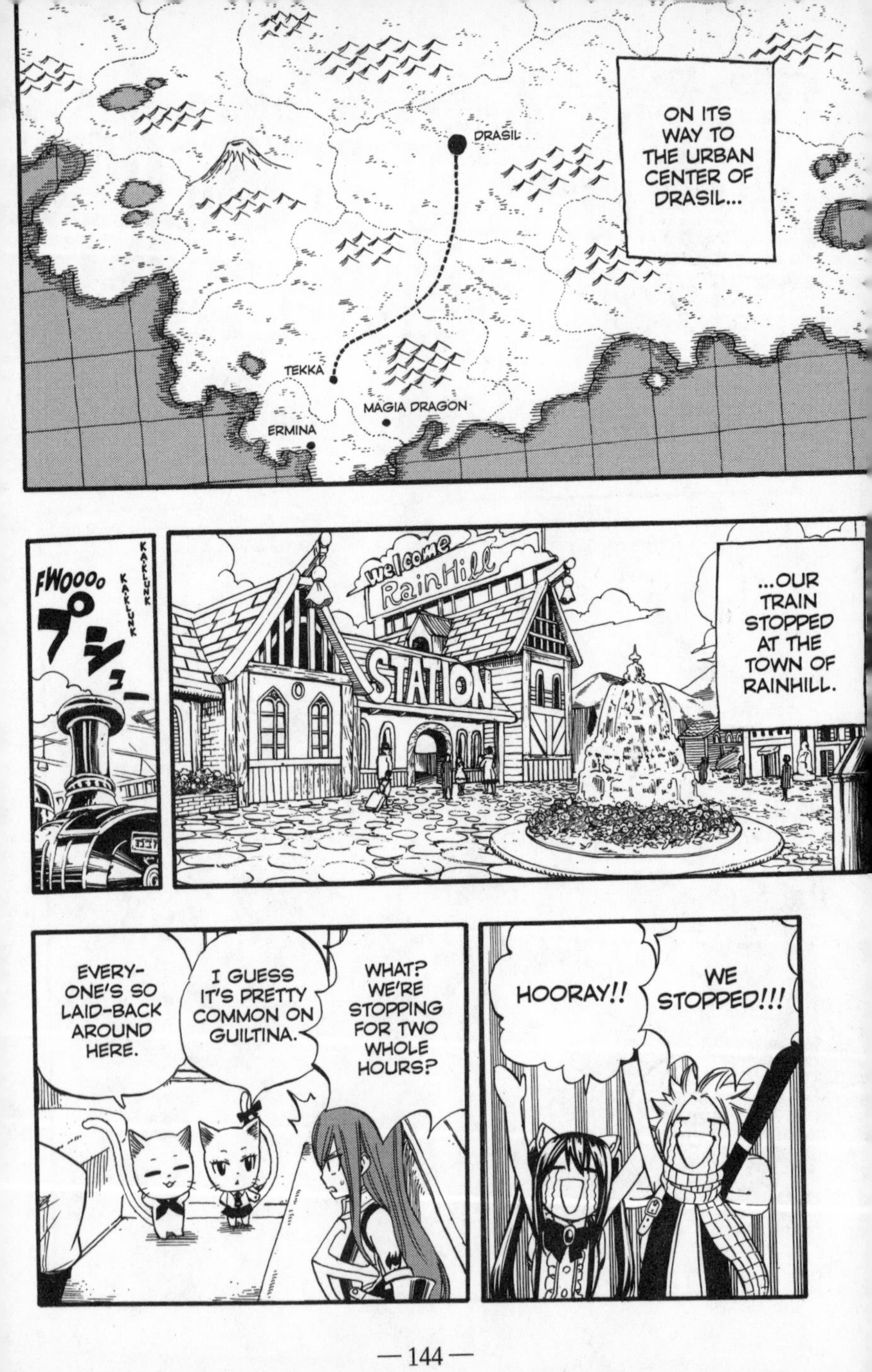
ON ITS WAY TO THE URBAN CENTER OF DRASIL...
DRASIL
TEKKA
MAGIA DRAGON
ERMINA
welcome RainHill
STATION
...OUR TRAIN STOPPED AT THE TOWN OF RAINHILL.
KAKLUNK KAKLUNK
FWOOOO
プシュー
WE STOPPED!!!
HOORAY!!
WHAT? WE'RE STOPPING FOR TWO WHOLE HOURS?
I GUESS IT'S PRETTY COMMON ON GUILTINA.
EVERY-ONE'S SO LAID-BACK AROUND HERE.

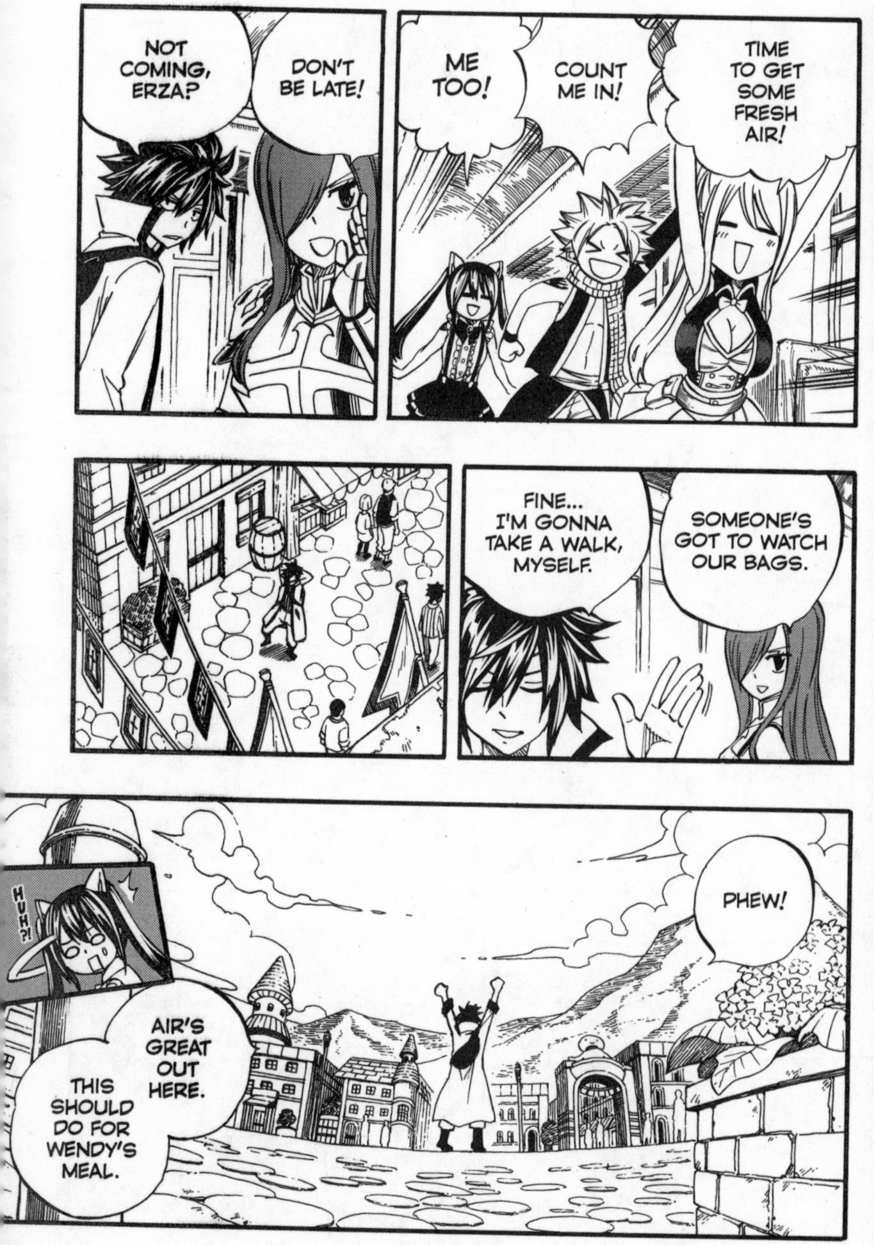
TIME TO GET SOME FRESH AIR!
COUNT ME IN!
ME TOO!
DON'T BE LATE!
NOT COMING, ERZA?
SOMEONE'S GOT TO WATCH OUR BAGS.
FINE... I'M GONNA TAKE A WALK, MYSELF.
PHEW!
AIR'S GREAT OUT HERE.
THIS SHOULD DO FOR WENDY'S MEAL.
HUH?!

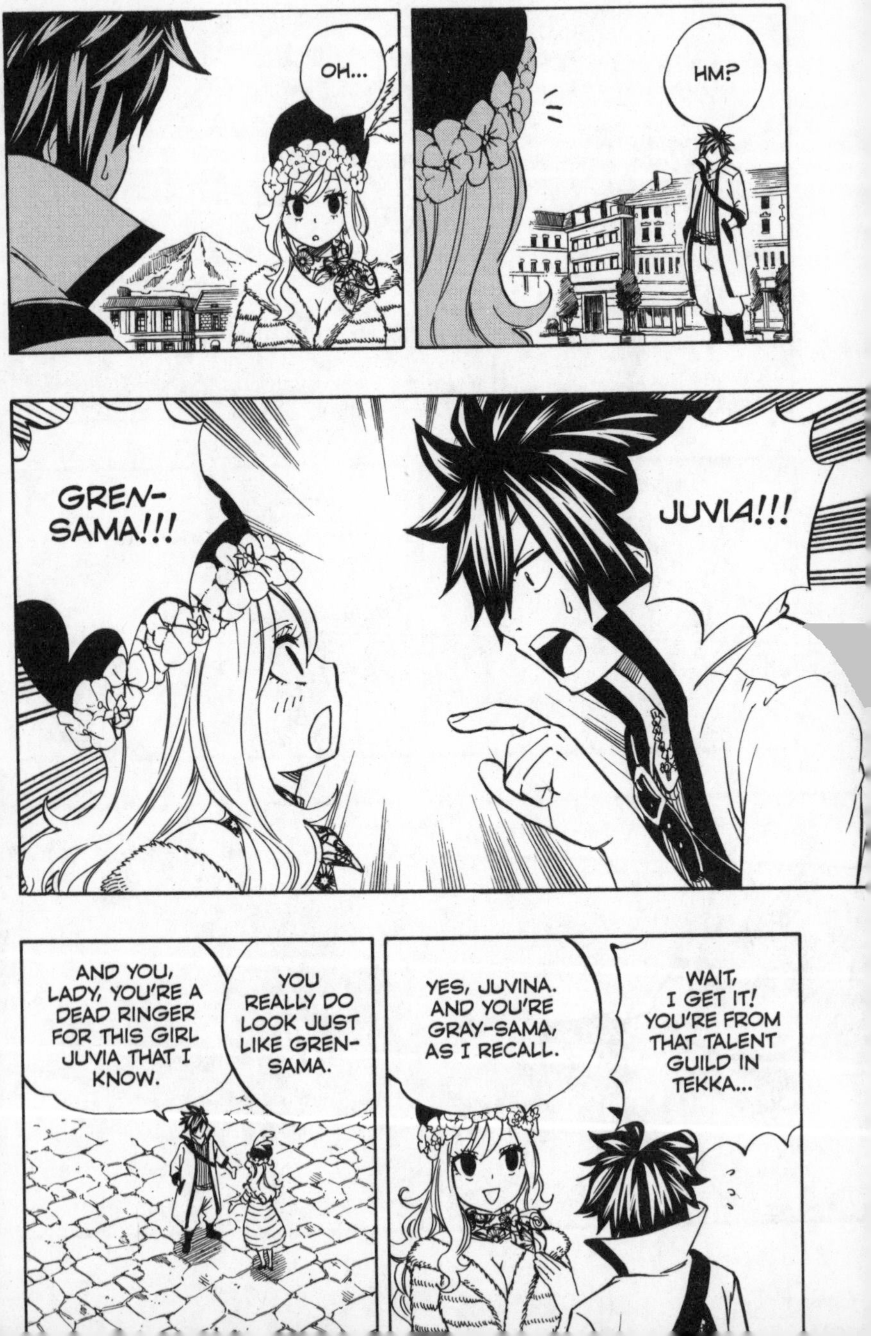
HM?
OH...
JUVIA!!!
GREN-SAMA!!!
WAIT, I GET IT! YOU'RE FROM THAT TALENT GUILD IN TEKKA...
YES, JUVINA. AND YOU'RE GRAY-SAMA, AS I RECALL.
YOU REALLY DO LOOK JUST LIKE GREN-SAMA.
AND YOU, LADY, YOU'RE A DEAD RINGER FOR THIS GIRL JUVIA THAT I KNOW.

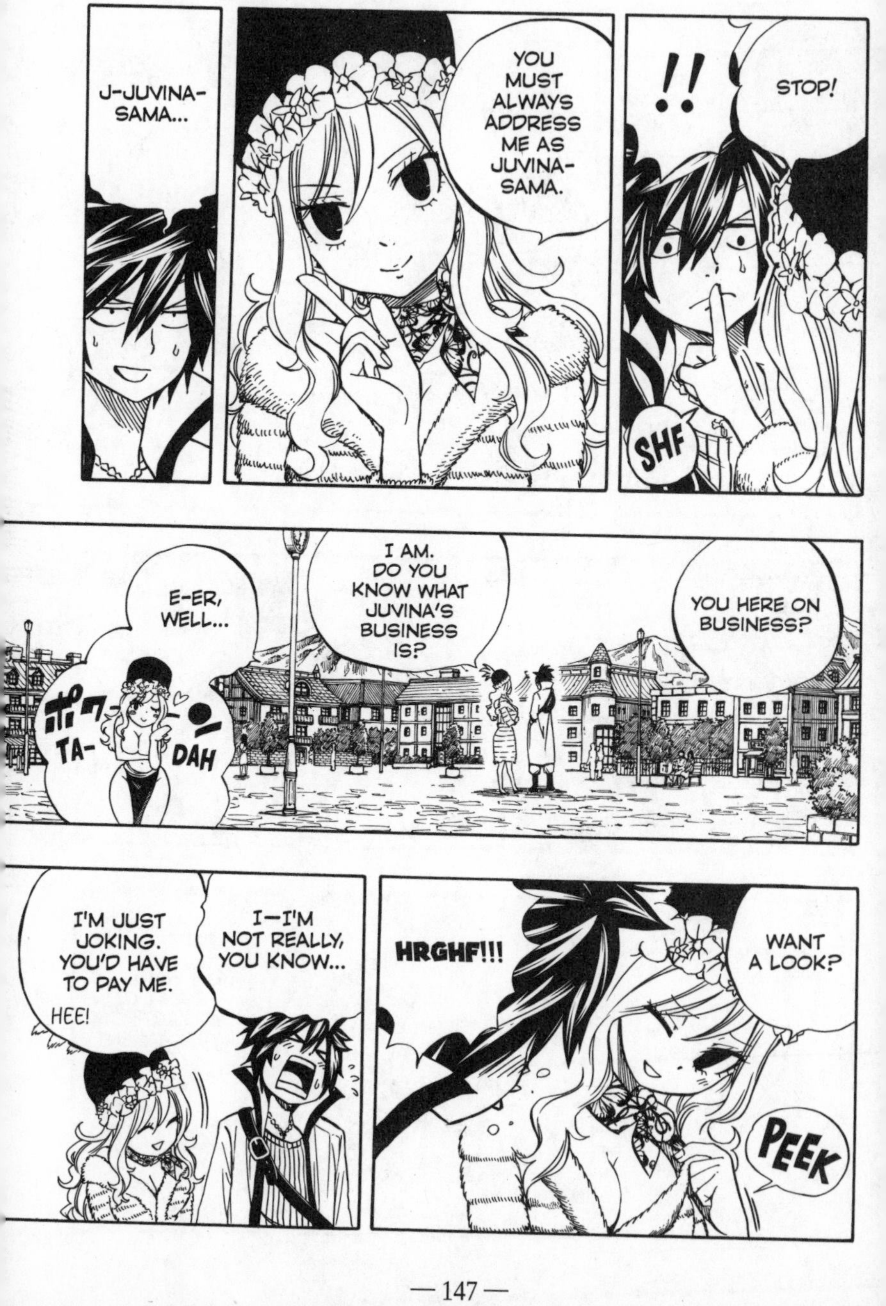
STOP!
!!
SHF
YOU MUST ALWAYS ADDRESS ME AS JUVINA-SAMA.
J-JUVINA-SAMA...
YOU HERE ON BUSINESS?
I AM. DO YOU KNOW WHAT JUVINA'S BUSINESS IS?
E-ER, WELL...
TA-DAH
WANT A LOOK?
HRGHF!!!
PEEK
I—I'M NOT REALLY, YOU KNOW...
I'M JUST JOKING. YOU'D HAVE TO PAY ME.
HEE!

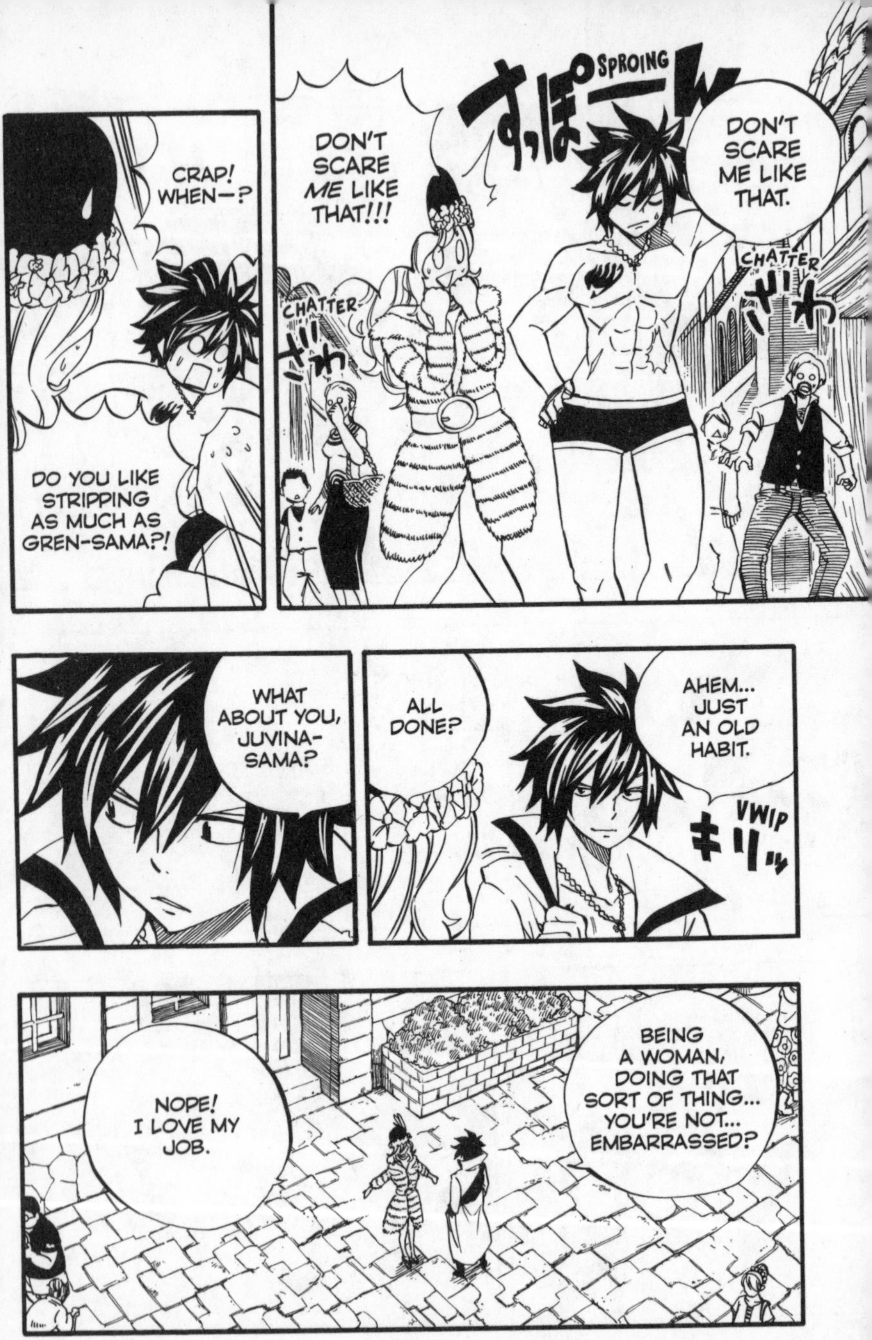
すっぽーん
SPROING
DON'T SCARE ME LIKE THAT.
CHATTER
ざわ
DON'T SCARE ME LIKE THAT!!!
CHATTER
ざわ
CRAP! WHEN—?
DO YOU LIKE STRIPPING AS MUCH AS GREN-SAMA?!
AHEM... JUST AN OLD HABIT.
キリッ
VWIP
ALL DONE?
WHAT ABOUT YOU, JUVINA-SAMA?
BEING A WOMAN, DOING THAT SORT OF THING... YOU'RE NOT... EMBARRASSED?
NOPE! I LOVE MY JOB.

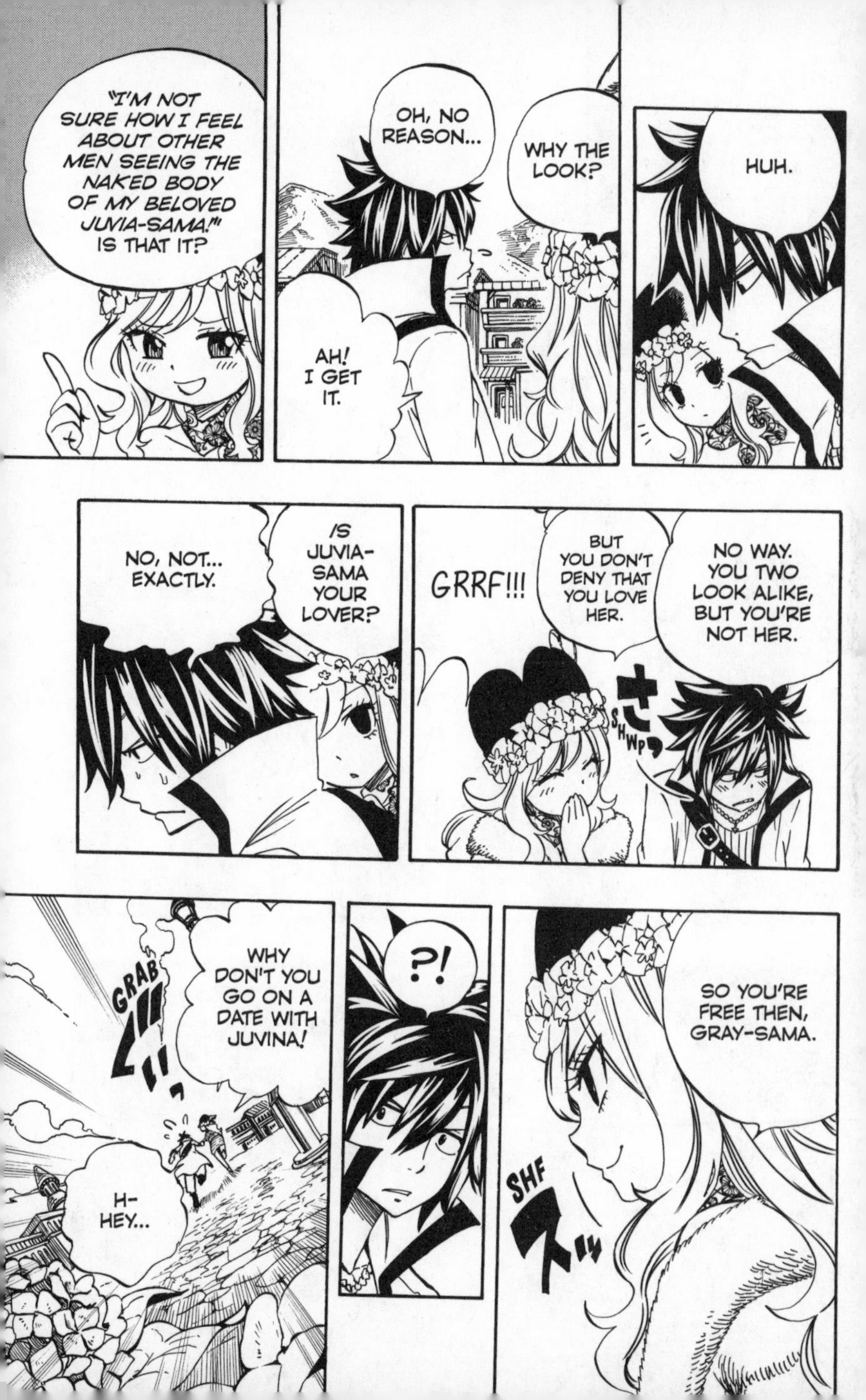
HUH.
WHY THE LOOK?
OH, NO REASON...
AH! I GET IT.
"I'M NOT SURE HOW I FEEL ABOUT OTHER MEN SEEING THE NAKED BODY OF MY BELOVED JUVIA-SAMA!" IS THAT IT?
NO WAY. YOU TWO LOOK ALIKE, BUT YOU'RE NOT HER.
BUT YOU DON'T DENY THAT YOU LOVE HER.
SHWP
GRRF!!!
IS JUVIA-SAMA YOUR LOVER?
NO, NOT... EXACTLY.
SO YOU'RE FREE THEN, GRAY-SAMA.
SHF
?!
WHY DON'T YOU GO ON A DATE WITH JUVINA!
GRAB
H-HEY...

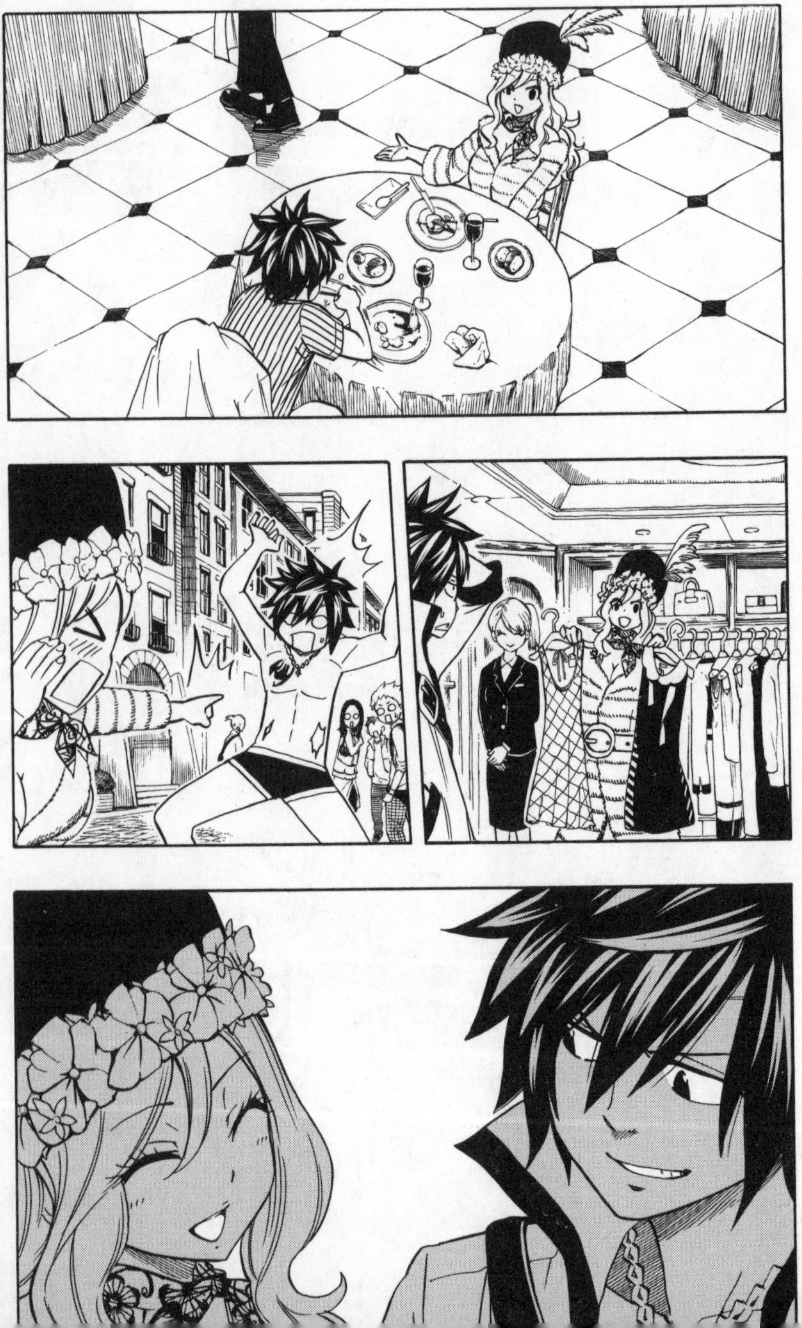

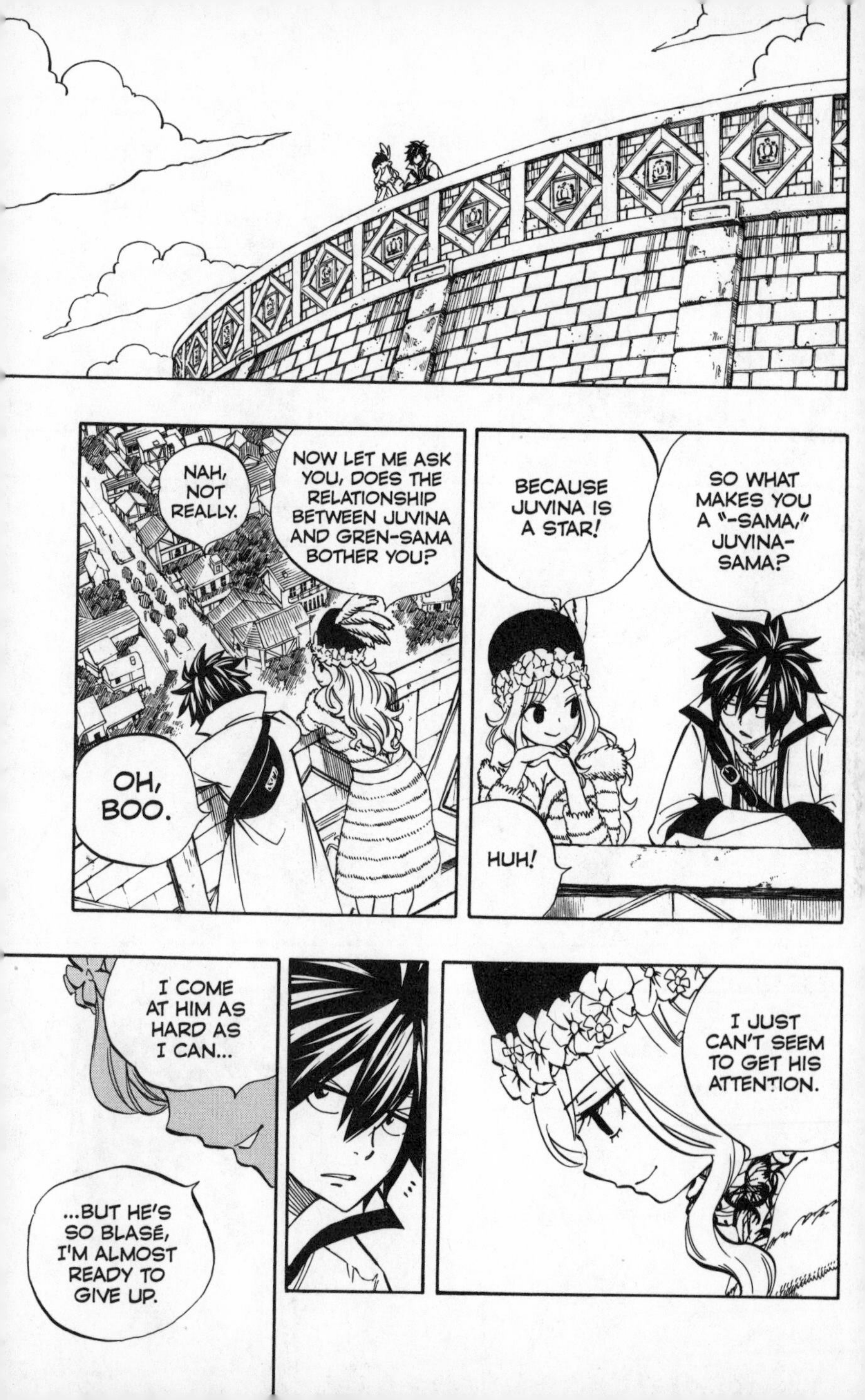
SO WHAT MAKES YOU A "-SAMA," JUVINA-SAMA?
BECAUSE JUVINA IS A STAR!
HUH!
NOW LET ME ASK YOU, DOES THE RELATIONSHIP BETWEEN JUVINA AND GREN-SAMA BOTHER YOU?
NAH, NOT REALLY.
OH, BOO.
I JUST CAN'T SEEM TO GET HIS ATTENTION.
I COME AT HIM AS HARD AS I CAN...
...BUT HE'S SO BLASÉ, I'M ALMOST READY TO GIVE UP.

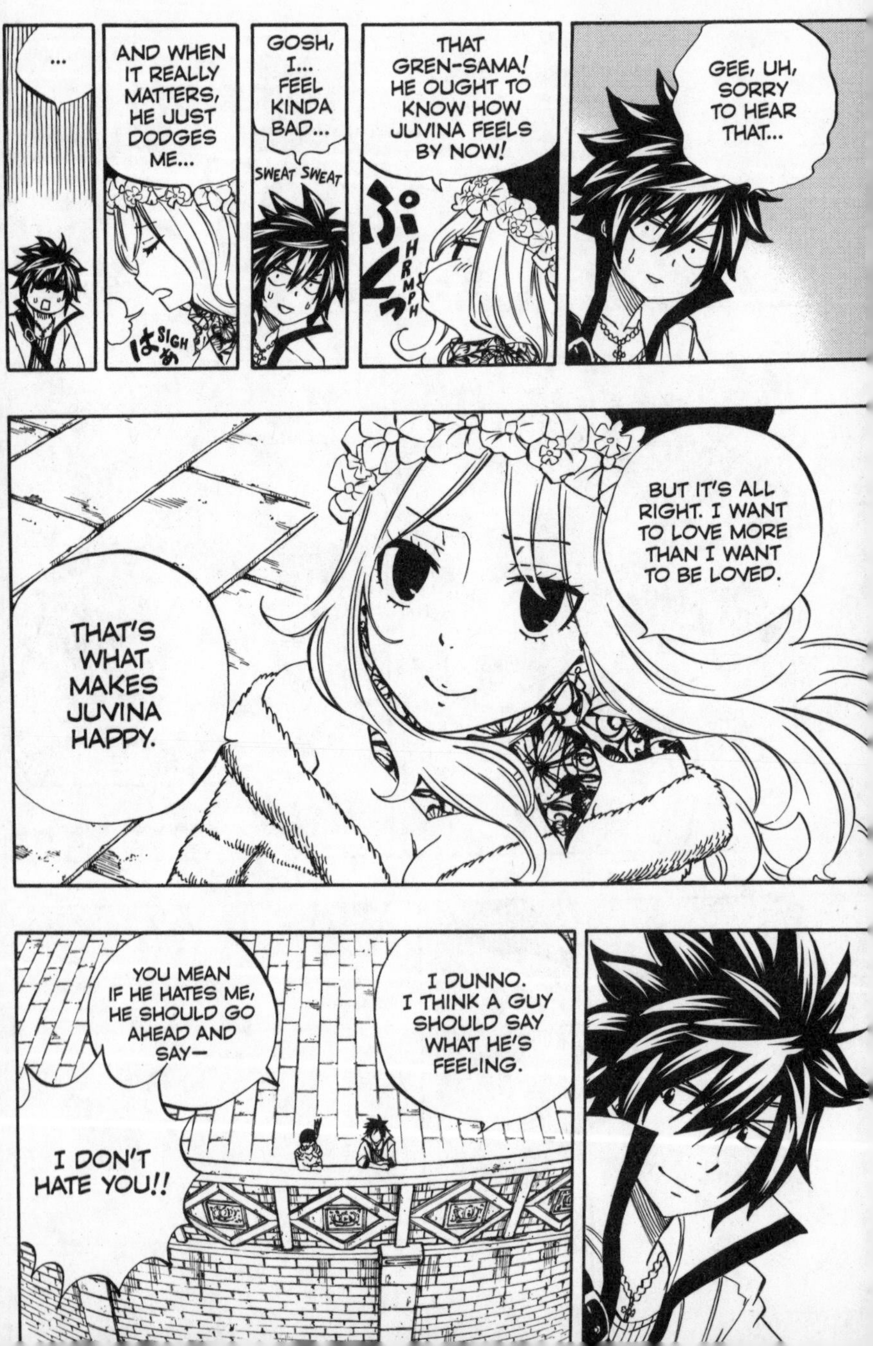
GEE, UH, SORRY TO HEAR THAT...
THAT GREN-SAMA! HE OUGHT TO KNOW HOW JUVINA FEELS BY NOW!
ぷくっ
HRMPH
GOSH, I... FEEL KINDA BAD...
SWEAT SWEAT
AND WHEN IT REALLY MATTERS, HE JUST DODGES ME...
はぁ
SIGH
...
BUT IT'S ALL RIGHT. I WANT TO LOVE MORE THAN I WANT TO BE LOVED.
THAT'S WHAT MAKES JUVINA HAPPY.
I DUNNO. I THINK A GUY SHOULD SAY WHAT HE'S FEELING.
YOU MEAN IF HE HATES ME, HE SHOULD GO AHEAD AND SAY—
I DON'T HATE YOU!!

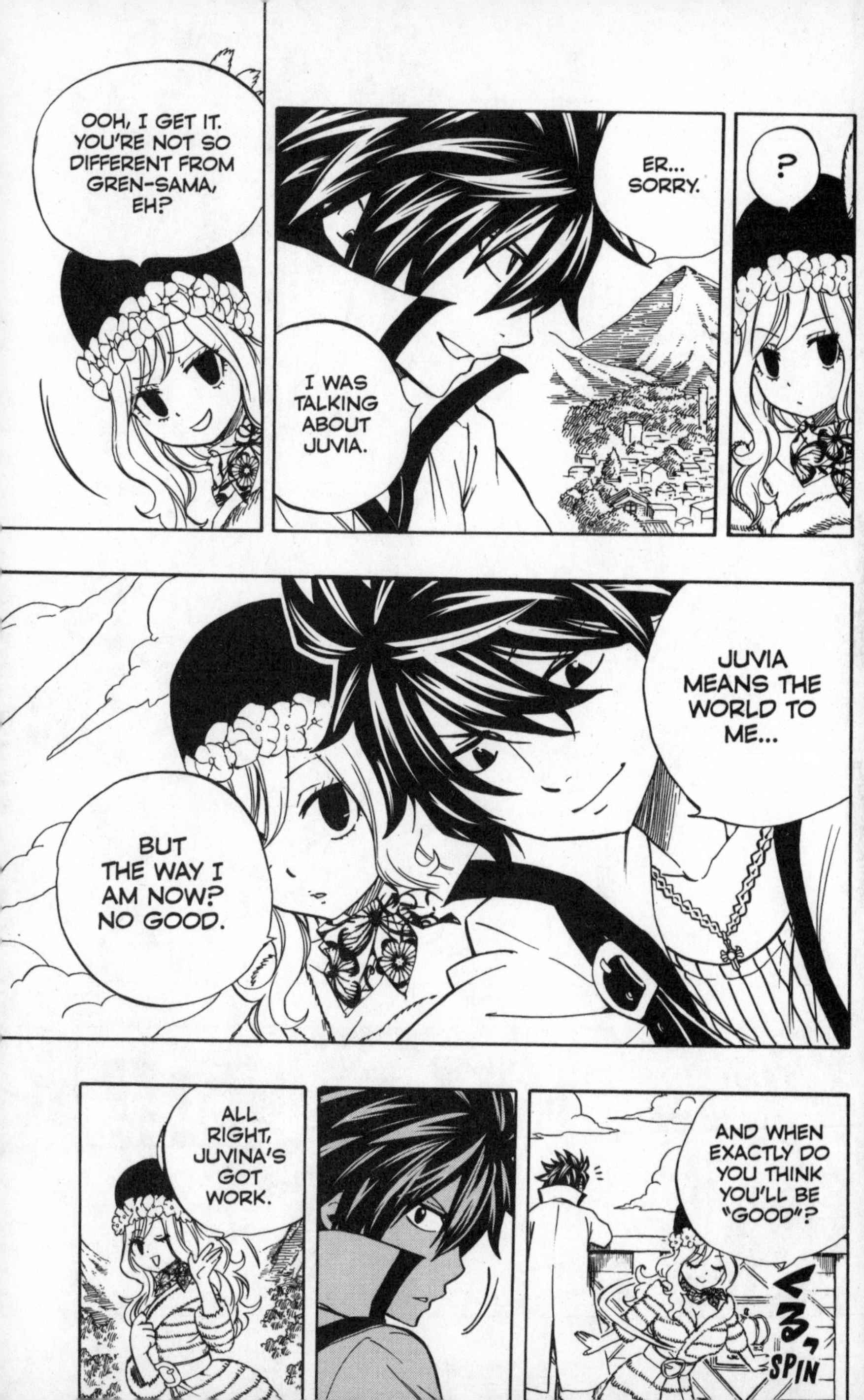
?
ER... SORRY.
I WAS TALKING ABOUT JUVIA.
OOH, I GET IT. YOU'RE NOT SO DIFFERENT FROM GREN-SAMA, EH?
JUVIA MEANS THE WORLD TO ME...
BUT THE WAY I AM NOW? NO GOOD.
AND WHEN EXACTLY DO YOU THINK YOU'LL BE "GOOD"?
くる
SPIN
ALL RIGHT, JUVINA'S GOT WORK.

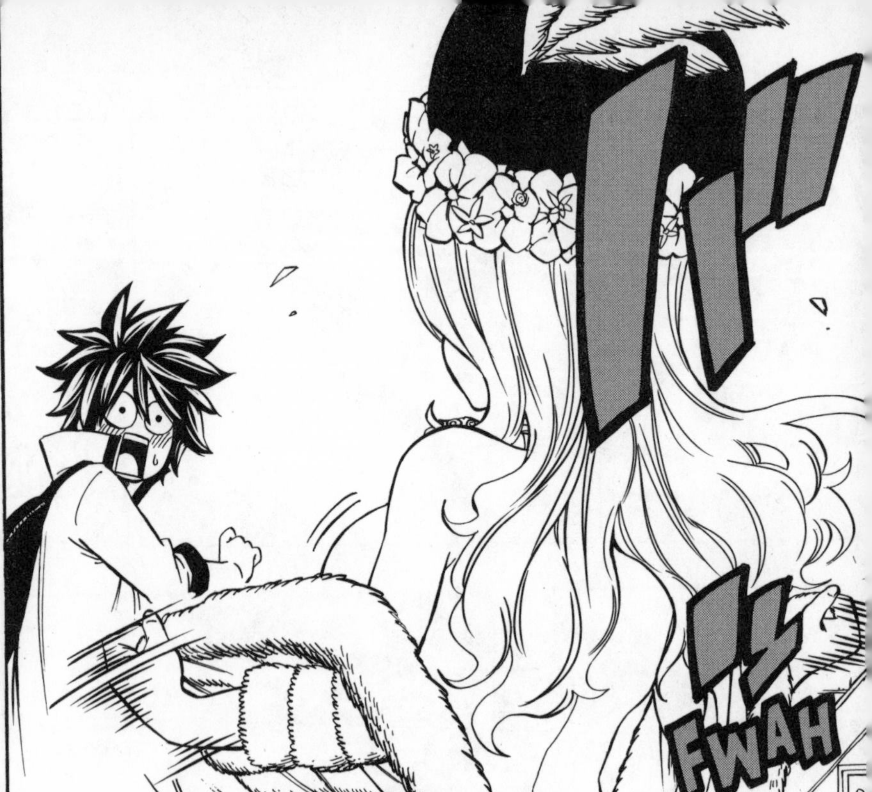
FWAH
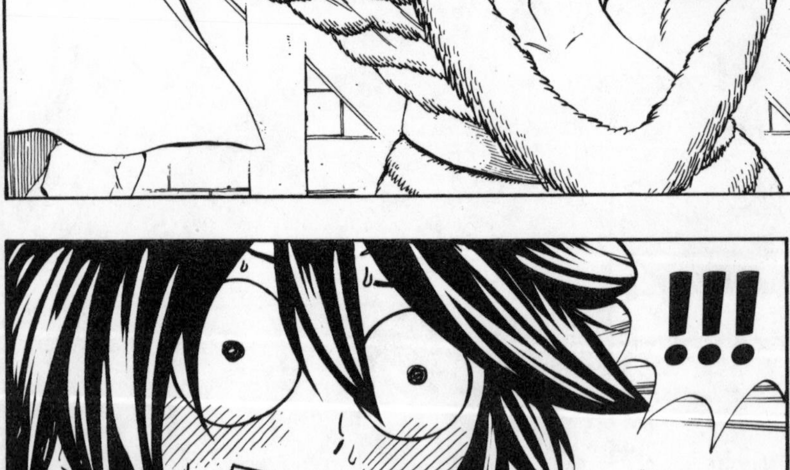
!!!

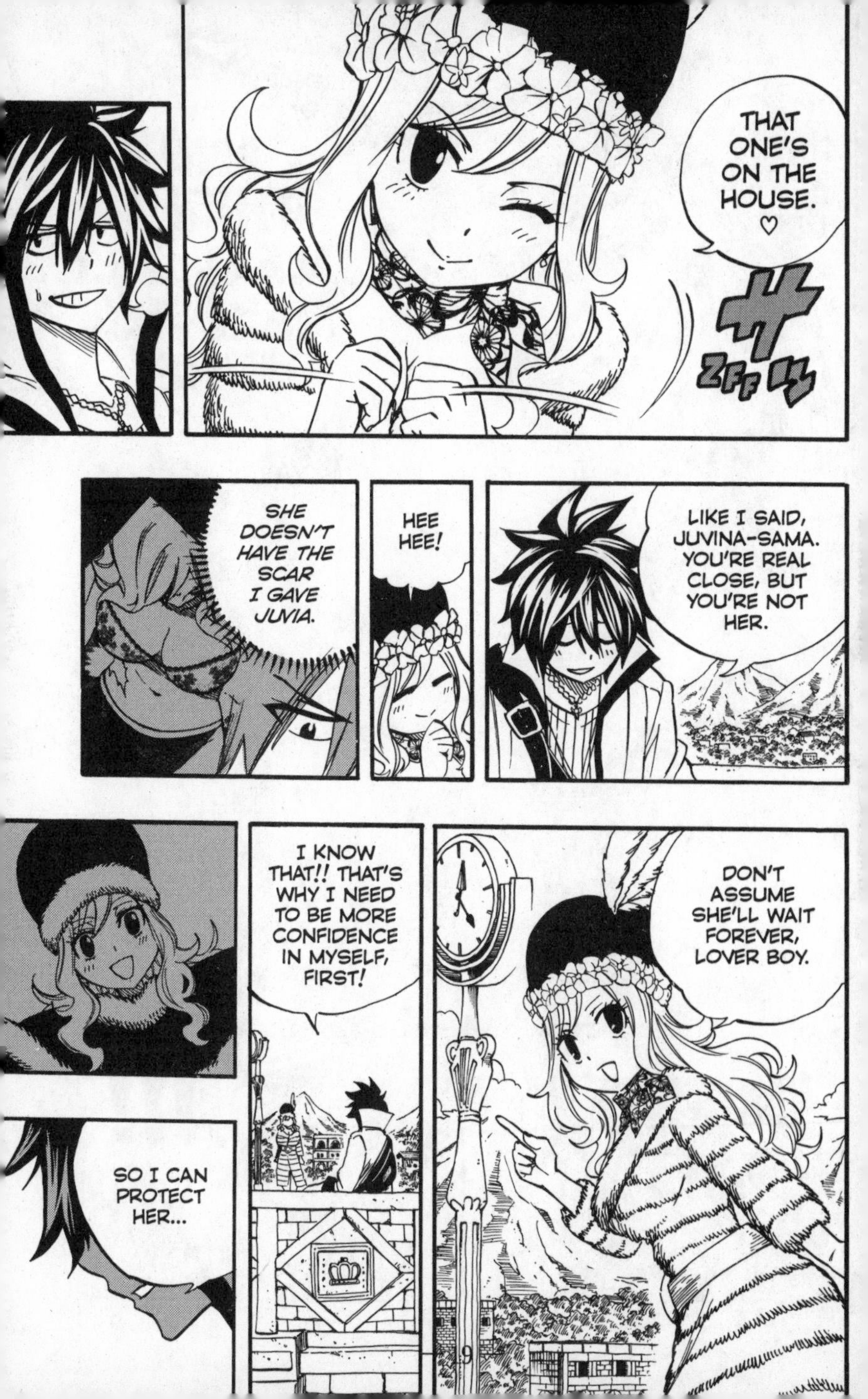
THAT ONE'S ON THE HOUSE. ♡
ZFF
LIKE I SAID, JUVINA-SAMA. YOU'RE REAL CLOSE, BUT YOU'RE NOT HER.
HEE HEE!
SHE DOESN'T HAVE THE SCAR I GAVE JUVIA.
DON'T ASSUME SHE'LL WAIT FOREVER, LOVER BOY.
I KNOW THAT!! THAT'S WHY I NEED TO BE MORE CONFIDENCE IN MYSELF, FIRST!
SO I CAN PROTECT HER...

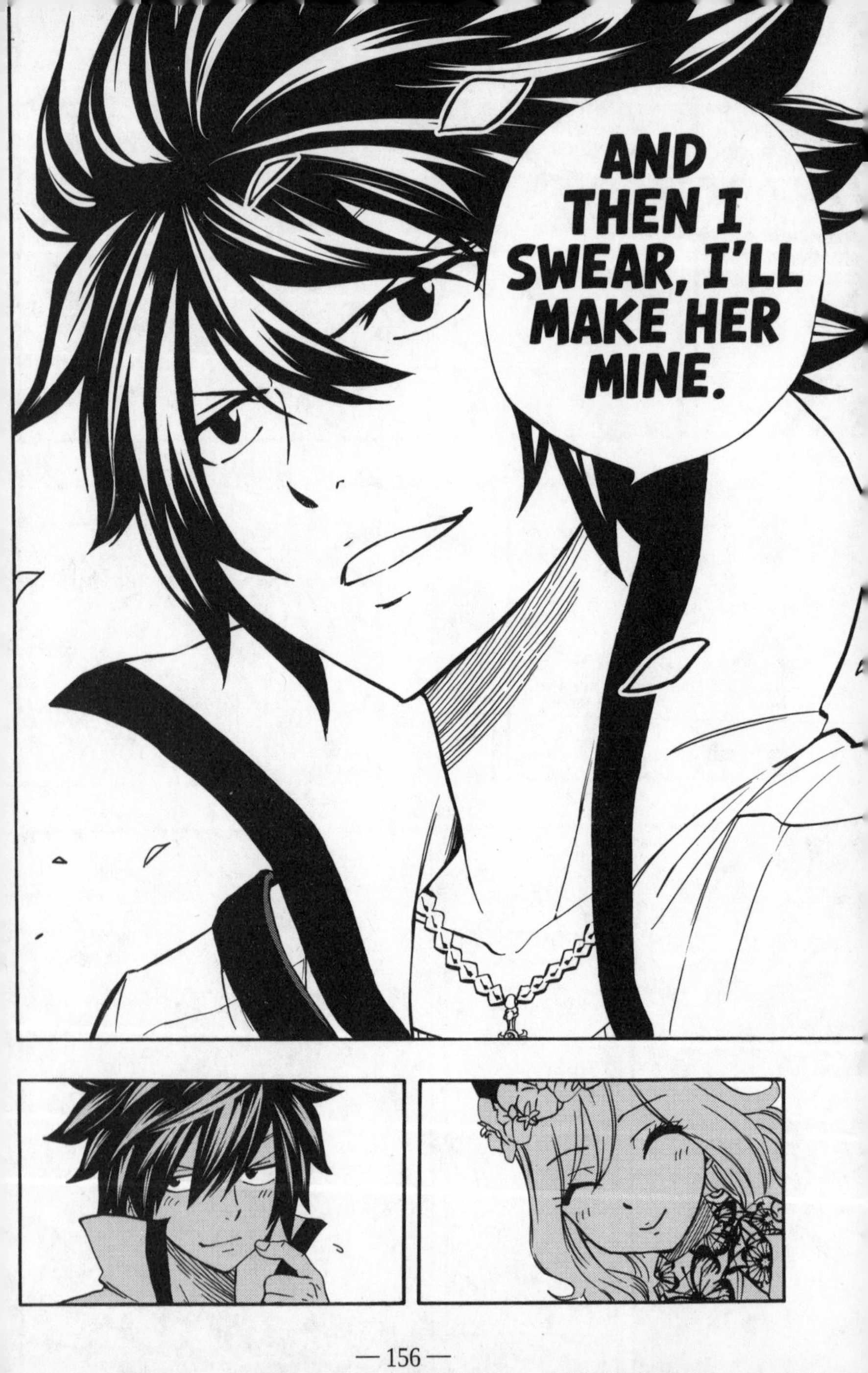
AND THEN I SWEAR, I'LL MAKE HER MINE.

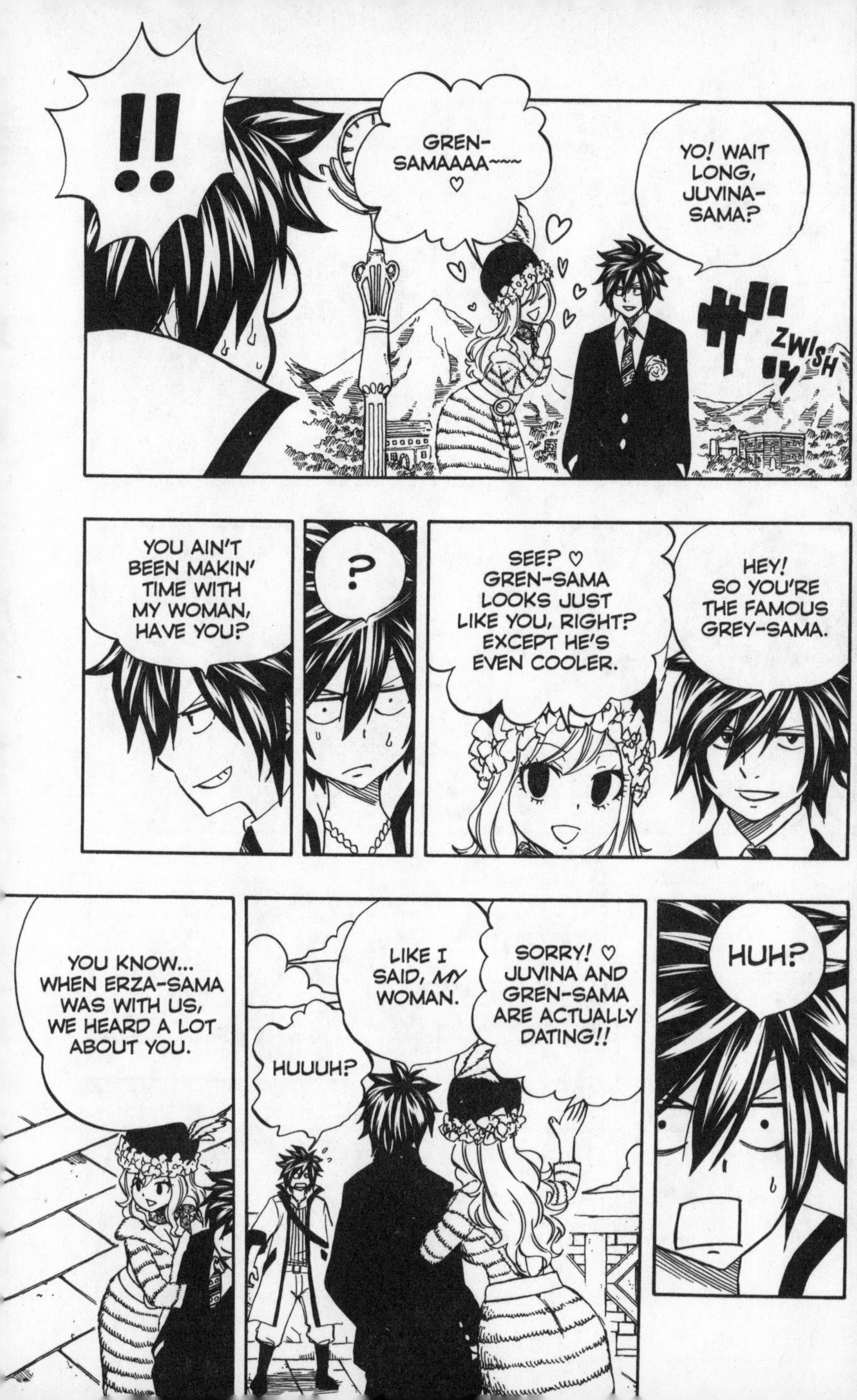
YO! WAIT LONG, JUVINA-SAMA?
ZWISH
GREN-SAMAAAA~~~ ♡
!!
HEY! SO YOU'RE THE FAMOUS GREY-SAMA.
SEE? ♡ GREN-SAMA LOOKS JUST LIKE YOU, RIGHT? EXCEPT HE'S EVEN COOLER.
?
YOU AIN'T BEEN MAKIN' TIME WITH MY WOMAN, HAVE YOU?
HUH?
SORRY! ♡ JUVINA AND GREN-SAMA ARE ACTUALLY DATING!!
LIKE I SAID, *MY* WOMAN.
HUUUH?
YOU KNOW... WHEN ERZA-SAMA WAS WITH US, WE HEARD A LOT ABOUT YOU.

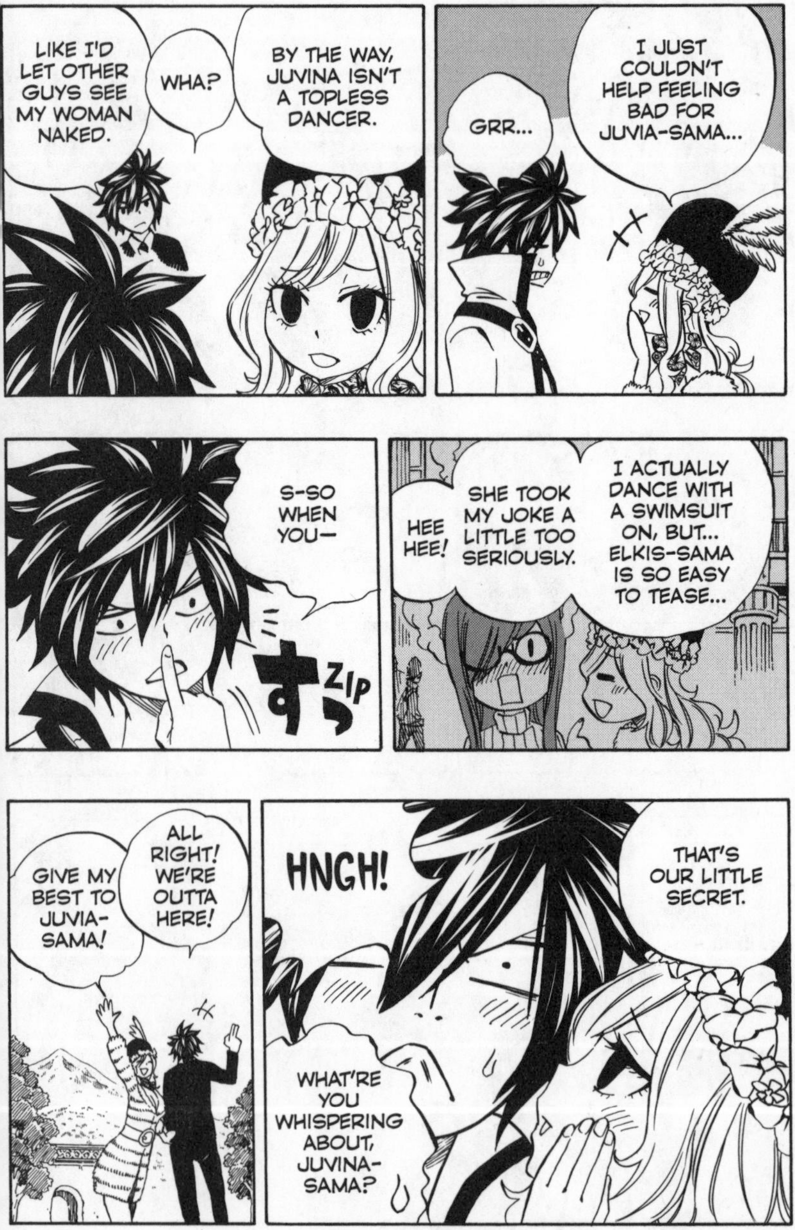
I JUST COULDN'T HELP FEELING BAD FOR JUVIA-SAMA...
GRR...
BY THE WAY, JUVINA ISN'T A TOPLESS DANCER.
WHA?
LIKE I'D LET OTHER GUYS SEE MY WOMAN NAKED.
I ACTUALLY DANCE WITH A SWIMSUIT ON, BUT... ELKIS-SAMA IS SO EASY TO TEASE...
SHE TOOK MY JOKE A LITTLE TOO SERIOUSLY.
HEE HEE!
S-SO WHEN YOU—
ZIP
THAT'S OUR LITTLE SECRET.
HNGH!
WHAT'RE YOU WHISPERING ABOUT, JUVINA-SAMA?
ALL RIGHT! WE'RE OUTTA HERE!
GIVE MY BEST TO JUVIA-SAMA!

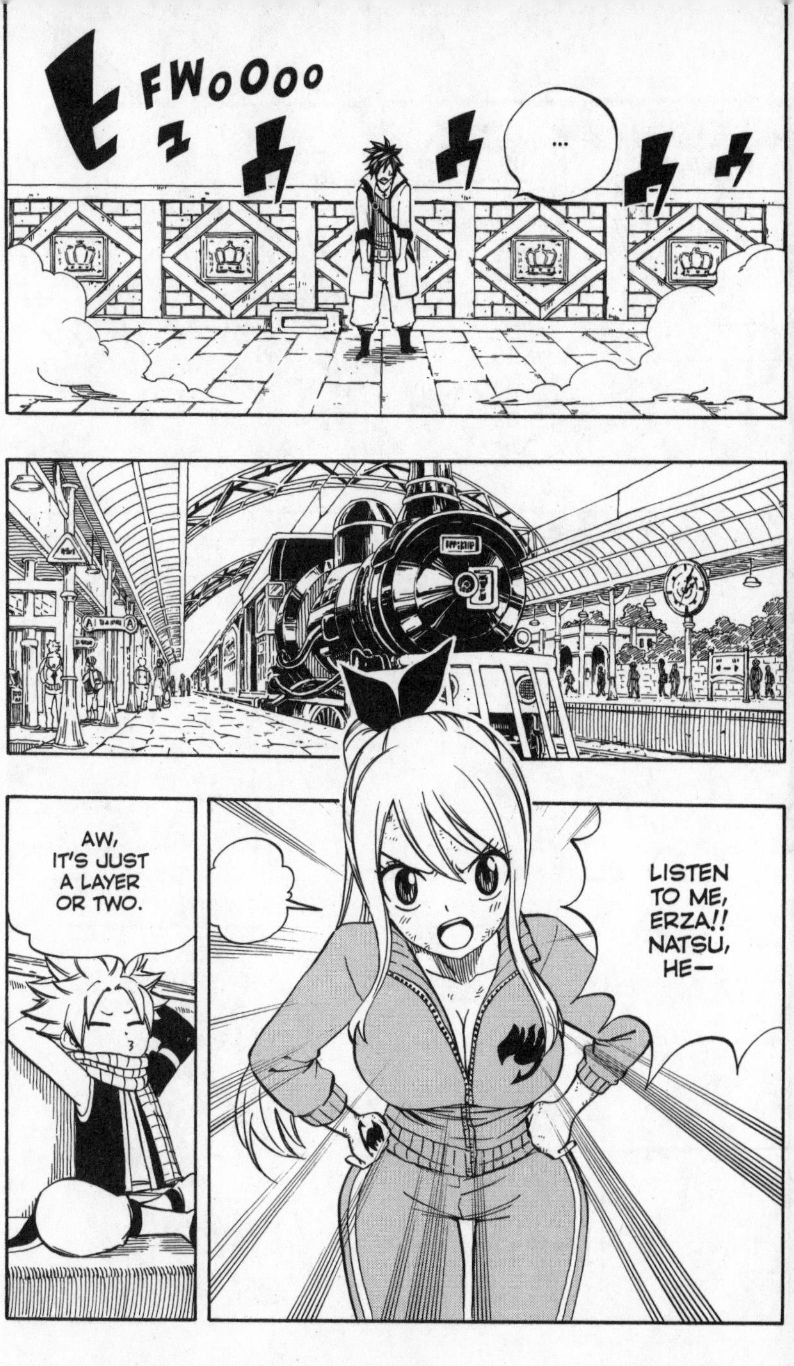
FWOOOO
...
LISTEN TO ME, ERZA!! NATSU, HE—
AW, IT'S JUST A LAYER OR TWO.

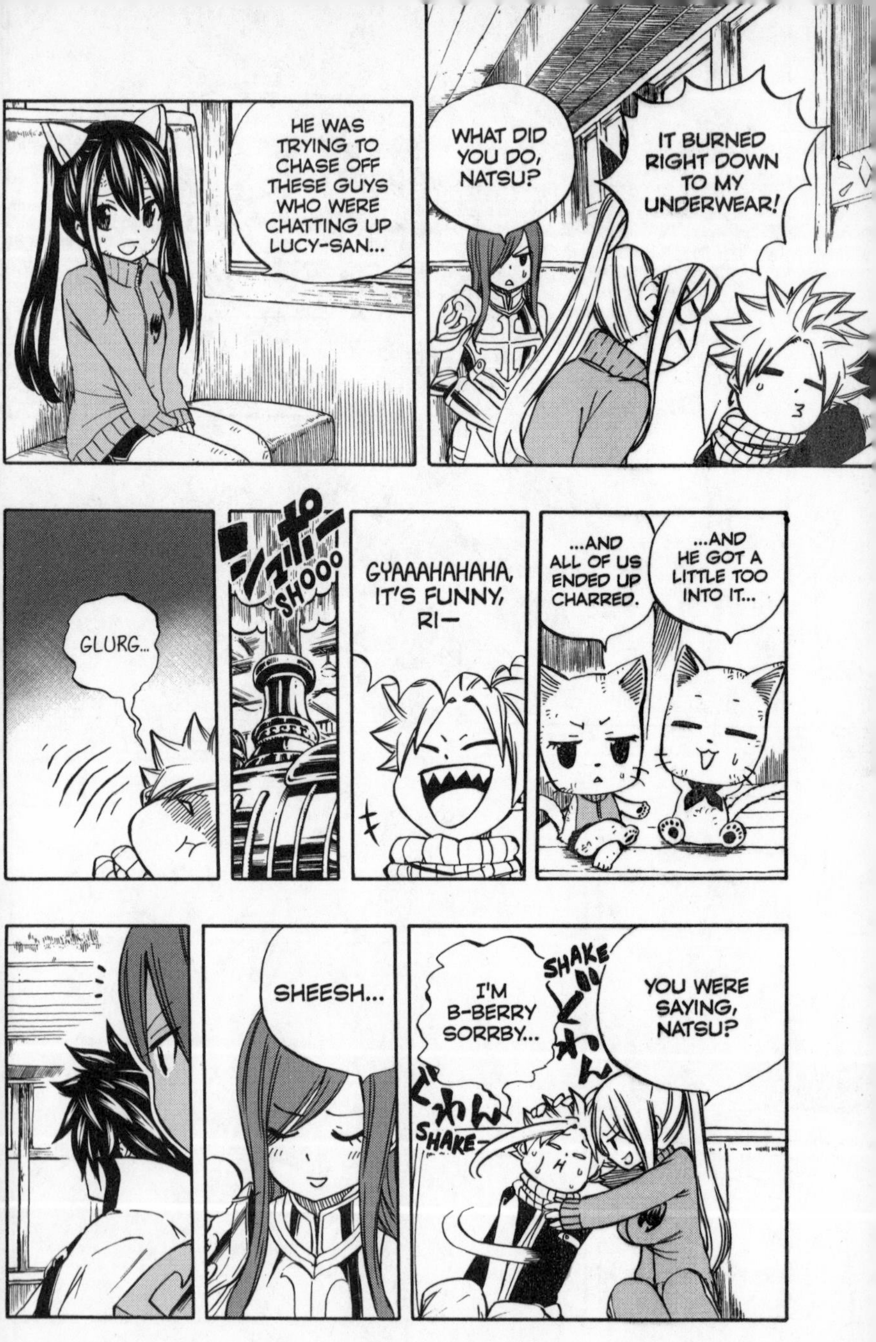
WHAT DID YOU DO, NATSU?
IT BURNED RIGHT DOWN TO MY UNDERWEAR!
HE WAS TRYING TO CHASE OFF THESE GUYS WHO WERE CHATTING UP LUCY-SAN...
...AND HE GOT A LITTLE TOO INTO IT...
...AND ALL OF US ENDED UP CHARRED.
GYAAAHAHAHA, IT'S FUNNY, RI—
SHOOO
GLURG...
YOU WERE SAYING, NATSU?
SHAKE
I'M B-BERRY SORRBY...
SHAKE—
SHEESH...

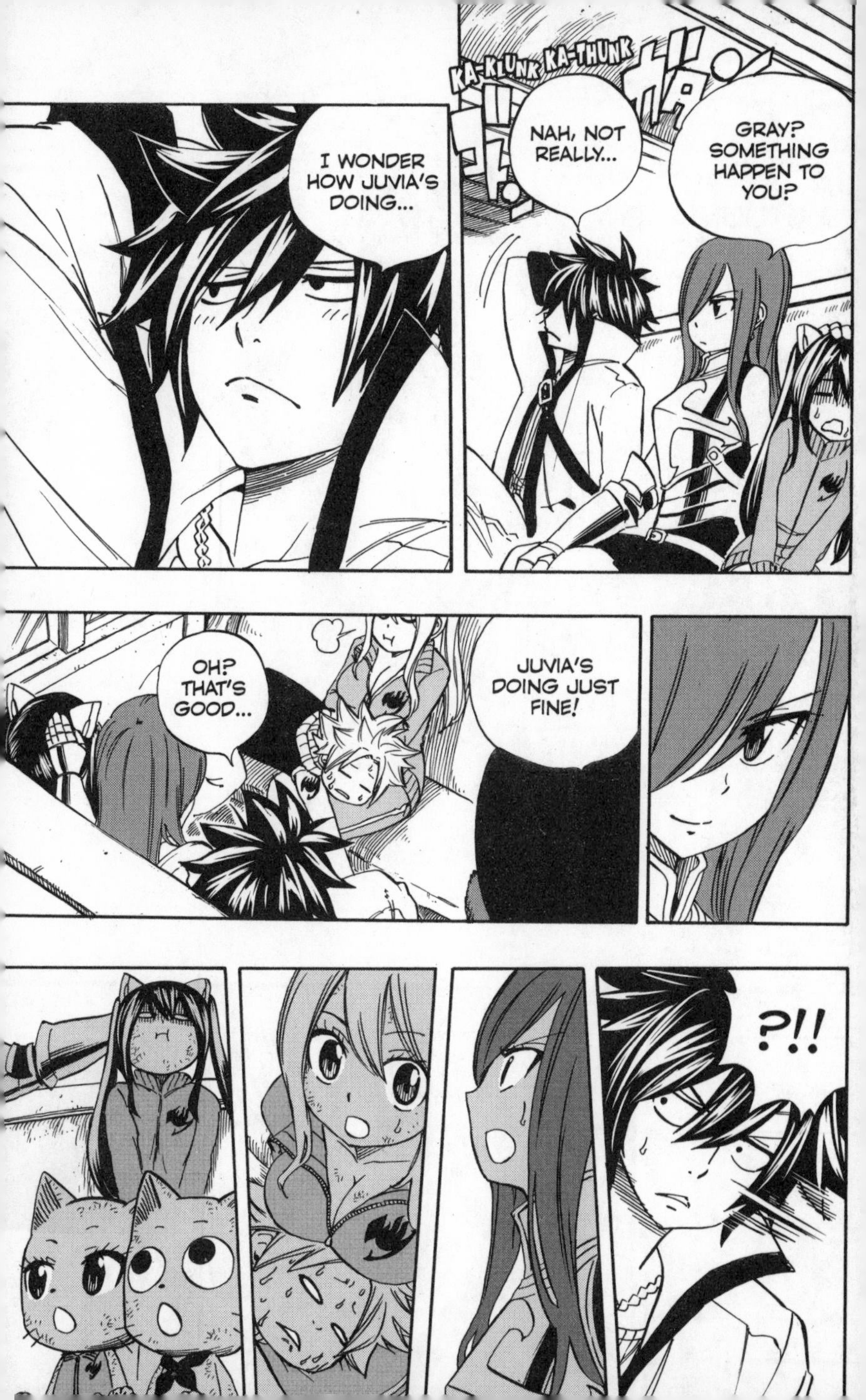
KA-KLUNK KA-THUNK
GRAY? SOMETHING HAPPEN TO YOU?
NAH, NOT REALLY...
I WONDER HOW JUVIA'S DOING...
JUVIA'S DOING JUST FINE!
OH? THAT'S GOOD...
?!!

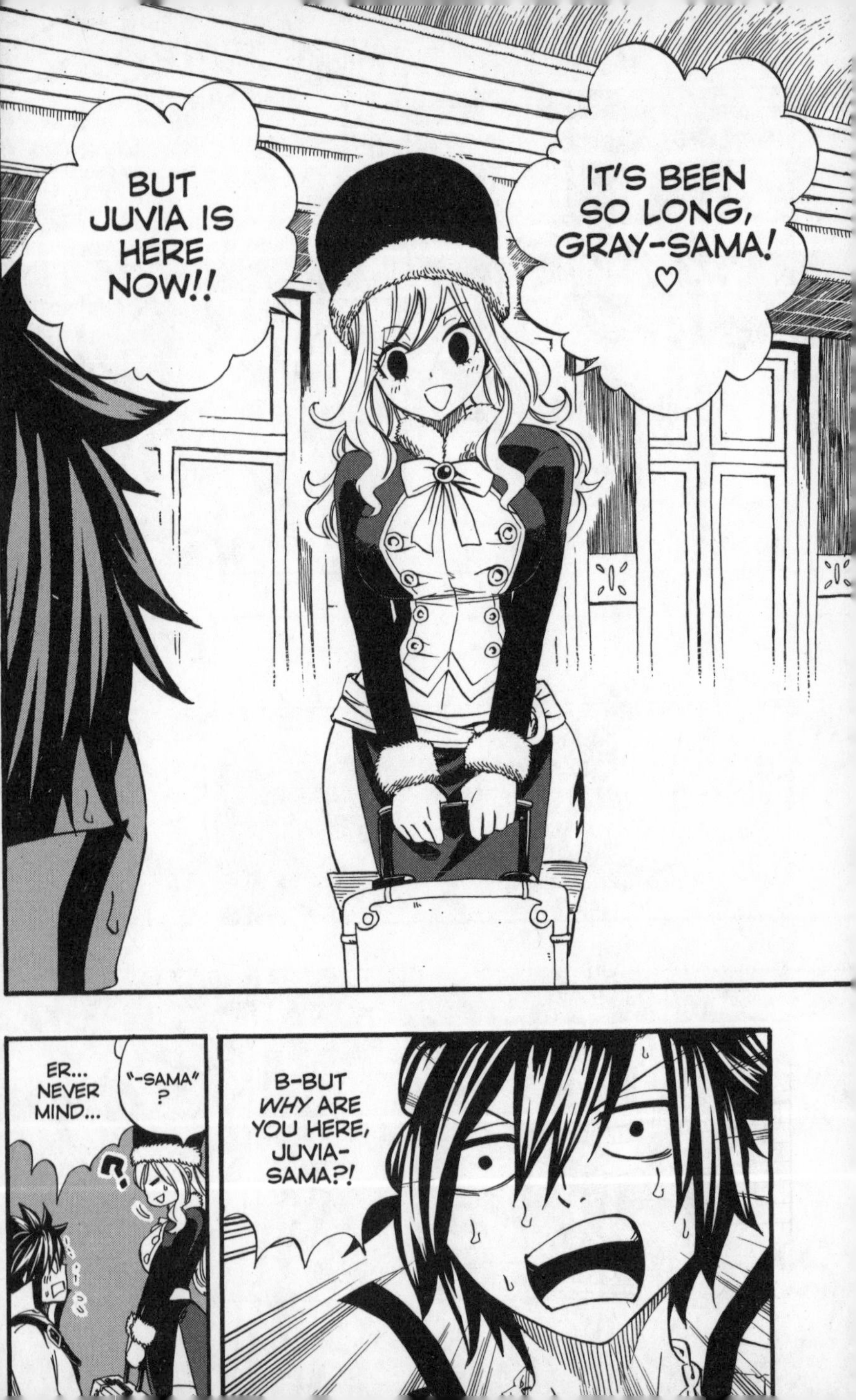
IT'S BEEN SO LONG, GRAY-SAMA! ♡
BUT JUVIA IS HERE NOW!!
B-BUT *WHY* ARE YOU HERE, JUVIA-SAMA?!
"-SAMA" ?
ER... NEVER MIND...

FAIRY TAIL 100 YEARS QUEST

Chapter 27: Aldoron, Wood Dragon God

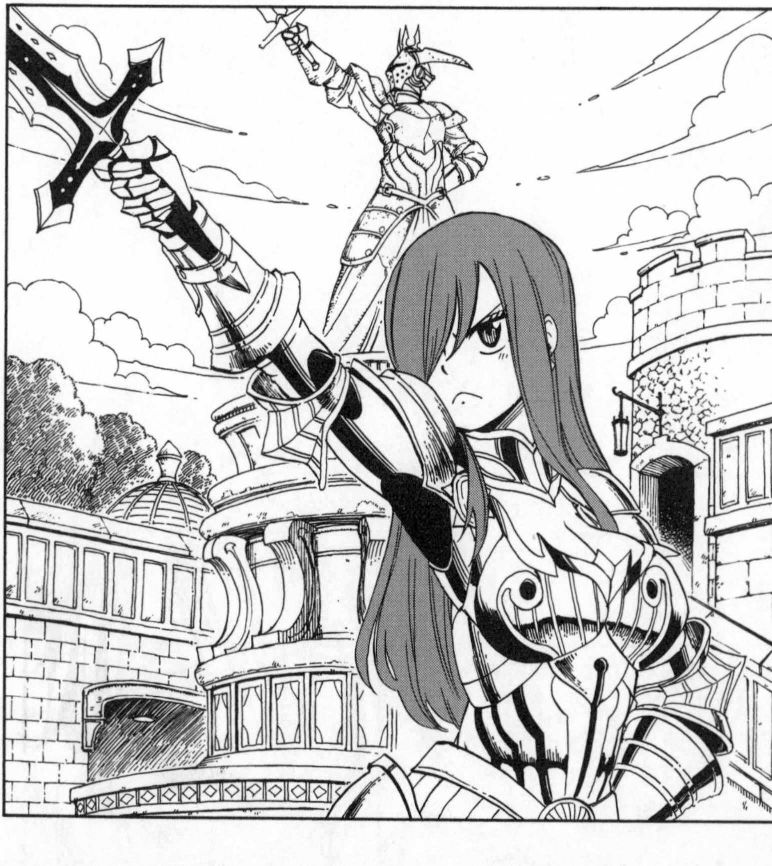

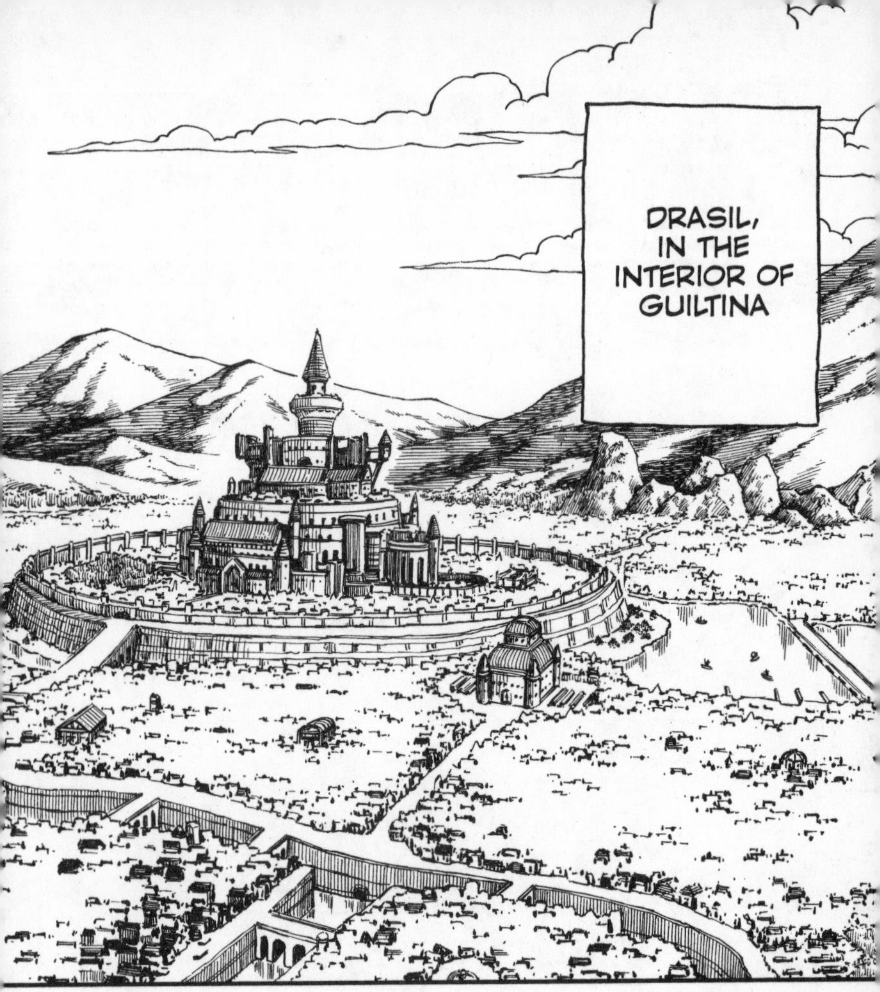
DRASIL, IN THE INTERIOR OF GUILTINA

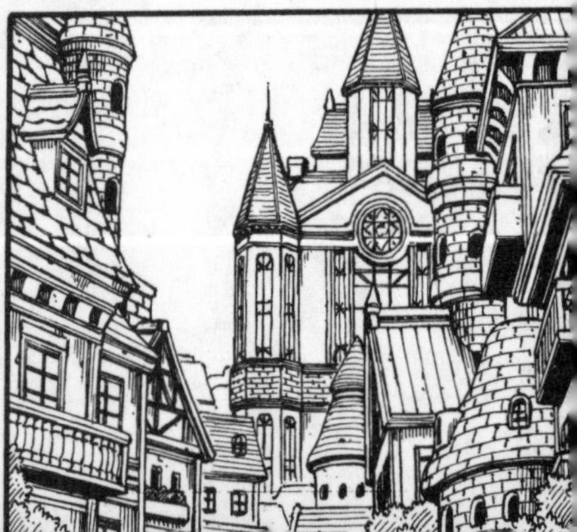

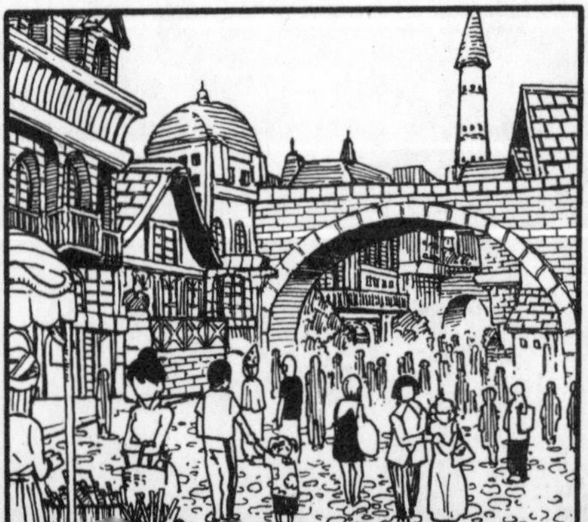

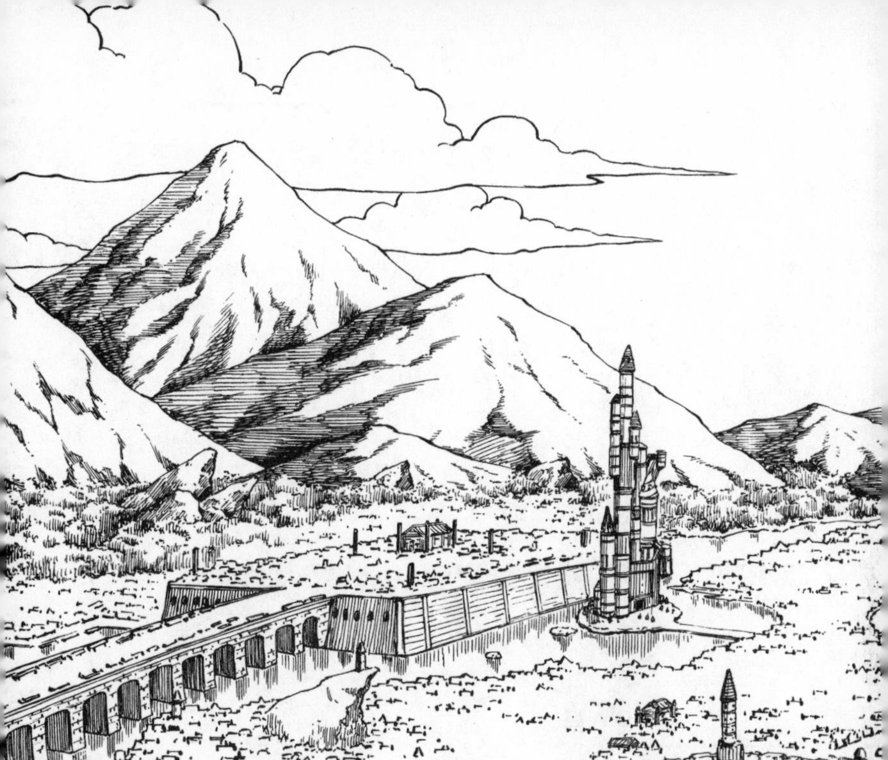

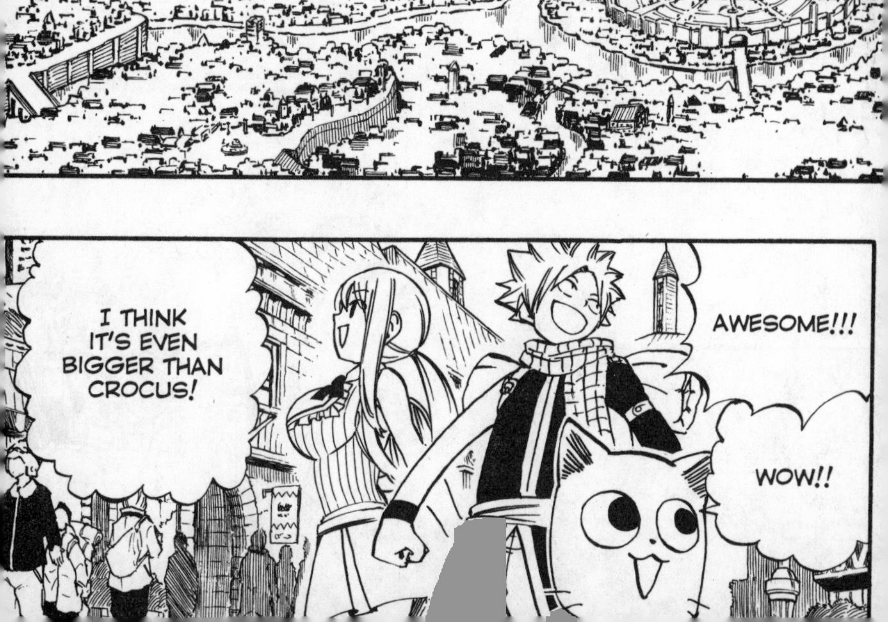
AWESOME!!!
WOW!!
I THINK IT'S EVEN BIGGER THAN CROCUS!

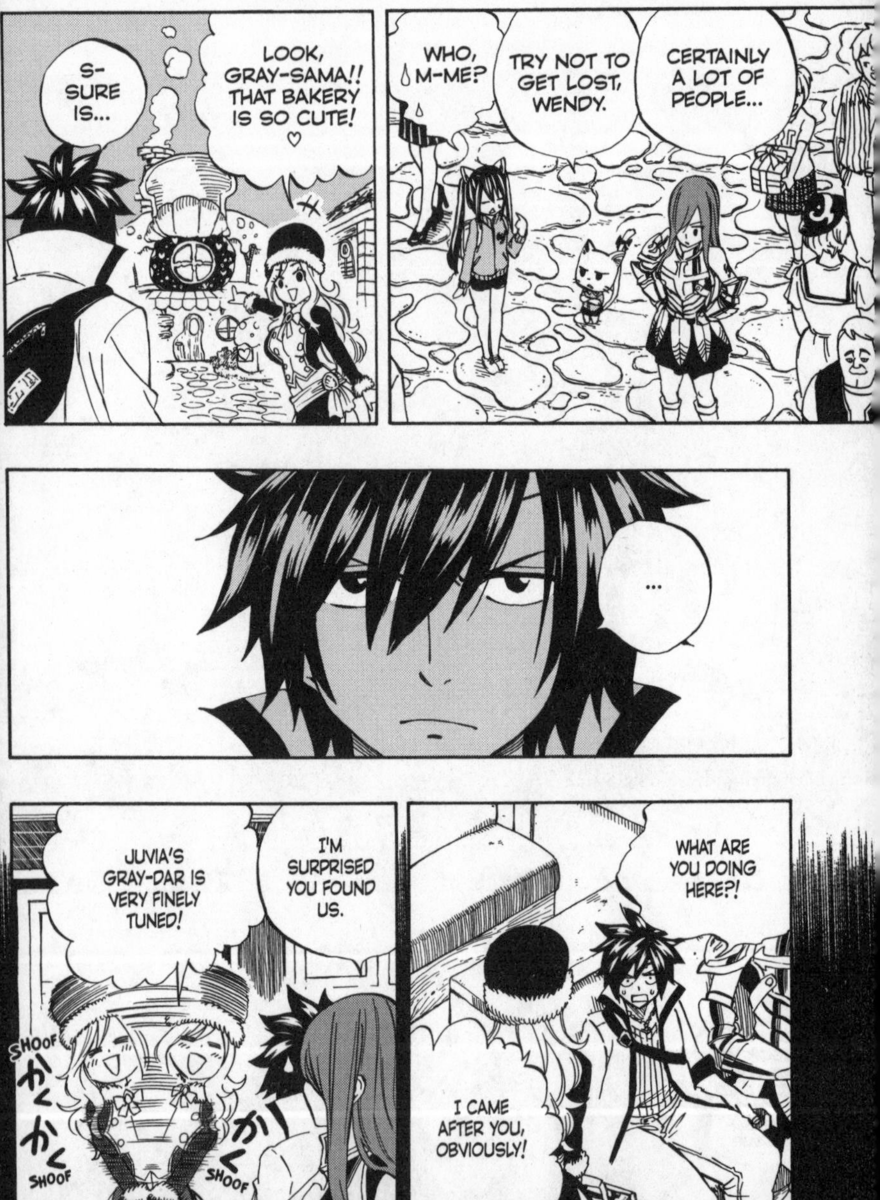
CERTAINLY A LOT OF PEOPLE...
TRY NOT TO GET LOST, WENDY.
WHO, M-ME?
LOOK, GRAY-SAMA!! THAT BAKERY IS SO CUTE! ♡
S-SURE IS...
...
WHAT ARE YOU DOING HERE?!
I CAME AFTER YOU, OBVIOUSLY!
I'M SURPRISED YOU FOUND US.
JUVIA'S GRAY-DAR IS VERY FINELY TUNED!
SHOOF
かく
かく
SHOOF
かく
SHOOF

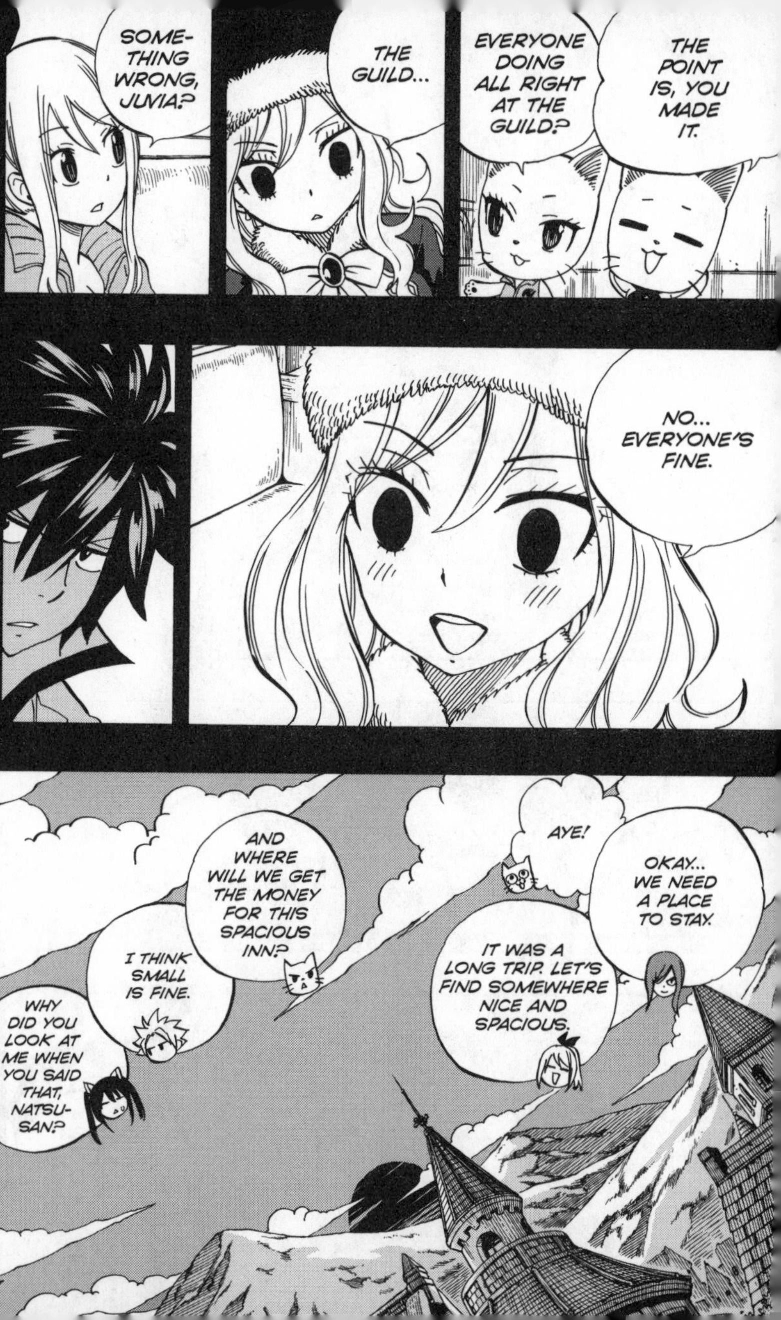
THE POINT IS, YOU MADE IT.
EVERYONE DOING ALL RIGHT AT THE GUILD?
THE GUILD...
SOME-THING WRONG, JUVIA?
NO... EVERYONE'S FINE.
OKAY... WE NEED A PLACE TO STAY.
AYE!
IT WAS A LONG TRIP. LET'S FIND SOMEWHERE NICE AND SPACIOUS.
AND WHERE WILL WE GET THE MONEY FOR THIS SPACIOUS INN?
I THINK SMALL IS FINE.
WHY DID YOU LOOK AT ME WHEN YOU SAID THAT, NATSU-SAN?

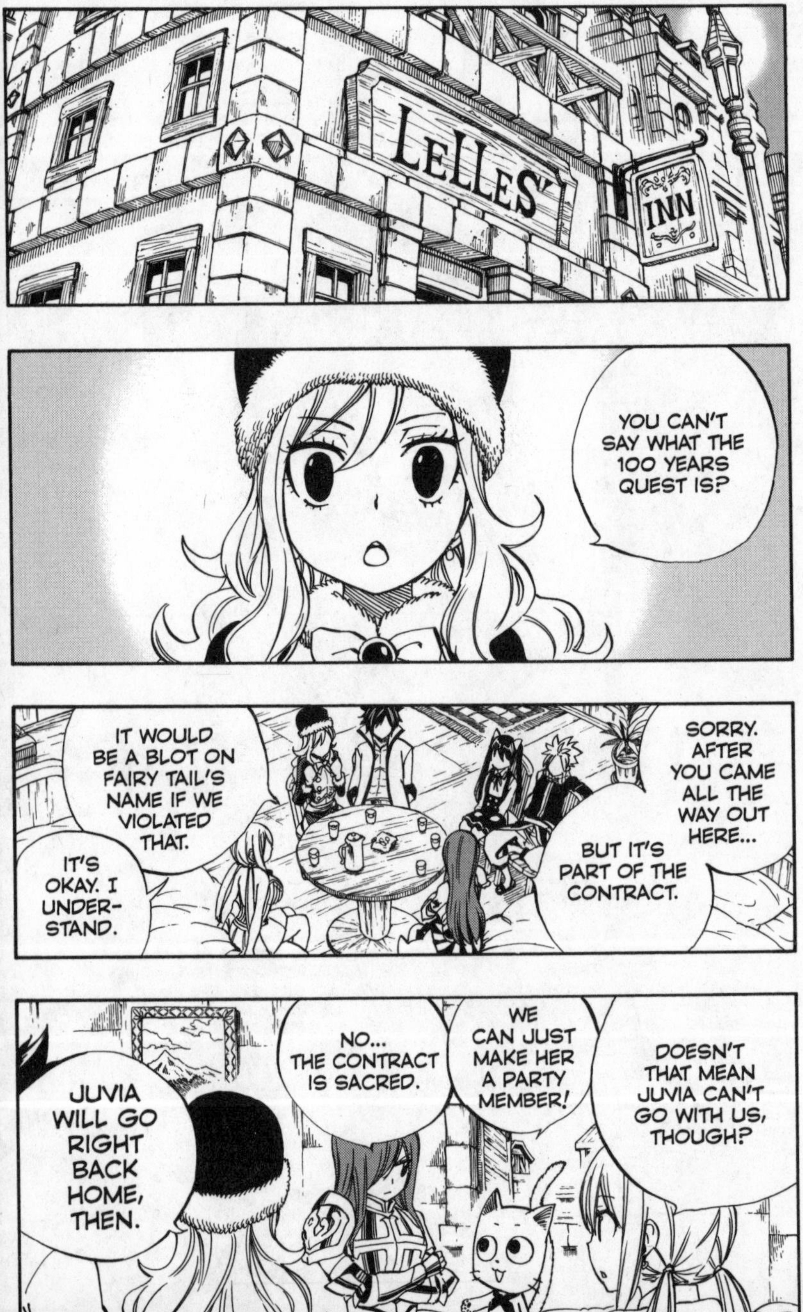
LELLES'
INN
YOU CAN'T SAY WHAT THE 100 YEARS QUEST IS?
SORRY. AFTER YOU CAME ALL THE WAY OUT HERE...
BUT IT'S PART OF THE CONTRACT.
IT WOULD BE A BLOT ON FAIRY TAIL'S NAME IF WE VIOLATED THAT.
IT'S OKAY. I UNDER-STAND.
DOESN'T THAT MEAN JUVIA CAN'T GO WITH US, THOUGH?
WE CAN JUST MAKE HER A PARTY MEMBER!
NO... THE CONTRACT IS SACRED.
JUVIA WILL GO RIGHT BACK HOME, THEN.

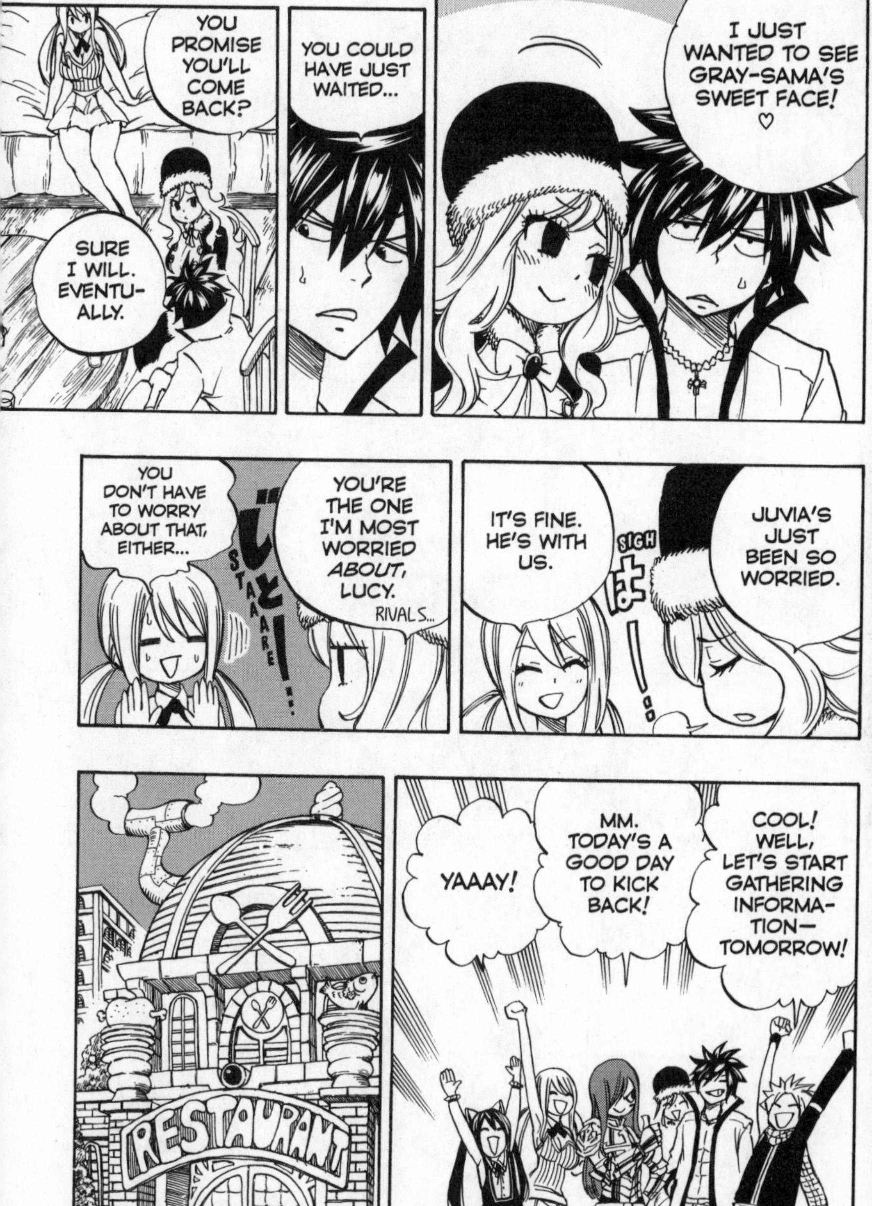
I JUST WANTED TO SEE GRAY-SAMA'S SWEET FACE! ♡
YOU COULD HAVE JUST WAITED...
YOU PROMISE YOU'LL COME BACK?
SURE I WILL. EVENTU-ALLY.
JUVIA'S JUST BEEN SO WORRIED.
SIGH
IT'S FINE. HE'S WITH US.
YOU'RE THE ONE I'M MOST WORRIED *ABOUT*, LUCY.
RIVALS...
STAAARE
YOU DON'T HAVE TO WORRY ABOUT THAT, EITHER...
COOL! WELL, LET'S START GATHERING INFORMA-TION— TOMORROW!
MM. TODAY'S A GOOD DAY TO KICK BACK!
YAAAY!
RESTAURANT

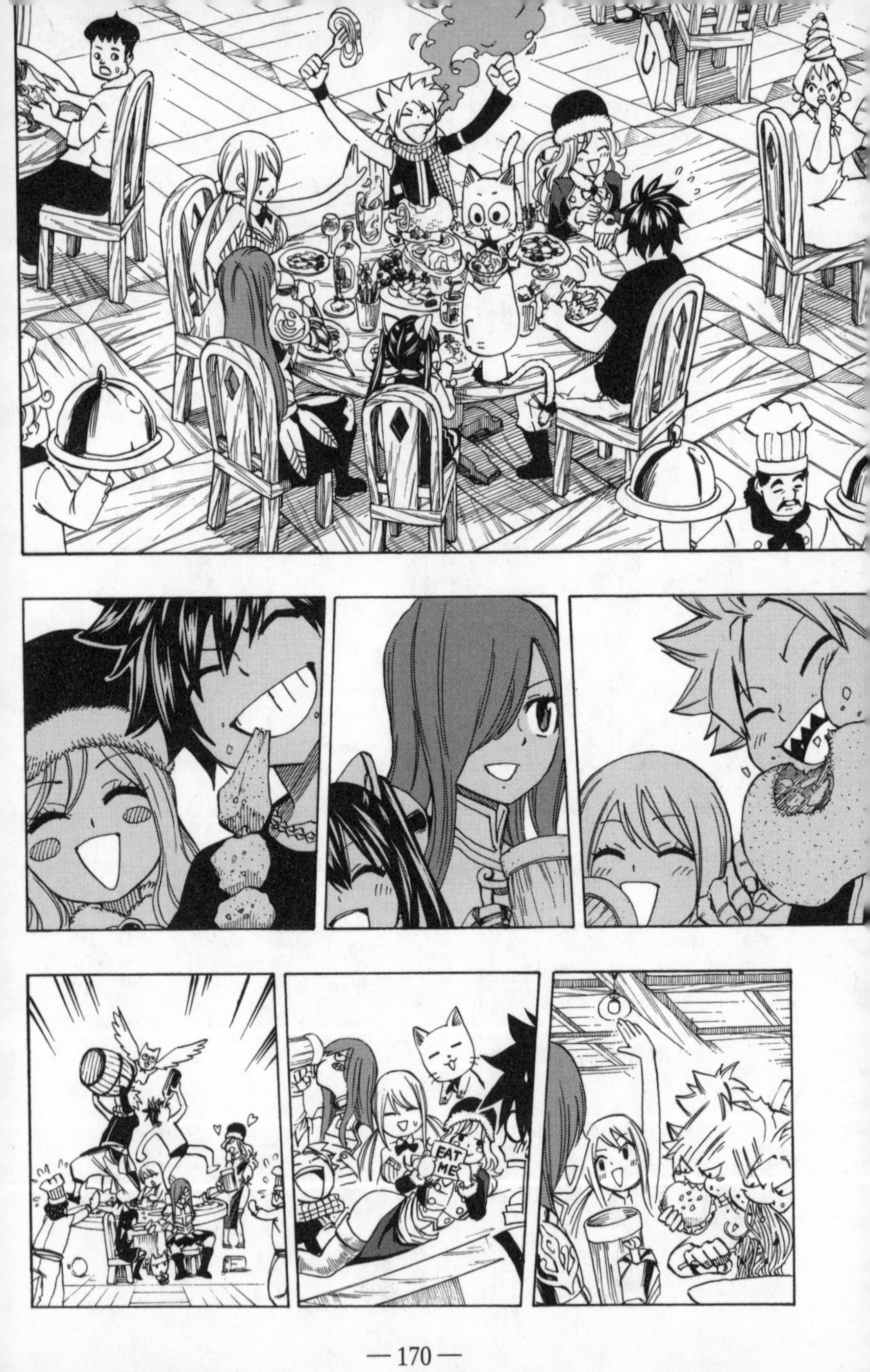
EAT ME

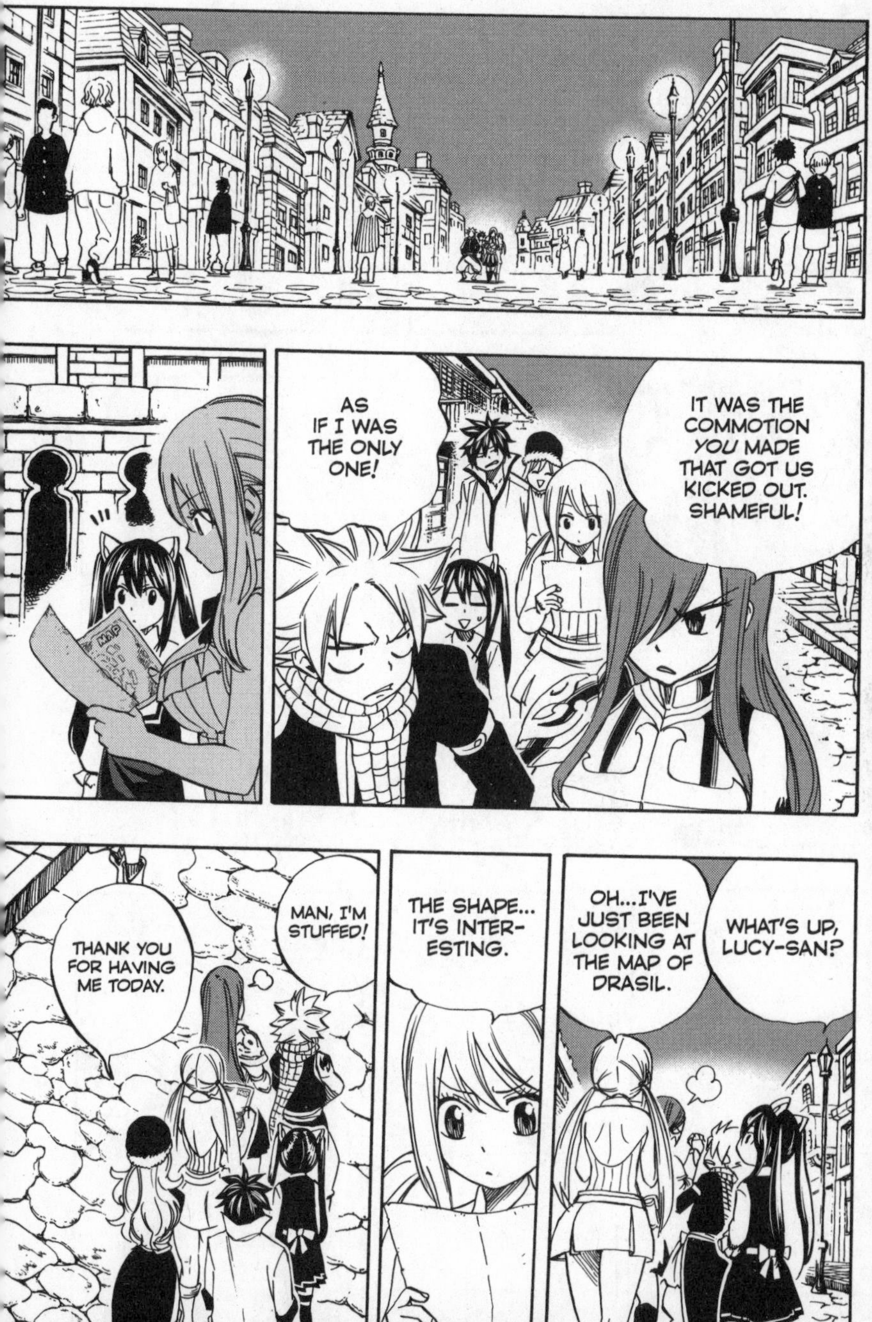
IT WAS THE COMMOTION *YOU* MADE THAT GOT US KICKED OUT. SHAMEFUL!
AS IF I WAS THE ONLY ONE!
WHAT'S UP, LUCY-SAN?
OH...I'VE JUST BEEN LOOKING AT THE MAP OF DRASIL.
THE SHAPE... IT'S INTER-ESTING.
MAN, I'M STUFFED!
THANK YOU FOR HAVING ME TODAY.

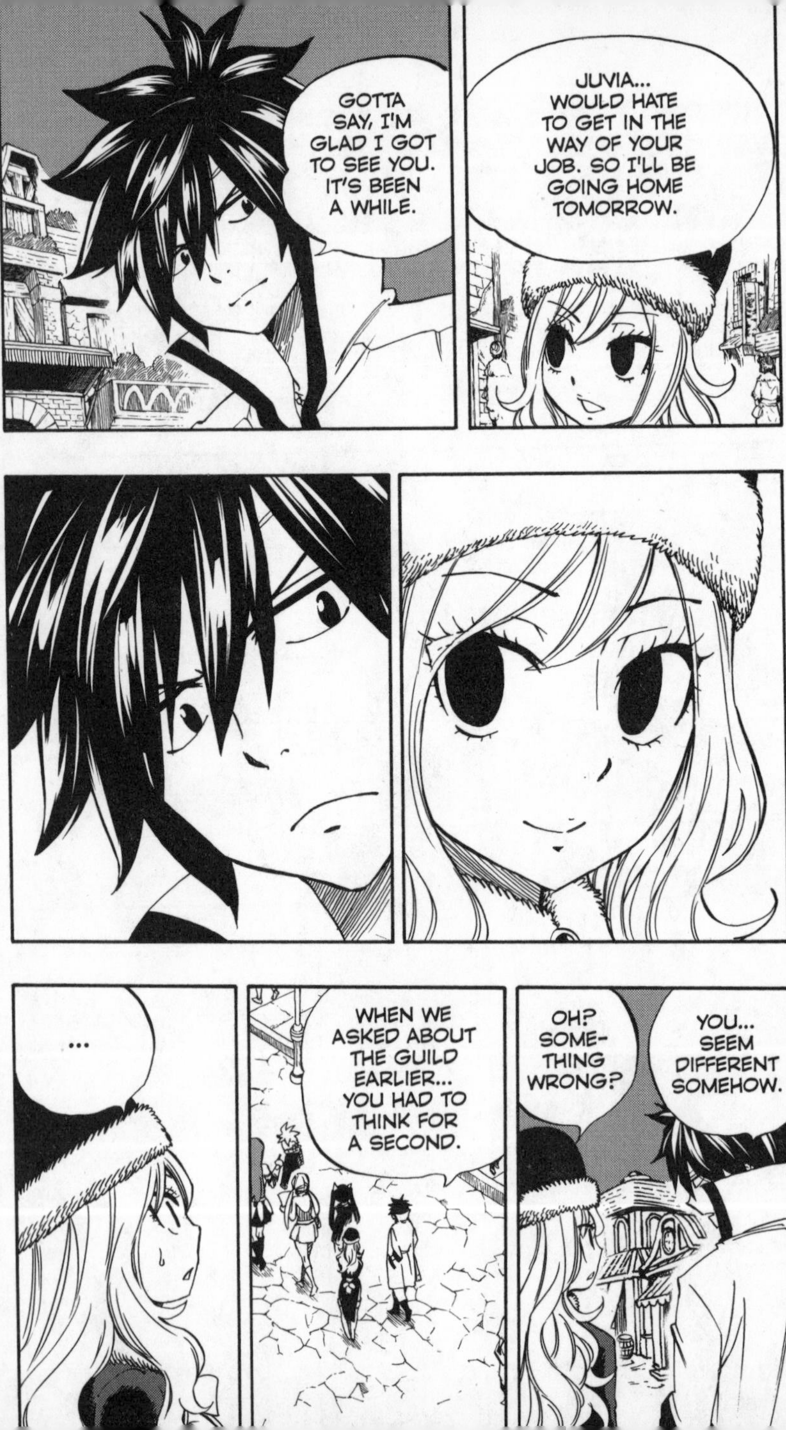
JUVIA... WOULD HATE TO GET IN THE WAY OF YOUR JOB. SO I'LL BE GOING HOME TOMORROW.
GOTTA SAY, I'M GLAD I GOT TO SEE YOU. IT'S BEEN A WHILE.
YOU... SEEM DIFFERENT SOMEHOW.
OH? SOME-THING WRONG?
WHEN WE ASKED ABOUT THE GUILD EARLIER... YOU HAD TO THINK FOR A SECOND.
...

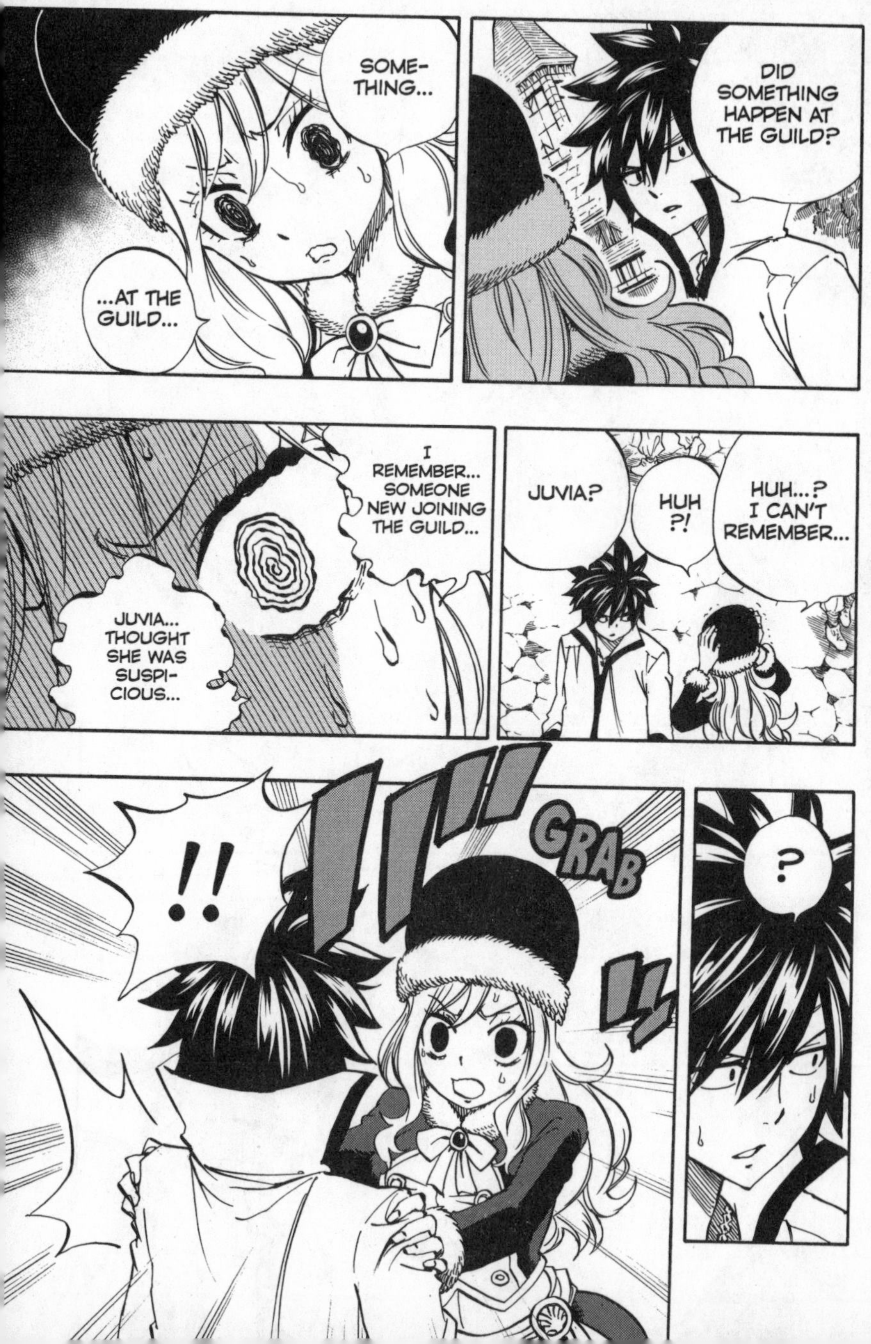
DID SOMETHING HAPPEN AT THE GUILD?
SOME-THING...
...AT THE GUILD...
HUH...? I CAN'T REMEMBER...
HUH ?!
JUVIA?
I REMEMBER... SOMEONE NEW JOINING THE GUILD...
JUVIA... THOUGHT SHE WAS SUSPICIOUS...
?
GRAB
!!

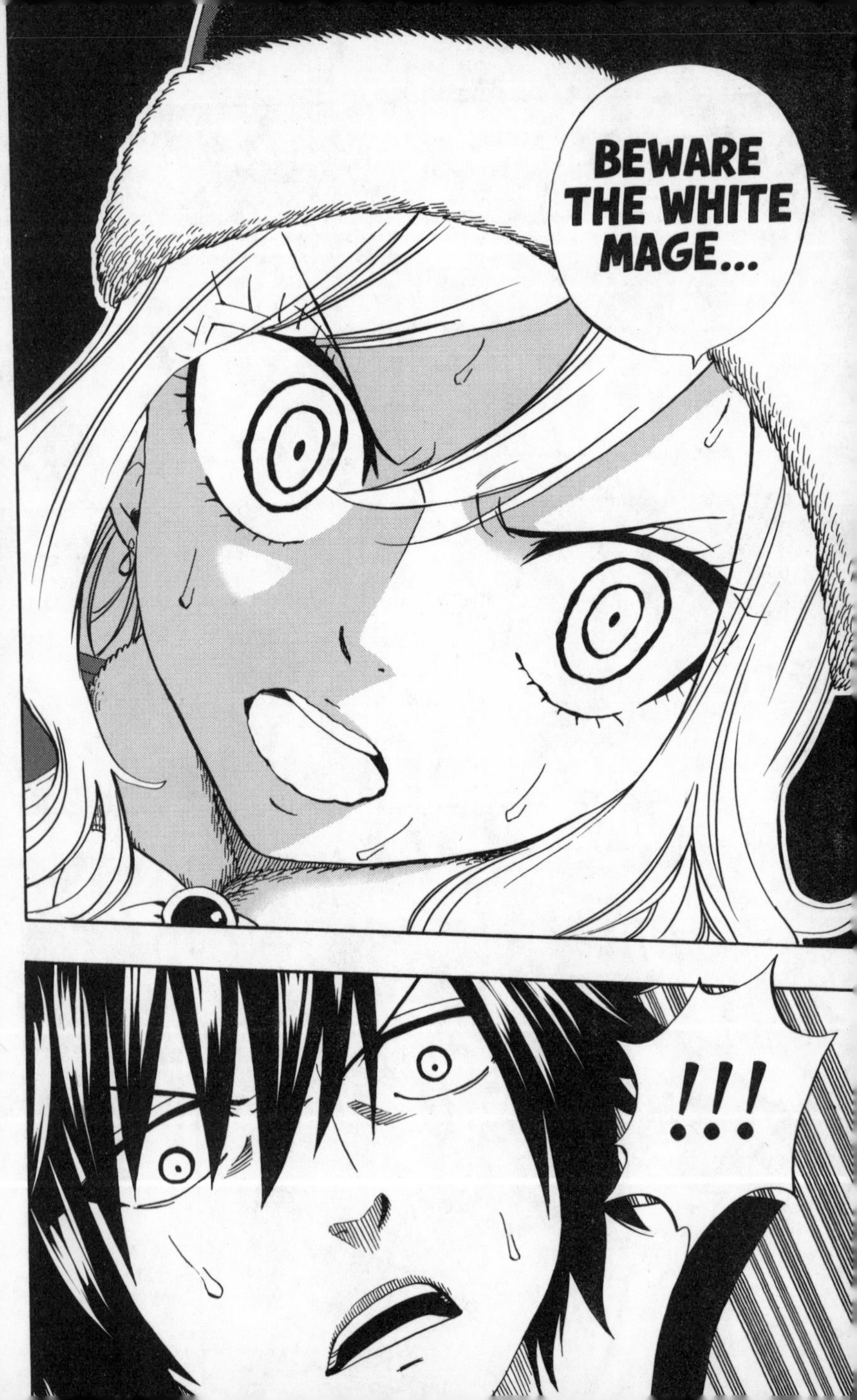
BEWARE THE WHITE MAGE...
!!!

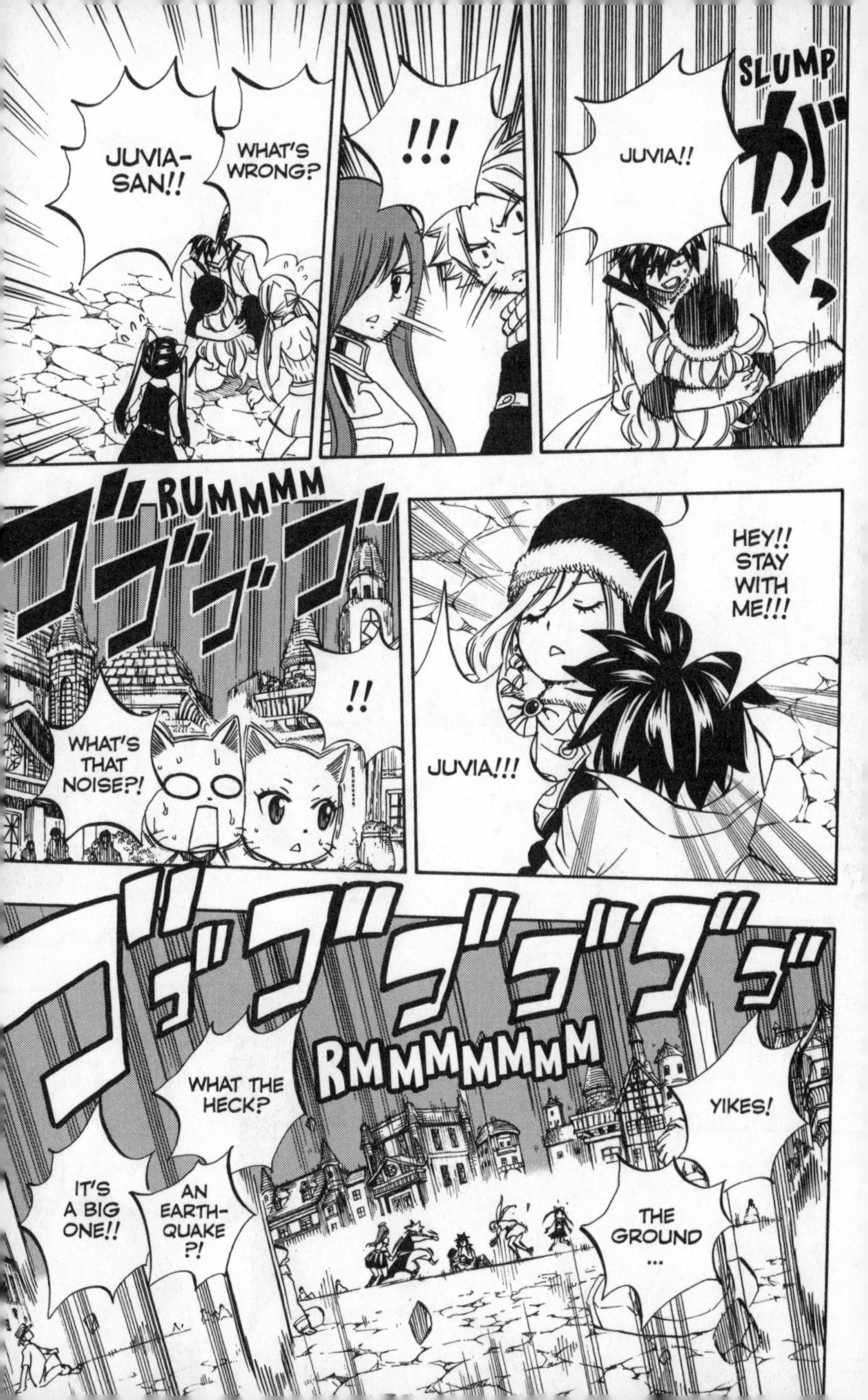
SLUMP
JUVIA!!
!!!
WHAT'S WRONG?
JUVIA-SAN!!
HEY!! STAY WITH ME!!!
JUVIA!!!
RUMMMM
!!
WHAT'S THAT NOISE?!
RMMMMMMMM
YIKES!
WHAT THE HECK?
THE GROUND ...
AN EARTH-QUAKE?!
IT'S A BIG ONE!!

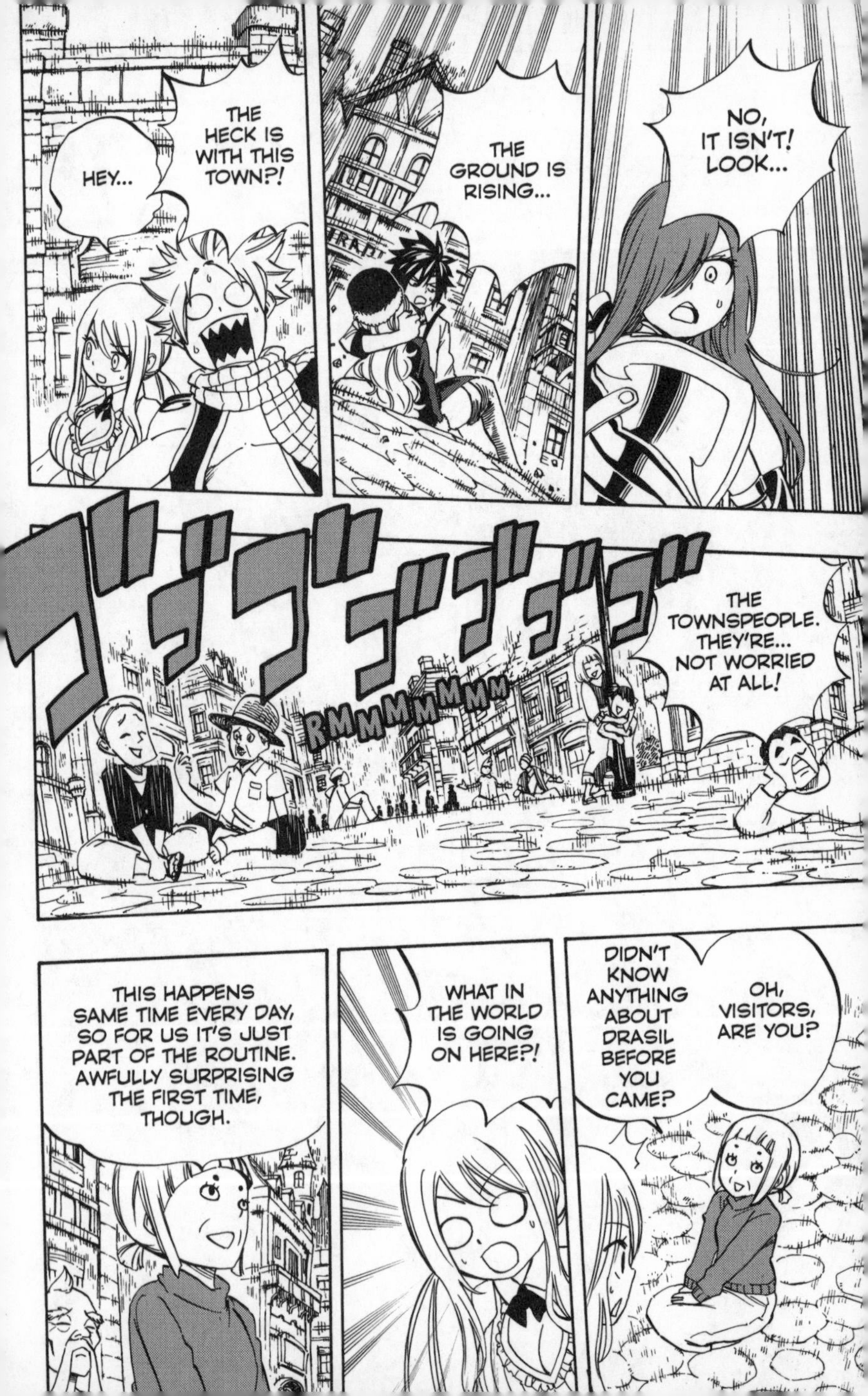
NO, IT ISN'T! LOOK...
THE GROUND IS RISING...
THE HECK IS WITH THIS TOWN?!
HEY...
THE TOWNSPEOPLE. THEY'RE... NOT WORRIED AT ALL!
ゴゴゴゴゴゴ
RMMMMMMMM
OH, VISITORS, ARE YOU?
DIDN'T KNOW ANYTHING ABOUT DRASIL BEFORE YOU CAME?
WHAT IN THE WORLD IS GOING ON HERE?!
THIS HAPPENS SAME TIME EVERY DAY, SO FOR US IT'S JUST PART OF THE ROUTINE. AWFULLY SURPRISING THE FIRST TIME, THOUGH.

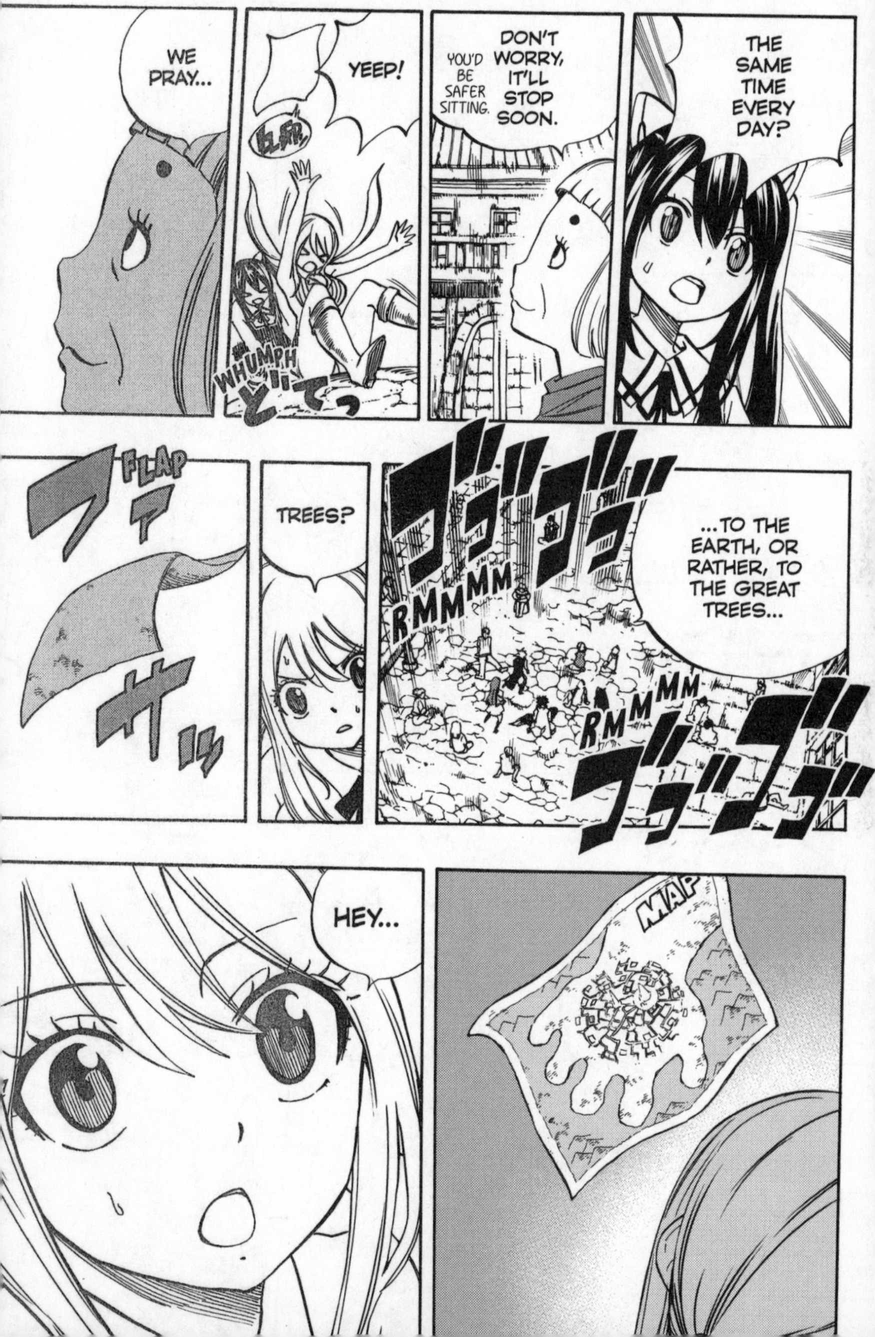
THE SAME TIME EVERY DAY?
DON'T WORRY, IT'LL STOP SOON.
YOU'D BE SAFER SITTING.
YEEP!
WHUMPH
WE PRAY...
...TO THE EARTH, OR RATHER, TO THE GREAT TREES...
RMMMM
RMMMM
TREES?
FLAP
MAP
HEY...

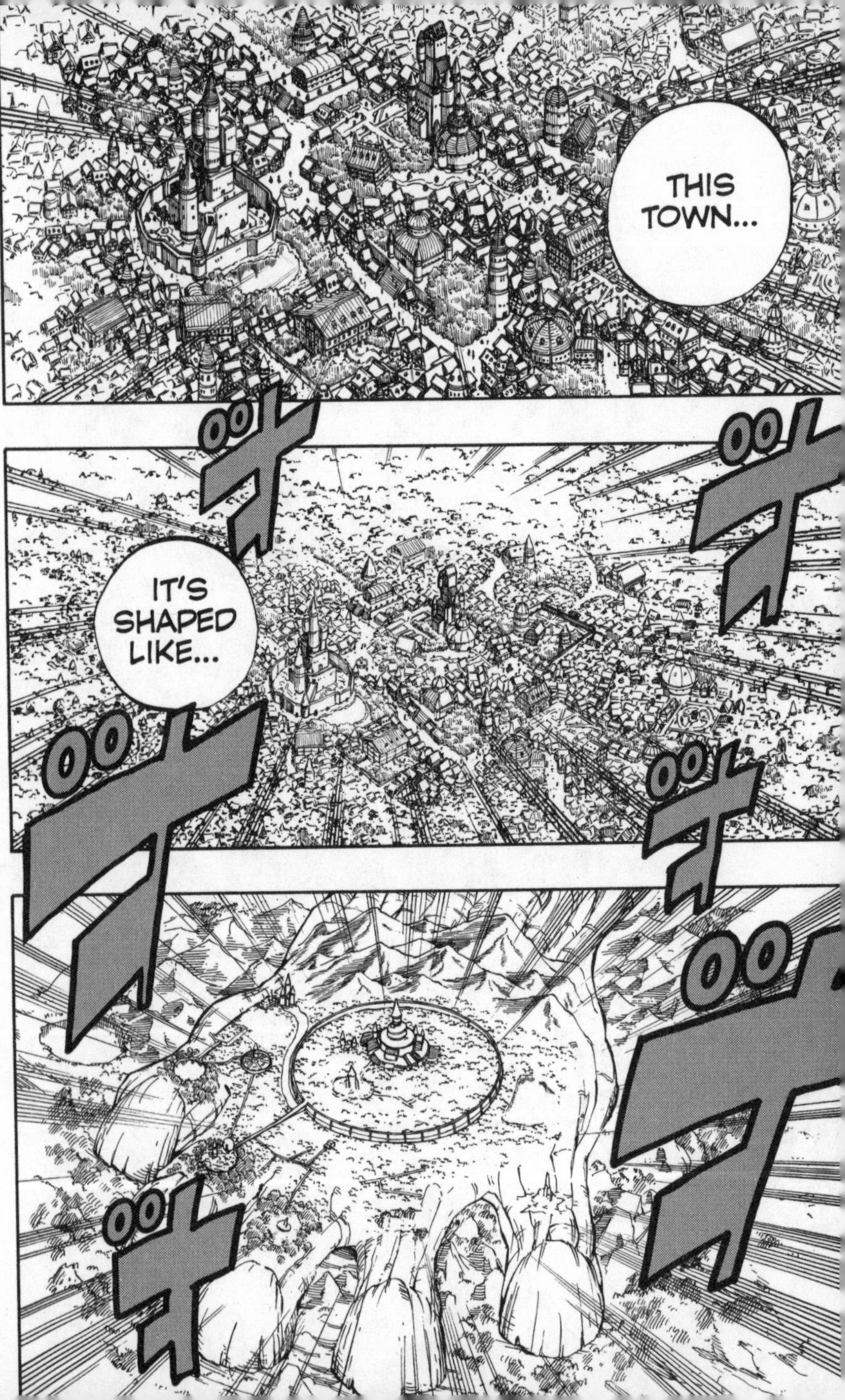
THIS TOWN...
IT'S SHAPED LIKE...

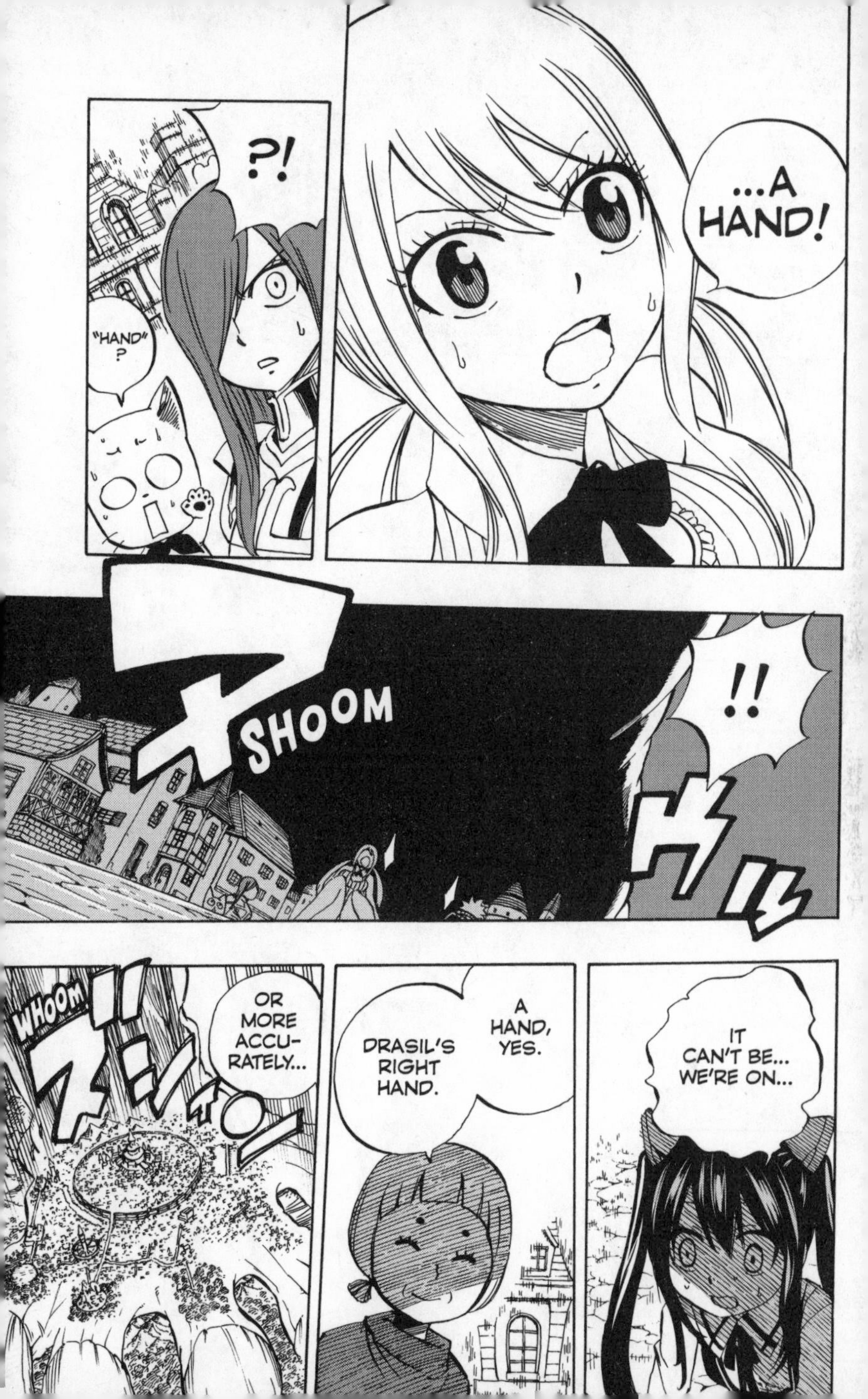
...A HAND!
?!
"HAND"?
!!
SHOOM
IT CAN'T BE... WE'RE ON...
A HAND, YES.
DRASIL'S RIGHT HAND.
OR MORE ACCURATELY...
WHOOM

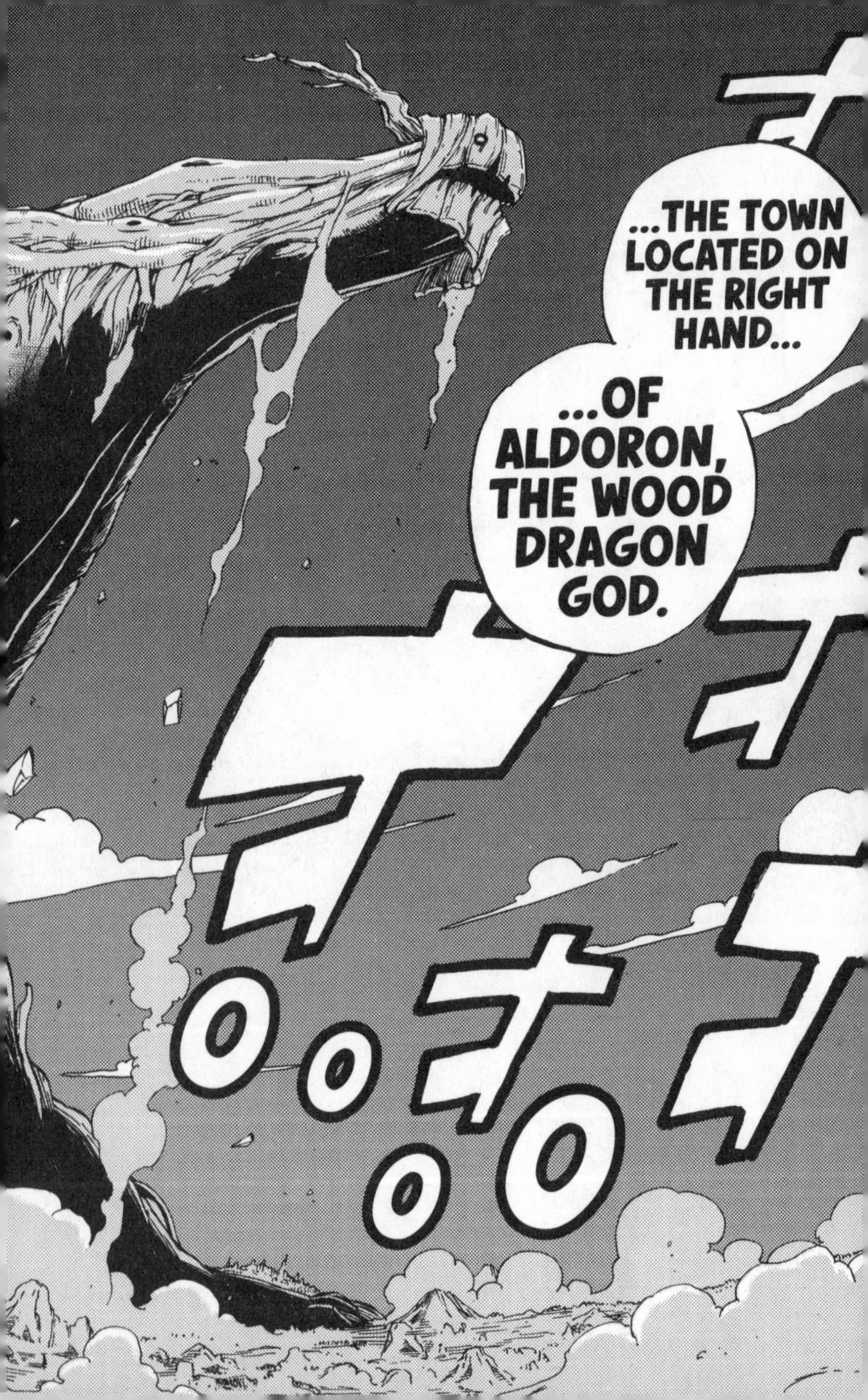
...THE TOWN LOCATED ON THE RIGHT HAND...
...OF ALDORON, THE WOOD DRAGON GOD.

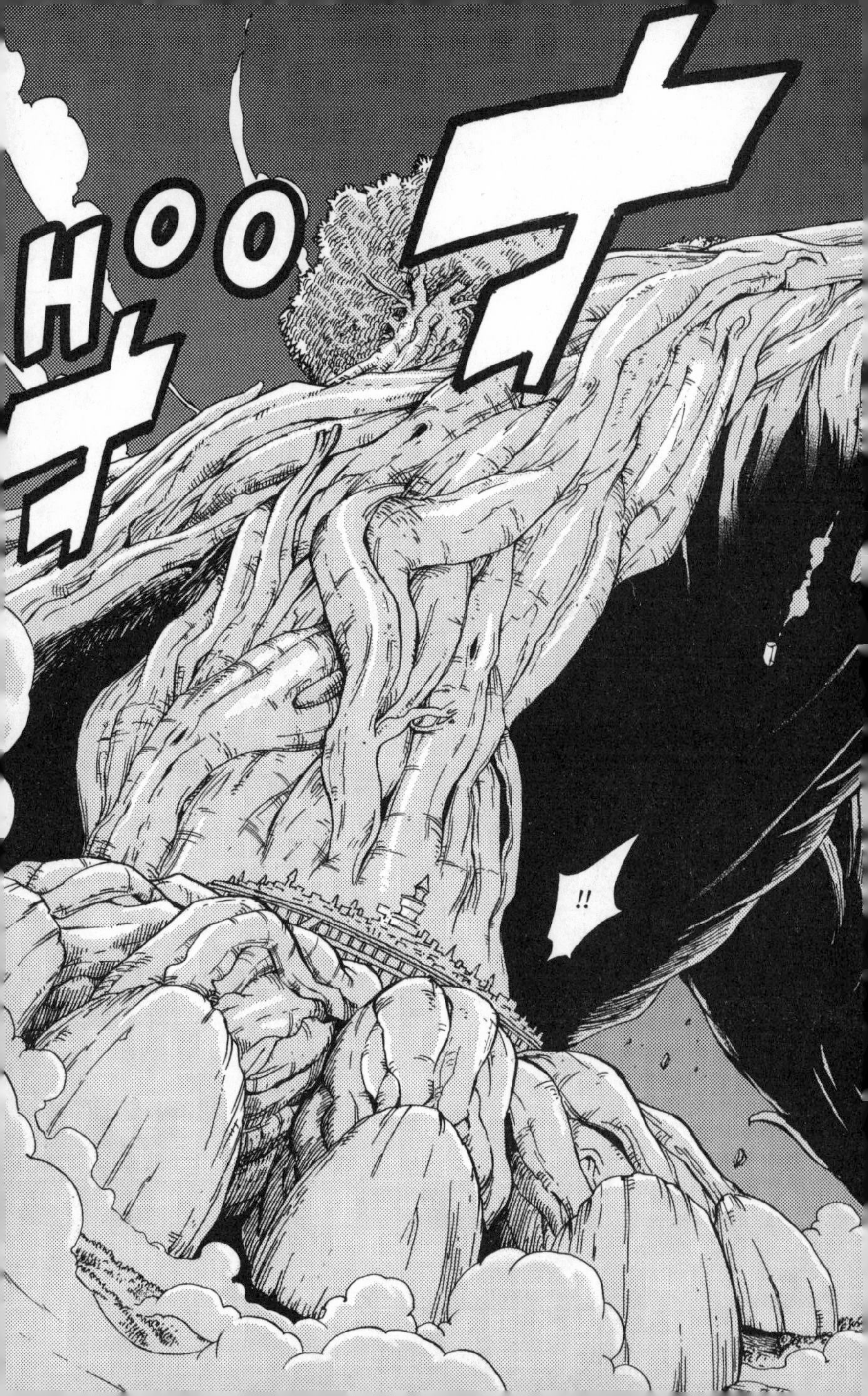
HOOT
!!

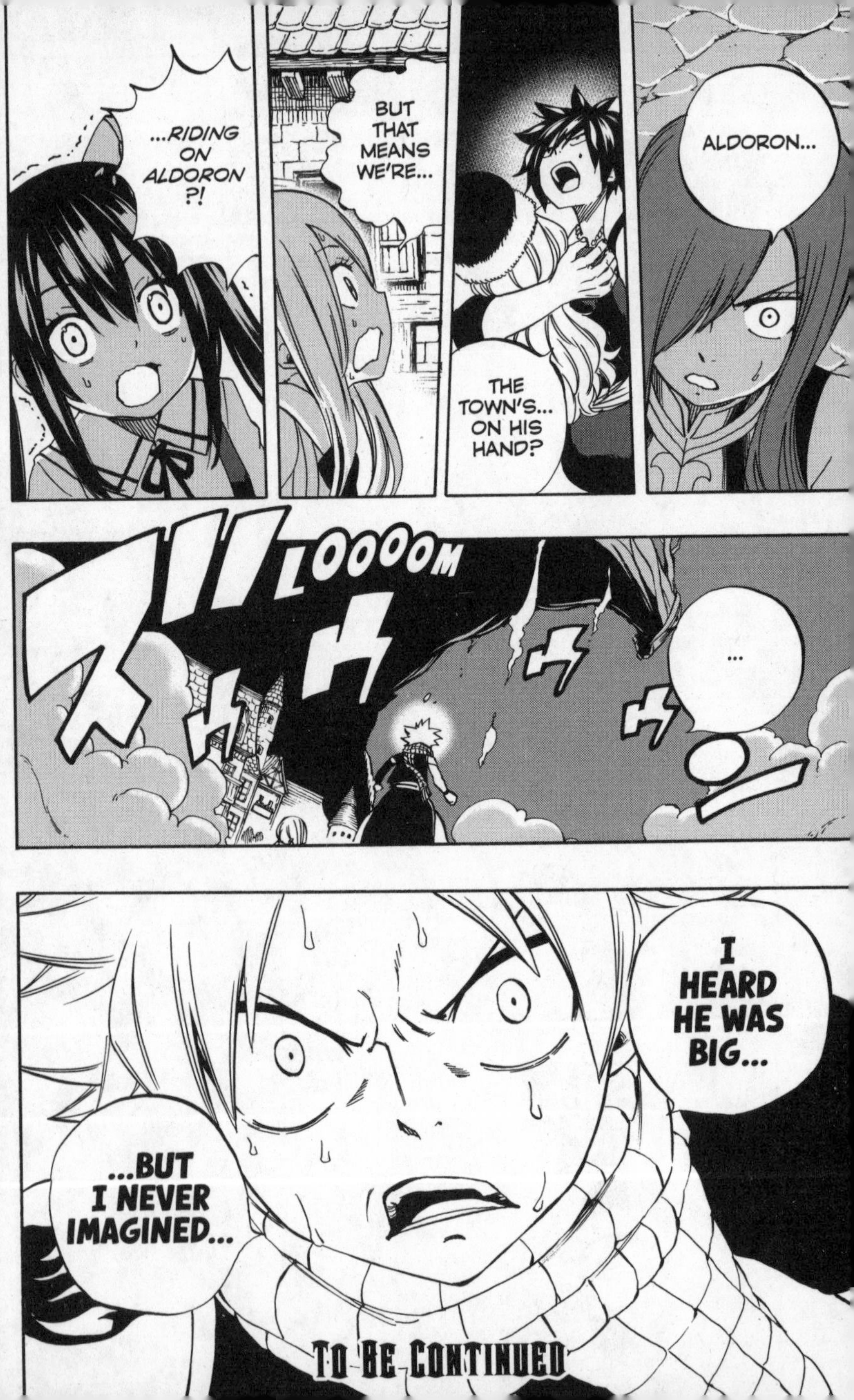
ALDORON...
THE TOWN'S... ON HIS HAND?
BUT THAT MEANS WE'RE...
...RIDING ON ALDORON ?!
LOOOOM
...
I HEARD HE WAS BIG...
...BUT I NEVER IMAGINED...
TO BE CONTINUED

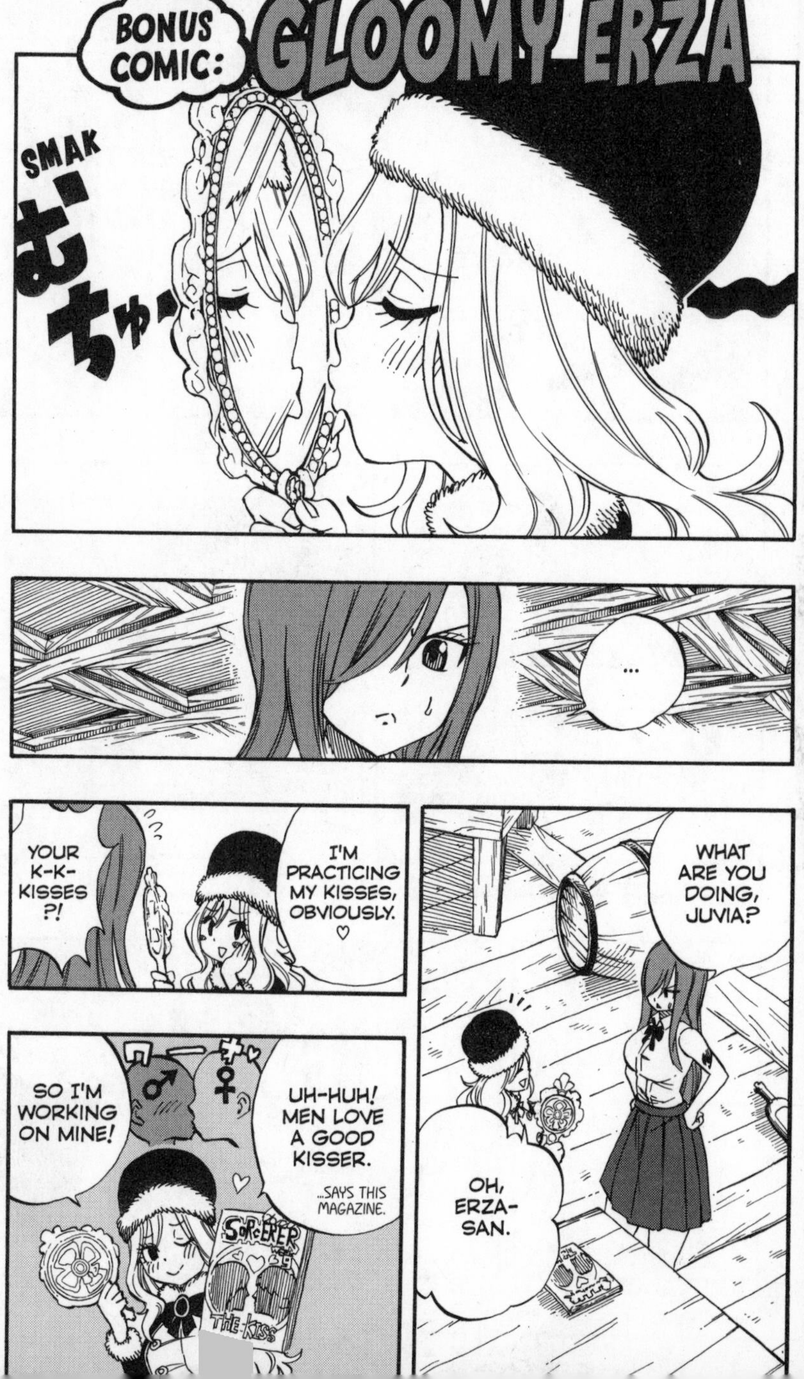
BONUS COMIC: GLOOMY ERZA
SMAK
...
WHAT ARE YOU DOING, JUVIA?
OH, ERZA-SAN.
I'M PRACTICING MY KISSES, OBVIOUSLY. ♡
YOUR K-K-KISSES?!
UH-HUH! MEN LOVE A GOOD KISSER.
...SAYS THIS MAGAZINE.
SO I'M WORKING ON MINE!
SORCERER
THE KISS

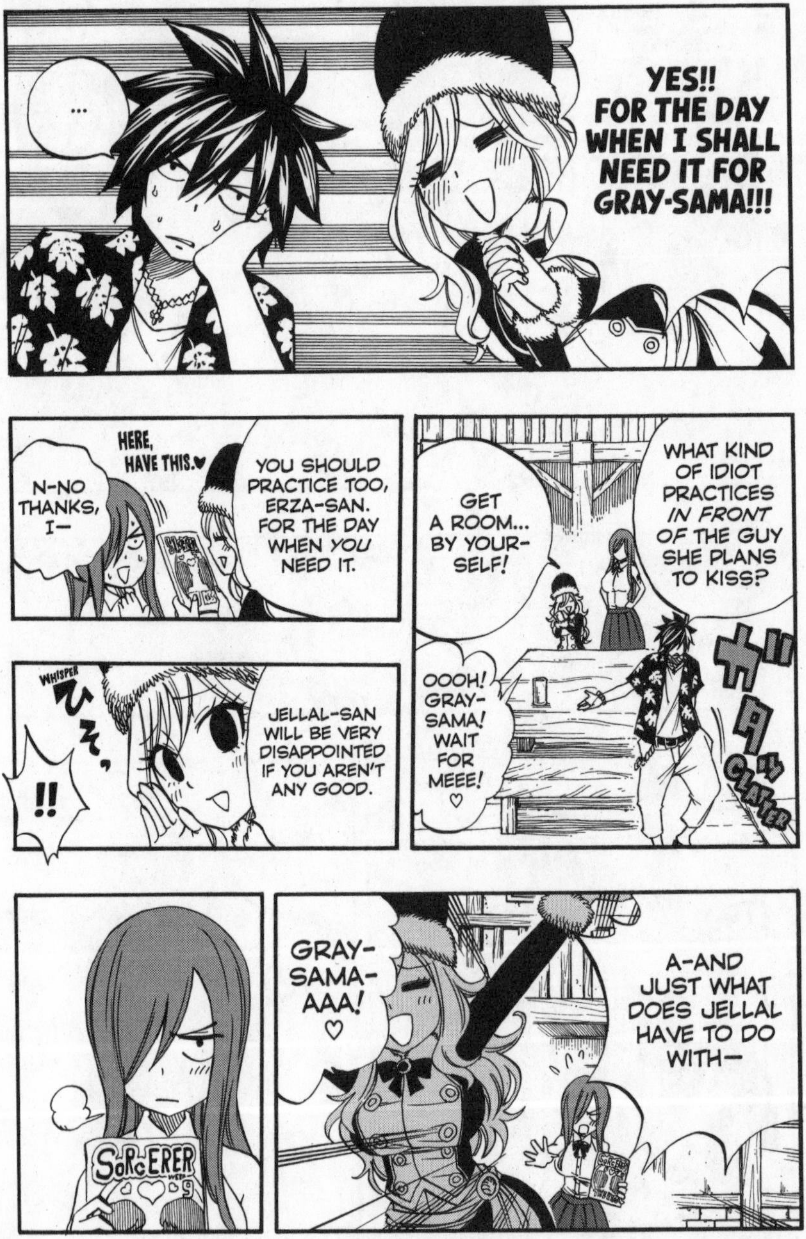
YES!! FOR THE DAY WHEN I SHALL NEED IT FOR GRAY-SAMA!!!
...
WHAT KIND OF IDIOT PRACTICES *IN FRONT* OF THE GUY SHE PLANS TO KISS?
GET A ROOM... BY YOURSELF!
OOOH! GRAY-SAMA! WAIT FOR MEEE! ♡
CLATTER
YOU SHOULD PRACTICE TOO, ERZA-SAN. FOR THE DAY WHEN *YOU* NEED IT.
HERE, HAVE THIS.♥
N-NO THANKS, I—
JELLAL-SAN WILL BE VERY DISAPPOINTED IF YOU AREN'T ANY GOOD.
WHISPER
!!
A-AND JUST WHAT DOES JELLAL HAVE TO DO WITH—
GRAY-SAMA-AAA! ♡
SoRcERER

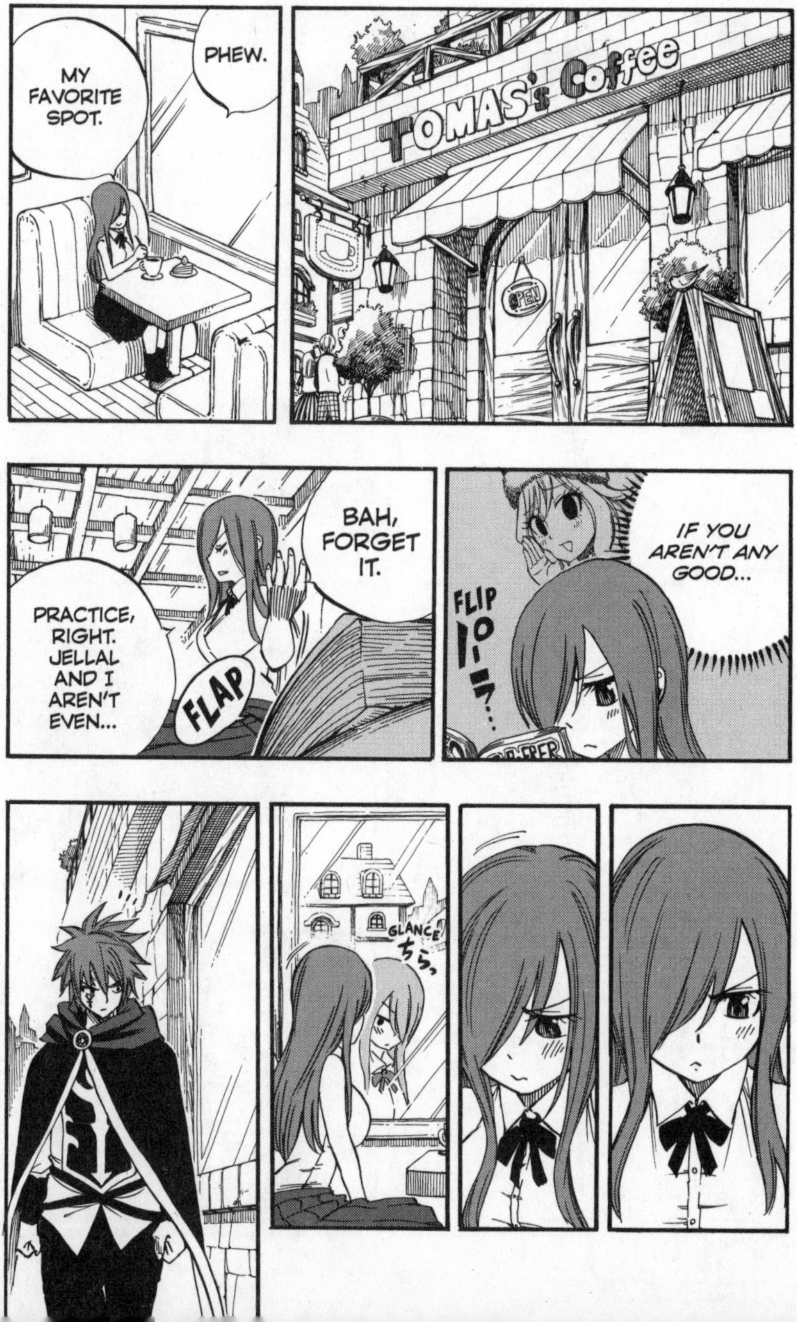
TOMAS's Coffee
OPEN
PHEW.
MY FAVORITE SPOT.
IF YOU AREN'T ANY GOOD...
FLIP
BAH, FORGET IT.
PRACTICE, RIGHT. JELLAL AND I AREN'T EVEN...
FLAP
GLANCE
ちらっ

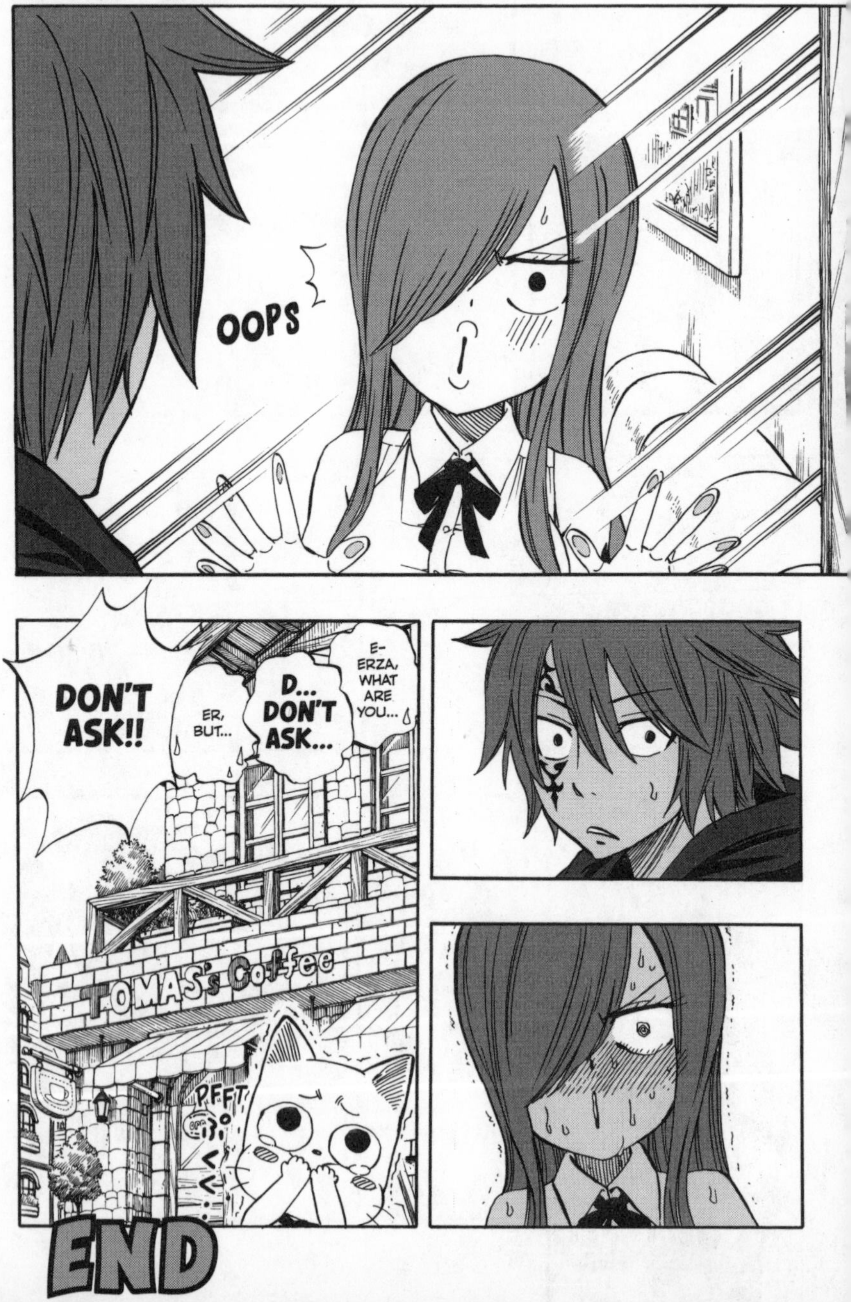
OOPS
E-ERZA, WHAT ARE YOU...
D... DON'T ASK...
ER, BUT...
DON'T ASK!!
TOMAS's Coffee
PFFT
END

FAIRY TAIL
100 YEARS QUEST

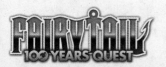

DE ART RETURNS

(MIE PREFECTURE TEN-SAN)

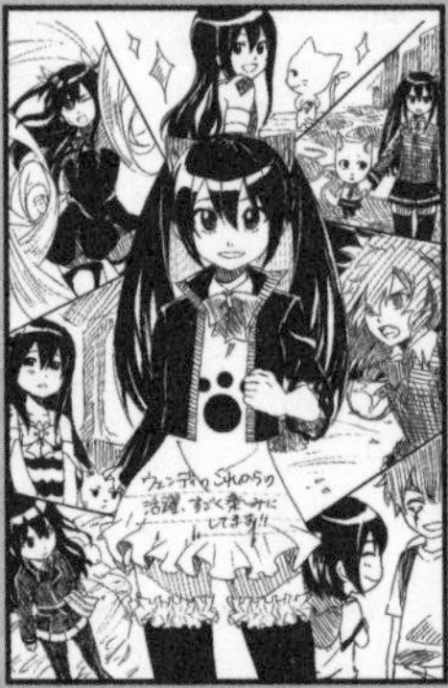

▲ THERE'S SO MUCH LOVE IN THIS PICTURE! THANKS!

▼ LOOKS REALLY COOL IN BLACK AND WHITE!

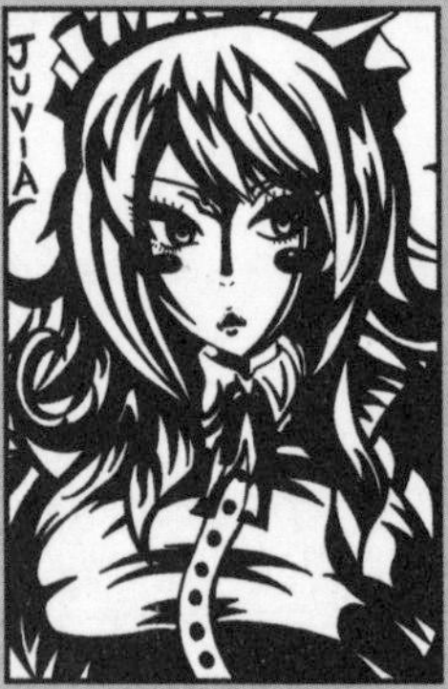
JUVIA

(AOMORI PREFECTURE YOSHIGO TAKEHARA)

(HOKKAIDO PREFECTURE FT LOVE BRIGADE CAPTAIN)

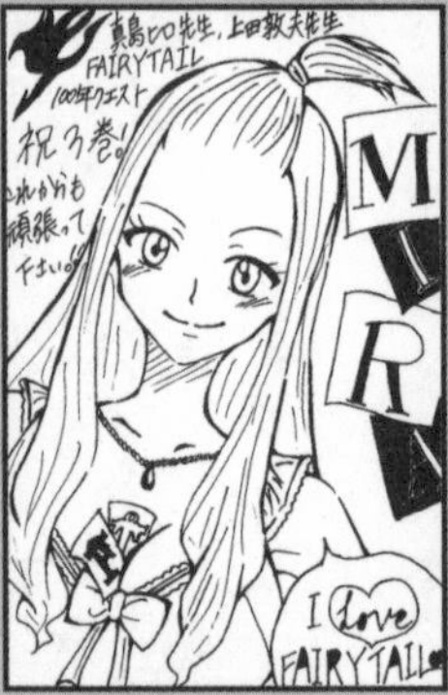
FAIRYTAIL
MIRA
I love FAIRY TAIL

▲ AHH, MIRA-SAN, NEVER-CHANGING. WONDERFUL.

▼ LOVE TO SEE THEM GETTING ALONG! EXCELLENT.

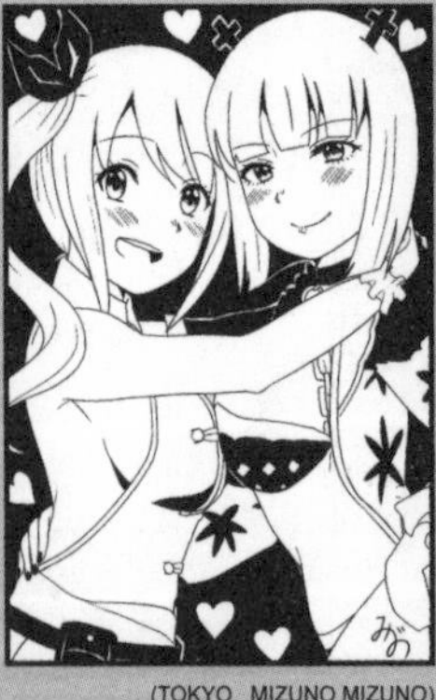

(TOKYO MIZUNO MIZUNO)

▼ SUIJIN-SAMA... I LOVE THE TOUCH OF MELANCHOLY HERE.

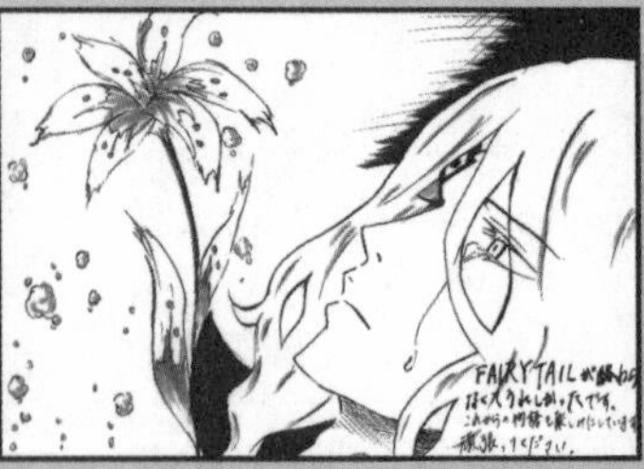
FAIRYTAIL

(SAITAMA PREFECTURE NOA SEKINE)

FAIRY TAIL 100 YEARS QUEST GUILD

(AOMORI PREFECTURE KOSHU)

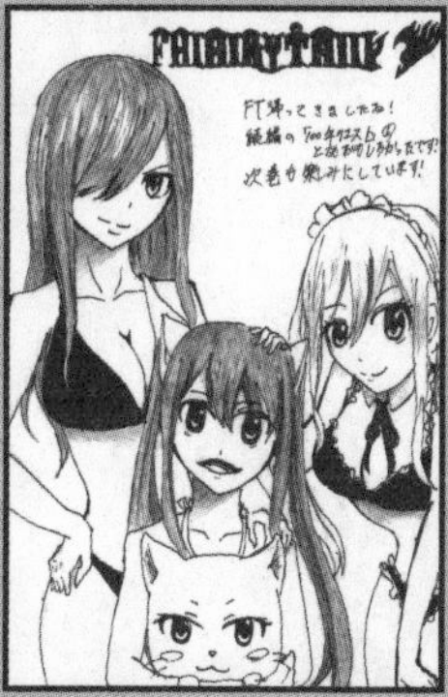

▲ IF I COULD HAVE THESE FOUR... ER, NEVER MIND.

▼ LIKE OIL AND WATER? WONDER IF THEY'LL GET ALONG.

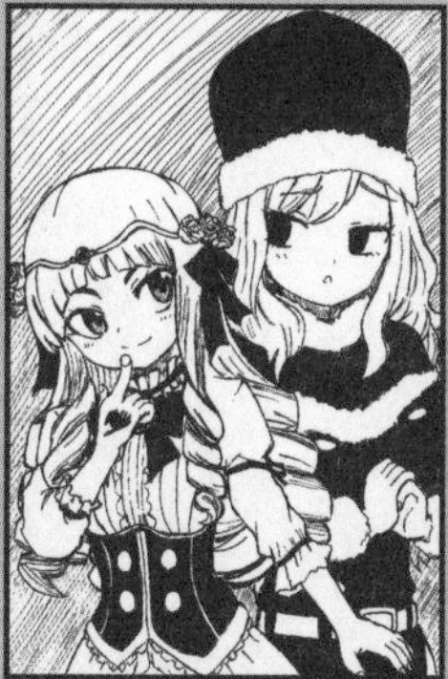

(IBARAKI PREFECTURE MIDORI-SAN)

(KAGOSHIMA PREFECTURE SHOJI MICHIO)

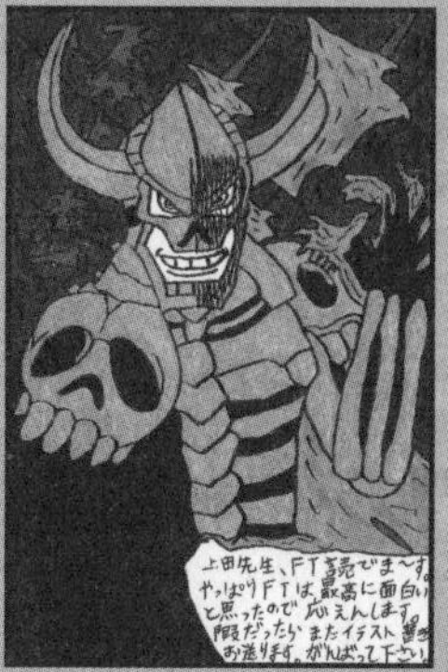

▲ OOH, INTIMIDATING!

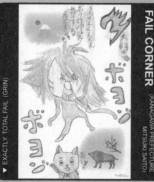

FAIL CORNER

(KANAGAWA PREFECTURE MITSUKI SAITO)

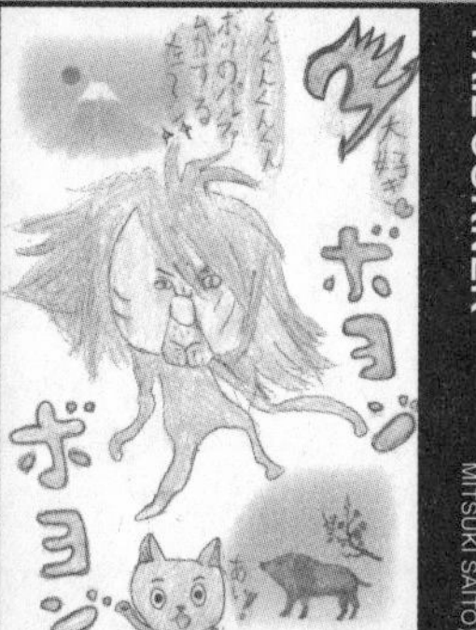

▼ EXACTLY. TOTAL FAIL. (GRIN)

(OSAKA PREFECTURE OTSUYU-SAN)

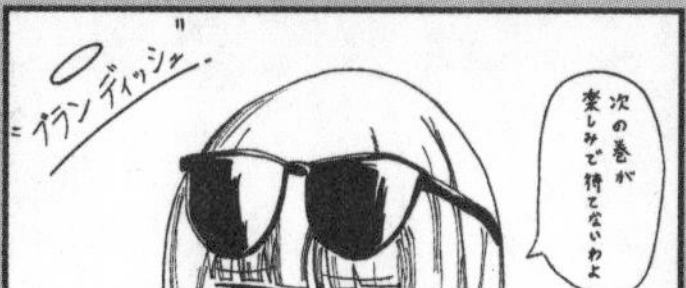
ブランディッシュ
次の巻が楽しみで待てないわよ

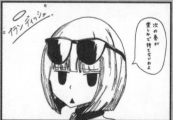

▲ THANKS FOR YOUR PATIENCE. VOL 3'S ON SALE NOW.

HERE'S OUR THIRD BATCH OF FAN DRAWINGS! ENJOY!

EDITOR'S NOTE: DRAWING SUBMISSIONS LIMITED TO JAPAN.

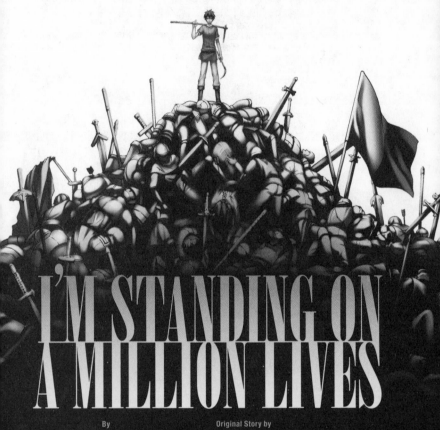

I'M STANDING ON A MILLION LIVES

By
Akinari Nao

Original Story by
Naoki Yamakawa